PERFORMANCE ACCOUNTABILITY AND COMBATING CORRUPTION

Introduction to the Public Sector Governance and Accountability Series

Anwar Shah, Series Editor

A well-functioning public sector that delivers quality public services consistent with citizen preferences and that fosters private market-led growth while managing fiscal resources prudently is considered critical to the World Bank's mission of poverty alleviation and the achievement of the Millennium Development Goals. This important new series aims to advance those objectives by disseminating conceptual guidance and lessons from practices and by facilitating learning from each others' experiences on ideas and practices that promote *responsive* (by matching public services with citizens' preferences), *responsible* (through efficiency and equity in service provision without undue fiscal and social risk), and *accountable* (to citizens for all actions) public governance in developing countries.

This series represents a response to several independent evaluations in recent years that have argued that development practitioners and policy makers dealing with public sector reforms in developing countries and, indeed, anyone with a concern for effective public governance could benefit from a synthesis of newer perspectives on public sector reforms. This series distills current wisdom and presents tools of analysis for improving the efficiency, equity, and efficacy of the public sector. Leading public policy experts and practitioners have contributed to this series.

The first 14 volumes in this series, listed below, are concerned with public sector accountability for prudent fiscal management; efficiency, equity, and integrity in public service provision; safeguards for the protection of the poor, women, minorities, and other disadvantaged groups; ways of strengthening institutional arrangements for voice, choice, and exit; means of ensuring public financial accountability for integrity and results; methods of evaluating public sector programs, fiscal federalism, and local finances; international practices in local governance; and a framework for responsive and accountable governance.

Fiscal Management

Public Services Delivery

Public Expenditure Analysis

Local Governance in Industrial Countries

Local Governance in Developing Countries

Intergovernmental Fiscal Transfers: Principles and Practice

Participatory Budgeting

Budgeting and Budgetary Institutions

Local Budgeting

Local Public Financial Management

Performance Accountability and Combating Corruption

Tools for Public Sector Evaluations

Macrofederalism and Local Finances

Citizen-Centered Governance

PUBLIC SECTOR
GOVERNANCE AND
ACCOUNTABILITY SERIES

PERFORMANCE ACCOUNTABILITY AND COMBATING CORRUPTION

Edited by ANWAR SHAH

THE WORLD BANK
Washington, D.C.

©2007 The International Bank for Reconstruction and Development / The World Bank
1818 H Street, NW
Washington, DC 20433
Telephone: 202-473-1000
Internet: www.worldbank.org
E-mail: feedback@worldbank.org

All rights reserved

1 2 3 4 10 09 08 07

This volume is a product of the staff of the International Bank for Reconstruction and Development / The World Bank. The findings, interpretations, and conclusions expressed in this volume do not necessarily reflect the views of the Executive Directors of The World Bank or the governments they represent.
 The World Bank does not guarantee the accuracy of the data included in this work. The boundaries, colors, denominations, and other information shown on any map in this work do not imply any judgement on the part of The World Bank concerning the legal status of any territory or the endorsement or acceptance of such boundaries.

Rights and Permissions
The material in this publication is copyrighted. Copying and/or transmitting portions or all of this work without permission may be a violation of applicable law. The International Bank for Reconstruction and Development / The World Bank encourages dissemination of its work and will normally grant permission to reproduce portions of the work promptly.
 For permission to photocopy or reprint any part of this work, please send a request with complete information to the Copyright Clearance Center Inc., 222 Rosewood Drive, Danvers, MA 01923, USA; telephone: 978-750-8400; fax: 978-750-4470; Internet: www.copyright.com.
 All other queries on rights and licenses, including subsidiary rights, should be addressed to the Office of the Publisher, The World Bank, 1818 H Street, NW, Washington, DC 20433, USA; fax: 202-522-2422; e-mail: pubrights@worldbank.org.

ISBN-10: 0-8213-6941-5
ISBN-13: 978-0-8213-6941-8
eISBN-10: 0-8213-6942-3
eISBN-13: 978-0-8213-6942-5
DOI: 10.1596/978-0-8213-6941-8

Library of Congress Cataloging-in-Publication Data
Performance accountability and combating corruption / edited by Anwar Shah.
  p. cm.
  ISBN-13: 978-0-8213-6941-8
  ISBN-10: 0-8213-6941-5
  ISBN-10: 0-8213-6942-3 (electronic)
   1. Total quality management in government. 2. Political corruption—Prevention.
I. Shah, Anwar.
JF1525.T67P43 2007
352.3'4—dc22
                                                      2006101263

Contents

Foreword xv

Preface xvii

Acknowledgments xix

Contributors xxi

Abbreviations and Acronyms xxv

Overview 1
Anwar Shah

Part I Ensuring Integrity and Improving the Efficiency of Public Management

CHAPTER 1

Performance-Based Accountability 15
B. Guy Peters
Central Place of Accountability in Governing 15
The Shift to Performance-Based Accountability 19
A Strategy for Change 21

v

vi   Contents

  Barriers and Perverse Consequences   27
  Conclusions   30
  Notes   31
  References   31

2 **Efficiency, Integrity, and Capacity: An Expanded Agenda for Public Management?**   33
  Willy McCourt
  Generating Commitment to Public Management Reform   34
  Creating the Conditions for Public Management Reform   40
  How Should Reforms Be Introduced and Sequenced?   52
  Conclusion: Embedding Reforms   55
  Notes   55
  References   55

3 **Can E-Government Make Public Governance More Accountable?**   59
  Helmut Drüke
  Accountability in Public Governance   60
  E-Government as a Comprehensive Concept of Modernization   62
  Fostering E-Government and Accountability   78
  Conclusions   81
  Notes   84
  References   84

4 **Networks and Collaborative Solutions to Performance Measurement and Improvement in Sub-Saharan Africa**   89
  Mark A. Glaser
  The Need for a Systems Approach to Community Improvement   90
  From Government to Governance: Networks and Collaborative Solutions   107
  Goals and Performance Targets   113
  Performance-Based Budgeting   116
  Tools for Engaging Citizens and Respecting Public Values   122

Improving Government Performance in Sub-Saharan
   Africa   124
Redefining Performance through Collaborative Networks   125
Notes   127
References   127

Part II Strengthening Oversight and Combating Corruption

5 The Role of Political Institutions in Promoting Accountability   135

Rob Jenkins

Key Concepts in Accountability Systems   136
Institutions: Functions, Pitfalls, and Innovative Remedies   148
Key Trends Affecting Efforts to Improve Accountability
   Systems   170
Diagnosing Accountability Failures in Political Institutions   176
Notes   179
References   179

6 Legal and Institutional Frameworks Supporting Accountability in Budgeting and Service Delivery Performance   183

Malcolm Russell-Einhorn

The Importance of Effective Citizen Voice to Budgeting and
   Service Delivery Performance   185
Cross-Country Experience with Legal and Institutional
   Frameworks That Support Citizen Voice Mechanisms   188
What Kinds of Mechanisms and Conditions Create Effective
   Citizen Voice?   205
Case Studies on Strengthening Citizen Voice Mechanisms to
   Improve Service Delivery   212
Conclusions   224
Annex: The ARVIN Framework   225
Notes   227
References   229

7 Tailoring the Fight against Corruption to Country Circumstances 233
Anwar Shah
What Is Corruption? 234
What Drives Corruption? 236
What Can Policy Makers Do to Combat Corruption? 243
Conclusions: Don't Use the "C" Word 249
Notes 250
References 250

8 Disrupting Corruption 255
Omar Azfar
Dealing with Incidental Corruption: Principal-Agent Theory versus the Economics of Crime 256
The Sale of Jobs and Its Effect on Mechanisms of Accountability 258
Dealing with Systemic Corruption 260
Case Study Evidence on Systemic Corruption 272
Elections and Revolutions 276
Recommendations 277
Notes 281
References 282

9 Corruption in Tax Administration 285
Mahesh C. Purohit
Causes of Corruption in Tax Administration 286
Administering Tax Policy 288
Impact of Corruption 290
Combating Corruption in Tax Administration 292
Conclusions and Policy Recommendations 298
Notes 300
References 301

10 Corruption and Fraud Detection by Supreme Audit Institutions   303
Kenneth M. Dye
The Rise in Fraud and Corruption   303
The Need for a Change in Audit Emphasis   305
What Are Fraud and Corruption?   307
The International Organization of Supreme Audit Institutions' Interest in Fraud and Corruption   309
Anticorruption Policies   310
Types of Audits   311
Detecting Fraud   314
Reporting Fraud and Communicating with Management   320
Recommendations for Improving SAI Anticorruption Performance   320
References   321

11 Public Sector Performance Auditing in Developing Countries   323
Colleen G. Waring and Stephen L. Morgan
Elements of a Performance Audit   324
Conducting the Performance Audit   333
Conducting Performance Audits in Sub-Saharan Africa   349
Notes   356
References   357

12 The Growth of Parliamentary Budget Offices   359
John K. Johnson and F. Rick Stapenhurst
The Role of Legislatures in the Budget Process   360
Examples of Specialized Legislative Budget Offices   361
Potential Value and Functions of Independent Budget Offices   371
Why Is the Number of Independent Budgeting Offices Growing?   372

Considerations in Establishing Effective Legislative Budget
Units   373
Conclusion   376
Notes   376
References   377

13 Strengthening Public Accounts Committees by Targeting Regional and Country-Specific Weaknesses   379
Riccardo Pelizzo and F. Rick Stapenhurst
Legislatures and Public Financial Accountability   380
Organization of PACs across the Commonwealth   381
What Factors Contribute to the Success of a PAC?   383
Obstacles to Effective Performance and Possible Ways of
Overcoming Them   391
Notes   392
References   393

Index   395

BOXES

2.1   The Four Phases of Civil Service Reform in Sri Lanka   35
3.1   Using E-Government to Fight Corruption around the World   71
5.1   Citizen Efforts to Improve the Electoral Process in Argentina and the United States   152
5.2   Civil Society Achievements in Mexico, South Africa, and Zambia   156
5.3   Does Participatory Budgeting Increase Accountability in Brazil?   157
5.4   Political Interference in Prosecuting Corruption in Malawi   162
6.1   Local Government Participation under the Uruguay National Agreement of 1992   198
6.2   The Everyday Effectiveness of the Peruvian Ombudsman   200
6.3   Goa's Right to Information Act   202
6.4   Promise and Pitfalls of Noninstitutionalized Participation: Mumbai's Action Committee for Rationing   204
8.1   Experimental Evidence on Controlling Corruption   259

Contents xi

8.2 Fighting Corruption Indirectly in Indonesia   265
9.1 Causes of Corruption in Tax Administration
     in Bulgaria   286
9.2 The Nature of Tax Fraud in India   289
9.3 Using Information Technology to Streamline Services and
     Reduce Corruption in India   295
9.4 Using an Independent Agency to Combat Corruption   296
10.1 The Risks of Whistle-Blowing   318
11.1 Does the Drug Abuse Resistance Education (DARE)
     Program Work?   332
11.2 Conducting a Performance Audit of Child Immunization
     Services at the Local Level   335
11.3 Cost of Child Immunization Services Clinic Staff: Site Visit
     Fieldwork Plan   345

FIGURES

6.1 Six Dimensions of Background Constraints   194
6.2 Voice Expression and Accountability Effects   206
6.3 Key Functional Institutions Necessary for Effective Stakeholder
     Participation/Consultation   209
11.1 Government Program Elements and Performance Aspects
     Subject to Audit   328
11.2 Interaction among Elements of an Audit Finding   348

TABLES

2.1 Application of Political Model of Reform to Civil Service
     Reform in Sri Lanka   37
2.2 Forces Driving and Restraining Civil Service Reform
     in Morocco   38
2.3 Responsibility for Staff Management in Central Government
     Agencies (Commonwealth Structure)   43
2.4 Sequencing of Public Management Reforms   53
3.1 Dimensions of Good Governance   63
3.2 Characteristics of Countries with "Restricted Stateness"   67
3.3 Ways in Which E-Government Contributes to
     Good Governance   69
4.1 Output Reporting by the Fairfax County Police Department   97
4.2 Output Reporting by the Fairfax County Fire and
     Rescue Department   98

4.3	Output Reporting by the Fairfax County Park Authority	99
4.4	Output Reporting by the Fairfax County Community and Recreation Services Cost Center	100
4.5	Output Reporting on Fairfax County Integrated Services Community Initiatives	108
6.1	Key Laws, Policies, and Institutions Supporting Voice Mechanisms	189
6A.1	The ARVIN Framework: A Way to Assess the Enabling Environment for Civic Engagement	225
7.1	Priorities for Anticorruption Reforms Given Level of Corruption and Quality of Governance	243
7.2	Empirical Evidence on Success of Selected Anticorruption Programs	245
7.3	Relevance of Anticorruption Programs Given Country Circumstances	247
8.1	Examples of Anticorruption Efforts Suggested by the Economics of Crime and by Principal-Agent Theory	257
8.2	Alternatives to Traditional Mechanisms of Accountability in Countries with Systemic Corruption	262
8.3	Rules That Might Have Prevented Democracy from Being Subverted in Belarus	274
11.1	Types and Examples of Audit Findings	327
11.2	Pre-audit Information-Gathering Activities and Their Benefits	336
11.3	Vulnerability Assessment of Risks Facing Child Immunization Services	338
11.4	Performance Objectives Based on Assessed Risks of Child Immunization Program	340
11.5	Methodologies for Gathering and Analyzing Data	341
11.6	Finding Elements, Data, and Analysis Methods Needed to Conduct Performance Audit of Child Immunization Program	343
11.7	Caveats about Conducting a Performance Audit	351
12.1	Characteristics of Selected Independent Budget Offices	375
13.1	Percentage of PAC Chairs Who Report that PAC "Frequently" Achieved Various Results, by Region	384
13.2	Percentage of PAC Chairs Who Consider Various Formal Factors "Very Important" to PAC Success, by Region	385

13.3 Percentage of PAC Chairs Who Consider Alternative Compositional Factors "Very Important" to PAC Success, by Region   388
13.4 Percentage of PAC Chairs Who Consider Various Practices and Procedures "Very Important" to PAC Success, by Region   389

Foreword

In Western democracies, systems of checks and balances built into government structures have formed the core of good governance and have helped empower citizens for more than two hundred years. The incentives that motivate public servants and policy makers—the rewards and sanctions linked to results that help shape public sector performance—are rooted in a country's accountability frameworks. Sound public sector management and government spending help determine the course of economic development and social equity, especially for the poor and other disadvantaged groups, such as women and the elderly.

Many developing countries, however, continue to suffer from unsatisfactory and often dysfunctional governance systems that include rent seeking and malfeasance, inappropriate allocation of resources, inefficient revenue systems, and weak delivery of vital public services. Such poor governance leads to unwelcome outcomes for access to public services by the poor and other disadvantaged members of society, such as women, children, and minorities. In dealing with these concerns, the development assistance community in general and the World Bank in particular are continuously striving to learn lessons from practices around the world to achieve a better understanding of what works and what does not work in improving public sector governance, especially with respect to combating corruption and making services work for poor people.

The Public Sector Governance and Accountability Series advances our knowledge by providing tools and lessons from practices in improving efficiency and equity of public services provision and strengthening institutions of accountability in governance. The series highlights frameworks to create incentive environments and pressures for good governance from within and beyond governments. It outlines institutional mechanisms to empower citizens to demand accountability for results from their governments. It provides practical guidance on managing for results and prudent fiscal management. It outlines approaches to dealing with corruption and malfeasance. It provides conceptual and practical guidance on alternative service delivery frameworks for extending the reach and access of public services. The series also covers safeguards for the protection of the poor, women, minorities, and other disadvantaged groups; ways of strengthening institutional arrangements for voice and exit; methods of evaluating public sector programs; frameworks for responsive and accountable governance; and fiscal federalism and local governance.

This series will be of interest to public officials, development practitioners, students of development, and those interested in public governance in developing countries.

Frannie A. Léautier
Vice President
World Bank Institute

Preface

Performance-based accountability is appealing because of its potential to improve government service delivery performance and to ensure the integrity of public operations. But implementation of such an accountability system represents a major challenge for any public sector organization; most such reforms fail as a result of difficulties in design and implementation. This volume provides advice on how to institutionalize performance-based accountability, especially in countries that lack good accountability systems. The volume describes how institutions of accountability may be strengthened to combat corruption.

The volume is organized into two parts. The first part deals with public management reforms to ensure the integrity and improve the efficiency of government operations. It outlines an agenda for public management reforms and discusses the roles of e-government and network solutions in performance improvements. The second part of the volume provides advice on strengthening the role of representative institutions, such as organs and committees of parliament, in providing oversight of government programs. It also provides guidance on how auditing and related institutions can be used to detect fraud and corruption. The book highlights the causes of corruption and the use of both internal and external accountability institutions and mechanisms to fight it. It provides advice on how to tailor anticorruption programs to individual country circumstances and how to sequence reform efforts to ensure sustainability.

This volume is the outcome of a partnership between the Swedish International Development Agency and the World Bank

Institute through the Public Expenditure Management and Financial Accountability (PEFA) program. It is hoped that the ideas for reform presented here will aid these institutions' client countries.

Roumeen Islam
Manager, Poverty Reduction and Economic Management
World Bank Institute

Acknowledgments

This book brings together learning modules on government performance accountability and combating corruption prepared for the World Bank Institute learning programs directed by the editor over the past three years. These learning modules and their publication in the current volume were primarily financed by the government of Sweden through its Public Expenditure and Financial Accountability (PEFA) partnership program, sponsored jointly with the World Bank Institute and directed by the editor. The government of Japan provided additional financial support for the editing of this volume. The editor is grateful to Hallgerd Dryssen of the Swedish International Development Agency (SIDA) in Stockholm, for overall guidance and support of the PEFA program. In addition, Bengt Anderson, Goran Anderson, Gunilla Bruun, Alan Gustafsson, and other members of the external advisory group for PEFA contributed to the design and development of the program. Thanks are also due to Cecilia Nordin Van Gansberghe for her contributions as a SIDA secondee to the PEFA program at the World Bank Institute.

The book has benefited from contributions to World Bank Institute learning events by senior policy makers and scholars from Africa and elsewhere. In particular, thanks are due to Ismail Momoniat, deputy director-general (acting) of the National Treasury of South Africa; Neil Cole, National Treasury of South Africa; Paul Boothe, former associate deputy minister of the Ministry of Finance of Canada; Tania Ajam, director of AFReC (the Applied Fiscal Research Centre of South Africa); Christina Nomdo of IDASA (the Institute for Democracy in South Africa); Anders Haglund,

PricewaterhouseCoopers, Stockholm; and Florence Kuteesa, public finance consultant, Ministry of Finance, Uganda.

The editor is grateful to the leading scholars who contributed chapters and to the distinguished reviewers who provided comments. Alta Fölscher, Adrian Shall, and Chunli Shen helped during various stages of the preparation of this book and provided comments and editorial revisions of individual chapters. Kaitlin Tierney provided excellent administrative support for this project.

I am grateful to Stephen McGroarty for ensuring a fast-track process for publication of this book. The quality of the book was enhanced by excellent editorial inputs provided by Barbara Karni. Production—including editing, typesetting, proofreading, indexing, and design—was managed by Janet Sasser. Denise Bergeron is to be thanked for the excellent print quality of the book.

Contributors

OMAR AZFAR is associate professor of economics in the department of public management at the John Jay College of Criminal Justice of the City University of New York. An expert on corruption, decentralization, and other aspects of governance, he regularly gives advice to the World Bank, the U.S. Agency for International Development (USAID), and other development agencies. He is the coeditor with Charles Cadwell of *Market-Augmenting Government: The Institutional Foundations for Prosperity* (University of Michigan Press, 2003), which suggests that markets work best when governments provide an effective legal infrastructure that allows exchange to be voluntary and reliable.

HELMUT DRÜKE is the head of e-government studies at the Institute of Electronic Business in Berlin, Germany. He is also assistant professor of political science at the Institute for Political Science at the University of Leipzig. He was part of the project team that supported the Federal Ministry for Economy and Technology in providing e-government at the local level in Germany. He is the editor of *Local Electronic Government: A Comparative Analysis*, with 50 case studies in seven countries.

KENNETH M. DYE is a chartered accountant with wide experience in the public and private sectors as an auditor, accountant, and senior executive. He is currently an independent international development consultant serving supreme audit institutions around the globe. He served as Auditor General of Canada from 1981 to 1991. He was the founder and first chair of the Development Initiative of the International Organization of Supreme Audit Institutions

(INTOSAI) and the Public Sector Committee of the International Federation of Accountants. He directed the Cowater Accountability Group from 1993 to 2003, where he specialized in strengthening of supreme audit institutions and ministries of finance in developing countries.

MARK A. GLASER is a professor of public administration at the Hugo Wall School of Urban and Public Affairs at Wichita State University, in Kansas. His research focuses on improving performance by strengthening connections between citizens and local government, particularly through the use of citizen surveys.

ROB JENKINS is professor of political science at Birkbeck College, University of London. His research focuses on the politics of development, particularly politics and political economy in contemporary India. He is the author of *Democratic Politics and Economic Reform in India*, the coauthor of *Reinventing Accountability: Making Democracy Work for Human Development*, and the editor of *Regional Reflections: Comparing Politics across India's States*. In addition to articles in academic journals, his work has appeared in the *Guardian*, the *Wall Street Journal*, and *Dissent*. He has worked as a consultant for the United Nations Development Programme, the U.K. Department of International Development, and other agencies.

JOHN K. JOHNSON is director of development for the Center for Legislative Development at the University at Albany, State University of New York. He has designed or managed democracy development activities for a variety of national and international organizations, including USAID, the United Nations Development Programme, the World Bank Institute, the Inter-American Development Bank, and the Ford Foundation. A former Foreign Service officer in Latin America, a USAID parliamentary project manager, a teacher in Kenya, and a committee director in the New York State Legislature, Mr. Johnson has management, consulting, and training experience in more than 25 countries.

WILLY MCCOURT is a senior lecturer at the Institute for Development Policy and Management at the University of Manchester. He has published on development policy, human resource management, and public management in developing countries.

STEPHEN L. MORGAN is the city auditor of Austin, Texas, where he directs a full scope audit office that conducts performance audits, investigates fraud, and engages in consulting. Before joining the City Auditor's Office, Mr. Morgan was an auditor in the U.S. Government Accountability Office's National Productivity Group, where he was responsible for auditing federal productivity programs. In 2002 he received the Harry Hatry Distinguished Performance Measurement Practice Award from the American Society of Public Administration, honoring his lifetime of contributions to public service.

RICCARDO PELIZZO is assistant professor of political science at the Singapore Management University and a World Bank consultant on legislative issues. He is the coauthor, with Gianfranco Pasquino, of *Parlamenti Democratici*.

B. GUY PETERS is the Maurice Falk Professor of Government at the University of Pittsburgh, as well as an adjunct professor at Bodo University College (Norway) and the City University of Hong Kong. Among his recent publications are *The Handbook of Public Administration* and *The Handbook of Public Policy*, both coedited with Jon Pierre, and *Institutional Theory in Political Science* (2nd ed).

MAHESH C. PUROHIT is director of the Foundation for Public Economics and Policy Research. Prior to this, he was a professor at the National Institute of Public Finance, New Delhi. He served as Member-Secretary of the Empowered Committee of State Finance Ministers to Monitor Sales Tax Reforms (1999–2001), Secretary to the Committee of Chief Ministers on VAT and Incentives to Backward Areas (1999), Member-Secretary to the Committee of Finance Secretaries on Backward Area Incentives (1999), and Secretary to the Committee of State Finance Ministers (1998). He is the author of many books and articles on public finance, industrial economics, and environmental protection.

MALCOLM RUSSELL-EINHORN is associate director of the IRIS Center at the University of Maryland, where he directs projects and conducts research on demand-driven strategies for improved delivery of government services. A lawyer and governance specialist who has worked on regulatory reform, administrative reform, and anticorruption projects around the world, Mr. Russell-Einhorn has written articles on comparative administrative law, government transparency, and legal reform. He has taught courses on law and development and comparative law at the law schools of Boston College, Boston University, Georgetown University, and American University.

ANWAR SHAH is lead economist and program leader for public sector governance at the World Bank Institute, Washington, D.C. He is also a member of the Executive Board of the International Institute of Public Finance in Munich, Germany, and a fellow of the Institute for Public Economics, Alberta, Canada. He has previously served the Canadian Ministry of Finance in Ottawa and the government of the province of Alberta, Canada. He has published books and articles dealing with governance, anticorruption, and public management reform issues. He is the lead author of a recent report evaluating World Bank assistance for corruption and governance reforms in developing countries. He has also lectured at Harvard, MIT, and Duke, as well as at other leading educational institutions.

F. RICK STAPENHURST is a senior public sector specialist at the World Bank Institute. Before joining the World Bank, he served as director of multilateral development banks at the Canadian International Development Agency. He is the coeditor, with Niall Johnston and Riccardo Pelizzo, of *The Role of Parliaments in Curbing Corruption*.

COLLEEN G. WARING is the deputy city auditor of Austin, Texas. She also trains government auditors and managers throughout the United States. She serves on the boards of the National Association of Local Government Auditors (NALGA) and the Regents of the Institute of Internal Auditors (IIA). She is the author of several research papers on the audit uses of evaluation and operations research methodologies.

Abbreviations and Acronyms

$	Unless otherwise designated, this symbol refers to U.S. dollars.
ADB	Asian Development Bank
CBO	community-based organization; also Congressional Budget Office (United States)
CEFP	Centro de Estudios de las Finanzas Publicas (Center for Public Finance Studies)
CenVAT	federal VAT
CPA	Commonwealth Parliamentary Association
CPI	Corruption Perception Index
CSO	civil society organization
DSMHS	Department of Systems Management for Human Services
EU	European Union
GNTP	Grupo Nacional de Trabajo para la Participacion
HRO	Human Rights Ombudsman
IFAC	International Federation of Accountants
INTOSAI	International Organization of Supreme Audit Institutions
LAO	Legislative Analyst's Office
LGTA	Local Government Transition Act
MDG	Millennium Development Goal
MP	member of parliament
NABO	National Assembly Budget Office
NBO	neighborhood-based organization
NGO	nongovernmental organization
NHM	National Health Ministry
NPM	New Public Management

OECD	Organisation for Economic Co-operation and Development
OTB	territorial grassroots organization
PAC	Public Accounts Committee
PBO	Parliamentary Budget Office
PDM	Municipal Development Plan
PETS	public expenditure tracking systems
POA	Annual Operation Plan
PRSP	Poverty Reduction Strategy Paper
SAI	supreme audit institution
UNDP	United Nations Development Programme
USAID	U.S. Agency for International Development
VAT	value added tax

Overview

ANWAR SHAH

The dysfunctionality of public sector governance is considered to be the root cause of corruption, inefficiency, and waste in developing countries. This dysfunctionality is attributed to a lack of citizen empowerment to hold the government to account. In earlier volumes in this series, Shah (2005) and Andrews and Shah (2005) presented a framework for citizen-centered governance to empower citizens to demand accountability from their governments. This volume presents the latest thinking of leading development scholars on operationalizing such a governance framework. The focus of this volume is creating performance-based accountability and oversight when there is no bottom line. Each chapter addresses an important dimension of such a framework.

Part I: Ensuring Integrity and Improving the Efficiency of Public Management

The four chapters in part I are concerned with integrity and efficiency in public management. In chapter 1, "Performance-Based Accountability," B. Guy Peters suggests that accountability is one of the central mechanisms for ensuring both democracy and effectiveness in the public sector. As implemented, however, accountability has relied heavily on political mechanisms that have tended to focus on exceptional events, notably exceptional failures. While those failures are worth noting, and are object lessons in what may need improvement in government, the more important issue is how government performs, on average, on a daily basis.

Performance management can be conceptualized as a means of converting accountability systems into more continuous assessment of what happens in government. The development of measures, however imperfect they may be, is a way of institutionalizing something other than strictly political judgments as the basis for assessing performance in the public sector. Performance measurement and management are not substitutes for political judgment and responsiveness, but they are important supplements to the existing means of understanding what transpires in government.

Although the ideas of performance-based accountability may be appealing to many people inside and outside government, implementing these ideas is often difficult because of both technical and political problems. Effective systems of indicators need to be developed that measure the performance of government programs without distorting the manner in which programs are implemented. Organizations whose programs are being assessed need to be convinced to cooperate with the exercise and to take performance issues seriously. Political leaders have to be trained to use these measures and to integrate them with other mechanisms for accountability.

Peters provides advice on how to institutionalize performance-based accountability, especially in developing countries that may not have a history of strong accountability systems. He emphasizes the importance of moving gradually toward a complete system of performance management, recognizing the need to build confidence in the system and a political coalition to support it.

In chapter 2, "Efficiency, Integrity, and Capacity: An Expanded Agenda for Public Management?" Willy McCourt examines the conditions necessary for public management reform to flourish. He highlights political economy issues, particularly the dense network of groups and institutions that enables policies to be implemented and the inevitable opposition of the groups whose interests those policies threaten to be overcome. McCourt examines the ways in which policy coalitions form and initial policy ideas are honed. Since worthwhile reform tends to generate opposition from powerful interest groups, he discusses the feasibility of different reform packages. He then examines what makes policy makers and other stakeholders committed to public management reforms.

McCourt then reviews available models of reform, illustrating them with empirical examples and showing what might be involved in introducing any of these models in any particular country. He examines three major approaches to public management reform: the efficiency, integrity, and capacity approaches.

McCourt concludes that policy analysis is as much a process of discovery as of prescription. Policy analysts, therefore, need to spend more time identifying and understanding promising policies that are country specific and the political economies in which those policies are embedded. Such homegrown policies stand a better chance of success than policies promoted from outside, however appealing those policies may appear to outsiders.

In chapter 3, "Can E-Government Make Public Governance More Accountable?" Helmut Drüke notes that developing countries in Africa, Asia, and Latin America are lagging behind other countries in providing the preconditions for e-government and establishing new ways to work internally and handle interactions with society. The reason for such slow progress is a complex interdependency of market imperfection and state failure.

E-government stands on the pillars of customer service, citizen engagement, and internal efficiency. It can provide a new level of quality of public administration, creating new relationships and encouraging cooperation between administration on the one hand and citizens and businesses on the other.

Applying e-government means both regulating the market (by eliminating the lack of transparency and unequal opportunities to pursue selfish economic interests) and strengthening the state's role in society (by facilitating the creation of market mechanisms). Doing so helps improve regulatory enforcement, reducing the discretion of officials and increasing transparency.

E-government facilitates innovative forms of cooperation between state and private actors (through public-private partnerships or agencification, for example). It strengthens legitimacy by sustaining public services and enlarging and deepening citizen participation. Corruption, one of the greatest hindrances to progress and accountability in developing countries, can be reduced significantly by applying e-procurement, online land use planning, and e-justice. Governmental competencies are clearly enhanced when communication with citizens is improved and more transparent; stakeholders are active partners in designing, monitoring, and steering e-government; and professional performance measurements are introduced to replace subjectivity and arbitrariness.

The right approach to e-government is extremely important, given the essential gaps in transparency, lawfulness, and objectivity in developing countries. Without a clear change in management that takes into account the need to implement e-government as a comprehensive modernization concept, e-government is likely to fail.

In chapter 4, "Networks and Collaborative Solutions to Performance Measurement and Improvement in Sub-Saharan Africa," Mark A. Glaser argues for a systems approach to the concerns of community that carefully balances competing dimensions of performance and a performance measurement system that articulates community values. He then shows how collaborative networks might be formed by combining the resources of community and governmental agencies that produce systems solutions to the concerns of community.

The chapter draws on the experience of Fairfax County, Virginia—a model of technical proficiency and community engagement facilitated by performance-based budgeting—for lessons that can be applied in Sub-Saharan Africa. The author concludes that if performance-based budgeting is to guide collaborative processes in Sub-Saharan Africa, it must be fundamentally changed to provide an accounting for the investments of all core agencies as collaborators in systems solutions to the concerns of community. Performance-based budgeting must address how local government and nongovernmental organization funds can be leveraged to secure investments by community-based organizations.

Part II: Strengthening Oversight and Combating Corruption

The nine chapters of part II are concerned with institutions and mechanisms to hold government to account. In chapter 5, "The Role of Political Institutions in Promoting Accountability," Rob Jenkins reviews the various ways in which political institutions can contribute—in theory and in practice—to greater accountability of public officials to the people on whose behalf they govern. He conceives of political institutions broadly (beyond merely representative bodies or the electoral arrangements through which political leaders are chosen), as even ostensibly nonpolitical institutions are often politicized (this is one of the reasons why accountability of governments to people is in such short supply). Situating political institutions within a broader understanding of political systems allows the de facto relationships in which key actors are embedded to be understood—and, as Jenkins shows, accountability is above all about relationships.

Chapter 5 introduces and unpacks key concepts associated with the idea of accountability. Jenkins then put these concepts into action by examining the functions that particular institutions are expected to play in commonsense theories of democracy, the reasons why these functions get undermined in practice, and some of the ways in which groups have sought to overcome these problems in order to improve accountability. He then overviews a number of contemporary trends that can affect efforts to improve accountability systems. The chapter ends with a procedure through which the concepts and issues raised in the chapter can be used in a given country context to survey the accountability landscape in order to better understand the prospects for advancing improvements.

In chapter 6, "Legal and Institutional Frameworks Supporting Accountability in Budgeting and Service Delivery Performance," Malcolm Russell-Einhorn notes that citizens throughout the world are demanding greater government accountability and responsiveness and better delivery of public services. Evidence has shown that properly focused citizen "voice" can result in better incentives for public officials to deliver services desired by the public. Appropriate legal and institutional frameworks can create significant participatory spaces and opportunities for citizens to exert such agency and make meaningful choices regarding service delivery quality, access, accountability, efficiency, and equity.

In general, legal and institutional frameworks must be constructed in such a way as to maximize *voice influence* (the ability of the public to actually have an impact on government policy) and *voice focus* (the ability for such influence to encompass broad interests in society, including those of the poor). The quality of these accountability effects is usually heavily dependent on the specific structure of the participatory mechanisms in question. Where participation is artificially circumscribed (because of high costs to citizens, controlled agenda-setting, forums that are difficult to access or tangential to actual policy making, and overly technical processes), the impact on governmental decision making will be relatively weak. Consequently, effective legal and institutional frameworks must involve formal or informal arrangements, highly practical in nature, by which citizen voice is incorporated into one or more stages of the regular policy cycle.

To intersect properly with the policy cycle, these arrangements must encompass (a) institutions providing for balanced representation; (b) notification and agenda-setting institutions; (c) affirmative information provision institutions; (d) transparency and documentation institutions; (e) voice elicitation institutions; (f) deliberation and decision-making institutions; (g) reporting, feedback, and evaluation institutions; and (h) complaint and redress institutions. Some of these institutions (a–d) are foundational and cross-cutting in nature, creating effective ground rules; others (e–g) are temporal, conforming to stages of the policy cycle itself.

A wide range of contextual factors complicates any straightforward emphasis on institutional arrangements, particularly formal ones. Politics and power relations among social and economic groups, sociocultural norms, resource issues, and citizen, government, and civil society organization capacity issues all have affected the nature of citizen participation. As a number of illustrative case studies demonstrate, citizen participation in a given context depends on the different interests and status of the individuals and groups involved, the specific types of issues in question (producing differential costs and benefits to particular citizens), and embedded social norms. These features also have a critical influence (in terms of political economy) on the introduction and implementation of voice mechanisms in a given jurisdiction.

In chapter 7, "Tailoring the Fight against Corruption to Country Circumstances," Anwar Shah argues that a lack of progress in eradicating corruption in developing countries could be the result of misguided strategies based on weak analytical underpinnings and still weaker appreciation of the institutional environments of individual developing countries. Public sector corruption, as a symptom of failed governance, depends on a multitude of factors, such as the quality of public sector management, the nature of accountability relations between the government and citizens, the legal framework, and the degree to which public sector processes are accompanied by transparency and dissemination of information. Efforts to address corruption that fail to adequately account for these "drivers" are unlikely to generate profound and sustainable results.

To understand these drivers, a conceptual and empirical perspective is needed to understand why corruption persists and what can be a useful antidote. At the conceptual level, a number of interesting ideas have been put forward. These ideas can be broadly grouped together in three categories: principal-agent or agency models, New Public Management perspectives, and neoinstitutional economics frameworks. All these models, especially the neoinstitutional economics approach, predict that the generally pursued anticorruption programs are unlikely to succeed, because they fail to change the incentives public managers face in conducting public business. The neoinstitutional economics approach argues that corruption results from the opportunistic behavior of public officials, which reflects the fact that citizens either are not empowered or face high transaction costs to hold public officials accountable for their corrupt acts. The empirical evidence supports these conclusions on past failures. Shah argues that tackling corruption requires an indirect approach that addresses the root causes of corruption. He argues that because corruption is itself a symptom of fundamental governance failure, the higher the incidence of corruption, the less an anticorruption strategy should include tactics that are narrowly targeted to corrupt behaviors and the more it should focus on the broad underlying features of the governance environment. He argues that there is a pecking order of reform strategies based on a recognition of the broader institutional environment in each country.

Chapter 8, "Disrupting Corruption," by Omar Azfar, distinguishes incidental from systemic corruption and proposes ways of dealing with each. In analyzing incidental corruption, he compares the economics of crime (prevention) and principal-agent theory. The economics of crime prevention focuses on incentives based on punishments meted out after corruption is observed and verified. The fundamental insight of principal-agent theory is that the agent can be induced to take the right action (that is, not be corrupt) by appropriate incentives, even if corruption cannot be observed. On the whole Azfar finds that principal-agent theory yields better ideas for combating corruption and recommends some concrete policies and reforms that could help alter incentives in incidentally corrupt systems.

Azfar then analyzes combating corruption when the principal is corrupt (that is, corruption is systemic). A frequent occurrence in countries with weak governance is the emergence of systems of rent extraction. Low-level bureaucrats buy jobs from their superiors, with the intention of collecting bribes; sometimes they even share the bribes with their superiors. In this situation, raising salaries is ineffective (or even counterproductive), as increasing the equilibrium price of a job leads low-level bureaucrats to become even more indebted, possibly increasing their demand for bribes. Accountability to corrupt supervisors can lead even honest bureaucrats to become corrupt.

Tackling systemic corruption is difficult, because any system to confront it can be captured. However, since the system is interconnected, exposure followed by a determined investigation can sometimes lead to the unraveling of the whole system and the dismissal or electoral defeat of the government. Only a small number of acts of corruption, therefore, needs to be exposed. Even if it is not possible to convict corrupt officials, a judicial process in which facts are found and publicized can create meaningful political consequences.

The usual mechanisms of external accountability—the justice system, anticorruption commissions, auditing agencies, inspectors general—are ineffective when corruption is systemic. Azfar therefore proposes alternative ways of dealing with corruption, such as the random assignment of judges and prosecutors, the direct election of prosecutors, opposition leadership of accountability committees in legislatures, and provisions for recalls and referenda. Based on case studies of systemic corruption in Belarus, Brazil, Kenya, and Turkey, he concludes that systems of corruption can sometimes be exposed, disrupted, and removed through a process of unraveling.

In chapter 9, "Corruption in Tax Administration," Mahesh C. Purohit examines five categories of corruption: political corruption, administrative corruption, grand corruption, petty corruption, and patronage corruption. He observes that the complexity of tax laws and procedures, the monopoly power of revenue officials, the degree of discretionary powers of the tax officials, the lack of accountability and transparency in administration, the role of political leadership, and staff-related factors are the key determinants of corruption.

Purohit focuses on corruption in tax administration in India, where too much discretionary power by officials and the lack of adequate monitoring and reporting mechanisms provide opportunities for corruption. He highlights the effect of corruption on tax revenue, tax officials, and taxpayers, noting that corruption affects not only the quality of governance but also investment and growth.

While each country has to develop measures best suited to its own local requirements, some policies are likely to prove useful in all developing countries in which corruption is a problem. The drivers of corruption within the tax administration should be the main target of anticorruption policies. Setting up an independent anticorruption organization, providing intensive training for tax officers, promoting a code of conduct, reorganizing tax departments on functional bases, and using information technology can help combat corruption.

Chapter 10, "Corruption and Fraud Detection by Supreme Audit Institutions," by Kenneth M. Dye, was written at the request of the World Bank Institute because there is a perception that supreme audit institutions are not detecting enough fraud and corruption when performing financial attest audits to give assurance about the fairness of financial statements. Too little fraud and corruption are identified in these audits because the legal burden of proof requirements are too high, causing auditors to shy away.

Fraud and corruption are often identified in public bodies, but they are usually identified by internal auditors or whistler-blowers, not by supreme audit institutions. Supreme audit institutions play an important role in conveying messages to parliaments, but they are not usually the original identifiers of the fraud and corruption. (China is an exception.) Dye suggests that public sector auditors should expand their audit programs and capabilities to seek out and report fraudulent and corrupt activities. He also suggests that public sector auditors should provide parliaments with explicit opinions on the adequacy of controls in government. He provides a number of recommendations for improving the capacity of supreme audit institutions to find and report fraud and corruption.

In chapter 11, "Public Sector Performance Auditing in Developing Countries," Colleen G. Waring and Stephen L. Morgan provide a practical guide to performance auditing and its role in supporting accountable, responsive, and responsible government. They identify the conditions and challenges to implementing performance auditing in Sub-Saharan Africa.

Waring and Morgan describe the basic elements of government programs, all of which can be subjected to a performance audit. These include inputs, processes, outputs, and outcomes. They emphasize the importance of the planning phase of auditing, in which key risks and controls are evaluated to select the most value-added audit objectives. They offer guidance for conducting effective planning, providing examples of the type of methods employed in the fieldwork phase and various means of reporting.

Implementing performance auditing in Sub-Saharan Africa requires both an existing governance infrastructure and an established administrative infrastructure. Public sector performance auditing serves an accountability function. A performance audit program depends to a great extent on the existence of certain prerequisites that form the foundation from which to apply accountability to government actions or omissions. These include the rule of law; clearly defined government organizations, with defined roles, responsibilities, and scopes of authority; the existence of policy and program planning structures; and the existence of basic accounting systems capable of tracking, categorizing, and reporting economic transactions.

The barriers to implementing and reaping the benefits of an effective government performance audit function stem from the same fundamental challenges facing development for any other aspect of African society. These include corruption; poverty; poor governance, at both the political and administrative levels; inadequate infrastructure; and brain drain.

Governance issues present a challenge to government auditing that can be overcome only from outside the audit function. Without strong independence, supported by legislative mandates and unwavering support from parliamentarians and citizens, performance auditors cannot survive long. Additional critical elements include administrative infrastructure and human resource development. Ultimately, implementing and supporting effective performance auditing in countries in Sub-Saharan Africa will require strong, committed leadership, energized by the political will to face the faults and flaws in the government.

In chapter 12, "The Growth of Parliamentary Budget Offices," John K. Johnson and F. Rick Stapenhurst show that independent, objective, nonpartisan legislative budget offices, first established in the United States in the 1900s, are being established in legislatures in other parts of the world—in many cases in legislatures with traditions quite different from those in the United States. They describe legislative budget offices in the state of California and in the national legislatures of Mexico, the Philippines, the Republic of Korea, Uganda, and the United States. These units may improve national budget processes.

Independent legislative budget offices provide several benefits. They help break the executive's monopoly on budget information, placing the legislature on a more equal footing with the executive. They simplify complexity, presenting complex budget information simply and clearly in formats that are useful for legislators. They promote budget transparency and executive accountability, making the budget process more straightforward and easier to follow. They also encourage greater discipline in public spending.

The functions of budget offices vary across locales, but they usually include making independent budget forecasts, establishing baseline budget estimates, analyzing executive budget proposals from a technical perspective, and making medium-term analyses to alert policy makers and the public to possible future consequences of proposed policy actions. Other functions include estimating the costs of policy proposals, preparing spending cut options for legislative consideration, analyzing the costs of regulations and mandates as well as the impacts of tax policies, producing policy briefs, making recommendations for government cost savings, and acting as institutional watchdogs.

If budget offices are to be effective, they must be nonpartisan. Establishing these offices by statute makes it much more difficult for executives to shut them down. Budget offices need access to executive budget information if they are to be effective; in some cases the statutes establishing them also grant them authority to compel the executive to provide budget information. When legislative-based, independent, professional, nonpartisan budget units succeed, they improve the quality of government budgets, make the budget process more transparent and easier to understand, and generally enhance government credibility.

In chapter 13, "Strengthening Public Accounts Committees by Targeting Regional and Country-Specific Weaknesses," Riccardo Pelizzo and F. Rick Stapenhurst investigate whether and under what conditions public accounts committees are able to scrutinize government accounts. Analyzing survey data collected by the World Bank Institute in 2002 from 51 Commonwealth countries, they find that the success of a public accounts committee depends on the behavior of committee members, the availability of independent sources of information, and the media's interest in scrutinizing government accounts.

In conclusion, this volume offers insights into ways policy makers can initiate governance reforms that introduce performance-based accountability in the public sector in order to both improve service delivery performance and eradicate corruption. The book should be of interest to those with a passion to make a difference in the lives of billions of voiceless people.

References

Andrews, Matthew, and Anwar Shah. 2005. "Citizen-Centered Governance: A New Approach to Public Sector Reform." In *Public Expenditure Analysis*, ed. Anwar Shah, 153–13. Washington, DC: World Bank.

Shah, Anwar. 2005. "On Getting the Giant to Kneel: Approaches to a Change in the Bureaucratic Culture." In *Fiscal Management*, ed. Anwar Shah, 211–28. Washington, DC: World Bank.

PART One
Ensuring Integrity and Improving the Efficiency of Public Management

Performance-Based Accountability

B. GUY PETERS

Accountability is a fundamental value for any political system. Citizens should have the right to know what actions have been taken in their name, and they should have the means to force corrective actions when government acts in an illegal, immoral, or unjust manner. Individual citizens should have the ability to have some redress when their rights are abused by government or they do not receive the public benefits to which they are entitled.

Central Place of Accountability in Governing

Accountability is also important for government itself. It provides government with a means of understanding how programs may fail and finding mechanisms that can make programs perform better.

An emphasis on accountability in government is one aspect of the growing emphasis on eliminating corruption and promoting transparency in government (Kaufman 2005). Transparency and openness are necessary, but perhaps not sufficient, to produce accountability in the public sector. If the public sector can maintain secrecy about its actions, there is little chance that political officials or the public will be able to impose effective control over government.

Transparency can be achieved in a number of ways. One of the most important is using performance data that can demonstrate to the public, and to political elites, just what government is doing. Information of this type may be more useful than more politicized information, which has been at the foundation of more conventional mechanisms of accountability.

What Is Accountability?

The term *accountability* can be used in a number of different ways, each with different implications for governing (see Thomas 2004). Some of the interpretations of accountability border on being incompatible with others, so that the choice of one form of accountability may preclude, or complicate, the use of others. A government, therefore, needs to exercise caution in designing a system of accountability and control in order to take into account all the contingencies that may arise from its choice.

The simplest form of accountability is the requirement for an administrative organization to render an account of what it has done. The report should be made to some external, independent organization—a legislature, an auditor, even the public at large—through a published report, so that the assessment can be reasonably public and objective. The accounting may be financial, or it may be expressed in terms of the services provided and the successes and failures of the program. In either case it involves making public what has been done in the public name. This form of accountability highlights the notion that at the most basic level, accountability is about transparency, about making it possible for actors outside a public organization to identify, and question, what has happened.

Accountability has also been conceptualized in terms of responsibility—ensuring that the behavior of officials corresponds to (is responsible to) the law or a code of ethics in office (Bovens 1999). While the conceptualization of accountability described above emphasizes the role of external actors in enforcing accountability, the concept of responsibility relies more on the internalized values of public servants and their understanding of the law and appropriate behavior in office.[1] Such a standard of personal responsibility may be acceptable and enforceable in countries with well-institutionalized public service systems; it may be risky to rely on such an approach when there is less agreement on standards of behavior.

Accountability can also be discussed in terms of responsiveness, or the willingness of civil servants to respond to demands from their political masters and perhaps from clients and the public at large. The idea of responsiveness is that the good civil servant is one who is willing to take direction from above, to attempt to serve the public, and, insofar as possible, to provide the public with what it wants. This conception points to the numerous pressures that impinge on the behavior of the public servant and the attendant difficulties he or she may face in determining an appropriate course of behavior.

These approaches to accountability may be in conflict with one another. If, for example, civil servants are motivated primarily by the responsiveness criterion, they may be guided by the interests of their clients, especially if they are "street-level bureaucrats" who may advocate the interests of their clients in the face of seemingly insensitive bureaucracies (Meyers and Vorsanger 2006). Civil servants strongly committed to legality may find it impossible to respond to the demands of a political leader if those demands are perceived to be beyond the law.

Importance of Accountability for Democracy

Accountability and transparency are essential to a democratic form of government. Opening up government to scrutiny from outside, independent actors provide a means for identifying and then questioning the government's actions. As party systems and legislatures in even fully democratic systems wane in importance with respect to the powers of the executive (see Peters 2007), the ability to scrutinize the activities of the executive becomes all the more important for democracy. Scrutiny and accountability are especially important as means of exercising control over the large and permanent public bureaucracy; they provide the public with its only means of exercising effective control over the professionalized public services that play a major role in preparing and implementing policy.

It is important to make unbiased empirical evidence about government actions available to the general public as well as to formal institutions in the public sector, "naming and shaming" poor performers. Countries that lack well-developed civil societies will encounter difficulties in using these measures of public services as instruments for accountability. The assumption behind these mechanisms is that once poor performance is identified, there will be some mobilization by the public, which will produce change. When public organizations are absent and the public is apathetic or cynical about government, mobilization will not naturally spring from evidence of poor performance.

Public sector elites also need to be mobilized. Effective use of any form of accountability requires a government elite with some sense of shame about inadequate performance. Such a sense of shame and responsibility is not universal among politicians, who can use their powers to suppress or "spin" the results of accountability exercises. Inadequate familiarity with performance management systems within government in many developing countries provides great opportunities to control and discount these efforts, scoffing at them as academic exercises that have little or nothing to do with the real work of governing.

Importance of Accountability for Effectiveness and Efficiency

Accountability mechanisms should also be conceptualized as a means of providing governments with feedback about their activities, providing them with the means of improving the delivery of public services. All organizations must be able to identify their successes and failures and to learn from these outcomes (Maula 2006); government perhaps more than others must be able to respond based on its own prior actions.

Accountability has all too often been conceptualized solely, or at least primarily, as a means of identifying malfeasance in office and punishing the individuals or organizations that did not perform adequately, especially if that action involved corruption. Accountability mechanisms should also be conceptualized as a means of assessing just what government has produced for its citizens. Are the programs adopted by government actually delivering goods and services, or are there major failures in delivery? If there are failures, what is the cause and how can it be corrected? These questions may identify malfeasance and corruption. In this case, punishments may be deserved. These questions may also identify poorly designed programs or poorly designed implementation systems that may not be able to deliver the services desired even with the most efficient and effective administrators.

Financial issues also play a role in accountability and have a central position in determining the efficiency of service provision. The question for this dimension of accountability therefore is, what services at what cost. If it is possible to provide high-quality service only at a prohibitively high cost, a government, especially in a developing country, may choose not to pursue a program. A number of techniques, notably cost-benefit analysis, can be used to assess the cost-effectiveness of a program, but good judgment remains central to assessment and enforcement of fiscal accountability.

Governments need to assess the quality of goods and services being produced through their actions. Evaluation research has developed an extensive repertoire of tools for assessing the quality of programs and advising governments about how well they are performing. These techniques are often considered luxuries by governments that want more immediate answers about their programs and the satisfaction of citizens with those programs. However, changes in the regimens associated with accountability are placing additional pressures for more effective assessment of programs and their impact on the public.

Importance of Accountability for Steering Society

Accountability is a central feature of governing, and steering, society. Governments need to learn from their own failures and successes; accountability is central to the process of detecting and correcting errors. It is important for the actors involved in this process to recognize that finding suboptimal results is not necessarily a cause for punishment, whether political or personal. Rather, it can be seen as an opportunity to learn and to find better means of providing service.

Accountability, especially accountability that focuses on improved performance rather than political punishment, is a means of institutionalizing a learning and steering approach to governance. Performance assessment fulfills the same need as policy evaluation, providing a measure of the success or failure of programs and at the same time preparing for the next round of policy making (Vedung 2006). There is some tendency for academic analysts to conceptualize policy as being made in discrete segments, beginning with problem identification and ending with evaluation; politicians talk in much the same language. In fact, policy making is a continuous process, with one round leading to the next.

Performance management as a mechanism for feedback from policy-making activities may be far from perfect, given the often very short-term measurements and the fact that the most significant effects of policy may occur far in the future. Still, performance measures may provide useful information for subsequent rounds of policy choices. Short-term information may underestimate the long-term consequences of programs and overvalue the short-term benefits. For this reason, performance measurement must be tempered with more subtle information about programs and their political setting.

The Shift to Performance-Based Accountability

Industrial country democracies have shifted away from traditional forms of accountability toward accountability based on performance and the quality of services rendered by government. This section discusses the reasons for these shifts, as well as the underlying logic of the new forms of accountability.

Weaknesses of Conventional Forms of Accountability

Part of the logic of moving toward performance-based management is that conventional forms of accountability have significant flaws, which can to some extent be rectified by performance-based accountability systems.

One flaw is the focus on exceptional events rather than average performance of organizations and their programs. The emphasis on political embarrassment in most conventional forms of accountability generally does not permit frank discussions of programs and their performance. Accountability may also be a function of political involvement rather than more objective analysis.

The logic of much of conventional accountability is punishment rather than improvement. The major political benefits of accountability are the exposure of the malfeasance or nonfeasance of political officials rather than the identification of problems in order to rectify them. If the real criteria to be used in accountability are political, there is little reason to focus on the measurement of outcomes and outputs of government. These more subjective elements of political criteria involved in accountability are certainly important, but they do not provide sufficient information with which to assess public programs.

Logic of Performance-Based Accountability

It is important to think through the process of managing performance and using performance as a means of accountability in a systematic manner. Without careful thought about the steps involved, the likelihood of committing mistakes—that is, inappropriately using performance information to make decisions and then making decisions that do not fully reflect performance—increases dramatically.

The process involved in performance management includes eight steps:

1. *Defining outcomes:* The process begins by defining what the organization, and government in general, wants the program to do and what types of outcomes are desired from a program.
2. *Defining outputs:* As well as defining the final outcomes of a policy choice, effective performance systems must also identify the intermediate steps in the process. For example, assessing the performance of the education sector requires identifying the number of teachers, the levels of funding, and all other components of an effective educational program.
3. *Developing effective measurement mechanisms:* If performance measurement is to move beyond the usual rhetoric about what government does and how well it does it, mechanisms for effective measurement must be developed. Good measures are difficult to develop and politically contentious; they may also be difficult to interpret, especially for outcomes.
4. *Linking programs to outputs and outcomes:* The actions of government have to be linked to the measures of outputs and outcomes. A program

may be called a health program, but health outcomes may depend on other programs, such as education or nutrition. A carefully constructed model of relationships is therefore required.

5. *Defining adequate standards:* What do measures of performance mean? How good is good enough? What is adequate performance? For political reasons, a standard may initially be set very low, in order to show improvements in performance.
6. *Defining adequate improvement:* How much improvement is adequate to indicate that a program and its management are performing adequately? How much improvement over what time period should be considered adequate?
7. *Defining responsibility:* The move from traditional forms of accountability to performance-based systems has shifted the emphasis away from blame to some extent. Still, one cannot ignore the fact that learning about performance provides a means for learning about the performance of individuals.
8. *Linking inputs to outputs:* In the past the budget process has been associated only with allocating inputs. The development of performance management systems provides the opportunity to better understand how those inputs are translated into programs and to make decisions accordingly.

A Strategy for Change

Given the local and national circumstances within which this chapter is considering implementing accountability systems, it is important to begin with a very fundamental set of choices. Attempting to make performance management successful may not be possible if there is not a clearly articulated strategy for making the program work.

Beginning with Basics

Given that performance management and the use of performance-based accountability systems constitute innovations in many political systems, the implementation strategy must begin with basics.

Choosing one or a few organizations or programs at a time

It is generally not feasible to initiate a program that includes all government programs at one time. Both the limited analytic capacity of government organizations in most settings and the political threat of a comprehensive approach make it advisable to begin implementing evaluation programs slowly. Advocates of performance management must have a clear plan for extending the program to other parts of government, however.

Choosing one indicator at a time

The initial phases of a performance project might begin with a single measure that captures a composite measure of performance (for example, completion rates in education). While any measure will have its weaknesses, this strategy permits some initial focus and enables would-be managers to launch the project. That said, the performance management program needs to be ready to expand quickly to multiple indicators to prevent excessive focus on a single measure and to provide a more rounded appraisal of performance.

Selecting programs

Everything else equal, it is better to begin with programs that have clearly identifiable and measurable outputs and that are central to public well-being. It may also be wise to select programs that can be improved with modest effort.

Negotiating measures

The indicator of performance needs to be negotiated and agreed upon. It is easy to impose an objectively useful indicator on a program and assume that it will work. Some agreement and negotiation will be useful to create "buy-in" by participants. Negotiation will enable the performance management exercise to draw on the organization's expertise. In the end, however, the center of government may have to use its power and its more extensive vision of the performance system to impose indicators.

Setting the bar low

Although the ultimate end of performance-based accountability is to make public programs as good as possible, it may be strategically useful to begin with very low demands on programs in order to ensure participation and allow programs to demonstrate improvement. The officials in charge of performance management can always raise the bar to drive improved quality. Indeed, officials should implicitly and explicitly have longer-range improvements in mind as they implement programs.

Making the process transparent

Part of the logic of accountability is legitimizing the actions of government, especially in countries that have not had transparent governments (see Curtis 1999). Therefore, making the process itself as transparent as possible can be important politically. Doing so is also a significant part of the learning process, both within government and for society as a whole.

Initiating a learning process

The performance management process should be seen as a way of initiating a learning process. This process may include a strategy for diffusing the results of the performance measurement, as well as linking this process with others within government as well as with international organizations and other governments to create benchmarks for good performance.

Making Other Strategic Choices

Additional choices will have to be made if performance-based management and accountability are to move from experiments to normal components of the governance process. Using a small number of programs to demonstrate the utility of the approach is an important first step, but extending the program and the concept of performance throughout government should be the ultimate goal.

Thinking about the issues below may appear to be premature given some of the challenges that will be encountered in even the more experimental stages of implementation. However, understanding how future implementation may have to be undertaken will help policy makers make more immediate decisions. That understanding will help prevent them from making decisions that will foreclose future options. Considering the future implementation strategy should also make it clear to civil servants in other parts of the government that performance management is coming.

Establishing responsibility for performance management

The question of who is to be responsible for a program may appear to be an insignificant concern, but structural decisions matter. It is therefore important to consider what impact the location of authority over performance management will have.

The first option for organizing performance management is to create a special unit that implements the program across all public organizations. This pattern, seen in a number of countries, such as New Zealand and the United Kingdom, has several virtues. In particular, it permits expertise to be concentrated in the organization that becomes the focus for developing measurement instruments, reporting, and interpreting the outcomes of performance evaluation in the government. When expertise is scarce, concentrating this function often represents the best use of this limited resource.

A potential problem with this approach is that placing the expertise for performance measurement and interpretation in a single organization outside of the operational elements of government may create line versus staff problems. Line departments producing services tend to view independent review organizations as lacking any real understanding of the problems that "real" agencies encounter. For their part, members of the performance assessment organization are likely to argue that the delivery agencies are insensitive to the demands for more scientific approaches to management and concerned only with their own limited perspective on policy and governing.

A second option for organizing performance management within government is to institutionalize it in a central government agency, such as a ministry of finance or the prime minister's office (see Campbell and Szablowski 1979; Savoie 1999). Doing so solves the obvious problem faced by a freestanding organization: the absence of the political power to encourage line organizations to participate in the system and to impose any recommendations that may arise from the information gained from performance appraisal. While expert, however, an independent agency may lack the power to make anything happen in government, especially a government with entrenched departments and agencies.

Locating performance management in a financial management agency, such as a ministry of finance or budget office, enables the organization to use the information yielded by performance management directly into the budget process. Furthermore, given that these organizations may have some responsibility for personnel management, the more individualized aspects of the process can be introduced into processes that assess and reward civil servants. The virtues of a linkage of this sort can be seen in the Government Performance and Results Act of 1993 in the United States (Roberts 2000). An elaborate set of performance targets and measures is now a part of the budget submission for each organization. Congress can use that information, linked with old-fashioned evaluation research, when setting annual budgets.[2]

There may, however, be some difficulties in locating performance management in a central agency. First, ministries of finance are dominated by issues of money and the financial health of the government. Performance management is a small, ancillary aspect of their business and may therefore be lost. In contrast, in a freestanding organization, these issues are the organization's only focus. Moreover, issues of performance may become conflated with issues of taxing and spending; they may lack the emphasis they require in order to be effective in improving performance. If performance management is located in a prime minister's office, it may become too tied to politics. Locating the function in an independent agency may allow it to provide more objective appraisal of the operations of government.

A third option is to establish a performance management unit within each ministry or agency and decentralize program implementation. This approach may seem to make sense, given that each of these units could specialize in the work of its own organization, becoming expert on the policy issues involved. In addition, this arrangement may be able to develop greater trust between the performance management staff and the programs being assessed and hence produce more detailed and useful evaluations of performance. Establishing a performance management unit within each ministry or agency may also make the institutionalization of performance management less threatening to the organizations involved in the process.

The obvious danger from organizing in this manner is that the evaluators and the evaluated are too close, potentially compromising their objectivity. The development of expertise may not offset the losses of detachment that are necessary to make a system of performance management effective and plausible to the public. For this reason, decentralization of performance management may be the least desirable of the organizational options presented here, although there may be instances in which the extent of hostility to the performance management may justify this choice.

In addition to these options, there are several other possibilities. One is to locate performance assessment and management in the legislative branch of government, as the Government Performance and Results Act did in the United States. This location may be the most appropriate, given that much of the logic of enforcing accountability is parliamentary, even in presidential systems. Performance management could also be located in the auditing and accounting organization of the public sector, generally associated with the legislative branch, as a means of ensuring greater financial accountability. In many countries, public auditing organizations have moved beyond simple financial accounting to engage in efficiency and effectiveness auditing. Adding the performance management function would be a natural extension of their approach to exercising control within government.

Linking performance management to budget and other allocation devices

Performance assessment should not be considered alone but as one component of the entire management and accountability regimen. Too often the measurement and understanding of organizational and personal performance in the public sector are isolated from other management processes, so that the information collected and interpreted is of little real consequence for the actual control of the system. This method of enforcing accountability can be threatening to managers and politicians, who segregate this information from the remainder of management.

The ultimate aim of implementing performance management in the public sector is to integrate it with financial management and personnel management (Hilton and Joyce 2004). For managing both organizations and individuals, the goal is to make the use of these criteria as central to everyday management as possible. In most governments there is a very long way to go before the measurement of performance is not perceived as exotic and foreign to the usual processes of governing. The financial constraints most governments face, especially in developing countries, make this linkage difficult. Ministers have more to worry about than these measurements, which they may perceive as abstract. Leaders of performance management programs will thus have to exercise substantial leadership to create the desirable integration.

Linkages may be easier to forge with personnel management than with financial management, given that the personnel constraints on government may not be as readily apparent as the financial constraints. Personnel managers are often committed to more traditional forms of managing personnel, such as civil service pay and grading systems, however, and may be less amenable to implementing performance-based systems that appear to be derived from the private sector. Some of this reluctance may be a result of sincere commitments to the principles of equality and to the notion that minimum qualification is sufficient for appointment at the heart of traditional personnel management. But reluctance may also represent fear of change. Training and leadership will be needed if the desired changes are to be implemented effectively.

If linkages with personnel management are to be effective and widely accepted, training opportunities should be provided for the civil servants being assessed. Performance systems should not become mere means of sanctioning civil servants and public organizations. If performance management merely provides the ammunition needed to discipline or dismiss some public employees, it will not have fulfilled its potential. Civil servants should be given the opportunity to correct difficulties detected in the review process, so that the process becomes one of feedback and error correction for individuals as well as organizations.

Linking performance management with traditional forms of accountability

Most political systems—and most citizens—still think about accountability in terms of traditional mechanisms, such as parliamentary oversight or legalistic controls. The evidence used in these traditional accountability exercises has tended to be more based on individual cases than on systematic consideration of the performance of organizations, programs, and individuals.

Making the linkage between conventional forms of accountability and performance-based accountability should not be difficult. The evidence from performance management simply becomes part of the information used to make the case that the officials in question have not, or perhaps, have performed adequately. The evidence being generated is more systematic and perhaps more quantitative, but it can be used for the same purpose—holding individuals and organizations accountable.

Demonstrating the benefits of performance management

Advocates and managers of performance-based accountability programs will need to demonstrate both that the program is not threatening and that it can produce real benefits for participants. One of the potential benefits of performance management is that it can demonstrate that performance in the public sector is good, or at least adequate. There is so much negative rhetoric about government that it is easy for citizens to assume that performance is weak. In fact, many public programs perform as well as or better than private programs. Even if the public may be reluctant to accept this reality, performance management can provide a basis for improving the image of government.

The commitment to performance management can be considered a commitment to improvement, as the goal of performance management is to identify both successes and failures and to address the failures. There can and should be some commitment to continuous improvement in the course of evaluating programs. Although the initial standards of performance can be minimal, the ability to drive performance with standards that are regularly raised is crucial to the success of the program.

Barriers and Perverse Consequences

Many barriers stand in the way of implementing performance management. Even in countries and organizations that have had extensive experience with performance techniques, questions about the impact of these techniques and their contributions to effective management arise in the public sector.

Barriers

Performance management goes against the traditions of government; it generally must be imposed in the face of opposition. Even in governments that emphasize accountability through more conventional means, the use of performance management may not be considered an appropriate means of achieving accountability. In particular, the performance approach may be seen as excessively technocratic and too removed from the political process that has defined accountability in the past.

Given the numerous, and very real, problems of measurement discussed above, a seemingly technocratic approach to accountability may be seen as trading a working, if imperfect, form of control over the bureaucracy for an equally if not more imperfect mechanism that has not really been implemented effectively in many settings. Most politicians and administrators are more comfortable with a system they know and generally prefer to modify it rather than embark on an entirely new system. The reluctance is perhaps most marked for politicians who have been able to use their accountability actions as a source of political power, as well as a source of appeal to the public.

For public administrators the use of performance-based ideas for accountability may be a source of protection as well as a potential source of concern. Rather than having to submit to the often arbitrary and capricious instruments for accountability associated with conventional political forms, the more objective information contained in performance assessments can provide a basis for more informed discourse about how to improve public programs. Rather than having to depend entirely on the goodwill of politicians for support, administrators can demonstrate that they are producing the services mandated at the level of quality mandated. This evidence may not be sufficient in the real world of politics and government, but it does provide a source of defense and a basis for argumentation.

In developing countries one of the major barriers to implementing performance management is that the process uses scarce resources that could be used to provide services to citizens, pay civil servants, or do the host of other things that need to be done. The obvious political question that arises is whether the improvement in performance that results from these techniques is sufficient to justify the investment of resources that could be used in other ways—particularly when the benefits of performance management may be reaped far in the future.

A second problem encountered by many would-be implementers of performance management in developing countries is that measurement is difficult, if not impossible, in many policy areas. Measurement is difficult in more affluent and urban societies; where there is less internal organization in civil society, it may be impossible to track the effects of a particular policy intervention (Bouckaert 1993). Even in affluent societies, some policy areas are less amenable to performance measurement. These programs must rely more heavily on less formal mechanisms to determine how well a program performs. Measures are politically contentious, and the choice of measurement to some extent implies the choice of a particular political stance.

Perverse Consequences

Almost all attempts at reforming management, whether public or private, have unintended consequences, and performance management is no different. It is important, therefore, that would-be reformers be cognizant of the difficulties that can arise from introducing this reform. Like many sets of unintended consequences, those produced by performance management occur when the basic ideas of the reform are taken to their logical extremes (Hood and Peters 2004). While perhaps unavoidable, these problems are manageable if they are understood. Being aware of their existence will enable evaluators to think more effectively about program design.

Indicatorism

The first, and perhaps most common, perverse consequence of performance measurement can be labeled *indicatorism*, the excessive reliance on indicators to make decisions about policies. In the complex world of public service provision, it is difficult to rely on a single indicator as an alternative to more thorough knowledge and careful reflection on the causes and consequences of organizational performance.

Creaming

If organizations and managers in the public sector are judged by how well they serve clients and produce identifiable outcomes, they will attempt to find as easy a way as possible to meet their goals, even if their actions fail to meet the true goals of the program. Employment programs that are assessed on their success in placing the unemployed, for example, are likely to focus on the more capable clients, who may not really need assistance, rather than the less capable clients, who really need help. Some programs may not be able to select their own clients, but those that can have strong incentives to select the clients that make their performance appear better.

Short-termism

To be useful for policy makers, and to some extent to be useful for purposes of accountability, the indicators that are developed must demonstrate changes over the short term. Unfortunately, some of the most successful programs in the long run do not necessarily show benefits in the short term. Many programs have "sleeper effects"—that is, the investment of public resources generates benefits only after years or even decades (Salamon 1979). Some programs that may be successful in the short term may produce effects that decay over time, so that short-term success is actually long-term failure.

The problem of time is related to the dominance of the political cycle in governing: politicians need to be able to demonstrate success in a limited time. Bureaucrats may need to be able to produce demonstrable outcomes within the confines of their normal budget cycle or the authorized lifetime of their program if they are to be able to defend the program and maintain its existence. For both politicians and bureaucrats, therefore, there is a need to identify short-term outcomes and use them as a central component of the political process.

Managerialism

Performance-based accountability systems tend to measure both the performance of policy delivery systems and the performance of the managers of those systems and to assume that the latter determines the former. In some instances, the underlying explanation for policy outcomes is the performance of the management of a program. In other instances, however, failure or success may stem from program design, inadequate funding, or other causes (Linder and Peters 1984).

The logic of focusing on the inadequacies of management goes back to the linkage between performance-based and conventional forms of accountability. If the goal of accountability is solely to establish blame, blaming managers makes sense. If, however, the goal is to focus on the overall performance of programs and the mechanisms for improving performance, excessive concern with blame will undermine the intentions of performance management.

Conclusions

Accountability is a central concept for governance. Although most closely associated with democratic governance, accountability can also be important for other types of systems. For both democratic and undemocratic governing systems, accountability is a means of identifying success and failure from past actions. This identification is a means of learning about governing and improving the capacity of the political system to govern. Accountability may also be a means of assigning responsibility for failures or, more rarely, identifying individuals responsible for success and then thinking about the personnel implications of the performance of the system.

The use of performance-based accountability systems changes the manner in which accountability is enforced. Performance systems require that rather than thinking about political consequences of choices and blame, the accountability system focuses on demonstrable indicators of success and failure. If implemented effectively, performance accountability should focus on improving performance and capacity. This emphasis would be a welcome change from punishment and blame. Of course, any system of accountability involves "naming and shaming"; the important question is the emphasis and the information that may be used in the process of blaming.

Notes

1. The difference between the two harkens back to the classic debate between Carl Friedrich and Herman Finer over the source of standards for conduct in public life (see Peters 2001).
2. The linkage here is not unambiguous. If an agency is performing poorly, should it be punished by having its budget reduced, or should it be given more money in order to be able to perform better in the future? One of the weaknesses of most performance appraisal systems is that they cannot determine the processes through which good or poor performance was produced and hence may need to be linked with more "old-fashioned" evaluation research.

References

Bouckaert, Geert. 1993. "Measurement and Meaningful Management." *Public Productivity and Management Review* 17 (1): 31–43.

Bovens, Mark A. P. 1999. *The Quest for Responsibility*. Cambridge: Cambridge University Press.

Campbell, Colin, and George G. Szablowski. 1979. *The Superbureaucrats*. Toronto: Macmillan.

Curtis, Donald. 1999. "Performance Management in Participatory Democracy: Thoughts on the Transformation Process in South African Local Government." *International Journal of Public Sector Management* 12 (3): 260–72.

Hilton, Rita M., and Philip Joyce. 2004. "Performance Information and Budgeting." In *Handbook of Public Policy*, ed. B. Guy Peters and Jon Pierre. London: Sage.

Hood, Christopher, and B. Guy Peters. 2004. "The Middle-Aging of New Public Management: Into the Age of Paradox." *Journal of Public Administration Research and Theory* 14 (3): 267–83.

Kaufman, Daniel. 2005. *Myths and Realities of Governance and Corruption*. World Bank Governance Program, Washington, DC.

Linder, Stephen H., and B. Guy Peters. 1984. "From Social Theory to Policy Design." *Journal of Public Policy* 4 (2): 237–59.

Maula, Marjatta. 2006. *Organizations as Learning Systems*. Amsterdam: Elsevier.

Meyers, Marcia, and Susan Vorsanger. 2006. "Street-Level Bureaucracy." In *Handbook of Public Policy*, ed. B. Guy Peters and Jon Pierre. London: Sage.

Peters, B. Guy. 2001. *The Politics of Bureaucracy*, 5th ed. London: Routledge.

———. 2007. "The Executive." In *European Politics*, ed. Colin Hay. Oxford: Oxford University Press.

Roberts, Nancy. 2000. "The Synoptic Model of Strategic Planning and the GPRA: Lacking a Good Fit with the Political Context." *Public Productivity and Management Review* 23 (2): 297–311.

Salamon, Lester M. 1979. "The Time Dimension in Policy Evaluation: The Case of New Deal Land Reform." *Public Policy* 8: 129–83.

Savoie, Donald J. 1999. *Governing from the Centre: The Concentration of Power in Canadian Politics.* Toronto: University of Toronto Press.

Thomas, Paul. 2004. "Accountability." In *Handbook of Public Policy*, ed. B. Guy Peters and Jon Pierre. London: Sage.

Vedung, Evert. 2006. "Evaluation Research." In *Handbook of Public Policy*, ed. B. Guy Peters and Jon Pierre. London: Sage.

2

Efficiency, Integrity, and Capacity: An Expanded Agenda for Public Management?

WILLY MCCOURT

This chapter reverses the conventional order of discussion by looking first at what makes policy makers and stakeholders committed to public management reforms. It then reviews some models of reform, illustrating them with empirical examples and discussing what might be involved in introducing any of these models in any particular country. The chapter then identifies the conditions necessary for reform to flourish and reviews three major approaches to public management reform that have been taken since the late 1950s and early 1960s, approaches that can be labeled efficiency, integrity, and capacity. While the emphasis is on the first two, which have attracted the most attention over the past 20 years, the chapter suggests that all three approaches are possible orientations for governments to adopt, depending on their circumstances and political priorities.[1] The chapter then considers some issues involved in introducing and sequencing public management reforms before providing a brief conclusion.

Generating Commitment to Public Management Reform

This section reviews some of the factors that affect government's commitment to reform. It argues that commitment needs to be examined more broadly than it usually is in the reform discourse.

Beyond "Buy-In": The Political Economy of Public Management Reform

One's view of the conditions that allow reform programs to succeed is all too often a truncated one. One observes that policy x has succeeded in country y and assumes that the policy can be transferred intact to country z as long as policy makers "buy into" the "correct" package. When that smooth process fails to work, observers frequently point their fingers at the lack of "commitment."

Commitment is important, but what such observers—outside observers perhaps in particular—fail to recognize is the dense network of groups and institutions that enabled the original policy to be implemented and then won over the inevitable opposition by the groups whose interests it threatened (groups such as civil servants' unions or students who have come to expect a guaranteed job in the government when they leave university). Only then did the program graduate to the status of a full-fledged model that governments elsewhere could consider adopting. The process of coalition formation and honing of the initial policy idea happens largely beneath the radar of policy analysts, especially external analysts. Despite being crucial, it thus tends to be overlooked, as the experience of civil service reform in Sri Lanka illustrates (box 2.1).[2]

Sri Lanka's informal coalition of political parties, senior civil servants, and staff associations, in which a small, radical, and formerly revolutionary party was pivotal, sustained the reform, because it responded to a need that they had identified themselves, the need to curtail patronage. As a civil service trade union leader conceded, "From time to time politicians have recruited without considering the need to recruit.... Politicians consider that government exists to provide jobs for their supporters" (McCourt 2006). A very senior official suggested that "the expectation that the public sector should provide jobs is the root." A donor's explanation for the failure of earlier reform was that "politicians had a vested interest in maintaining a patronage system."

Making a strengthened Public Service Commission the centerpiece of reform was not a Sri Lankan invention, but it was an indigenous initiative. As such, while still precarious, it was more stable than the donor-sponsored reform phases that preceded it. Ironically, it was also deeper and more radical.

BOX 2.1 The Four Phases of Civil Service Reform in Sri Lanka

Sri Lanka has gone through four phases of reform since the mid-1980s, supported at different times by the United Nations Development Programme (UNDP), the World Bank, and the Asian Development Bank (ADB). The first two phases of reform "receded as fast as they came," as the Cabinet Secretary noted (quoted in Wijesinghe 1997: 15). The first phase was the very comprehensive report of the Administrative Reforms Committee (1987–88). Its chairman subsequently exclaimed that "the recommendations concerning the increase of salaries were embraced with glee! But . . . more important recommendations were glossed over . . . . When it came to biting the bullet, the political will evaporated" (quoted in Wijesinghe 1997: 21, 26).

The second phase was a structural adjustment–era downsizing program. When this phase ended, the government had more employees than when it began. It had also, according to an official, mistakenly offered a generous voluntary retirement package to all its surprised but grateful regular retirees.

The third phase was "managerialist." It featured mission statements and strategic objectives, management restructuring, and performance appraisal. Eight years later, these measures existed mainly on paper. The management restructuring, according to an official closely connected with the reform, "couldn't be done. The new government actually increased the number of ministries."

By 2004 donors had drifted away, denied the results they believed they had been promised; even a very senior Sri Lankan official conceded that "there is not much room for satisfaction." From outside, prospects looked bleak. Yet this was the point at which the government took a new turn, entirely under its own steam, in a fourth phase of reform, gaining the two-thirds majority necessary to pass the Seventeenth Amendment to the Constitution in 2001. This reform restored the independence of the Public Service Commission, previously the plaything of politicians. It created parallel Police and Judicial Service Commissions, with the leader of the opposition having a real say in the appointment of their members, who would serve three-year terms separate from the electoral cycle. The Public Service Commission's first chair was a retired ambassador, forthright and politically unaligned.

The three main parties and civil servants through their staff associations all supported the reform: "The Public Service Commission means we have justice" was one representative view. In one uniformed service, political interference had gone down "from 90–100 percent to 5–10 percent," according to a very senior officer in that service. However, this effective centralization of staffing authority came at the cost of some loss of local discretion and an increase in bureaucratic delays. Moreover, citizen "voice" had not been harnessed to create a constituency for the reform that would have helped it survive.

Source: McCourt 2006.

An important lesson from Sri Lanka's experience is the need for public management reform to be congruent with a country's own political economy. Reform need not always be internally generated—successful reforms can be borrowed from elsewhere—but it must at least be borrowed on the country's own terms and therefore owned (World Bank 1998a). Reforms imposed from outside, however worthy in the abstract, will almost certainly fail: "vice may be virtue uprooted," in the words of the Anglo-Welsh poet David Jones (1974: 56).

The successful transplantation of democracy to Japan after World War II is a well-known historical example of this point. Key institutions were retained to which citizens could give allegiance. These institutions included the monarchy (the emperor's acquiescence in the new dispensation was crucial) and the apparatus of civilian government (the American military governor ruled through the Japanese civilian administration, which was legitimized in a general election soon after the war ended) (Moore and Robinson 2002).

One reform package cannot be said to be better or worse than another without noting the political economy in which it is embedded. This may appear a stark view, but it is arguably the mainstream one among political scientists (Gulhati 1990; Killick 1998; Nelson 1990; Williamson 1994). It is in line with the views of the World Bank's (1998a) *Assessing Aid* report, as well as with the view of a recent and very relevant World Bank strategy: "The Bank Group's strategy is to help developing country governments, in light of their distinct national challenges, to identify their own priorities for improving governance and to articulate and implement programs responding to those priorities, in a manner that is effective and sustainable over the long term" (World Bank 2006: iii).

A Political Model of Public Management Reform

Policy analysts have tended to assume a rational systems model of the policy process that gets public management and other kinds of reform on the statute book. An example is the model of Jenkins (1978), with its stages of initiation, information, consideration, decision, implementation, evaluation, and termination. In contrast, the model presented in table 2.1, which is based on a study of seven cases of successful public policy reform, is a political model. It summarizes the political policy message of this section.

Feasibility

The question of political commitment matters only when the program to which a leader is asked to commit is challenging and has powerful opponents,

Efficiency, Integrity, and Capacity 37

TABLE 2.1 Application of Political Model of Reform to Civil Service Reform in Sri Lanka

Policy stage	Example	Threat to success
An upsurge of "social energy" ...	Election victory in 2000	Policy lacks popular roots or is imposed (structural adjustment policies).
generates a policy idea or highlights an existing idea ...	Reform of the Public Service Commission	Sterile oppositionism, in which social activists confine themselves to criticizing government policy
around which a coalition assembles ...	Political parties, senior officials, and staff associations	Coalition may disintegrate (following an election defeat, for example).
that throws up a leader who gets the idea on the policy agenda ...	(No single leader identified with the reform)	Weak leadership may fail to carry reform over inevitable challenges.
and overcomes opposition from supporters of the old dispensation.	Sidelining of "pork-barrel politicians in two major parties	Patrons or rent seekers (especially pork-barrel politicians) may capture the policy.
The coalition is institutionalized, empowering beneficiaries and deflecting patrons and rent seekers.	Seventeenth Amendment to the Constitution	
It is consolidated using feedback to adapt the policy to changing circumstances.	(Complaints of bureaucratic inflexibility and delays not acted on)	Policy rigidity and entropy.

Source: Based on Bebbington and McCourt 2007.

so that the possibility of failure and ignominy is real. No particular vision is needed to implement a popular policy, such as pay raises for civil servants, cherry-picked at the expense of more difficult recommendations from the report of an administrative reform commission in Swaziland (McCourt 2003).

Leaders are wise to look before they leap where difficult reforms are concerned. Benin's experience with pay reform in the public sector, in particular the role played by President Nicéphore Soglo, shows how the better part of a leader's valor can be discretion. Despite sharing the World Bank's neoliberal ideology (Soglo was a former regional director of the Bank), President Soglo could not implement that ideology as a politician. When he tried to implement austerity measures, he met with stiff opposition from unions and members of parliament. Political forces "were wary about his structural adjustment policies and the transformation envisaged towards the existing system, including the civil service" (Kiragu and Mukandala 2004: 97). Soglo's defeat suggests that social political pressures affected voters. His personal commitment to reform was not enough to make reform stick when the strain on the political system became too great. Political feasibility rather than political commitment or will on the part of the government was lacking.

Assessing the feasibility of reform does not mean throwing in the towel, ruling out opportunities to improve the way the public service is managed because they are politically difficult. Rather, it means having a clear understanding of the political factors that facilitate or constrain reform. In reaching that understanding, it helps to have a sense of the stakeholders involved (in Benin they included civil servants, politicians, the army, public service unions, students, church, regions, donors).

It is also helpful to use standard organizational change techniques, as Morocco did in attempting to implement staff reform. "Force-field analysis" techniques identify the forces that supported and opposed reform in Morocco (table 2.2). Such an analysis may appear mechanical on paper, but in real life it requires sensitivity, suppleness, and judgment.

Morocco's experience shows that a human resource reform can succeed even where previous attempts have failed, if officials present ministers with a feasible proposal that takes account of what stakeholders will countenance while sacrificing as little as possible of the essence of reform. It bears out the observation that "in many respects, political will is a function of the quality of advice provided [by officials] to politicians" (World Bank 1998b: iii).

TABLE 2.2 Forces Driving and Restraining Civil Service Reform in Morocco

Driving forces	Restraining forces
Royal authority and commitment to overall reform	Royal reluctance to impose reform
Growth of civil society	Passivity ("*attentisme*") of some key political actors
Able technocrats in key positions	Rural notables' hostility to innovation
Indigenous ownership	Fragmented political parties
Political liberalization under new king	
Participative approach that allowed islands of good practice to emerge	

Source: Al-Arkoubi and McCourt 2004.

Commitment

Even when the stars of the political firmament are in alignment, public management improvements such as Sri Lanka's constitutional amendment still require the commitment of politicians and senior officials. When allowance is made for reforms that were never feasible in the first place, the World Bank's conclusion that lack of political commitment was the single most important explanation for the failure of about 40 percent of the Bank's civil service reform projects in the mid-1990s should be taken seriously (Nunberg 1997).

What is commitment, and what can governments do to increase it? A study of staffing reform in Swaziland provides some answers. When a given reform is feasible and the "antecedents" of reform are sufficiently present, leaders may choose to make a realistic commitment that can be expected to lead to concrete reform. That commitment will be binding to the extent that it is

- voluntary (not imposed by a donor or other outside agent against the government's better judgment);
- explicit (clear and straightforward, not hedged with qualifications or riders);
- challenging (leading to substantial, not trivial improvement);
- public (leaders have publicized their commitment in the mass media and in other ways); and
- irrevocable (leaders have not allowed themselves an easy line of retreat if the going gets rough).

The first step to increasing commitment is to analyze the politics of reform on a case-by-case basis: "Answers must be invented for each country individually," as Nelson notes (1990: 361). After that, governments will proceed in ways that make political sense to them. To take one example, a study on Swaziland (McCourt 2003) suggests that the government needs to distinguish between its fundamental interest in continuing the monarchical political system and its contingent interest in perpetuating a system of patron-client relations in the allocation of government jobs. It points to the need to restore the independence of the Civil Service Board, the equivalent of Sri Lanka's Public Service Commission, as an "irrevocable" step that would demonstrate the government's commitment to reform.

So much space has been devoted here to the political antecedents of successful reform in terms of political economy, feasibility, and political commitment, because they are insufficiently recognized in treatments of public management reform. When canvassing a public management reform, it is necessary to assess the balance of political forces, the feasibility of the proposed reform, and what will be necessary to obtain the commitment of key leaders and groups to the reform. There is room for leaders to place an issue on the political agenda and persuade others to adopt it. It is only when all of the political antecedents are favorable, however, that the necessary "buy-in" will occur that will allow reforms to succeed.

Creating the Conditions for Public Management Reform

Public management reforms have followed a rough historical sequence. Taking the independence era of the 1960s in Africa and Asia as a starting point, four phases can be identified:[3]

1. *The nation-building phase of the 1960s and 1970s:* Basic provision of public services was created or at least scaled up from the rudimentary provision the colonial rulers had bequeathed. This was the era of capacity building.
2. *The structural adjustment phase of the 1980s:* Accumulated overspending exacerbated by the oil price shocks of the 1970s required governments to reduce or restrain public spending. This was the era of employment reform—downsizing and "civil service reform" in the narrow sense of the phrase.
3. *The integrity phase (overlapping with phase 2):* The perception of corruption rose in the consciousness of the public and development agencies. This was the era of anticorruption strategies.
4. *The millennium phase:* Adoption of the Millennium Development Goals renewed the emphasis on capacity, targeted more narrowly on education and health services than earlier capacity-building efforts.

Although this phasing is somewhat artificial—the phases overlap, and governments may need to emphasize integrity at the same time as efficiency—it may be analytically helpful.

Attempts to reform the size and cost of the public sector have had pride of place over the past quarter-century. Between 1987 and 1996, the World Bank assisted no fewer than 68 developing countries and transition economies with staffing reform programs (Nunberg 1997). Even in industrial countries, the scale of reform has been spectacular: between 1987 and 1992, staff retrenchment programs were carried out in the public sectors of 22 of the 27 member countries of the Organisation for Economic Co-operation and Development (OECD), making it by far the most widespread human resource initiative during that period (OECD 1994). Manning and Parison (2003) find that measures to control wage bills remain very important in the

21st century, featuring in the reforms of all 14 countries they surveyed, 11 of which are OECD members. The OECD's own reporting suggests that reforms to control wage bills had tailed off somewhat (OECD 2004).

A 1994 OECD survey ranked measures to improve human resource management in government only slightly behind size and cost initiatives and ahead of such widely publicized initiatives as privatization. By 2001 retrenchment initiatives were less prominent, presumably indicating that the battle had been won, at least in some countries. Other human resource management measures reported in the 1994 survey (notably devolution of management authority to line ministries and agencies and the introduction of performance management and appraisal, sometimes including a performance-related pay element) were joined by new measures, such as increasing the gender and ethnic diversity of the workforce, increasing the use of staff attitude surveys and employee forums, and adopting an overall strategic framework for managing staff. Manning and Parison (2003) list the following measures: improving service delivery (13 countries), tackling corruption (4 countries), improving employment contracts (3 countries), tackling patronage (3 countries), and improving monetary incentives (2 countries).

Enhancing the Legal Framework So That Performance Can Flourish

In trying to explain why performance management has had so little effect in three former communist countries, the authors of a World Bank study conclude that "instituting performance management in environments where the foundations of public administration have not been established may be inconsequential at best or risky at worst" (Anderson, Reid, and Ryterman 2003: 16). A clear legal framework is the indispensable foundation for public management, because it establishes the basic parameters for the day-to-day actions of both managers and employees. It may be necessary to specify the remit of basic institutions in the national constitution and to amend the constitution when those institutions prove inadequate, as Sri Lanka's constitutional amendment improving the status of the Public Service Commission did.

In a democracy, appointed officials must be subservient to the politicians whom the people have elected. But it is also appropriate to separate the political and administrative spheres. In the classic New Public Management phase, politicians should "steer but not row"—that is, establish the policy framework and set targets where necessary but then let officials implement the policy and meet the targets. For their part, officials should implement policies faithfully, within reason, and not set themselves up as a power base in their own right. This separation is spelled out in civil service codes of practice.

Balancing central and line agencies

Devolution of management responsibility to line agencies is a central plank in the New Public Management formula for managing public services, and it is reflected in the practice of many industrial countries. In the civil service in the United Kingdom, for example, delegation has been a gradual process. It began in 1964, when the recruitment of clerical staff was devolved to departments. The central Civil Service Commission continued to approve appointments until 1983. In 1991 all recruitment below grade 7 (a middle-management level) was also devolved; in 1995 the cut-off point was raised to grade 5 (a senior-management level). In addition, the center has progressively delegated power over pay and grading to departments. The role of the Civil Service Commission is now merely to issue standards of conduct, make appointments down to grade 5, hear appeals, commission selection audits, and promote best practice within departments by issuing guidelines on selection.

Within line agencies in the United Kingdom, managers are responsible for selection, discipline, performance rewards, and career development. Personnel management units have come into their own as contributors to departmental personnel strategies and policies and providers of support services to line managers. These units are responsible for pay and grading below grade 5; succession planning, auditing, and monitoring of line performance; and provision of advice on selection, discipline, and training when managers need it. Thus, after a full quarter-century of gradual devolution, the idea of a uniform, centrally managed civil service is coming to an end in the United Kingdom. Professional peer pressure, rather than central control, now maintains the integrity of staffing.

The experience of Nepal shows why devolution is not a panacea. Nepal's Public Service Commission is a stable institution with an unbroken history going back to 1956. In a country where nepotism and political favoritism are rampant, the commission has a constitutional status that allows it to keep its distance from politicians. Commissioners are appointed by a committee whose members include the prime minister, the leader of the largest opposition party, and the chief justice. Politicians cannot remove them, and their term of office is separate from the electoral cycle. Nepal has resisted donor pressure to tinker with its structure by devolving or even privatizing recruitment, mindful that an earlier donor-inspired devolution turned the public enterprises into a patronage playground (McCourt 2001a).

Devolution may be appropriate in countries that implement it gradually (an incremental approach is desirable) and in which the mechanism of professional peer pressure is able to operate. In Nepal, and other countries where maintaining nepotism and favoritism is a priority and respect for the rule of law and a culture of transparency are not ingrained, central control may still be appropriate.

The remit of central agencies

When governments discuss where to put responsibility for human resources, they often do so in terms of how much authority the center should have relative to line departments and agencies. But governments also need to decide on the appropriate division of responsibility between the central departments and agencies themselves. Taking staff management as an example, in many countries that have not devolved responsibility to line ministries and agencies, the respective roles of government ministries look broadly like those shown in table 2.3.

This structure is particularly close to the Commonwealth model, especially with respect to the role of the Public Service Commission, but even non-Commonwealth countries, such as the Republic of Korea and Thailand, have very similar structures.

From a strategic or corporate point of view, this type of structure may appear to "balkanize" public management and be a recipe for conflict between agencies. In the structural adjustment era, when many governments tried to reduce staff numbers, ministries for the civil service were often seen by their finance counterparts as Trojan horses inside government, acting as an informal civil servants' trade union to frustrate the aims of reform (Corkery and Land 1996). Staff in the Ministry of Finance in Ghana, for example, openly declared that their public service colleagues were the greatest single threat to the success of reform (McCourt 2001b).

From a strategic point of view, the remedy would appear to be simple: bring all these functions together in a single strategic agency, possibly the

TABLE 2.3 Responsibility for Staff Management in Central Government Agencies (Commonwealth Structure)

Entity	Function
Office of the Prime Minister	Overall government policy
Ministry of Finance	Pay and pensions
Ministry for the Civil Service	Deployment and conditions of service for public servants
Public Service Commission	Appointment, promotion, transfer, and discipline
National Administrative Staff College	Training and development

Source: McCourt 2006.

Office of the Prime Minister or similar office. Some governments, such as that of South Africa, have moved in this direction, but no government has taken this argument to its logical conclusion. Ministries of finance everywhere are reluctant to surrender their power over public servants' pay, which consumes a large share of public expenditure. Governments may also prefer to leave well-established bodies with a tradition of competence, such as national administrative staff colleges, alone, even though their very existence weakens the strategic thrust of government.

Implementing Employment Reform

Although the frequency of employment reform (downsizing) programs has probably declined in recent years, in both industrial and developing countries, the perennial need to restrain public spending means that from time to time governments will need to reduce spending on staff. Yet downsizing efforts have not always been appropriate. As governments such as Tanzania's have found, there may be more scope to reduce government deficits by improving revenue collection (Dia 1996). The structural adjustment loans that downsizing programs were so often part of may have disappeared, but that does not mean that downsizing itself should be a thing of the past. Factors such as economic recession resulting from the business cycle; external shocks, such as bad harvests or increases in the price of oil; and new technology that makes it possible to reduce the number of people needed to carry out standardized tasks such as sending out tax demands all make downsizing an intrinsic feature of the reform landscape.

Experience of employment reform during the 1980s and 1990s suggests three principles that should underlie it. Effective employment reform should be strategic (that is, start from a strategic view of where government or an individual department is going and a sense of the implications of strategy for staff employment); it should deliver real savings, not simply reduce the employee headcount; and it should minimize hardship on employees.

Something approaching a consensus has developed that turning around an organization is a two-stage process, in which emergency action to stem decline leads to strategic planning for the future. This process has been called "recovery strategy." What does a strategic approach mean in practice? In a strategic model based on a review of experience in both private and public sectors in both industrial and developing countries, employment reform begins with the overall strategy and staffing strategy of the government or the individual department. In that strategic context, a management review is conducted and used to generate an employment reform plan where appropriate, one that includes measures to minimize hardship to employees. Job reduction is not a necessary outcome of a review.

"Process" measures run alongside all of this, since they will be a continuous concern. They include measures to generate ownership of and commitment to the program, as well as consultation and communication with staff and their representatives. The appropriate pace of the program, which the timetable in the strategy action plan will address, is another process issue.

Once the strategic framework is in place, the next step is to try to avoid making job reductions altogether, through the following measures:

- Conduct human resource forecasting in order to anticipate a declining need for staff in some areas or a declining ability to pay for them.
- Seek functional flexibility through multiskilling. The Ford Motor Company in the United Kingdom took action to reduce the number of separate job categories from 516 in 1986 to 45 in 1988 (Slatter 1984).
- Set up a redeployment procedure in which staff in a redeployment "pool" have to be considered before a post is advertised. It is important to prevent such pools from being used as dumping grounds for staff who have fallen from political favor, such as senior civil servants identified with the party previously in power.
- Provide retraining (to retool, for example, a redundant administrator into a computer programmer).
- Anticipate redundancy by having procedures in place that will enable government to deal with the problem systematically. Such procedures take time to develop, especially where trade unions have to be consulted. They should be drawn up as a part of day-to-day human resource management practice. In one local authority in the United Kingdom, the redundancy agreement enabled the authority to reduce jobs over a period of several years without making compulsory redundancies.

In addition, governments need to control new appointments. Governments have sometimes had the depressing experience of finding that after making painful cuts, the overall number of staff has hardly been reduced at all; as in a leaking boat, water seeps in as fast as it is baled out. This problem can be avoided by the following:

- Identifying where the power to make appointments is located (in a central agency or at the local level)

- Specifying the precise circumstances in which new appointments can be made (managers may continue to evade the new controls, by using the staff transfer mechanism, for instance)
- Monitoring the operation of the new controls (after a brief period of central oversight, controls may be relaxed and the number of staff may begin to creep upward again; indeed, there may be a rush of appointments as departments try to "catch up" on the posts they feel are owed to them).

If after taking these steps, a government still finds that it needs to reduce jobs, it should consider the following actions (see McCourt 2001b; Nunberg 1994):[4]

- Delete posts that have been vacant for some time and are no longer needed.
- Enforce the retirement age. Uganda discovered several thousand staff still working beyond the official retirement age (McCourt 1998).
- Introduce part-time and flexible positions.
- Appoint new staff on temporary contracts.
- Impose a freeze on recruitment.
- End guaranteed entry. Some countries, such as Benin, guarantee entry to the civil service by all graduates. Given the increased number of graduates, such a guarantee is probably no longer appropriate in most countries.
- Suspend automatic advancement. Many countries provide automatic, seniority-based promotion, which, apart from its salary implications, weakens the link between promotion and merit.
- Encourage voluntary redundancy, which staff often welcome. In the United Kingdom and elsewhere, quotas were achieved more rapidly than expected (McCourt 1998). Such programs can be expensive, however: in Ghana voluntary redundancy consumed 2 percent of total government expenditure over the first five years of reform.
- Privatize or contract work out. These measures will reduce staff numbers, but they may not reduce spending, as contracted out services are not necessarily cheaper.
- Freeze salaries.
- Make compulsory redundancies.

A striking feature of this list of options is that compulsory redundancy is only the last item in a long menu. It may never be necessary, if the government manages to make sufficient savings through other means. If redundancies are needed, responsible employers will minimize the hardship caused to staff who are laid off. Generally speaking, once government has consulted trade unions and others on its plans, it is probably well advised to concentrate assistance in the lump-sum payment and pension that retrenched workers receive: there is evidence that people make better decisions about how to use such a payment than government makes on their behalf (Younger 1996). Advice and information are also important, to remove misconceptions and prepare staff for the change. Retraining schemes to help retrenched workers acquire new skills are desirable in theory, but they can be expensive, difficult to administer, and poorly targeted, often providing workers with little practical benefit.

Adopting a Holistic Approach to Integrity in Public Management

Measures to promote greater commitment to impartiality and honesty within the public service—in short, to promote integrity—have increased since the late 1990s. The section focuses on how to give force to the provisions on ethical behavior that most governments have in one form or another.

Controlling corruption

Other things equal, a holistic approach is probably best in curbing corruption. Such an approach should consist of the following elements:

- Demonstrable or "public" political commitment by political leaders against corruption, regardless of who is involved
- Comprehensive anticorruption legislation implemented by an autonomous agency endowed with strong legal powers (Pope 1999)
- Identification and targeting of government functions that are most susceptible to corruption and a review of procedures to minimize the scope for abuse
- Maintenance of public salaries that are adequate and not too far below private sector levels (though effective action against corruption can be taken before this condition is met)
- Adoption of additional legal deterrents against corruption, such as the nullification of contracts, licenses, or permits obtained corruptly. Such a measure would force overseas export guarantee agencies to closely monitor the international transactions they underwrite, and it would give the public an incentive to avoid corrupt behavior and report demands for bribes (Pope 1995).

Establishing public service values

Ironically, some of the improvements discussed in this chapter run the risk of eroding the foundation of public service values that support the efficiency of government and the trust that citizens are prepared to place in it. Governments in many developing countries and transition economies face another threat as well, in the form of the damage done to government by the culture of corruption, nepotism, and favoritism.

Some governments have found it helpful to produce a clear statement of what they mean by "values." In Singapore the Chambers of the Attorney-General (2003) has drawn up a code of conduct for its staff. That code, which requires that personal conduct be "beyond reproach," includes the following tenets:

- We shall conduct ourselves with honor, integrity, and dignity at all times.
- We shall not engage in conduct that may adversely affect public trust and confidence in the offices of the Attorney-General and Public Prosecutor.
- We shall not abuse our office to advance our personal interests.
- We shall not disclose confidential information acquired in our official capacity for any purpose unrelated to the discharge of our duties.
- We shall not engage in conduct that may cause harm to the proper administration of justice.
- We shall treat our colleagues, staff and others we meet in our work with respect, sensitivity and courtesy.

Such codes should be short statements rather than detailed rule books, the sanctions that apply if a public servant breaks the code should be clear to everyone, and employees should be taught what the code says and why it exists. A code may be a necessary but not a sufficient condition of honest public service, however: it must be complemented by other improvements to public management, such as upgrading the professional quality of recruitment, selection, and training.

Operationalizing the code of conduct

A critical element of the code of conduct is the establishment of an independent anticorruption body (Pope 1999). Such a body would monitor adherence to the code and initiate appropriate action in cases of failure to observe its provisions. Setting up an enforcement agency along such lines is necessary for two reasons. First, civil servants may interpret the absence of such a mechanism as a signal that they need not take the code seriously or alter their conduct to conform with its provisions. Second, public cynicism will emerge if the government is not seen to be tackling corruption and other abuses of public office notwithstanding the existence of the code. Such cynicism may then extend to other aspects of public service reform, undermining efforts to forge a partnership for reform with civil society.

Examples of the use of enforcement mechanisms in Hong Kong (China), Singapore, and in the United Kingdom reveal several important lessons.

CONTROLLING CORRUPTION IN HONG KONG (CHINA) AND SINGAPORE. Corruption was perceived as a serious problem in both Hong Kong (China) and Singapore. In Singapore there was a high incidence of unethical behavior in the immediate postwar period, partly as a result of high inflation and declining real salaries during the Japanese occupation in World War II. In both jurisdictions, corruption was brought under control following sustained efforts to deal with the problem in the 1960s and 1970s. As a result of those efforts, corruption is no longer seen as a serious threat to the integrity of the state.

Governmental resolve has been crucial in the process (Quah 1994). The government's response was to pass new legislation providing for, among other things, the recovery of the proceeds of corrupt behavior from the estates of deceased persons.

Both Hong Kong and Singapore passed comprehensive anticorruption legislation setting up investigation agencies and vesting in them considerable legal powers (for instance, the right to obtain statements from witnesses [Singapore] or to require government organizations to alter working procedures to reduce the potential for corruption [Hong Kong]). In Singapore the penalties for corrupt behavior include provision for the surrender of illegal earnings in return for a shorter prison sentence.

In the 1980s Hong Kong's Independent Commission against Corruption had 1,087 staff and a budget of HK$109 million (about $14 million). Singapore's counterpart, the Corrupt Practices Investigation Bureau, was much smaller, with 71 officers and a budget of S$6 million (about $4 million). Although these bodies were larger than in most other countries, the results achieved in Singapore suggest that good results can be achieved by organizations considerably smaller than that of Hong Kong.

Both bodies carry out other roles in addition to their core activity of investigating malpractice and supporting prosecutions. These include prevention (recommending changes to government procedures to make them less vulnerable to corruption) and awareness building, through training programs for civil servants and the use of the media.

Hong Kong's Independent Commission against Corruption reached out to the public, community organizations, and professional bodies. It opened local offices joining together agency staff, local council members, and representatives of civic associations in order to develop trust and gather reliable information. Six bodies with membership from auditors and accountants associations oversaw various activities, bringing with them both specialized knowledge and credibility.

The establishment of Singapore's Corrupt Practices Investigation Bureau was supported by a Ministry of Finance directive to other ministries to take a variety of measures to reduce corruption in vulnerable areas. These measures included better supervision, reduction in procedural delays, regular rotation of staff, and surprise checks. Such measures had to be reviewed regularly every few years to ensure that they remained effective.

CONTROLLING CORRUPTION IN THE UNITED KINGDOM. In the United Kingdom, the primary institution concerned with fairness and impartiality in the government's dealings with the public is the ombudsman, known officially as the Parliamentary Commissioner for Administration. It is not specifically an anticorruption agency. Cases of corruption are dealt with by the normal investigative and judicial machinery of the state.

No organization is concerned specifically with corruption in public administration. This may reflect the fact that, notwithstanding recent concerns about misconduct by members of parliament (MPs) and the weakness of parliamentary oversight of government, public administration is still viewed as relatively clean. A code of conduct for civil servants was set out in 1995, in response to concerns about the maintenance of a proper relationship between ministers and civil servants rather than concerns about corruption as such.

In response to recent concerns over improper behavior by politicians, Parliament has also set up an internal committee to investigate MPs accused of misconduct. This committee has bipartisan support, reflecting the current perception that the public will punish a party that appears soft on alleged misconduct by its MPs.

Others Mechanisms for Promoting Integrity

Several other mechanisms can promote integrity. They include prosecuting offenders, decentralizing and controlling corruption, and raising the prestige of public service.

Prosecuting offenders

Both Hong Kong (China) and Singapore continue to rely on the normal judicial processes for prosecuting those accused of corrupt activities. Attempting to do otherwise might encounter constitutional obstacles, and it would probably be considered unacceptable in a democratic country (though it may be possible to use disciplinary mechanisms against civil servants independently of criminal proceedings).

Weaknesses in the judicial system—excessive length of cases or the unpredictability of verdicts—could become the Achilles heel of anticorruption campaigns, as they have in a number of countries. The judicial system may need to be strengthened as a component of a strategy to curb corruption. Since the credibility of initiatives to control corruption often depends on their ability to bring about quick results, alternative means to deliver sanctions should also be sought. These could include disciplinary proceedings in the case of civil servants and dismissal in the case of political appointees to office.

Decentralizing and controlling corruption

Can management decentralization increase corruption? The incidence of corruption is sometimes related to the extent of discretion officials are able to exercise in decision making; reducing officials' discretion is often prescribed as a means of reducing the potential for corrupt behavior. In some countries the centralization of management authority in the public service is justified as a way of minimizing discretion and the possibility of corruption.

However, Transparency International notes that centralization may generate corruption, as people seek to overcome delays and inefficiencies. It cites two extreme cases: "One [bureaucracy] perhaps may be characterized by the presence of chaos, with an absence of rules, with poor record-keeping and rapidly changing personnel, all dictating a payment of bribes as an antidote to uncertainty. At the other extreme, another might suffer from overrigidity: possessing a clear hierarchy and an abundance of rules, but with decision making only at the highest levels, so encouraging pay-offs to bypass bottlenecks and ensure that resources are not depleted by going through the system" (Pope 1995: 285). These cases are consistent with findings from other countries that a high degree of centralization is ultimately self-defeating, since people faced with a multiplicity of rules and regulations will seek ways to subvert them.

Raising the prestige of public service

It is not enough for the public service to be efficient and fair; it should also be seen as such. The image of the public service in the eyes of the public matters a great deal. Citizens need to feel confidence in the government that provides public services on their behalf. Government will attract good-quality recruits only if government service is perceived as a worthwhile career by young people and their families.

It was perhaps inevitable and even desirable that the prestige of government as an employer should decline relative to the private sector. Apart from the value of private sector–led economic growth in itself, the growth of the private sector in many countries means that many young people have career options that were not available to their parents. But the public sector's prestige has also declined in absolute terms, not only relative to the private sector.

There is no quick fix for the poor image that government has acquired in many countries; no Web site or advertising campaign will change the perception overnight. In the long run, it is the patient, long-term developmental activities that this chapter sets out that will make a difference.

Two countries show how decisions about public management can, over time, dramatically improve the prestige of government. Both Botswana and Singapore have opted for a relatively small, elite civil service, recruiting from among the most talented graduates and school-leavers.

Botswana used pay as a key lever. The 1990 Presidential Commission on the Review of Incomes Policy was crucial in allowing market forces to determine pay rates. It decompressed salaries, widening the ratio between the highest and lowest paid salary from 15:1 in 1984 to 39:1 in 2002. Its pay rates are now among the highest in Sub-Saharan Africa (Kiragu and Mukandala 2004).

In 1988 Singapore had 493 "supergrade" officials at the top of the hierarchy, constituting less than 1 percent of the civil service. These officials were drawn from the top graduates of elite universities; indeed, the Public Service Commission gave scholarships for study at such universities on condition that recipients join the government after graduating.

Not surprisingly, levels of corruption in government, as reported by Transparency International, are low in both Botswana and Singapore. Strong anticorruption policies have also helped.

It will not be as easy for many countries as it was for Botswana and Singapore, which have enjoyed good economic growth, to take steps such as these. However, the two countries represent models whose features other governments might apply selectively, in line with their own circumstances and needs.

How Should Reforms Be Introduced and Sequenced?

Even where a public management reform is feasible and policy makers have committed themselves to it, leadership is needed to see it through. While countries that have been successful in strengthening public administration have pursued different reform strategies (table 2.4), they have all had leadership that possessed the capacity to make difficult decisions and implement them.

TABLE 2.4 Sequencing of Public Management Reforms

Objective	First-stage reform	Second-stage reform
Facilitate career management.	Enhance job security and protection from political interference.	Decrease tenure and link to continuous performance assessment.
Achieve unity of the civil service.	Create a legally defined cadre with common terms and conditions.	Devolve and diversify pay arrangements to provide flexibility to employers.
Provide individual incentives.	Apply standard merit promotion and reward rules consistently.	Establish annual performance targets.
Create openness.	Encourage career development within a closed system and avoid nepotism.	Move toward position-based systems and encourage lateral entry.

Source: Manning and Parison 2003.

A good public official, trained to emphasize predictability, regularity, and the following of rules, is not necessarily a good leader. Whereas management is concerned with consistency and order, leadership is about purposeful and constructive change (Kotter 1990). Where a manager may have an impersonal and functional attitude to work, a leader is personally engaged and committed; where a manager may seek to administer an existing arrangement efficiently, a leader will seek to break the mold to find new ways of tackling problems (Zaleznick 1997).

An important element in the successful leadership of reform is vision, one of the three factors identified by Williamson (1994) in his 11-country study of the political economy of reform. Vision is about being able to see the shape of things to come over the heads of the jostling stakeholders who consume so much of leaders' time, and to motivate others, so that they share the leader's vision. Vision is one of the elements labeled "transformational leadership" (Burns 1978). It is very different from the skills of day-to-day management.

The experience of reform shows that successful leaders are hands-on leaders; leadership can be delegated only up to a point. In Malaysia Prime Minister Mohamed Mahathir chaired all 10 meetings of the committee that reformed Malaysia's civil service pay and introduced performance appraisal with a performance pay element (Government of Malaysia 1991). Ten years later, he personally ordered officials to make radical changes to the scheme in response to complaints from the civil servants' trade union about unfair subjectivity in the way it operated. In the United Kingdom,

Prime Minister Margaret Thatcher's admired staffing reforms in the 1980s were not very different from those of Harold Wilson in the 1960s. What was different was that she gave them "quality time" and followed them through to full implementation.

Senior officials who seek to lead cannot be hands on if their hands are kept off the organizational levers: they need some delegated authority. In Mauritius even a very senior central official complained that "the actual centralized system favors 'passing the buck.'" The head of a large service department commented, "You want people to behave as managers, but you're not giving them the opportunity.... I have to bear with people like x, y, z, and others. They are chosen elsewhere.... People are even removed from my organization without my knowledge!" (McCourt and Ramgutty-Wong 2003: 608). Unless central control remains appropriate, leaders should have the authority and management systems to exercise leadership in support of reform.

In complex political and institutional conditions—in which, for example, reform depends on a loose and shifting coalition of supporters—forceful leadership becomes more rather than less important as a way of cutting the Gordian knot of institutions. Leaders are the public faces those coalitions must have if their ideas are to translate into concrete reforms. Leaders such as Carlos Salinas in Mexico capitalized on the widespread perception of economic crisis, used patronage power to place supporters in key appointments, and sidelined hostile party leaders and trade unions (Grindle 2007). In short, they pull all the levers that their formal positions grant them in order to break stalemates and face down rent seekers.

The reality of leadership of public management reform, even where it is forceful, is more complex than the crudely heroic image that airport bookstalls portray (though such leaders do exist: Mahathir is an example). Rather than the property of an individual leader, leadership may be "distributed" among several members of a policy coalition (Barry 1991). This seems to have been the case with a local planning, financing, and governance model in Nampula province, Mozambique (Jackson forthcoming), where the provincial political leadership, civil servants, the Dutch government (the principal long-term funder), and two donor-funded technical advisors all contributed to the direction of reform. Leadership may also be "sequential," with different individuals having more or less power at different stages of policy development. In Brazil a scheme to provide cash transfers to poor families was placed on the agenda by a senator but implemented initially at the municipal level before being taken up by the federal government (Melo forthcoming).

While some aspects of leadership may be universal, others appear to differ from country to country. Leonard (1991) notes that successful public managers in Kenya had good political connections and access to donor resources; Kanungo and Conger (1995) suggest that in countries with a collectivist orientation, leaders should adopt a "family approach," making themselves available to staff by attending social occasions, for example. Pascal's observation that what is true in one country can be false in another (*vérité en-deçà des Pyrénées, erreur au-delà* [truth on this side of the Pyrenees is error on the other]) applies strongly to leadership.

Conclusion: Embedding Reforms

As noted already, one reform package cannot be said to be better or worse than another without reference to the political economy in which it is embedded. The models of reform presented in this chapter can be viewed as alternatives that governments can adapt to suit their own circumstances.

The innovations and proposals of policy analysts and external agencies, including development agencies, will continue to be a fertile source of ideas for policy makers. However, policy analysis is as much a process of discovery as of top-down prescription. A challenge for policy analysts, therefore, will be to identify and understand promising policies at the country level in their own terms and to understand the political economies in which those policies are embedded. Supporting reform becomes more a matter of identifying promising ideas that have already attracted the interest of local policy makers than of encouraging—let alone compelling—policy makers to adopt some international reform model, however appealing such a model may appear to outsiders.

Notes

1. Other options are, of course, also possible. It is convenient to separate options for analytical purposes; in real life, governments frequently adopt a mixture of approaches, one of which may predominate at any given point.
2. Sri Lanka is not presented here as a model of successful reform, although its experience is positive in some respects, but rather as an illustration of the domestic political factors involved in getting reforms to take root in local soil.
3. This scheme does not apply as well to Latin America or to countries that obtained independence a little earlier or later, such as India and Zimbabwe.
4. In keeping with the political economy approach taken in this chapter, these steps are listed in order of likely political difficulty.

References

Anderson, James, Gary Reid, and Randi Ryterman. 2003. *Understanding Public Sector Performance in Transition Countries: An Empirical Contribution*. World Bank, Washington, DC. www.worldbank.org/wbi/governance/govdonors/pdf/reid.pdf.

Al-Arkoubi, Khadija, and Willy McCourt. 2004. "The Politics of HRM: Waiting for Godot in the Moroccan Civil Service." *International Journal of Human Resource Management* 15 (6): 978–95.

Attorney-General's Chambers. 2003. "Code of Conduct." Singapore.

Barry, David. 1991. "Managing the Bossless Team: Lessons in Distributed Leadership." *Organizational Dynamics* 21 (1): 31–47.

Bebbington, Anthony, and Willy McCourt, eds. 2007. *Development Success: Statecraft in the South*. London: Palgrave Macmillan.

Burns, James. 1978. *Leadership*. New York: Harper and Row.

Corkery, Joan, and Anthony Land. 1996. *Civil Service Reform in the Context of Structural Adjustment*. European Centre for Development Policy Management, Maastricht.

Dia, Mamadou. 1996. *Africa's Management in the 1990s and Beyond: Reconciling Indigenous and Transplanted Institutions*. Washington, DC: World Bank.

Government of Malaysia. 1991. *Report of the Special Committee of the Cabinet on Salaries for the Public Sector*. Kuala Lumpur: National Printing Department.

Grindle, Merilee. 2007. "When Good Policies Go Bad, Then What? Dislodging Exhausted Industrial and Education Policies in Latin America." In *Development Success: Statecraft in the South*, ed. Anthony Bebbington and Willy McCourt. London: Palgrave Macmillan.

Gulhati, Ravi. 1990. "Who Makes Economic Policy in Africa and How?" *World Development* 18 (8): 1147–61.

Hyden, Goran, Julius Court, and Kenneth Mease. 2004. *Making Sense of Governance: Empirical Evidence from 16 Developing Countries*. Boulder, CO: Lynne Rienner.

Jackson, David. Forthcoming. "The Nampula Model: A Mozambique Case of Successful Participatory Planning and Financing." In *Development Success: Statecraft in the South*, ed. Anthony Bebbington and Willy McCourt. London: Palgrave Macmillan.

Jenkins, William. 1978. *Policy Analysis*. London: Martin Robertson.

Jones, David. 1974. "The Tribune's Visitation." In *The Sleeping Lord and Other Fragments*, ed. David Jones, 42–58. London: Faber and Faber.

Kanungo, Rabindra, and Jay Conger. 1995. "Modal Orientations in Leadership and Their Implication for Developing Countries." In *New Approaches to Employee Management*, vol. 3, ed. Rabindra Kanungo, 155–70. Greenwich, CT: JAI Press.

Kaufmann, Daniel. 1999. *Governance Redux: The Empirical Challenge*. World Bank Institute, Washington, DC. www.worldbank.org/wbi/governance/pubs/govredux.html.

Killick, Tony. 1998. *Aid and the Political Economy of Policy Change*. London: Routledge.

Kiragu, Kithinji, and Rwekaza Mukandala. 2004. *Pay Reform and Policies Report*. OECD Development Assistance Committee, Paris.

Kotter, John P. 1990. *A Force for Change: How Leadership Differs from Management*. New York: Free Press.

Leonard, David. 1991. *African Successes: Four Public Managers of Kenyan Rural Development*. Berkeley: University of California Press.

Manning, Nick, and Neil Parison. 2003. *International Public Administration Reform: Implications for the Russian Federation*. World Bank, Washington, DC. www.worldbank.org/publicsector/civilservice.

McCourt, Willy. 1998. "Civil Service Reform Equals Retrenchment? The Experience of 'Rightsizing' and Retrenchment in Ghana, Uganda and the United Kingdom." In *Beyond the New Public Management: Changing Ideas and Practices in Governance*, ed. M. Minogue, C. Polidano, and D. Hulme, 172–87. Cheltenham, United Kingdom: Edward Elgar.

———. 2001a. "The New Public Selection? Anti-corruption, Psychometric Selection and the New Public Management in Nepal." *Public Management Review* 3 (3): 325–44.
———. 2001b. "Towards a Strategic Model of Employment Reform: Explaining and Remedying Experience to Date." *International Journal of Human Resource Management* 12 (1): 56–75.
———. 2003. "Political Commitment to Reform: Civil Service Reform in Swaziland." *World Development* 31 (6): 1015–31.
———. 2006. *The Human Factor in Governance: Managing Public Employees in Africa and Asia*. London: Palgrave.
McCourt, Willy, and Anita Ramgutty-Wong. 2003. "Limits to Strategic Human Resource Management: The Case of the Mauritian Civil Service." *International Journal of Human Resource Management* 14 (4): 600–18.
Melo, Marcus. Forthcoming. "Political Competition Can Be Positive: Embedding Cash Transfer Programmes in Brazil." In *Development Success: Statecraft in the South*, ed. Anthony Bebbington and Willy McCourt. London: Palgrave.
Moore, Ray, and Donald Robinson. 2002. *Partners for Democracy: Crafting the New Japanese State under MacArthur*. New York: Oxford University Press.
Nelson, Joan, ed. 1990. *Economic Crisis and Policy Choice*. Princeton, NJ: Princeton University Press.
NEPAD (New Partnership for African Development). 2004. "Country Self–Assessment for the African Peer Review Mechanism." Bamako, Mali. www.nepad.org/2005/files/documents/156.pdf.
Nunberg, Barbara. 1994. "Experience with Civil Service Pay and Employment Reform: An Overview." In *Rehabilitating Government: Pay and Employment Reform in Africa*, ed. D. Lindauer and B. Nunberg, 119–59. Washington, DC: World Bank.
———. 1997. *Rethinking Civil Service Reform: An Agenda for Smart Government*. World Bank, Poverty and Social Policy Department, Washington, DC.
OECD (Organisation for Economic Co-operation and Development). 1994. *Public Management Developments*. Paris: OECD.
———. 2004. *Issues and Developments in Public Management: Canada 2001*. Paris: OECD. www.oecd.org/dataoecd/39/25/1923850.pdf.
Pope, Jeremy. 1995. "Ethics, Transparency and Accountability: Putting Theory into Practice." In *Civil Service Reform in Anglophone Africa*, ed. Petter Langseth, Sandile Nogxina, Daan Prinsloo, and Roger Sullivan. Pretoria: Economic Development Institute, Overseas Development Administration, and Government of South Africa.
———. 1999. "The Need for, and Role of, an Independent Anti-corruption Agency." Transparency International Working Paper, Berlin, www.transparency.org/working_papers/pope/jpope_iaca.html.
Quah, Jon. 1994. "Controlling Corruption in City-States: A Comparative Study of Hong Kong and Singapore." *Crime, Law and Social Change* 22 (4): 391–414.
Slatter, Stuart. 1984. *Corporate Recovery*. Harmondsworth, United Kingdom: Penguin.
Wijesinghe, D. 1997. *Administrative Reforms: International Perspectives and the Case of Sri Lanka*. Colombo: Government of Sri Lanka.
Williamson, John. 1994. *The Political Economy of Policy Reform*. Washington, DC: Institute for International Economics.
World Bank. 1998a. *Assessing Aid: What Works, What Doesn't, and Why*. Washington, DC: World Bank.

———. 1998b. *Public Expenditure Management Handbook*. World Bank, Poverty and Social Policy Department, Washington, DC.

———. 2004. *World Development Report 2004: Making Services Work for Poor People*, Washington, DC: World Bank.

———. 2006. "Strengthening Bank Group Engagement on Governance and Corruption." Draft Development Committee strategy, World Bank, Washington, DC.

Younger, Stephen. 1996. "Labour Market Consequences of Retrenchment for Civil Servants in Ghana." In *Economic Reform and the Poor in Africa*, ed. David Sahn, 185–202. Oxford: Clarendon Press.

Zaleznick Abraham. 1997. "Managers and Leaders: Are They Different?" *Harvard Business Review* 55 (3): 67–78.

3

Can E-Government Make Public Governance More Accountable?

HELMUT DRÜKE

Globalization, changes in information and communication technology, the declining importance of ideologies, new ideas on the reasons for efficiency in organizations, and a changed understanding of the relation between the state and society demand an extensive restructuring of public administration. The challenge is to change the structure and function of public administration in a way that affects all societies and all nations.

Initiatives to modernize public administration are being carried out around the world. The first generation of changes, implemented in the 1980s, focused on public sector modernization, based on the concepts and instruments of New Public Management. New Public Management had two main tracks. The first was to restructure the relationship with external actors by sharpening the customer focus and introducing alternatives to the in-house production of services, such as contracting out, corporatization, agencification, and privatization (Naschold, Jann, and Reichard 1999). The second was to optimize the processes and organization within public administration by applying transparent financial management with cost-benefit assessment, improved transparency of administrative processing, and reformed incentive structures.

E-government represents the second generation of reform. The main effect of e-government is "simply better government by enabling better policy outcomes, higher quality services, greater engagement with citizens and by improving other key outputs identified. Governments and public administrations will, and should, continue to be judged against these established criteria for success" (OECD 2003: 12).

Developing countries are making great efforts to modernize their public administration with the aid of e-government. The extraordinary challenge is to both modernize the public sector and progressively democratize public life. The adoption of Web-based technologies in public administration in developing countries has already begun to create a new interface between government and society. Whether e-government will unambiguously lead to a more transparent, interactive, open, and hence accountable government remains to be seen.

This chapter discusses the extent to which e-government can contribute to achieving accountable public governance. The first section discusses the notion of accountability in public governance. The second section describes e-government as a comprehensive modernization concept and identifies the preconditions needed before it can be introduced in developing countries. The third section discusses what the state can do to foster the development of e-government in developing countries. The last section addresses what must be done to ensure that e-government improves accountability.

Accountability in Public Governance

Political scientists agree in defining *accountability* as "holding people to account for their impact on the lives of people." People who are affected have the right to be heard and to have their views taken into account. People with power have the obligation to listen and respond. To enforce these rights and obligations, societies have established sanctions.

Accountability and Democracy

Accountability is a cornerstone of modern democracy. According to Brin (1998), accountability is the fundamental principle of a transparent society. Brin cites Karl Popper, for whom accountability is the rational principle in dealing with systems of administration and economy in democratic societies: "Only by insisting on accountability, [Popper] concluded, can we constantly remind public servants that they are servants. It is also how we maintain some confidence that merchants aren't cheating us or that factories aren't poisoning the water. As inefficient and irascibly noisy as it seems at times, this habit of questioning authority ensures freedom far more effectively than any of the older social systems that were based on reference or trust" (Brin 1998: 12).

Accountability is not restricted to public governance; it is a basic principle of regulation and expectation in all social relations. Private sector, nonprofit, and civic organizations must all be accountable to the public and to their institutional stakeholders.

Who is accountable to whom varies, depending on whether decisions or actions taken are internal or external to an organization or institution. In general, an organization or institution is accountable to those who will be affected by its decisions or actions. The fact that accountability is a basic principle in society is the precondition that accountable public governance can work and is accepted and expected by the actors in society.

Accountability is essential for the legitimacy of governance. The difference between internal and external accountability is important in this context. Internal accountability refers to the fact that actors in government and corporations are accountable to those who have assigned them their tasks. More difficult in terms of legitimacy is external accountability, meaning that those who do not participate directly or indirectly in the networks of politics but who are affected by decisions have a chance to influence these decisions. External accountability can be achieved only by increased transparency and openness.

Accountability and Good Governance

That citizens have the right to good governance should be understood. The fact that the quality of public administration must be good instead of bad should be accepted without question. Public administrations must deliver high quality in social services and allow participation in political processes. In this sense the notion of good governance is an old and familiar term. But *good governance* is a recent term, reflecting the new expectations that the governed have with regard to governing actors. "Given that the prevailing mentality was that citizens were subjects of government . . . and that free choice and free argumentation were the cornerstones of the organization of government, the process of concretely guiding governments toward serving the citizenry was overlooked in many if not in fact most countries" (Saarenpää 2002: 10).

Good governance regards the governed as citizens with dedicated aspirations and expectations with regard to the result and the process of governance. It has eight main characteristics, according to the United

Nations Economic and Social Commission for Asia and the Pacific (UNESCAP): it is "participatory, consensus oriented, accountable, transparent, responsive, effective and efficient, equitable and inclusive, and follows the rule of law" (UNESCAP 2006: 1).

This definition makes clear that accountability is an important feature of good governance, not only in the sense of effective bureaucracy but also in the sense of democratic governance. Democratic governance "emphasizes the interactions between citizens, political representatives, and administrative machinery, providing a special view of citizens' opportunities to influence and participate in policy making, development, and service processes" (Anttiroiko 2004: 25). Accountability facilitates good governance insofar as active involvement of citizens in transparent decision making shapes good governance. It is pursuant to this understanding of good governance that citizens have an enforceable right to take an active part in governance and to have public services of good quality.

What does good governance mean in concrete terms? In an effort to define concrete action to achieve good governance, Fuhr and Stockmayer (2002) identify four dimensions of good governance and propose indicators for each (table 3.1).[1]

The first dimension (state tasks and their reform) touches the rooting of subsidiary structures of task fulfillment and the strengthening of legitimacy by enlarging effective citizen participation. The second dimension (governmental competence) refers to the ability to formulate a coherent policy and the configuration of a reform-oriented government organization. The third dimension (civil society) involves civil society and its institutions. The fourth dimension (law) addresses the establishment of property rights, which is especially relevant for transparent and reliable interaction within society and between society and the state.

E-Government as a Comprehensive Concept of Modernization

E-government stands on the pillars of customer service, citizen engagement, and internal efficiency. It creates a completely new quality of public administration. New ways of using information and knowledge are the basis of reshuffling front and back offices, creating cooperation among administrators across different levels of government and enlarging citizen participation in decision-making processes. Completely new relationships and forms of cooperation between the administration on the one hand and citizens and businesses on the other are now possible.

TABLE 3.1 Dimensions of Good Governance

State tasks and their reform	Governmental competence	Civil society	Law
Implementation of subsidiary structures of task performance	Consultation in the design of a coherent policy	Creation of a climate for civil engagement	Creation of a self-standing order of economic property rights
Strengthening of legitimacy by provision of sustainable public services	Configuration of a reform-oriented governmental organization	Introduction of procedures of constructive interaction between state institutions and civil society	Attribution of rights and guarantee of their application
Strengthening of legitimacy by more effective citizen participation	Continuous improvement		Lawfulness of the state
Abolition of corruption			
Abolition of generalized violence by a few actors			

Source: Based on Fuhr and Stockmayer 2002.

E-administration defines the intraorganizational relationships, or the internal and public sector management component. E-governance refers to the interaction between citizens, government organizations, and elected officials. It focuses on the decision-making and policy-making process. Information and communication technologies support the phases of the decision-making process (information seeking, forming of opinions, joint decision making, negotiation, conflict handling, and voting).

E-government is a means to increase the transparency of public administration. It makes it easier for public administration to give an account of its activities to the governed. Transparency is supported by implementing a monitoring role of the citizen in administrative processes, which is then integrated into workflow systems. Another method is to implement a track and trace system, with which applicants for governmental services, permits, or franchises can follow the processing of their applications. Increasing the responsiveness of public administration toward "customer" inquiries helps government become aware of the expectations that society has with regard to public services. An active complaint management system can induce citizens to file complaints and generate a transparent processing of complaints received, to name but a few applications.

Dealing with public administration is less stressful and complicated for individuals and businesses when a single-window solution is implemented, meaning that applicants can obtain information from one access point. A single-window solution requires integration of front and back offices so that demands, when they are standardized or semicustomized, can be processed by the front office. The new distribution of responsibilities and activities between an empowered call center dealing face to face with the customer and the back-office organization opens completely new potentials for reorganizing the distribution of activities within public administration.

Cooperation between public authorities from different jurisdictions on different levels (local, regional, federal) is also possible. External cooperation partners can also be connected electronically, irrespective of distance.

There is a tendency to overestimate the potential that digital governance might have. E-government is an organizational concept based on a strong political will and a clear vision to change the way governments and the governed interact. The OECD formulates it aptly: "E-government is more about government than about 'e'" (OECD 1993: 6).

E-Government in Developed Countries

E-government in its most developed form means that all aspects of government and administration (public policy formation, decision making, development and provision of services, participation) are supported by information and communication technology. This includes seamless transactions between the administration and its customers, as well as participation of citizens in policy formation and decision-making processes at the local level through the Internet and digital television.

Measured by these standards, throughout the developed world, e-government is on the verge of moving from the stages of information and communication to the stage of transactions. The first stages of development focused on creating municipal information systems, such as administrative guidance, forms, municipal portals, and facilities for communication (e-mail, chat rooms). Simple e-transactions such as registration of births, changes of address, and company registration are widespread.

More sophisticated transactions (such as payment of taxes and charges and e-procurement) are taking place only in countries in which the statutory and technical obstacles to transaction security, legally binding transactions, and authenticity are relatively low, such as Canada, the United Kingdom, and the United States, which are among the world leaders in benchmarking studies of online services. According to the online availability study conducted by Capgemini for eEurope in 2004 (Capgemini 2005), countries in the European Union have realized two-way interaction using downloadable forms, but full electronic case handling remains rare. Online availability of services is higher for businesses than for citizens, reflecting the shifting focus of e-government to business-oriented services.

Participation services also vary widely in character. In many countries, citizens can directly reach council members and administrative staff over the Internet; in some countries, citizens participate in building permission procedures. Broad participation facilities are found in Finland. A special form of public participation in the e-government project itself has been developed in Virginia Beach, Virginia, where a citizen committee monitors project work. E-voting, once regarded with high hopes, has been used or tested only in minor elections because of the high investment and low demand (Malkia, Anttiroiko, and Savolainen 2004).

Only if e-government is designed as a comprehensive program of administrative modernization can it be a success. All of the progressive local communities studied in the volume edited by Drüke (2005) have a written e-government strategy, in most cases based on a vision. E-government is considered a major success factor if the top political and administrative leadership identifies with e-government and modernization. This commitment is a major condition to ensure coherence between the modernization project and other reform projects in politics.

E-Government in Developing Countries

Until recently, with some exceptions, e-government had been used largely in Australia, Europe, Japan, New Zealand, North America, and Singapore. On the basis of a solid structure of state interaction with society, the new potential of reorganizing the inner workings and interaction with society is about to be changed significantly by e-government. The channels are in place for information to be spread more easily and rapidly to users. If "material democracy" is provided (in the sense that everyone is given a chance to raise his or her voice in the political process) and a strong state is in place, e-participation gives the governed a stronger voice. The legal system and market regulation are developed to the degree that online transactions are managed effectively and transparently.

Developing countries in Africa, Asia, and Latin America are lagging the developed countries of the world in creating the preconditions for e-government and establishing new ways to work internally and to handle interactions with society. The reason for such slow progress is a complex interdependency of market imperfection and state failure. Promoters of modernization face special conditions and challenges: "E-government in the developing world must accommodate certain unique conditions, needs and obstacles. These may include a continuing oral tradition, lack of infrastructure, corruption, weak educational systems and unequal access to technology. Too often, the lack of resources and technology is compounded by a lack of access to expertise and information" (Pacific Council on International Policy 2002: 1).

Public Governance in Developing Countries

The traditional rubrics of Newly Industrialized Countries (NICs), Less Developed Countries (LDCs), and Least Developed Countries (LLDCs) are outdated, because they are restricted to a monocausal approach—the performance of national economies. Two trends demand a different approach: the increasingly differentiated reflections about the state in the development process (Messner 1995; Rotberg 2004; World Bank 1993; World Bank Institute 2004) and the significance of "good governance" as a major requirement by the governed (Chesterman 2004; Minogue and McCourt 2002; OECD DAC 2002).

Risse and Lehmkuhl (2006) propose a new categorization that focuses on the development level of the state. Countries with "restricted stateness" are characterized by a lack of authoritative decision competence and the lack of a state monopoly on violence (table 3.2).

In some countries in Latin America, market structures are imperfect and the regulatory system is underdeveloped (Fuhr 1998). Corrupt elites abuse state privileges for rent seeking and rent appropriation, establishing rent-distribution alliances with the middle class and trade unions, thereby integrating strong social groups and neutralizing the potential of resistance. "Populism controlled by the state and corporatism is the political pendant to market limitation and protectionism in import substituting industrialization" (Fuhr 1998: 5). Accountability is lacking, because decisions are made within these broad alliances. Political responsibility is covered and success attributed only to members of the political class.

In most countries in Latin America, this path has led to economic disaster, with long-lasting economic decay and deep national debt resulting in

TABLE 3.2 Characteristics of Countries with "Restricted Stateness"

Type of state	Characteristics	Examples
State in decay	Neither the state monopoly on violence nor the ability of political actors to effectively enforce political decisions is in place.	Afghanistan, Colombia, Democratic Republic of Congo, Nigeria, Tajikistan
Weak state	Serious deficiencies exist in the state monopoly on violence and the ability to effectively enforce political decisions in many transition economies and developing countries, often as a result of the lack of political-administrative capabilities.	Argentina, Armenia, Azerbaijan, Georgia, India, Indonesia, Mexico, Pakistan
Emerging state	The state monopoly on violence and authoritative cannot be effectively enforced everywhere.	Brazil, China, Republic of Korea, South Africa

Source: Risse and Lehmkuhl 2006.

severe budgetary restrictions. Problems of legitimacy have accumulated. Consequently, a wave of state modernization has taken place, in some cases starting with the far-reaching restructuring of economic direction and the reshuffling of political power.

New Public Management, with its cornerstones of redefinition of public tasks and internal modernization, was widely accepted as a way out of this dilemma, especially in Latin America. The results have been modest, however. Fuhr (1998) concludes that state modernization did not really succeed, partially because of the specific power constellation in most of these countries and because of the inability of New Public Management to address fundamental problems, such as low investment in human capital, deficiencies in the fight against corruption, low level of connection to civil society, and the lack of checks and balances in the formally democratic systems.

Market imperfection and state failure create significant obstacles to the development of an information society. Countries that retain telecom monopolies, hamper free entry of competitors, and restrict competitive markets are penalized by slow growth and the consequent decline in social development.

A special role is played by the bureaucracy in emerging countries. Countries such as Brazil and South Africa are controlled by a kind of bureaucratic community that makes the state a dominant and effective institution. This bureaucracy carries out its control function over and above its coordinating and support functions, a condition that is a product of the narrow experience with parliamentary democratic structures. Competent and qualified civil servants are often frightened away by this attitude, choosing the more attractive salaries, career paths, and working conditions offered by the private sector. High turnover, especially at the level of middle management in public administration, creates a serious strain on the cooperative relationships in these and other countries.

The Contribution of E-Government to Good Governance

E-government works on the double problem of market imperfection and state failure. Applying e-government means both regulating the market (creating transparency and equal opportunities to pursue one's economic interests) and strengthening the state's role in society (enabling market mechanisms to work). This, in turn, helps improve regulatory enforcement, reduce the discretion of officials, and increase transparency. E-government plays a significant role in addressing deficiencies in countries with restricted stateness, better involving citizens in the decision-making process through e-participation. E-government contributes to the reformulation and modernization of state tasks and their reform, increases governmental competencies, develops civil society, enforces a new legal structure, and introduces lawfulness in public administration (table 3.3).

Reforming state tasks

Due to the new potential for networking and new opportunities for cooperation by authorities at different administrative levels and within a single administrative level, the discussion of the 1980s, which was stuck in the dichotomy of public or private, now takes place in a broader context. E-government, to a far greater extent than New Public Management, is about new relationships with the external world. Alternatives to high vertical integration or regulated autonomization of state activities include agencification and the formation of private-public partnerships. Agencification is a form of devolution of public activities to civil society; public-private partnerships are a way to connect public authorities and private initiative.[2]

What makes agencies an interesting alternative to the complete privatization is their greater flexibility compared with public authorities. Public agencies in the United Kingdom operate with framework documents that determine their competencies, duties, political targets, financial resources, and outputs and performance. They differ significantly with regard to functions (administration of penitentiaries, patent offices, land surveys, customs clearance,

TABLE 3.3 Ways in Which E-Government Contributes to Good Governance

Dimension of good governance	E-government application
State tasks and their reform	
Implementation of subsidiary structures of task performance	Contracting out, agencification, public-private partnerships
Strengthening of legitimacy by providing sustainable public services	Access to records, gazetteer, mobile service delivery, e-procurement
Strengthening of legitimacy by more effective citizen participation	More effective and uncontrolled access to information and government services, e-procurement, urban land planning procedures, e-parliament
Abolition of corruption	E-procurement, interborder checks, e-justice, tax systems, electronic register of corruption cases
Abolition of generalized violence by a few actors	E-justice
Governmental competence	
Consultation in the designing of a coherent policy	Stakeholder involvement, active communication
Configuration of a reform-oriented governmental organization	Professional performance measurement, e-justice, public-private partnership
Continuous improvement	Professional monitoring, civil monitoring of accountability mechanisms
Civil society	
Creation of a climate for civil engagement	E-participation, stakeholder involvement
Introduction of procedures of constructive interaction between state institutions and civil society	Formation of public-private partnerships, market development for information and communication technology products and services, economic development
Law	
Creation of a self-standing order of economic property rights (see abolition of corruption)	Market liberalization through the use of tools such as e-signatures, e-transactions, licensing, and cybercrime legislation; e-procurement
Attribution of rights and guarantee of its application	Electronic registration of voters to prevent voters from being left off voter lists
Lawfulness of state as attribute of good governance	Definition and transparency of competencies and responsibilities, access to records, e-justice

Source: Author.

labor offices, and so forth) as well as in size (from 40 to 40,000 employees). They get their resources from taxes, fees, or sales on the open market.

Private-public partnerships—cooperation of public authorities and private companies to run joint projects with investment from both sides—are not a new instrument.[3] They have been used for some time in the construction sector, for example. The advantages for both sides of private-public partnerships in e-government are that each partner has restricted risk and brings special know-how and interests. Private-public partnerships are of high relevance in the process chain connecting public authorities and private businesses (examples include the issuance of building permits, creation of portals, and e-procurement). The experience in countries such as Finland and the United Kingdom indicates the tremendous opportunities this instrument provides for pursuing common interests (Drüke 2005).

A third aspect of the new relationships between public administration and the external world is cooperation, which does not necessarily fall within the strict legal forms or processes discussed above. Finland, with its long experience of cooperation, pushed cooperation to a new level with the introduction of e-government. E-government in Finland builds on that nation's traditional cooperative structures as well as a working relationship among stakeholder organizations. "We may even say that the trend seems to be that a large part of local e-government in Finland will be built upon co-operation, networks and partnerships" (Anttiroiko 2005: 53). All of these variants of cooperative forms for carrying out government functions introduce competition and innovation into the public sphere, and break up nontransparent and often corrupt inner circles of a few privileged circles.

A second aspect of state reform and the increase of efficiency and accountability in state action is the fight against corruption. E-government is an excellent tool in this challenge, as the examples in box 3.1 reveal.

E-procurement ensures the anonymity of participating suppliers, even to buyers, until bids are opened. It ensures transparency, since anyone associated with the transaction can access the status of the transaction. It enhances efficiency, since time is saved and inventory planning is improved due to the transparency of the bid process. Compared with the manual procurement process, subjectivity, favoritism, and discrimination have been reduced, resulting in a more secure, reliable, and accountable process.

An online tendering and bidding process for procurement of goods and services for public administration is one of the most important applications for fighting corruption and installing a lawful market mechanism. According to estimates by the National Counter Corruption Commission

BOX 3.1 Using E-Government to Fight Corruption around the World

Several countries have begun using e-government to fight corruption. They include Colombia, Germany, India, the Republic of Korea, Mexico, Namibia, the Philippines, and Thailand.

Colombia
Colombia achieved budget transparency by publishing information (working plans, revenues, expenditures). It rationalized payment and accounting procedures by introducing software for financial management and cost calculation. Verifiability and citizen orientation were increased by decentralizing registration, processing, and data provision (von Richter, Breckner, and Friedland 2002).

Germany
Implementation of an online debt collection system in Bremen allowed the municipality to reduce the number of courts from three to one. Online debt collection has also replaced contacts with often dubious debt collectors (Grabow and Siegfried 2003).

India
In Gujarat trucking companies encouraged transporters to load their trucks beyond the permissible axle load in order to maximize their earnings from each vehicle. The government installed a video camera system to register all trucks coming to the border and to check the permissible weight for each truck using the data from a central database. An electronic weighbridge weighs the vehicle, and a computer automatically issues a fine. Drivers can use a stored value card for payments, obviating the need for them to carry large sums of cash, thereby reducing corruption at the border. The system increased tax collection from $12 million to $35 million over two years and reduced the average time required to clear a vehicle from 30 minutes to 2 minutes (Kumar and Sushil 2005).

Republic of Korea
The Online Procedures Enhancement for Civil Applications (OPEN) in Seoul allows citizens to monitor the progress of their applications over the Internet. With real-time information available to everyone, officials can no longer sit on cases without justifiable reasons or make arbitrary decisions. An open record of all stages of administrative procedures eliminates the need for personal contact with particular officials and does away with "express fees." Transparency is used to deter corruption (Wescott 2003: 4).

Mexico
Mexico's Compranet system "allows the public to see what services and products the government is spending its resources on and what companies are

(*Box continues on the following page.*)

providing them with these services" (Pacific Council on International Policy 2002: 10). It logs more than 6,000 public sector tenders a day and has more than 20,000 service-providing firms as regular users. Lessons learned from successful experiences reveal the tremendous contributions that e-procurement can make to fighting corruption and improving bureaucratic efficiency.

Namibia
Namibia used information technology to strengthen the efficiency and transparency of its court trials. The administration of justice is being restructured as part of the Legal Capacity Building Program funded by German Technical Cooperation. The main outcome of the program is that the administration of justice, including financial transfers to subcourts, is being restructured to facilitate electronic procedures and monitoring, increasing transparency (BMZ 2006).

The Philippines
A database used in the Philippines matches a company's declared sales with its purchases, real property transactions, tax credits, refunds granted, import entries, and government incentives. In the case of a significant discrepancy, the false statement is detected and the company subject to a fine or penalty.

Thailand
A pilot project has been set up to register corruption cases, making it easier to identify corrupt practices, as the registry is available throughout Thailand.

in Thailand, up to 30 percent of the government procurement budget may be lost to corrupt practices (ADB 2001). E-procurement introduces transparency, accountability, and predictability of rules and procedures into both tendering and bidding.

The online processing of tax processes is another important instrument in the fight against corruption. The objective is to bring more transparency, mainly into business taxation, and to reduce tax evasion in customs clearance.

Improving governmental competence

Transforming service delivery by introducing e-government and increasing transparency by reducing corruption are likely to enhance governmental competencies. Public authorities all over the world are characterized by a distinct silo orientation and island solution in organizational and technical aspects. E-government facilitates horizontal (between authorities on the same level) and vertical (between authorities on different levels) cooperation. Cooperation can be as simple as exchanging information through a Web site. An example is the Web site of the municipality of Surrey, in the United Kingdom, which allows the county council, district councils, local police, ambulance services, health authority, and army to rapidly share information about major incidents or emergencies, such as flooding (Ferguson 2005).

The next step in establishing cooperation between public authorities can be the formation of shared service centers. In Auckland, New Zealand, seven district councils share services, including a contact center (Socitm and I&DeA 2002). In the United Kingdom, a partnership in Cumbria among six districts and borough councils, the fire and police departments, and the county council "is exploring co-operative working between the organizations to improve address management/geographical based systems and data, which will be fundamental to future customer centered e-government services" (I&DeA 2004).

In times of budgetary restrictions and higher expectations from society with regard to efficiency of public administration, it is no longer affordable to operate a full-fledged administration with high fixed and variable costs. Cooperation by authorities helps overcome the high costs of integration.

Another area in which governmental competence can be improved is the professionalization of the monitoring and controlling system. A case in point is the use of e-reporting in Germany. E-reporting is a system for distributing information for controlling costs and investment by administrative units. Data are forwarded from the data-gathering point to the program responsible for consolidating and interpreting the data. Reports for defined receiver groups are compiled automatically. In order to create a well-functioning process, all relevant structures, processes, and information technology systems must be aligned. The seamless connection between the participating information technology systems is critical. In addition to the technological specifications, the functional and organizational specifications of the new information technology process must be taken into account.

Empowering civil society

Reformers seek to create a climate of civil engagement and to introduce constructive interaction between state institutions and civil society. With the reform of public administration through e-government, the interaction between administration and civil society changes dramatically in the direction of greater customer orientation, transparency, efficiency, and lawfulness. But civil engagement and interaction between state institutions and civil society require reorganizing the political decision-making process, which helps open up closed circles of the political class and give the governed a stronger voice. E-government supports e-participation. Stakeholder involvement strengthens the connection between public administration and its users.

E-participation has three objectives: increasing e-information, enhancing e-consultation, and supporting e-decision making. The aim of e-participation must be to establish "civic publicness." "Citizens should be able to assume an active and creative role as participants in and as (co)producers of the public sphere, allowed to take part in the definition of the domain and agenda of public discussion" (Ridell 2004: 96).

Systems for e-information ensure that citizens are fully informed on policies and programs, budgets, laws, and regulations. But it is not enough to guarantee openness of procedures and access to documents. Freedom of information requires active delivery of information on issues of public interest. Public authorities must therefore guarantee timely access and use of public information by installing effective procedures.

E-consultation is an obligation for governments that want to develop and maintain accountability. Two methods have proven useful and feasible in developed countries: direct e-mail contact from the administration and political representatives and Web-mediated consultation and discussion. In Amersfoort, the Netherlands, "citizens are regularly asked to give their opinion on various local issues and, for the last two years, it has been possible to submit complaints about public areas and environmental issues by e-mail to the particular departments or private sector service provider involved. This process has been deemed successful by both citizens and the departments and organizations concerned" (Socitm and I&DeA 2002: 101).

Web-mediated consultation goes a step further. Topics of public interest are put online for discussion, with real-time and archived access in public meetings. Unorganized citizens, citizens in associations or stakeholder committees, and decision makers participate in chat room discussions of service provision.

In the United States citizens have used e-government applications to organize themselves. In Uniontown, Alabama, the government provides the financial support for the city's Web site. But citizens, as members of Uniontown Cares, maintain and update the page. "This is certainly a way the citizens of Uniontown feel empowered to participate and work with government officials to achieve their goals . . . . The citizens feel connected to each other, to their broader community, and to their government through the access the Web site provides" (Slaton and Arthur 2004: 128).

The Manse Forum in Tampere, Finland, encourages dialogue among city representatives, politicians, residents, and economic actors. It also creates a forum for trying out citizen-oriented forms and contents (Ridell 2004). Web-mediated discussion complements rather than substitutes for face-to-face communication between Web editors and local grassroots citizen groups.

Web queries are linked to city representatives and economic actors and to offline activities using the Web in a "complementary way to advance the public treatment of given issues, especially by drawing into collective conversation those parties that choose not to take part in face-to-face gatherings or are not 'disturbed' by the producers of the mass-mediated public sphere" (Ridell 2004: 99). The Manse Forum also created an open bulletin board and a public participants' guidebook. The bulletin board posts events, mostly by local citizen groups and associations. The guidebook offers easily accessible information about local resident issues, such as legal rights in land-use projects.

Other examples in Tampere also demonstrate how citizen initiatives and creativity can be supported. The city has organized moderated discussion forums on topical issues, which constantly change, depending on what themes are at stake in the political discussion of the city. It also uses the Internet to measure public opinion on specific questions every year. "For example, in the inquiry on municipal economy and finance in spring 2002, citizens sent over 1,000 answers or opinions on municipal finance issues. These opinions were taken into account in the preparation of the municipal budget. Citizens' ideas gathered in public inquiries and surveys even brought certain new emphases to the budget" (Anttiroiko 2004: 48).

The city administration of Hamburg, Germany, conducted three moderated online discussion forums, on the growing metropolis, the family-friendly city, and the 2007 budget. Participation by inhabitants was high. More than 2,000 proposals for a city budget were given within two weeks of opening the Web discussion (interview with the e-government manager of the city of Hamburg, March 2006).

The use of the Web to support decision making by local and regional authorities is illustrated by the TeamWest project in Australia. A regional Web site for the initiative in Greater Western Sydney was designed, "making the site a public face to an accessible and transparent structure of linked regional organizations and communities"(Sproats, Cairney, and Hegarty 2004: 208).

E-participation at the highest, most binding level is defined as e-decision making. In this form of e-government, government takes citizen input into account in making decisions and gives feedback on the outcome of specific issues. An example is online participation in land-use planning in Frankfurt, Germany, where a draft of a land-use plan was put on the Internet during the planning process. The public was invited to take part in the discussion and to make comments and raise objections. Online participation is especially useful in the case of a regional zoning plan, in which thousands of square kilometers of area are to be planned, hundreds of authorities and bodies with public interest are involved, and millions of citizens are affected.

By using the Internet, significant advantages for increasing accountability can be achieved. More and different groups of the population, such as elderly people or people who work, can be reached, and they can participate anonymously.

Increasing stakeholder involvement through e-government

"Civic engagement" means giving civil society and its stakeholders a strong and influential voice in issues of public interest. The involvement of stakeholders (citizens, businesses, and interest groups) is clear evidence of a vital democracy.

The special commission on e-government in Virginia Beach, Virginia, was created to increase the influence of the community in the development of e-government itself. Although this body plays only an advisory role, it is, nevertheless, an important channel of communication between the political and administrative establishment on the one hand and civil society groups on the other. "The commission members represent a wide range of interest groups, and they use their contacts to meet these groups and discuss e-government in face-to-face meetings" (Brown and Schelin 2005: 236).

To achieve the same objective, the municipality of Tameside, in the United Kingdom, created an e-team, with representatives from different stakeholder groups (Ferguson 2005). The municipality of Espoo, Finland, maintains Extranet services for key stakeholders, which means that only registered users have access to a Web room protected against entry by nonauthorized users (Anttiroiko 2005). The Wireless Philadelphia Executive Committee is serving as an advisory or advocacy group seeking to "develop a public and private partnership to achieve wireless access throughout the City and to enhance economic development in neighborhoods, help overcome the digital divide, and improve quality of life for all Philadelphians" (Wireless Philadelphia Executive Committee 2004: 7).

Strengthening civil rights and lawfulness

E-government is a strong instrument for strengthening the lawfulness of state action as well as accountability. E-government addresses state failure and market imperfection by implementing regulations that safeguard and realize citizens' rights, such as freedom of information and free and equal voting; introducing property rights for market regulation; and enhancing citizens' participation in decision making.

E-government creates new opportunities to introduce or strengthen civil rights, such as equal access to information. People with access to the Internet can now have access to public information. The goal is to achieve freedom of information as an essential and inherent element of democracy. Freedom of information is the basic precondition to forcing the government to disclose, within reasonable and defined limits, information about its activities. Openness correlates closely with accountability. An informed society is able to control state action and to influence actively the decision-making process. Legal regulation on freedom of information will result in a more effective and uncontrolled access to information and government services. What is essential is the active role of government, which must inform citizens of what it is doing, not expect citizens to try to obtain the information they need to take part in public life.

A second civil right is the right to have requests for information be decided upon within a reasonable time. This right is normally secured by introducing rules for answering e-mail and installing track and trace software, all of which require a functioning public information system.

Political rights can be strengthened by using e-government systems. An example is the electronic registration of voters. The government of Madagascar plans to use e-government to address corruption issues inherited from the former regime. It is creating an electronic registry of voters to ensure that all citizens can vote in the 2007 elections and that their names will not be missing from electoral lists (DOT-COMments 2005).

Setting up a powerful and legally binding juridical system is a means of installing and improving market mechanisms in developing countries. Regulation is needed to protect personal rights. Data warehousing, for example, which enables authorities to use the same database as a customer relation management system, poses a risk to privacy, insofar as citizens are no longer able to control the use of their data.

Property rights and labor rights are essential to accountability in the market relationships between government and economic actors. E-government facilitates transparent market transactions and impartiality in information delivery. A prime example is e-procurement.

Another area in which to introduce lawfulness is e-government itself. Doing so requires ensuring data security and privacy, to name but the most important aspects. Technological and organizational potentials related to e-government need to be regulated to protect fundamental rights. Administrative procedures must be regulated by law and decrees that give documents signed with an e-signature the same status as handwritten documents. New forms of cooperation, such as public-private partnerships, need strict legal frameworks. A desired effect of the regulation of e-government is to enhance transparency in the market mechanism.

Fostering E-Government and Accountability

Only the state can design and execute a program modernizing public governance. Especially in countries with restricted stateness, however, it needs support from, and cooperation with, international donors, consultants, and other experts.

Instruments at the State's Disposal

The state, in cooperation with empowered actors in society, has a variety of means with which to establish and carry out a change management process to make reform happen. These include financial resources, regulation, and, increasingly, the state's role as negotiator and motivator.

Improving e-government readiness

The successful implementation of e-government depends largely on having a high level of general e-readiness.[4] Access to tools for information and wealth creation, which remain highly skewed across the regions and countries of the world, is critical. Although the number of fixed and mobile telephones increased by a factor of more than 30 in developing countries between 1980 and 2005, only one in three people in the developing world has a telephone (UNDESA 2005). In the Republic of Korea, half of the population uses the Internet, while just 1 in 1,250 Cambodians ever goes online. "The stark reality [is] that many people in developing countries, especially in the rural areas, have zero access to information and communication technologies" (UNDESA 2005: 4).

A second area in which e-readiness must be improved is e-skilling. Civil servants with adequate skills are key to the real transformation of public administration. Media competence is essential for users to take full benefit of the new potentials. In addition to training, efforts in basic education are indispensable. A program such as an e-school is needed, in which children are trained to use computers in a group environment, thereby strengthening team cooperation.

Governments have to do the best they can to achieve significant progress in promising application fields such as e-health. An important government task is to make sure that the technological framework is being developed to achieve the level of technology needed to deliver e-government services: broadband investment, market preparation for new media, third-generation (3G) technologies, and technologies to manage digital rights.[5] Some developing countries understand that the state has to provide basic technologies. India, for instance, has established a wide area network with broadband technology and has nearly completed the computerization of most government departments.

Stimulating demand for e-government services

The state can play an important role as an economic actor. By switching its public procurement from paper to online tendering and bidding, government can dramatically boost innovation in the field of e-government. Such a radical change requires that the legal framework be in place and that suppliers accept the system and implement standardized systems for online transactions with public entities.

Investment can also transform conventional public activities into e-activities that are likely to boost innovation in the national economy. Important fields for such innovation include fostering of Internet penetration in schools and the health care sector, support for e-learning, and the use of e-government in internal procedures.

Funding e-government initiatives

Governmental authorities at all levels spend a huge volume of resources to promote e-government at the central, regional, and local levels. Between 2000 and 2004, the Ministry for Economics and Labor in Germany funded three pilot projects totaling €25 million; regional governments collectively allocated about the same amount to support regional initiatives. The United Kingdom increased the Local Government Online fund to £675 million (about €1 billion) through 2006. The Japanese government allocated massive financial resources for e-government in its e-Japan strategy (Fujita, Izawa, and Ishibashi 2005).

Organizing the playing field

Organize the playing field means negotiating, moderating, and bringing together partners. Essential to the promotion of e-government is the empowerment of civil society and organized stakeholders to build a coalition of those who want to transform a weak state into an enabling state and to enhance governmental competencies. Very early in the process, the state must implement appropriate institutions and official positions to foster the development of an information society in general and e-government in particular. This strategy embraces authorization bodies, standardization bodies, benchmarking groups, state reform committees, information technology task forces, and e-government steering groups. The aim is to motivate important players within the public sector administration and civil society and to organize the strategic and operational process very clearly from the beginning.

Guaranteeing standards and interoperability

The market is not able to generate commonly accepted rules on how to act in the networked environment: tell 100 systems engineers to organize interoperability and they will come up with 100 solutions. Alignment is the key to achieving network traffic at reduced costs and efforts. The state can set and declare standards unilaterally or organize a collaborative process on developing standards and interoperable systems. Without standards, it is not possible to achieve economies of scale, as ineffective island solutions will continue to exist.

Obstacles to Success

State action affects interests and power constellations, and it endangers common practices in politics and civil society, especially in developing countries with restricted stateness. Indigenous structures and attitudes can constrain public governance reform by e-government.

Coordination and cooperation are the core challenges to regulating e-government, according to Eifert and Püschel (2004). Within certain limits, it is easier for a strong central government to impose standards and interoperability on the different administrative levels (local, regional, central) than for individual federal states, which must deal with a higher complexity of political and legal influences, to do so.

Administrative culture has to do with how authorities in public administration understand their function and how they see their relationship to society. The ideal types of culture range from managerialism, found largely in Anglo-Saxon and some Scandinavian countries, to moderate modernism, found in Germany, to the double structure of modern elite and predominant state-socialist attitudes found in Eastern Europe.[6] In Germany the strong constitutional position of autonomous municipalities typically discourages initiatives to establish cooperation with other jurisdictions. Instead, municipalities generally prefer to find solutions on their own, even if they are expensive and suboptimal. The other pole is represented by Finland, where jurisdictions handle issues of common interest cooperatively, in close cooperation with the private sector.

Misunderstandings, false orientations, misjudgments, and overestimations have characterized the history of public administration and e-government in developed countries. Sources of policy failure include misguided focus, late implementation, the setting of unrealistic goals, the overestimation of citizens' willingness to pay for e-government services, and resistance from civil servants and public administrators.

The significance of the economics (cost-benefit ratio) of e-government projects has not been addressed adequately. The budgetary restrictions that many decision makers face should motivate them to determine what e-government costs and what benefits it provides. Financial resources have too often been lacking, and flanking measures, such as training, have been left out. Governments in developed countries are about to learn their lessons from these mistakes. In many countries the hype to focus on the online availability of public services leads to an approach that gives highest priority to the benefit of online services for different user groups, such as citizens and businesses. Step-by-step e-government is better understood as a comprehensive concept of modernization of the administration and its relationship to society, not a distribution channel for public services. This understanding is especially important when it comes to coping with the more complex transactions in government to business, government to citizen, and government to government relations.

Conclusions

Transparency and accountability depend on a better relationship between state administration and society, between governors and governed. E-government is the key to reaching a new level of public governance. E-government can significantly enhance accountability and help improve governance. It helps rationalize government reform by facilitating innovative forms of cooperation between state and private actors, strengthening legitimacy through sustainable public services, and enlarging and deepening citizen participation. E-procurement, online land-use planning, and e-justice can significantly reduce corruption, one of the greatest hindrances to progress and accountability in developing countries. Governmental competencies are clearly enhanced when communication with citizens is improved and made more transparent; when stakeholders are active partners in designing, monitoring, and steering e-government; and when professional performance measurements are introduced to replace subjectivity and arbitrariness.

E-participation and stakeholder involvement help put interaction with citizens on a rational and objective basis. Lawfulness, instead of ambiguity and lack of transparency, shapes governmental actions. Clear and legal regulations structure the interaction within society and between state authorities and society.

The description of good practices in this chapter gives some idea of the potential of e-government. These examples show that technology is not the core enabler in this transformative process of public governance.

E-government is not an information technology project but a comprehensive and far-reaching program of transformation of the way state authorities work and organize their relationships with civil society.

Many developing countries face massive gaps in transparency, lawfulness, and objectivity. "E-government . . . is no panacea for those societies with congenitally corrupt and defective political, social and economic systems and structures. . . . It is patently absurd to think that e-government could, and indeed would, transform a (failed state) into an efficient, credible, development-oriented super state. . . . E-government realistically is a function of capacity, capability and political will to break away from an existing condition" (Aziz 2003: 2).

If e-government is not approached as a comprehensive concept for modernizing public governance, failure is likely. If flanking measures are missing and essential reforms left out, e-government will be no more than a passing phenomenon, another overestimated innovation project. A case in point is China. The national government has achieved tremendous progress in preparing for e-government, with more broadband lines operating there than anywhere but the United States. The government is preparing the next step for digital administration. But an essential element is missing: policy makers have not established national interoperability standards. "The current lack of e-government standards is leading to a proliferation of information islands at a civic level—digitized pools of information that remain entirely inaccessible to related organizations. As a result, one of the e-government's key benefits—the liberalization of citizen information from legacy data silos—is failing to be realized" (Public Sector Technology and Management 2004: 10).

The first guideline in developing e-government must therefore be to coordinate and standardize the effort. "All the pieces—infrastructure, security, transparency, innovation and skills—must be properly interlaced to ensure e-readiness" (Economist Intelligence Unit 2005: 4).

The second guideline is to put a high priority on increasing e-government readiness in civil society and public administration. To do so, a strong political will, a clear strategy based on a persuading vision, and a clear distribution of responsibilities are needed. The development of an information society, even under the complex circumstances of developing countries, has to be the overall goal of all initiatives. Telecommunication infrastructure has to be developed, human resources made available, and training intensified. An umbrella program integrating initiatives in school, health care, and infrastructure must be developed. The climate for e-business must be fostered. The speed of introduction of e-government will greatly affect countries' ability to get into e-business activities. E-procurement is of critical importance in this process.

The third guideline is to base e-participation on "material democracy" (Ridell 2004). This aspect refers to the preeminent problem of developing countries: the need to guarantee equal access to online services and digital democracy. "It is hard to imagine how digitally mediated communication could function democratically unless everybody, regardless of his or her material wealth, social status, and cultural competencies, has access to new communication and information technologies as well as opportunities to obtain adequate computer literacy and navigating skills" (Ridell 2004: 86).

The authors of the *UN Global E-Government Readiness Report 2005* connect good governance in the sense of socially inclusive governance to access to all. "Participation is possible only if political, economic, technological and social barriers are removed and access to these opportunities is equitably distributed" (UNDESA 2005: xiii).

In his evaluation of the initiatives undertaken by the Indian government to foster e-government, Haque (2002: 244) concludes that because of the insurmountable problems of guaranteeing access to all, e-government in India "has not shown any promising results." Implementation of e-government has increased the distance between the governing circles and the governed, because "under e-governance, the nature of the relationship between politicians and public servants may have changed from one based on neutrality and accountability to one of a fused power structure with the dominance of bureaucrats empowered by information expertise" (Haque 2002: 245).

The fourth guideline, therefore, is to give the fight against the digital divide the appropriate priority in the e-government strategy. E-government provides the instruments to cope with the digital divide between skilled and less skilled, rural and urban areas, old and young people.

The lack of Internet access at home can partially be compensated for by installing public Internet access points in shopping malls, recreation centers, factories, and offices, where users, guided by instructors, can use e-government services for information, communication, and even business transactions.

Another way of increasing access is the Internet bus, which is being used in Bahia, Brazil; Liverpool, United Kingdom; and Tampere, Finland. In Bahia these mobile units have access to computer networks and databases that allow citizens to access identification cards and birth certificates. Mobile health units with access to electronic patient records treat people in the state's poorest communities, bringing services to millions of people (Pacific Council on International Policy 2002).

Without a clear change in management that takes into account these four guidelines, innovators in developing countries run the risk of failure. Resistance by representatives of closed political circles in weak states who defend the existing system of public governance, discouragement on the part of serious innovators, and lack of acceptance by ordinary civil servants who must live with new public governance will endanger preparedness to innovate public administration for a long time.

Notes

1. These dimensions are similar to those used by the World Bank in assessing governance: voice and accountability, political instability and violence, government effectiveness, regulatory burden, rule of law, and graft (see Kaufmann, Kraay, and Zoido-Lobatón 1999).
2. Agencies are public autonomous organizations that have enlarged spaces of action in the fields of management, personnel administration, and budget and financial management because they are set free from bureaucratic restrictions.
3. Given this definition of *public-private partnerships* (PPP), permanent cooperation as given with the so-called "institutional PPP" instead of a PPP for projects is not included.
4. According to the United Nations Department of Economic and Social Affairs, "E-government readiness is a function of not only a country's state of readiness but also its technological and telecommunications infrastructure and the level of its human resource development, among other factors, and at a minimum should be based on the level of all three" (UNDESA 2005: 14).
5. Third-generation services provide the ability to simultaneously transfer both voice data (a telephone call) and nonvoice data (such as downloading information, exchanging e-mail, and instant messaging).
6. In managerialism, public administration is regarded as similar to the administration of a private company. In moderate modernism, politics are widely shaped by negotiation between the state and associations of industry, workers, or nongovernmental organizations.

References

ADB (Asian Development Bank). 2001. "Technical Assistance to Thailand for Strengthening Accountability Mechanisms." Working Paper R86-01, Manila.

Anttiroiko, Ari-Veikko. 2004. "Introduction to Democratic E-Governance." In *E-Transformation in Governance: New Directions in Government and Politics*, ed. Matti Malkia, Ari-Veikko Anttiroiko, and Reijo Savolainen. Hershey, PA: Idea Group Publishing.

———. 2005. "Urban E-Government in Finland." In *Local Electronic Government: A Comparative Study*, ed. Helmut Drüke, 19–59. New York: Routledge.

Aziz, Tunku Abdul. 2003. "E-Government: Impact on Transparency and Anti-corruption." Paper presented at the World Bank Workshop "E-Government: Impact on Transparency and Anti-Corruption," Washington, DC, January 28.

Bikshapathi, Shri K., Bala P. Ramaraju, and Subash Bhatnagar. 2006. "E-Procurement in Government of Andhra Pradesh, India." World Bank, Washington, DC. http://web.worldbank.org.

BMZ (Bundesministerium für Technische Zusammenarbeit). 2006. "Korruptionsbekämpfung." ("Fight against Corruption"). http://www.bmz.de.

Brin, David. 1998. *The Transparent Society: Will Technology Force Us to Choose between Privacy and Freedom?* Reading, MA: Addison-Wesley.

Brown, Mary Maureen, and Shannon Schelin. 2005. "American Local Governments: Confronting the E-Government Challenge." In *Local Electronic Government. A Comparative Study*, ed. Helmut Drüke, 229–69. New York: Routledge.

Capgemini. 2005. *Online Availability of Public Services. How Is Europe Progressing? Web-Based Survey on Electronic Public Services*. Report of the Fifth Measurement October 2004, prepared by Capgemini for the European Union Commission Directorate General for Information Society and Media, Brussels.

Chesterman, Simon. 2004. *You, the People: The United Nations, Transitional Administration, and State-Building*. Project of the International Peace Academy. New York: Oxford University Press.

DOT-COMments. 2005. "Pushing the Envelope on E-Government." http://www.dot-com-alliance.org/index.htm.

Drüke, Helmut, ed. 2005. *Local Electronic Government. A Comparative Study*. New York: Routledge.

Economist Intelligence Unit. 2005. "The 2005 E-Readiness Rankings." White Paper. http://www.eiu.com.

Eifert, Martin, and Jan Ole Püschel. 2004. *National Electronic Government. Building an Institutional Framework for Joined-Up Government: A Comparative Study*. New York: Routledge.

Ferguson, Martin. 2005. "Local E-Government in the United Kingdom." In *Local Electronic Government: A Comparative Study*, ed. Helmut Drüke, 156–97. New York: Routledge.

Fuhr, Harald. 1998. "Staatsreform und Verwaltungsmodernisierung: Zur Neuen Rolle des Staats in Lateinamerika." ("State Reform and Administrative Modernization: On the New Role of the State in Latin America.") Working Paper, Department for International Politics, University of Potsdam, Germany.

Fuhr, Harald, and Albrecht Stockmayer. 2002. "Reformen im Öffentlichen Sektor: 'Good Governance' und Die Beratungsaufgaben der GTZ." ("Reforms in the Public Sector: 'Good Governance' and the Consulting Task of GTZ.") Paper written for the Society for Technical Cooperation (GTZ) Eschborn, Germany.

Fujita, Masahiro, Takahiro Izawa, and Hiroki Ishibashi. 2005. "The E-Public Administrative Process in Japan." In *Local Electronic Government: A Comparative Study*, ed. Helmut Drüke, 197–229. Milton Park, UK/New York: Roultedge.

Grabow, Busso, and Christine Siegfried. 2003. "Re-Engineering der Aufbauorganisation." ("Re-engineering of the Organizational Structure.") In *Success Model Local E-Government*, ed. Busso Grabow, Helmut Drüke, and Christine Siegfried. http://medikomm.difu.de/erfolgsmodell/index.php?m=2,12,3,18&highlight-=Mahnverfahren.

Gupta, M. P., and Prabhat Kumar. 2005. "E-Governance in Gujarat." Department of Management Studies, Indian Institute of Technology Delhi Huaz Khas, New Delhi. http://www.egovonline.net/articles/article-details.asp?articleid=507&typ=In%20Practice.

Haque, M. Shamsul. 2002. "E-Governance in India: Its Impact on Relations among Citizens, Politicians and Public Servants." *International Review of Administrative Sciences* 68 (2): 231–50.

Hill, Hermann. 2002. "Electronic Government: Strategie zur Modernisierung von Staat und Verwaltung." ("Electronic Government: Strategy for Modernizing the State and Administration.") *Aus Politik und Zeitgeschichte* B 39–40: 24–37.

I&DeA (Improvement and Development Agency). 2004. "The Building Blocks of E-Government." London. www.idea-knowledge.gov.uk.

Kaufmann, Daniel, Aart Kraay, and Pablo Zoido-Lobatón. 1999. *Governance Matters.* Washington, DC: World Bank.

Malkia, Matti, Ari-Veikko Anttiroiko, and Reijo Savolainen, eds. 2004. *E-Transformation in Governance: New Directions in Government and Politics.* Hershey, PA: Idea Group Publishing.

McCourt, Willy, and Martin Minogue, eds. 2002. *The Internationalization of Public Management: Reinventing the Third World State.* Northampton, MA: Edward Elgar.

Messner, Dirk. 1995. *Die Netzwerkgesellschaft: Wirtschaftliche Entwicklung und Internationale Wettbewerbsfaehigkeit als Probleme Gesellschaftlicher Steuerung.* (*The Network Society: Economic Development and International Competitiveness as Problems of Social Steering.*) Cologne: Deutscher Wirtschaftsdienst.

Naschold, Frieder, Walter Jann, and Christoph Reichard.1999. *Innovation, Effektivität, Nachhaltigkeit: Internationale Erfahrungen Zentralstaatlicher Verwaltungsreform.* (*Innovation, Effectivity, Sustainability: International Experiences of Central State Administrative Reform.*) Berlin: Sigma.

OECD (Organisation of Economic Co-operation and Development). 2003. *The E-Government Imperative.* Paris: OECD.

OECD DAC (Organisation of Economic Co-operation and Development Development Assistance Committee). 2002. "Note DCD DAC." 11/REV1, May 16, Paris.

Pacific Council on International Policy. 2002. "Roadmap for E-Government in the Developing World: 10 Questions E-Government Leaders Should Ask Themselves." Los Angeles.

Popper, Karl. 1945/1995. *The Open Society and Its Enemies.* London: Routledge and Kegan Paul.

Public Sector Technology and Management. 2004. "Chinese E-Government: Too Hot to Handle." Alphabet Media, Singapore, October 9–10.

Ridell, Seija. 2004. "ICTS and the Communicative Conditions for Democracy: A Local Experiment with Web-Mediated Civic Publicness." In *E-Transformation in Governance: New Directions in Government and Politics*, ed. Matti Malkia, Ari-Veikko Anttiroiko, and Reijo Savolainen. Hershey, PA: Idea Group Publishing.

Risse, Thomas, and Ulrike Lehmkuhl. 2006. "Problemstellung." ("Problem.") Free University, Berlin. www.sfb-governance.de.

Rotberg, Robert I. 2004. *When States Fail: Causes and Consequences.* Princeton, NJ: Princeton University Press.

Saarenpää, Athi. 2002. "E-Government: Good Governance? An Impossible Equation?" Paper presented at the Public Policy Forum "Integrating Government with New Technology: How Is Technology Changing the Public Sector?" Commonwealth Centre for Electronic Governance, Ottawa, February 25.

Schmidt, Manfred G. 1995. *Wörterbuch zur Politik.* (*Dictionary of Politics.*) Stuttgart: Kröner.

Slaton, Christa Daryl, and Jeremy L. Arthur. 2004. "Public Administration for a Democratic Society: Instilling Public Trust through Greater Collaboration with Citizens."

In *E-Transformation in Governance: New Directions in Government and Politics*, ed. Matti Malkia, Ari-Veikko Anttiroiko, and Reijo Savolainen. Hershey, PA: Idea Group Publishing.

Socitm, and I&DeA (Improvement and Development Agency). 2002. *Local E-Government Now: A Worldwide Perspective*. London: Socitm Ltd.

Sproats, Kevin, Trevor Cairney, and David Hegarty. 2004. "Building Regional Communities in an Information Age: The Case of Greater Western Sydney." In *E-Transformation in Governance: New Directions in Government and Politics*, ed. Matti Malkia, Ari-Veikko Anttiroiko, and Reijo Savolainen. Hershey, PA: Idea Group Publishing.

UNDESA (United Nations Department of Economic and Social Affairs). 2005. *UN Global E-Government Readiness Report 2005: From E-Government to E-Inclusion*. Division for Public Administration and Development Management, New York.

UNESCAP (United Nations Economic and Social Commission for Asia and the Pacific). 2006. "What Is Good Governance?" Bangkok. http://www.unescap.org.

von Richter, Wolfgang, Elke Breckner, and Carsten Friedland. 2002. "E-Government: Ansätze für die Deutsche Entwicklungszusammenarbeit." ("Approaches for the German Development Cooperation"). Presentation to the workshop titled "Electronic Government: Herausforderungen für die deutsche Entwicklungspolitik," ("Electronic Government: Challenges for German Technical Cooperation") December 4, Bonn.

Wescott, Clay G. 2003. "E-Government to Combat Corruption in the Asia Pacific Region." Paper presented at the 11th International Anti-Corruption Conference, Seoul, May 25–28.

Wireless Philadelphia Executive Committee. 2004. "Wireless Philadelphia Business Plan. Wireless Broadband as the Foundation for a Digital City." Working Paper, Philadelphia.

World Bank. 1993. *The East Asian Miracle*. Oxford: Oxford University Press.

World Bank Institute. 2004. *Governance Matters*. Washington, DC. www.worldbank.org/wbi/governance/pdf/govmatrs.pdf.

4

Networks and Collaborative Solutions to Performance Measurement and Improvement in Sub-Saharan Africa

MARK A. GLASER

The world is rapidly changing, driven in no small part by globalization and the global economy (Birdsall 2003; Kettl 2000). While these changes are global in nature, actions taken at the local level will have much to do with community prosperity.

This chapter shows how performance-based budgeting and a systems approach to the concerns of community can be instrumental in organizing, orchestrating, and applying the resources of a community, forming symbiotic relationships between governmental and nongovernmental agencies. It builds on the understanding that meaningful community improvement begins with civil society, which rests on the foundation of good government (Baker and others 2002). Performance-based budgeting is of little consequence unless government is committed to serving citizens. A symbiotic relationship between government and community must be formed.

The first section argues for a systems approach to the concerns of community that carefully balances competing dimensions of performance and a performance measurement system that articulates community values. The second section explores how collaborative networks might be formed by combining the resources of community and governmental agencies that produce systems solutions to the concerns of community. The third section examines how targeting can be used to improve performance. The fourth section demonstrates how performance measurement and budgeting must be continuously adjusted and shaped to fit the changing decision-making needs of dynamic organizations and presented in a format that can be understood by citizens. The fifth section explores how various research tools, such as survey research, can be used to infuse public decisions with the values of community. The sixth section identifies barriers to performance improvement in Sub-Saharan Africa. The last section discusses how performance-based budgeting can be tailored to facilitate collaborative solutions to the problems of community, including citizen engagement.

The Need for a Systems Approach to Community Improvement

Globalization provides communities in Sub-Saharan Africa with a unique opportunity to improve their economic position in the world. To take advantage of this opportunity, these communities must form networks that include collaboration between government and community agencies and the strategic application of limited resources. Collaborative ventures and networked solutions necessarily include coproduction—the willingness of citizens to join with government and other community agencies (nongovernmental organizations [NGOs], community-based organizations [CBOs], and neighborhood-based organizations [NBOs]) to improve the community. Coproduction is essential to communities in developing countries, and it is becoming increasingly important in developed countries. Citizens can be transformed from liabilities to assets by finding creative ways to involve them in the collaborative production of goods or services that benefit community.

A systems approach to the concerns of community changes the nature, but does not diminish the importance, of local government leadership. Leadership by local authorities will be instrumental in bringing community agencies together to define and address community concerns. In many cases, solutions will require joint leadership on the part of local government and nongovernmental agencies.

Local governments that actively engage the community must embrace change (Melkers and Willoughby 2005). Performance-based budgeting can be a tool that orchestrates change, including the application of the resources of government and community collaborators for community improvement. Transparency in the actions of government is essential if citizens are to be actively involved in the decisions of community. Involvement is critical to the functioning of civil society in Sub-Saharan Africa.

The Choice of Fairfax County

This chapter examines the model of a performance-based budgeting system used in Fairfax County, Virginia. This community was selected for a number of reasons, including its technical proficiency and the transparency of its performance-based budgeting. Fairfax County is also a model in the way that it relates to the community it serves. Community engagement is integral to Fairfax County's mission and a central influence on almost every aspect of its operations, including performance-based budgeting. The relationship between local government and community is dynamic in nature.

Fairfax County uses strategic planning and performance-based budgeting to integrate and shape the products of government to promote consistency between organizational mission and community well-being. Strategic planning is embedded in performance-based budgeting, contributing to an organizational culture that focuses on the future, embraces change, and encourages collaboration within government and between government and the community.

The decision to use Fairfax County as the model for this discussion was done with the clear understanding that there are vast differences between it and communities in Sub-Saharan Africa. While it is unreasonable to expect communities in developing countries to match the accomplishments of Fairfax County, it is reasonable to expect them to lay the foundation for change and to begin the continuous improvement process, guided by a model with considerable merit.

Dimensions of Performance

Performance improvement begins with establishing common definitions of performance. While there is shared support for performance, there are vast differences between constituencies over how it is defined. Performance measurement begins with a clear understanding of the natural tension between dimensions of performance. Public leadership is defined, in part, by choices related to the relative value assigned to competing dimensions of performance. Therefore, it is important to recognize how the various dimensions of performance interact and to make conscious choices about how best to balance competing dimensions using input from an engaged community. The discussion that follows highlights the dimensions of performance and encourages thoughtful action on the part of public leaders, including reflections on public values and how best to shape performance-based budgeting in light of these values.

Efficiency

Efficiency is the extent to which public agencies deliver a good-quality product at the lowest possible price. Generally speaking, those who argue that government should perform more like business value improved efficiency. Efficiency focuses on actions that reduce the unit costs of products or services. *Productivity*, the number of labor hours required to produce a particular good or service, is often used interchangeably with efficiency. While public agencies are not motivated by profit, they are responsible for delivering the best possible product using the fewest public dollars.

There is a natural tension between improvements in efficiency and other dimensions of performance. For example, public agencies are also responsible for democratic processes and responsiveness to citizens. When government takes the time to listen to citizens, efficiency usually suffers (Berry, Portney, and Thomson 1993; Burke 1989; Pecorella 1986). Therefore, governments that assign disproportionate value to efficiency tend to deemphasize responsiveness.

Responsiveness

Unwillingness on the part of public agencies to involve citizens in the decisions of government breeds distrust and discontent, and it undermines citizen support for the actions of government. Responsiveness includes actions taken by public agencies to listen to citizens and to act in ways that are consistent with the will of the people. Generally speaking, responsiveness is good, but governmental agencies that are responsive to one segment of the population at the expense of others contribute to inequality (Andrews and Shah 2003a). Advantaged classes of citizens who benefit from governmental inequality pressure government for more of the same. Disadvantaged classes of citizens react to unequal treatment with distrust of government and withdrawal from civil society, focusing more on self-interest. To protect against promoting inequality and withdrawal from civil society, government must scrutinize the way it uses limited resources.

Governmental responsiveness is of particular importance in Sub-Saharan Africa. Governmental reform that shifts responsibility from central to local governments, including local selection of leadership, increases responsiveness (Andrews and Shah 2003a; Schou 2000). Responsiveness is further advanced when local government encourages citizen involvement in the decisions of government. While it is impossible for government to listen to the unique concerns of every citizen, citizen participation vehicles can be used to organize and prioritize citizens' demands.

Neighborhoods and NBOs are potentially effective vehicles for organizing the voice of community and simplifying communication between citizens and government. NBOs can be used to engage citizens in the decisions of government and to encourage coproduction for community improvement. Neighborhoods tend to be fairly homogeneous, including citizens of similar socioeconomic standing and value systems. Symbiotic relationships among neighbors, neighborhoods, community agencies, and government potentially create the critical mass of resources necessary to produce meaningful change.

Effectiveness

In many ways, effectiveness has the most obvious connections to performance measurement. Performance measurement is driven by logical connections among goals, objectives, and measures. Effectiveness is the extent to which governmental agencies successfully meet the goals of the organization. From a systems perspective, effectiveness is advanced when decisions are made and resources allocated based on the long-term well-being of the community (Berman and Wang 2000). Effectiveness is advanced by infusing performance measurement with strategic planning (Kelly and Rivenbark 2003; Poister 2003). Strategic planning should be community based as opposed to government based. Effectiveness is improved when government engages in strategic planning to promote consistency of action for the long run, engages citizens and community organizations in strategic planning processes, integrates the results of strategic planning into performance-based budgeting, and forms integrated performance measurement systems blending the activities of governmental and community agencies.

Unilateral actions on the part of government often contribute to suboptimal use of community resources. Suboptimization results from the expenditure of public resources without regard for the actions or use of resources by other governmental or community agencies. Effectiveness is facilitated by blending governmental and community resources and using these resources in ways that are consistent with the long-term well-being of the community.

Equity

Equity—the fair and equal treatment of citizens, regardless of their station in life—is an often neglected dimension of performance. Inequality and unequal treatment come in many forms, including discrimination based on race, ethnic origin, religion, gender, and socioeconomic standing. Responsiveness to the demands of more advantaged segments of society represents an important performance concern. The functioning of society is facilitated through governmental actions that promote equal opportunity for all classes of citizens (Simonsen and Robbins 2000).

Issues of equity are especially troublesome in developing countries, particularly in Sub-Saharan Africa. Unequal opportunity is a formidable barrier to development (Foster 1980). When those who lack opportunity lose hope, chaos reigns (Balogun 2003). All too often, governments in developing countries use limited resources to promote economic development while disregarding the plight of the disadvantaged (Andrews and Shah 2003a).

Community

Community, as discussed here, is less about geography and more about the paradoxical tension between societal well-being and self-interest that resides in every individual (Wheatley and Kellner-Rogers 1998). This tension is best viewed as a continuum, with community at one end and self-interest at the other. Those who are detached from community and have retreated into self-interest are less likely to be concerned about the plight of their fellow citizens or future generations; those who are attached to community recognize that their well-being is tied to the well-being of others. Those who are attached see children as the future and press for societal behavior that is cognizant of the future. They are more likely to feel that society has some responsibility for caring for those who are disadvantaged.

The behavior of government has much to do with the behavior of citizens. Public leaders who make decisions and invest resources in ways they feel are consistent with the long-term well-being of the community are more likely to elicit similar behavior on the part of citizens (Berry, Portney, and Thomson 1993; Denhardt and Denhardt 2000).

Community attachment is universally important but particularly crucial in Sub-Saharan Africa, where civil society is weak (Baker and others 2002; Balogun 2003). Government reform in Tanzania has laid the foundation for positive change, including increased responsiveness as a result of local government autonomy from central government (Baker and others 2002). Unfortunately, the local tax base tends to be weak, contributing to local government dependency on central government transfers. This dependency is mitigated somewhat through the use of block grants, which attach fewer strings to spending.

Baker and others (2002) provide evidence of strengthened citizen engagement and democratic processes in Tanzania. They recognize the changes that have taken place as positive but advise local governments to depend less on unilateral action and more on collaborative ventures that build the capacity of community agencies.

The revenue side of performance-based budgeting is driven by the health of the economy, the strength of the local tax base, and the willingness on the part of citizens to pay taxes. Tax-demand discontinuity occurs when citizens demand more from government than they are willing to pay for (Glaser and Denhardt 1999; Glaser and Hildreth 1996). Weak democratic processes in developing countries contribute to tax-demand discontinuity (Andrews and Shah 2003a). Healthy democratic processes fortified by governmental actions that are transparent, equitable, and focused on the long-term well-being of community will increase the willingness to pay, as well as the willingness of citizens to coproduce community improvement consistent with a sustainable society (Glaser, Aristigueta, and Miller 2003–04; Glaser, Aristigueta, and Payton 2000; Glaser, Denhardt, and Hamilton 2002; Glaser, Parker, and Payton 2001; Thomas 1992). Performance measurement and performance-based budgeting potentially contribute to transparency, creditability, and trust in local government (Holzer and Yang 2004).

Types of Performance Measures

The discussion of types of performance measures focuses on two themes that interact in ways that make performance measurement challenging. The first demonstrates why it is important for public agencies to recognize and carefully balance the weight assigned to the various dimensions of performance. The second focuses on the technical side of performance measurement, such as issues of validity and reliability.

Technical considerations focus on developing the appropriate mix of measures that capture performance in a valid and reliable way. Individual measures, as well as combinations of measures, must be evaluated based on the extent to which they capture the critical activities and assign the appropriate weight to the various dimensions of performance. Any one measure viewed in isolation can misrepresent performance. Multiple measures, including various types of measures, are often necessary to accurately assess performance, sometimes referred to as *triangulation of measures* (Glaser 1991; Holzer and Yang 2004; Melkers and Willoughby 2005; Poister 2003; Wholey and Hatry 1992).

Discussion of triangulation of measures raises many questions about how many and what types of measures are necessary to accurately reflect performance. Poister (2003) proposes the use of "program logic models" to systematically approach triangulation. His program logic models are much like the impact models associated with program evaluation, which explain the logical connections between interventions and expected outcomes. These models force the integration of processes and logic associated with program design, delivery, and measurement.

Consistent with this approach, Yang and Holzer (2006) argue that consideration should be given to measuring alternative or nonprogram influences on performance. Performance outcomes are driven by a combination of program- and nonprogram-related influences. Some of these influences are controllable by the agency, others are not. Despite efforts to more fully understand what drives performance, measurement is not designed to deliver airtight causal determinations of program or service delivery outcomes (Kelly and Rivenbark 2003). Generally speaking, measurement is designed to track performance variation and alert decision makers when performance outcomes vary from expectations (based on goals and performance targets).

Output measures

Measures of output or workload are the most basic and the most commonly used performance measures. Output measures focus on the amount of a service or product delivered (Berman and Wang 2000).

Performance measurement has been criticized for depending too heavily on output measures, which do not address costs, quality, or effectiveness. Increasingly, proponents of performance measurement challenge public agencies to include more robust measures of performance and to advance beyond basic measures of output (Kelly and Rivenbark 2003). Although there are limits to the usefulness of output measures, they do provide valuable indicators of changes in workload or service volume, information that is important for management and budgetary decisions.

Fairfax County continuously strives to reduce its dependency on output measures. Its agencies use various types of measures to assess performance.[1]

To the extent possible, agencies should standardize the format for presenting performance measures, as Fairfax County does. Standardized presentations of measures make possible the exchange of intra- and interorganizational information that is critical to collaboration. In addition, a standardized format increases the transparency necessary for involving citizens with limited knowledge of government.

TABLE 4.1 Output Reporting by the Fairfax County Police Department

Indicator	FY2003 actual	FY2004 actual	FY2005 estimate	FY2006 estimate	FY2007 projection
Output					
Cases assigned	11,848	12,106	11,723	11,706	11,805
Cases cleared	7,556	7,949	8,089	7,648	7,718
Robbery cases investigated	423	482	448	451	454
Robbery cases cleared	102	133	133	123	124
Aggravated assault cases investigated	46	42	44	44	44
Aggravated assault cases cleared	16	34	29	28	28
Efficiency					
Cases per detective	174	178	172	172	172
Outcome					
Percentage of all cases cleared	64.0	66.0	69.0	65.0	69.0
Percentage of robbery cases cleared	21.1	27.6	29.6	65.0	69.0
Percentage of aggravated assault cases cleared	34.8	81.0	63.4	67.0	63.4

Source: www.fairfaxcounty.gov/dmb/advertised/FY2007/pdf/Volume1/00190.pdf.

The Fairfax County Police Department collects data on various measures of output (table 4.1). Its workload measures are driven in no small part by issues and concerns that are beyond the control of the police department. Crime is attributable to any number of environmental concerns, many of which are beyond the control of law enforcement agencies (at least in the short run). Although many environmental influences contribute to fluctuations in crime, the workload measures provided are good indicators of changes in the burden of the organization and will ultimately influence resource allocation. The subcategories related to types of crimes reveal trends, changes in the composition of crime, and changes in the difficulty of caseloads. Output reporting of the number of cases cleared edges toward a more robust measurement of outcome. The qualitative narrative associated with performance and budgetary reporting provides details about crime-related trends and strategic actions of the department.

Fire and rescue reporting is similar to police reporting, with one important exception (table 4.2). These activities have a more direct connection to the

TABLE 4.2 Output Reporting by the Fairfax County Fire and Rescue Department

Indicator	FY2003 actual	FY2004 actual	FY2005 estimate/actual	FY2006 estimate	FY2007 projection
Output					
Fire investigations conducted	465	372	465/380	380	390
Fire inspection activities conducted	21,330	20,816	21,000/20,052	20,800	20,800
Systems testing activities conducted	10,164	10,872	10,000/11,738	10,000	10,000
Revenue generated by inspection activities	$2,486,047	$3,032,272	$2,900,000/$3,308,634	$3,000,000	$3,100,000
Efficiency					
Net cost per inspection (revenues in excess of average cost)	($0.72)	($14.60)	($9.89)/($23.17)	($8.64)	($8.64)
Service quality					
Percentage of total fire investigation cases closed	69.5	57.7	60.0/59.0	52.0	60.0
Outcome					
Percentage of fire criminal cases prosecuted successfully	—	74.1	60.0/90.0	60.0	60.0
Total fire loss for commercial structures	$949,010	$1,153,350	$1,250,000/$5,296,600	$4,000,000	$4,000,000

Source: www.fairfaxcounty.gov/dmb/adopted/FY2007/pdf/Volume1/00192.pdf.
— Not available.

budget through measures that indicate which activities produce revenue. As a result, concerned taxpayers are easily able to determine that businesses are shouldering a portion of the increased burden for fire safety.

Output measures are some of the most common and straightforward measures of performance. Table 4.3 provides examples of output measures from park services, including maintainable linear feet of trail and number of athletic fields maintained. Output measures become more meaningful when coupled with qualitative measures, such as those reported at the bottom of the table. Qualitative descriptions help the reader understand the interaction between performance quality and quantity. Decision makers may elect to sacrifice output quantity for improved quality or vice versa.

TABLE 4.3 Output Reporting by the Fairfax County Park Authority

Indicator	FY2003 actual	FY2004 actual	FY2005 estimate/actual	FY2006 estimate	FY2007 projection
Output					
Maintainable linear feet of trail[a]	1,067,485	1,076,294	1,076,294/1,077,194	1,114,182	1,154,182
Number of athletic fields	274	274	275/275	289	291
Efficiency					
Cost per linear foot of trail	$0.12	$0.10	$0.11/$0.11	$0.11	$0.11
Cost per athletic field	$6,882	$7,885	$7,840/$7,840	$7,881	$8,382
Service quality					
Percentage of customers satisfied[b]	65	67	75/69	70	70
Outcome					
Percentage of trails maintained to standard	32	19	20/17	20	20
Percentage of athletic fields available for use	97	98	96/97	96	96

Source: www.fairfaxcounty.gov/dmb/adopted/FY2007/pdf/Volume1/00151.pdf.

a. In FY2005, 1,077,194 linear feet of trails were maintained, with a projected increase of 36,988 linear feet in FY2006 and 40,000 linear feet of new trails in FY2007. The cost per linear foot of trail is projected to remain at its FY2005 level of $0.11 per linear foot in FY2006 and FY2007.

b. A satisfaction survey was used to determine the service quality of trails and athletic fields. The quality outcome of this survey reflects the percentage of respondents who rated their satisfaction as 8, 9, or 10 on a scale of 1–10, with 1 being the worst and 10 being the best quality. Satisfaction ratings increased slightly in fiscal year 2005 to 69 percent, closer to the goal of 70 percent for the next two fiscal years.

Table 4.4 includes two measures of output that differ from the measures presented in the first three tables. It can be argued that the first measure of output (volunteer hours provided) is really a measure of outcome, in that it

TABLE 4.4 Output Reporting by the Fairfax County Community and Recreation Services Cost Center

Indicator	FY2003 actual	FY2004 actual	FY2005 estimate/actual	FY2006 estimate	FY2007 projection
Output					
Volunteer hours provided	14,981	9,122	11,403/15,667	16,450	17,273
Community center attendance	119,685	116,185	139,422/142,531	149,658	164,624
Efficiency					
Average hours of service per volunteer	57.0	60.0	60.0/56.5	60.0	60.0
Community center cost per attendee	$8.23	$9.81	$8.29/$8.14	$8.73	$6.55
Service quality					
Percentage of volunteers satisfied	90.0	78.0	85.0/84.0	85.0	85.0
Percentage of participants satisfied	91.0	86.0	85.0/87.0	85.0	85.0
Outcome					
Percentage change in volunteer hours provided in community center programs	(43.0)	(39.0)	25.0/72.0	5.0	5.0
Percentage change in citizens attending activities at community centers	(13.0)	(3.0)	20.0/23.0	5.0	10.0

Source: www.fairfaxcounty.gov/dmb/adopted/FY2007/pdf/Volume1/00150.pdf.
Note: **Qualitative explanation**—Community center attendance and volunteer hours increased substantially, due primarily to the grand reopening of the James Lee Community Center. **Goal**—to provide Fairfax County children, youth, and families with affordable leisure opportunities that will facilitate socialization and physical, mental, and personal growth, while creating a feeling of well-being, community, and community responsibility; to design and implement leisure programs and activities that will provide lifelong leisure skills and foster the development of a personal leisure philosophy that will assist individuals in making appropriate leisure choices; and to provide intervention, early intervention, crisis intervention, and referral services to youth and their families. **Objectives**—(a) to increase by 5 percent the number of hours provided by both adult and teen volunteers who supply activity and program support to instill community ownership and pride in programs and services provided by community centers; and (b) to increase by 10 percent the attendance at all community centers to ensure that residents have access to programs and services that reinforce healthy and positive choices for leisure and recreation.

indicates coproduction (the extent to which citizens are willing to join with local government to coproduce recreational services).

In contrast to variations in crime, variations in community center attendance can be influenced by the actions of the agency. Projected increases in attendance reflect expectations of increased use of facilities, although it is not clear to what extent these increases are driven by population growth, marketing, or the quality of service delivery.

These output measures reveal just how varied output measures can be and provide evidence of the importance of using a triangulation of measures. In reference to the dimensions of performance discussed previously, there are obvious connections to responsiveness through registered demand for recreational activities (community center attendance) and community as measured through coproduction, the willingness of members of the community to volunteer to improve the quality of life of their fellow citizens.

Productivity measures

Measures of productivity and efficiency are particularly important in accounting for the expenditure of public dollars. Most measures of productivity focus on the number of employee hours required to deliver a product or service. Organizations focused on performance from the perspective of productivity concentrate on reducing the number of employee hours required to produce a product or unit of service.

Building on the concept of productivity, measures of efficiency translate employee hours into labor costs associated with the production of goods and services. Accordingly, gains in efficiency include reducing the number of hours required for production or lowering the costs per hour. Hourly costs can be limited to actual wages paid to employees, or they can more fully capture associated labor costs, including fringe benefits, such as sick leave, medical insurance, and retirement. In some cases, administrative or supervisory costs are added to the costs of hourly employees in an attempt to more fully capture the costs of production.

Fairfax County is trying to establish a direct cost method. Direct labor costs are calculated by multiplying the total annual salary of employees associated with the production of a particular good or service by the percentage of each employee's time used to produce the good or service. This percentage can be estimated or tracked through the maintenance of daily logs by individual employees. Daily logs require employees to report the number of hours they spend each day on particular products or services.

Fringe benefits are commonly considered direct labor costs and therefore included in the calculation of measures of efficiency. Fairfax County has developed standardized rates to assign fringe benefits based on employee classifications. The fringe benefit rate is multiplied by the total labor cost associated with a particular position to obtain the value of fringe benefits assigned to a product or service. Fairfax County also assigns a percentage of its operating and capital costs to the delivery of products or services. Direct costs are summed, and total direct costs are divided by the total number of units produced to provide the cost per unit of service.

Fairfax County provides electronic spreadsheets with built-in formulas to minimize errors and time associated with calculating efficiency. This process forces managers to become aware of the implications of engaging additional personnel or incurring other direct costs associated with the production of a particular good or service (Fairfax Country Department of Management and Budget 2005a). Measuring efficiency is not particularly challenging once the spreadsheet formulas have been encoded. Local governments in developing countries may not have agencywide access to computers, making performance measurement in general, and assessments of efficiency in particular, more challenging.

Measures of efficiency are some of the most straightforward measures of performance, but they are often difficult to implement, for several reasons. First, the quality of measures of efficiency hinges on the diligence of employees in keeping daily logs that accurately reflect the time invested in the production of a particular service, product, or project. Certain types of jobs or activities do not lend themselves to this type of reporting. Second, employees fearing job-related consequences may manipulate the number of hours assigned to a particular product or service in ways that are consistent with favorable outcomes. Local governments that promote intra-agency competition for limited resources and use efficiency measures in punitive processes will taint reporting practices.

In most cases, barriers to efficiency reporting are less about technical capacity and more about the political implications of resource allocation. The diverse nature and creative processes that efficiency reporting requires will challenge communities in Sub-Saharan Africa.

Performance reporting is a dynamic process that is influenced by agency capacity and the nature of the product being delivered. The measure reported in table 4.1 under the heading "efficiency" (cases per detective) more accurately reflects productivity or output. Detectives simultaneously work on multiple cases with varying degrees of difficulty: some cases are cleared and some crimes are never solved. In theory measures of efficiency are straightforward; in practice they are not.

The efficiency measure associated with fire and rescue comes closer to a textbook approach, with a twist. In this case, efficiency is measured based on whether average net revenues per inspection are neutral, negative, or positive. In other words, agency assessments focus on whether inspections produce net gains per inspection after subtracting average cost per inspection. The first efficiency measure reported in table 4.3 (the average cost to maintain a linear foot of trail) is more consistent with textbook definitions of efficiency.

The Department of Community and Recreation Services (see table 4.4) provides two additional measures of efficiency. The first focuses on coproduction, or the average number of hours contributed per volunteer. The second measures community center cost per attendee. Reality often dictates that textbook definitions of productivity or efficiency be replaced by creative measures developed by the agency.

Outcome measures

Outcome measures are particularly valuable, because they are some of the best indicators of goal achievement. Establishing validity (accuracy in capturing the essence of the concept) and reliability (consistency of the measure in capturing the concept) can be more challenging in the case of outcome measures. The quality of the measurement process rests, in no small part, on the alignment or consistency among agency activities, goals, objectives, and measures. The program logic models discussed earlier are designed to help agencies logically connect organizational activities with measures of outcome. Misalignment between agency activities, associated goals and objectives, and the actual measures used to assess goal achievement misrepresents performance and can be counterproductive to goal achievement (Holzer and Yang 2004; Streib and Poister 1999).

Difficulty in resolving issues of validity and reliability also hinges on the extent to which the activities being measured are direct observables versus constructs. Direct observables tend to have obvious measurement solutions. For example, there is little room for dispute over the measurement of the number of citations issued by law enforcement officers. In contrast, constructs, such as fear of crime, are not as easily measured, raising concerns about validity and reliability.

The valid measure of impact also presents measurement challenges. It is relatively easy to track changes in crime rates (although many crimes go unreported); it is difficult to ascertain the extent to which variations in crime are a function of law enforcement or attributable to environmental fluctuations, such as the health of the economy. As a result, tracking variations in the crime rate has value as a social indicator, but agencies should be careful about taking credit or accepting blame for these variations.

Finally, outcomes can vary considerably based on the extent to which an agency establishes and verifies adherence to data collection and reporting protocols. Measures of outcome often require detailed instructions (including decision rules), training, and periodic verification to ensure accuracy and adherence to protocol. These challenges commonly force prudent agencies to rely on intermediate measures of outcome, such as those presented in table 4.1.

Increasingly, agencies are encouraged to measure the quality of service delivery. Performance measurement systems that focus on quantity while disregarding quality potentially invite problems with service delivery satisfaction. Service quality is commonly viewed as a measure of outcome. In some cases Fairfax County reports service quality separately from measures of outcome. The Department of Fire and Rescue, for example, reports the percentage of total fire investigation cases closed as a measure of service quality.

While effectiveness at extinguishing fire is generally accepted as a performance outcome, prevention represents an advanced form of effectiveness. Much like law enforcement, success associated with fire prevention is contingent on a variety of environmental issues, many of which are not easily controlled by fire departments. As a result, Fairfax County uses two intermediate measures of fire prevention (see table 4.2). First, it reports outcomes related to deterrence, the percentage of fire-related criminal cases successfully prosecuted. Second, it examines trends related to total commercial fire losses in dollars. Local governments can use statistical analysis to shed light on or discriminate between environmental and departmental influences. For example, they can examine overall changes in square footage of commercial space, the age of buildings, changes in the mix of commercial activities, and other factors to try to explain variations in losses due to fire. If fire losses are rising faster than the growth in commercial space, the fire department might want to examine protocols for fire inspections. Findings indicating that certain types of commercial activities pose greater fire risks or that some fire suppression systems are more effective than others may result in changes in the frequency of or protocols on fire inspections. Analysis of areas within the county may reveal that some may have disproportionately high fire losses, triggering more detailed investigation to better understand if systematic deviations in protocols are associated with particular fire inspectors.

In some ways, citizen satisfaction with service delivery is one of the most important measures of effectiveness (Swindell and Kelly 2005). Unfortunately, citizens usually lack the knowledge of services necessary to support valid and reliable service ratings (Morgan and England 1987). For example, if citizens were surveyed regarding their satisfaction with the performance of fire and rescue operations, most would be unable to respond in a valid or reliable fashion because of lack of knowledge. In contrast, citizens often have considerable knowledge and are better able to provide insight about park and recreation services. Therefore, it is important to assess the extent to which citizens can reasonably be expected to have sufficient knowledge of a service before using service delivery satisfaction as a performance outcome.

Table 4.3 provides an example of how Fairfax County uses citizen survey research findings to provide an assessment of customer satisfaction. It supplements quantitative with qualitative evidence to provide insight about service delivery.

The first outcome item in table 4.3 gives the reader a general understanding of service delivery quality, although many readers may not understand exactly what it means for the park service to maintain nature trails "to standard." The description indicates that the percentage of trails maintained to standard is decreasing. The table note explains that the number of linear feet of trail has increased. This explanation helps readers understand the conflict between efficiency and effectiveness. Decision makers may choose to emphasize efficiency and deemphasize effectiveness by choosing to lower professional standards for parks in order to increase access. Decision makers have measures that allow them to choose where to place the fulcrum balancing efficiency (reduced cost per linear foot of trail) and effectiveness (percentage of trails maintained to standard). These decisions are less about good versus bad performance and more about measures that allow decision makers the opportunity to decide how best to balance competing dimensions of performance.

In most cases, performance measures are and should be quantifiable. The intent is to provide decision makers with empirical evidence that can be reviewed easily and that summarizes the activities of an agency. While the bulk of performance reporting should be quantitative, qualitative reporting is often useful for preserving measurement quality and informing decisions. In many cases, variations in performance are the product of forces that are not easily controlled by the organization. Qualitative reporting promotes honesty in agency reporting by providing agencies the opportunity to explain conditions or performance problems and associated corrective action.

Process measures

Performance measurement systems in general, and outcome measures in particular, alert users to variations in performance, but they often provide limited explanations for change (Behn 2003). Performance measurement is improved when measures capture both program and environmental contributors to change. If process measures were used in performance measurement much as they are used in evaluations research, they could better inform decision making. While applied research rarely reaches airtight causal determinations, process measures should be selectively used to enhance understanding of the relationship between programming and outcomes. Many attributes associated with the logic of program evaluation can be blended with performance measurement to aid decision making (Glaser 1993).

Process measures rooted in program evaluation are designed to determine if a program or service is being delivered to the intended target in the designed way. Process measures are particularly helpful in determining if variations in program delivery protocols (intended or unintended) are responsible for variations in outcomes. Process measures provide valuable information about the extent to which services or program delivery protocols are being followed. Without measures of process, it is difficult to determine if failure to achieve targeted outcomes is a function of poor program-related logic (impact model) or deviations from the program delivery protocol. Program evaluation uses impact models to describe program logic—why it is reasonable to expect the designed program to address a particular problem or concern. Impact models provide specific instructions or protocols for program delivery, including defining the intended target.

Variations in program delivery protocols, including deviations from the intended target, potentially have important performance implications. The reasons for deviations in program delivery protocols are many and varied, ranging from poor quality control to intentional acts of deception. It is not uncommon for stakeholders who are responsible for program delivery to manipulate the target in an effort to make the program appear to be more or less successful than it really is. Accordingly, agencies should consider using process measures in performance-based budgeting when tracking the performance of programs that represent important investments of resources.

Process measures can also be used to address concerns related to equity. For example, if there is reason to believe that services may be withheld from a particular segment of the targeted population or that a service or program might be altered to the benefit or detriment of one segment of the intended target, process measures can be used to test for deviations from service delivery protocol. If process measures reveal that a particular subpopulation is being underserved, adjustments can be made to ensure equity in service delivery. In the example presented in table 4.4, if the intended target of youth-related programming is low-income youths living in particular neighborhoods, process measures can be used to determine if the targeted youths are actually receiving the benefits of the programming and if program delivery protocol varies with the segment of the population being served.

From Government to Governance: Networks and Collaborative Solutions

The concerns of community usually outstrip the resources available to public agencies to address them. To fill the gap, unilateral action by government must give way to collaborative ventures in which governmental and community agencies jointly lead and invest resources based on a shared vision of community well-being.

Community Development and Collaborative Networks

Many factors contribute to poverty, interacting in ways that defeat piecemeal solutions. A weak civic infrastructure is a formidable barrier to improved quality of life in Sub-Saharan Africa (Balogun 2003). Community development driven by collaborative community networks with contributions from local government and a variety of community agencies (NGOs, CBOs, and NBOs) offers the best opportunity for improving quality of life. Coproduction is an essential resource for community development and the strengthening of civic infrastructure.

A stakeholder is anyone who has something to win or lose as a result of the activities of an agency (Aristigueta 1999). When community is viewed as a system and performance measurement as a tool to promote collaboration, views of stakeholders become more inclusive and the walls between government and community agencies become more permeable. Performance measurement used in support of collaborative networks documents and directs interaction among core agencies. In network analysis terminology, core agencies are organizations whose products or services are critical to network performance (Provan and Milward 2001). Collaborative networks build civic infrastructure and optimize the use of resources from the perspective of community as opposed to government. Accordingly, performance measurement must be changed to more fully capture interactions between government and community agencies. Local governments acting in concert with other core actors (NGOs) would be well advised to take steps to facilitate the formation and enrichment of CBOs as coproducers of networked solutions. The discussion that follows draws on insight from Fairfax County to better understand steps local governments can take to measure and promote community engagement.

Transforming Citizens through Coproduction

Coproduction can be instrumental in strengthening civil infrastructure and community attachment in support of community development in

108 Mark A. Glaser

Sub-Saharan Africa. Performance measurement can be instrumental in lowering the barriers of self-interest by increasing understanding of how citizens working in concert with government and various community agencies can become coproducers of community improvement.

Tables 4.4 and 4.5 provide evidence of Fairfax County's commitment to community engagement and recognition of value-added through coproduction. Two cost centers associated with the Department of Community

TABLE 4.5 Output Reporting on Fairfax County Integrated Services Community Initiatives
(*number of hours volunteered*)

Indicator	FY2006 estimate	FY2007 projection
Efficiency		
Return of total service hours on investment	83,103	87,258
Percentage of total Community and Recreation Services (CRS) programs provided with direct support from community partners	30	33
Service quality		
Percentage of community leaders and volunteers satisfied with service experience	85	90
Percentage of community partners satisfied with specific partnership experiences	85	90
Outcome		
Percentage change in the number of community leaders and volunteers that support the provision of programs, services, and activities	5	5
Percentage change in the number of programs provided with direct support from community partners	—	20

Source: www.fairfaxcounty.gov/dmb/adopted/FY2007/pdf/Volume1/00150.pdf.
Note: **Qualitative explanation**—Volunteerism is essential to the successful provision of CRS programs and services. Community involvement in the planning and implementation of programs leads to partnerships where the broader community identifies and provides for its own needs. Building leaders allows for this process to sustain itself, thus strengthening the community. To that end, CRS seeks to increase the number of community leaders and overall volunteers who are directly involved in the provision of programs and services. Additionally, CRS seeks to build upon these efforts to ensure at least 25 percent of all CRS programs are provided through direct support from its community partners. Community leadership development opportunities are being expanded to include training and education in addition to community involvement activities such as advisory councils, community planning teams, Youth Speaks Out, and various volunteer positions. **Goal**—To build community capacity to advocate for and meet its own needs by developing community leaders, facilitating community involvement, and providing integrated services that utilize partnerships with a variety of community, public, and private organizations. **Objectives**—(a) to increase by 5 percent the number of community leaders and volunteers who provide support for the provision of programs, services, and activities; (b) to increase by 20 percent the number of programs provided with direct support from community partners.
— Not available.

and Recreation Services are used to demonstrate coproduction on the part of individuals (see table 4.4) as well as contributions through CBOs (table 4.5). Performance-based budgeting facilitates transparency and citizen engagement through budgetary presentations organized around programs or bundled activities sometimes referred to as cost centers (Melkers and Willoughby 2005).

Table 4.4 provides examples of how a governmental agency such as the Department of Community and Recreation Services can enlist coproduction on the part of citizens to improve access to and the quality of recreational services. This example also improves understanding of the importance of continuity between goals, objectives, and dimensions of performance, as well as the use of triangulation in performance measures, including qualitative and quantitative reporting. The goal statement that appears at the bottom of table 4.4 indicates that the intent of the agency is to engage citizens (adults and youths) by encouraging them to join with government to coproduce improved access to leisure and recreational opportunities. This recreational venture recognizes the special needs of disadvantaged youths. The objectives indicate that the intent of the programming is to engage citizens of all ages to provide increased access to leisure activities and to increase cost-effectiveness by substituting coproduction for governmental service delivery, thereby reducing the costs per participant. The objectives also indicate that the intent of volunteerism is to build civic capacity by strengthening connections to community for both program participants and volunteers assisting in program delivery. In other words, Fairfax County hopes not only to improve service delivery but also to build allegiance to community through volunteerism—citizens assisting citizens. This approach produces convergence between performance dimensions (effectiveness, efficiency, and community) and triangulates measures for an improved understanding of performance. Output measures track volunteer hours and the number of volunteers. Efficiency measures track gains in productivity associated with increased volunteerism and success at reducing costs per participant. Measures of effectiveness focus on satisfaction from the perspective of both volunteers and participants. That is, in addition to improving the quality of life on the part of program participants, volunteers are expected to reap intrinsic rewards through their contributions to the community. Performance outcomes include quantifiable increases in volunteers and program participants. Finally, triangulation includes qualitative reporting that offers explanations for changes in quantitative measures of outcome. Any one of these measures in isolation provides an incomplete picture of performance; the combination of measures more clearly articulates goal achievement.

Building the Capacity of Community-Based Organizations

The Chr. Michelsen Institute in Bergen, Norway, has conducted considerable research on Tanzania. It concludes that community development through collaborative networks between government and community agencies presents important opportunities for improving quality of life. A study of the policy of Tanzania's central government that attempts to institutionalize the involvement of community organizations warns that governmental policy must take care to avoid actions that interfere with the grassroots nature of these organizations, thought to be key to their effectiveness (Lange, Wallevick, and Kiondo 2000). Autonomy, or independence from government, is often an important condition for preserving the effectiveness of community agencies and an important consideration for collaborative networks (Glaser, Soskin, and Smith 1996; Warren, Rosentraub, and Weschler 1992).

A second study by the Chr. Michelsen Institute (Baker and others 2002) points to the successes of informally organized CBOs, many of which are organized by women. This study makes the case for governmental support of grassroots ventures, which could be instrumental in strengthening the civic infrastructure in Sub-Saharan Africa.

Fairfax County values community engagement and uses local government policy to facilitate community development through CBOs (Kelly and Rivenbark 2003). The following discussion of the Departments of Systems Management for Human Services (DSMHS) and the Department of Community and Recreation Services sheds light on what it means for local government to use performance-based budgeting to act aggressively to build the capacity of CBOs.

DSMHS serves in a support role, improving the internal functioning of county government and bridging the divide between government and community. Like all other agencies associated with the Fairfax County government, DSMHS merges strategic planning with performance measurement through performance-based budgeting. It introduces reporting related to the strategic agenda by accepting responsibility for strengthening partnerships between government and community agencies. DSMHS describes its responsibilities for intra- and interorganizational system coordination as follows:

> DSMHS supports integration of service delivery systemwide coordination of planning, management and operations across Human Services regions and among the various Human Services and non-Human Services agencies. The Department uses a project management approach to perform these functions, and work is based on specific agency or community requests, or on an identified systemwide need. The Department's Research, Analysis, and Project Services

(RAPS) staff will continue to focus on the collection, analysis, and dissemination of information useful to the Human Services systems as a whole; coordination of cross-system or multiagency collaboration work; building partnerships between County agencies and the community; and helping agencies redesign work processes to achieve greater efficiency, improve service quality, and to better align service delivery with strategic goals and capacity in the context of constrained resources. (Fairfax County Department of Systems Management for Human Services 2006: 410)

Fairfax County's commitment to community becomes tangible through performance-based budgeting. Local governments are often unwilling to engage or strengthen CBOs, because they are concerned that community agencies will usurp their political power (Logan and Rabrenovic 1990; Sharp 1990). Fairfax County approaches community as a system and CBOs as important components of that system that must be engaged and strengthened to coproduce community improvement. Consistent with this understanding, it aggressively engages CBOs. It has developed a unique financial tool—the Consolidated Community Funding Pool—to support these ventures. This pool builds the capacity of CBOs; it is designed "to usher in a new era of strengthened relations and streamlined processes between the County and private, nonprofit organizations" (Fairfax County Department of Systems Management for Human Services 1999: 7).

Fairfax County recognizes that despite its considerable resources, it does not have the capacity to address all of the county's needs itself. Accordingly, Fairfax County in general and DSMHS in particular collaborate with CBOs to identify the needs of the community and to enhance the capacity of community agencies to address identified concerns.

In many ways, investments through vehicles such as the Consolidated Community Funding Pool strengthen the capacity of community agencies to solve problems. This process simultaneously strengthens the civic infrastructure while improving the capacity of CBOs. Fairfax County articulates CBO capacity-building through a Web site (http://www.fairfaxcounty.gov/ccfp/NPODInitiative.htm) that delineates 15 key management capacity elements:

1. The CBO's mission and its business plan for accomplishing the mission
2. The strategic planning process
3. The financial management system (including budgeting, tax reporting, audit readiness, and other related aspects of the CBO's current financial condition), prospects for the future, and ability to respond to change
4. Past performance and the ability to measure performance outcomes
5. The CBO's service delivery system, including customer satisfaction, quality control, and sensitivity to community needs

6. The involvement of the CBO's board of directors in policy planning and fundraising
7. The adequacy and utilization of operational procedures
8. The adequacy of recordkeeping and reporting systems and the accuracy and timeliness of reports
9. The adequacy of fundraising capacity and success in leveraging other support
10. The adequacy of personnel and related human resources management capabilities
11. The accessibility of the CBO's operating facilities and adequacy in meeting future needs
12. The adequacy (and utilization) of technological resources
13. The adequacy of cooperation with other organizations
14. The adequacy of organizational and cultural diversity
15. The adequacy of client information and data analysis capabilities.

The success of collaborative networks and community development is tied to community leadership. In recognition of the leadership deficit that is typical of struggling CBOs and disadvantaged communities, Fairfax County has initiated programming that strengthens volunteerism and CBO leadership. The goal and objectives statements in table 4.5 indicate that the intent of county government is to leverage public dollars to build the capacity of CBOs for purposes of community development and to give disadvantaged citizens a more powerful voice in shaping the future of their community. The measures associated with this newly launched venture clarify government expectations, including improved community leadership and increased capacity for coproduction. Consistent with a systems approach, Fairfax County is intent on promoting collaborative ventures with self-sustaining CBOs.

Networked solutions necessarily require critical assessments of the contractual relations between local government and community agencies. A recent study (Snyder and Flentje 2000) provides insight into how contractual relations between local government and nonprofit agencies might be improved. It explores how performance monitoring and evaluation can be used to alert local government to performance concerns. The study proposes actions that can be taken to build the capacity of community agencies and develop collaborative solutions to community concerns, including "improving accountability for services delivered by nonprofit providers that combines standards/compliance models with outcome/performance models" (Snyder and Flentje 2000: 29).

Ultimately, collaborative solutions that jointly apply the resources of government, NGOs, and CBOs require interlocking performance measurement systems. Interlocking performance measurement systems reach beyond transparency through transformed accountability that optimizes the use of resources from the perspective of community rather than government. This more inclusive approach to performance measurement promotes communication and alignment of the strategic agendas of NGOs, CBOs, and governmental agencies to advance the well-being of the community.

Goals and Performance Targets

Goals, as operationalized through objectives, give direction to the actions of government and collaborating agencies. Performance targets define expectations for achieving goals, as operationalized in units of measurement. Stakeholder involvement in processes associated with setting goals, developing measures, and establishing performance targets enlists commitment to goal achievement (Aristigueta 1999). If NGOs are to collaborate with governmental entities to coproduce systems solutions to the concerns of community, they must be intimately involved in strategic planning and decision-making processes (Lacey, Adeyemi, and Adewuyi 1997). Inclusive processes take more time than unilateral actions, but they are more likely to secure commitment to decisions and will help participants make the necessary transition from governmental to community orientation.

Presentation of goals is critical if performance-based budgeting is to provide transparency and to signal the intent of government. Goal statements are especially critical to prevent suboptimization associated with collaborative solutions. Agencies that form the collaborative network, especially core agencies, must be able to understand the intent of the activities of network partners in order to improve interface, avoid duplication, and make sure that they are filling an identified community need. Goal statements that lack specificity or are convoluted can be counterproductive.

The goal statement shown in table 4.4 is particularly effective in describing program intent. It presents a wealth of information about the intent of recreational activities. The goal of recreational activities offered through the community centers is not limited to short-run improvements in quality of life but instead is designed to promote lifestyle changes, including long-term health benefits.

Performance Improvement Trends and Targets

If performance measurement is to have meaning, performance targets must be established and actual and targeted performances compared. While there is little dispute about the need to establish targets, there are important differences in approach.

One of the most common approaches involves establishing performance-related trends, which are used to establish targets. Two or more historical data points are necessary to establish a trend.

Regardless of the method used to establish targets, it is important to provide the opportunity for targets to be adjusted. The organization and the organizational environment are continuously changing; these changes necessarily influence performance. As a result, performance targets must be adjusted to reflect the changing reality, including changes in the environment.

It is important to carefully define protocols for change. Performance targets that are too easily adjusted or that can be adjusted without adherence to protocols invite abuse. Conversely, performance targets that are inflexible invite dishonesty in performance reporting.

Table 4.4 provides an example of legitimate target adjustment related to actual and projected increases in community center attendance. The qualitative reporting in this table explains the large variances in outcomes, driven primarily by increased capacity associated with the reopening of a community center. Target estimates associated with current and future operations are adjusted to reflect the added capacity of community centers in addition to the overall growth in community center usage. The goal statement calls for a 10 percent increase in community center usage.

Benchmarking Performance

Benchmarking involves identifying organizations that are recognized for their performance in particular activities, functions, or programming. For example, if a community is dissatisfied with the performance of law enforcement and after investigation decides to transition from traditional law enforcement to community policing, it might initiate a search for what could be considered a model agency with respect to community policing. The transferability of the model depends in no small part on the extent to which the communities are comparable (Behn 2003; Folz 2004; Kelly and Rivenbark 2003; Poister 2003). Communities and agencies that appear similar on the surface may have important contextual differences that are critical to performance (Poister 2003). Nevertheless, much can be learned from functional comparisons across communities (Ammons 1995; Kopczynski and Lombardo 1999; Wholey and Hatry 1992).

Despite the usefulness of interagency comparisons, government would be ill advised to implement rigorous benchmarking in Sub-Saharan Africa. These approaches include standardized measures and rigid comparisons across communities. While standardization of measures and measurement systems may one day be feasible, the technical challenges and political implications are likely to do more harm than good in developing countries. Communities in Sub-Saharan Africa are more likely to benefit from innovation and creativity that capture the unique character of the community, governmental agencies, NGOs, and CBOs.

Strategic Planning and Performance Targets

Performance measurement and performance-based budgeting are most effective when nested in strategic planning processes (Kelly and Rivenbark 2003; Poister 2003). Collaborative approaches and networked solutions necessarily require community-based, as opposed to government-based, strategic planning. Agenda setting necessarily involves key stakeholders from core agencies, including governmental and nongovernmental agencies that are critical to goal accomplishment and community improvement. Performance-based budgeting driven by a strategic agenda developed by a broad base of stakeholders strengthens commitment to the community and the civil infrastructure.

Policy makers, community agencies, and citizens tracking the activities of government are particularly interested in products associated with the strategic agenda, as opposed to some of the more mundane activities of government. Success breeds success; it is therefore important that citizens, either as individuals or as participants through engaged community agencies, be able to track progress on strategic items through performance measurement (Holzer and Yang 2004). Citizens who are stakeholders in participating community agencies that monitor investment and track community improvements will be more likely to trust government and to coproduce community improvement (Yang and Holzer 2006).

Unintended Consequences

An unintended consequence and common concern associated with performance measurement involves "playing to the measure," which occurs when agencies become more concerned with performance reporting than actual results (Kelly and Rivenbark 2003). It is not uncommon for an agency to modify its behavior in ways that influence the measurement of performance while disregarding performance. For example, standardized testing is commonly used to assess educational performance. In an effort to give the appearance of performance, teachers often focus on subject matter that is likely to appear on a standardized test. Educational content important to good citizenship or labor-force quality may be displaced by narrowing the curriculum to improve the match between class and standardized test content. In addition, in an attempt to boost the scores of their students, some schools offer special classes that emphasize test content and test-taking skills and encourage students to take practice examinations to prepare for standardized testing associated with college entrance. It is thus possible to increase scores on standardized tests without improving labor-force capacity. This example demonstrates the importance of critical thinking and logic about the connection between measures and organizational behavior. Kelly and Rivenbark (2003) recognize these concerns and other performance measurement shortcomings but argue that governments must nevertheless press ahead with performance measurement improvements.

Performance-Based Budgeting

Several actions can be taken to strengthen the connection between performance-based budgeting and improved performance. These include steps to involve citizens in decision making.

From Generic Information to Information Germane to Decisions

The success of performance-based budgeting and positive organizational change rests heavily on the shoulders of leadership. Leadership must embrace change and value performance; it must work to establish an organizational climate that is conducive to change (Behn 2003; Melkers and Willoughby 2005). This means that both policy makers and administrators must consistently support actions that enhance performance, including performance-based budgeting, if performance is to improve (Berman and Wang 2000).

The information available through performance-based budgeting should be used to aid, not displace, the decision-making responsibilities of leadership (Melkers and Willoughby 2005). Performance-based budgeting feeds the decision-making process, but it is only one of many considerations that drive decisions (Klay 2001). The nature of the decision will have much to do with the level of influence of rational systems such as performance-based budgeting. Some decisions rest heavily on knowledge of human behavior and are fed by an intimate understanding of the organization and its environment.

The usefulness of performance measurement and performance-based budgeting will depend on how germane the information is to the decision. Initial versions of performance measures tend to be generic. They must be shaped through iterative processes. Governmental organizations are wrapped in an environment that is continuously changing; performance-based budgeting must therefore be continuously shaped to fit the changing informational needs of the organization. This means that intra- and interorganizational stakeholders must be actively involved in a continuous process of adjusting performance-based budgeting. All too often, local government leadership fails to recognize this dynamic process. The result is performance measures that are not germane to decisions (Glaser 1991).

Financial and Programmatic Accountability

If citizens are to play an active role in shaping the actions of government and performance-based budgeting is to be instrumental to citizen engagement, budgetary evidence must be presented in a form that invites understanding. Kelly and Rivenbark (2003) describe performance-based budgeting as a way of capturing both budget variance (financial accountability) and performance variance (accountability for program or service delivery). They believe that both line-item and program-based budgeting are necessary to form a complete picture of performance.

They describe financial accountability as a plan for how resources are to be used. Line-item budgets provide a detailed assessment of adherence to the plan. Expenditures and encumbrances (a commitment to pay) are generally tracked on a monthly basis to allow for adjustments to ensure annual compliance. When an agency uses public resources for items that are not a part of the plan or exceeds its budget, it is not in compliance with the plan, and those who are responsible for the deviations must be held accountable. In some cases, deviations from the plan can be justified. The budget must then be revised to reflect the new reality, such as organizational or environmental changes or priority adjustments. Line-item budgets are useful for making sure that government operates within the boundaries of available resources and that public resources are spent on intended or budgeted items.

Program budgeting is the second form of accountability. It measures performance based on goal achievement. Performance targets are set using one or more of the methods discussed earlier, and performance measurement is used to assess achievement of goals. Goals are operationalized through measures and performance targets.

Financial auditing is necessary to ensure that the discipline of the line-item budget is maintained. Auditing promotes spending within budgeted limits and on designated items. Internal auditing is generally conducted by an independent agency within local government. Such agencies are usually structurally insulated or set apart from other agencies within local government, in an effort to limit the influence that internal agencies are able to exert on the auditing function. Internal auditors have the advantage of knowledge of the organization and its operations. The primary disadvantage of internal audits stems from difficulties in ensuring that these agencies and the outcomes of the audit are truly independent. Fjeldstad and others (2004) find that internal auditing associated with local government in Tanzania is weak. Audits associated with line-item budgets focus on financial accountability.

External audits are used when independent assessments are essential; financial accountability usually requires guarantees of independence. External auditing of financial considerations is especially important in developing countries, where government is attempting to strengthen the bonds of trust between citizens and government. Fjeldstad and others (2004) report that external audits in Tanzania in 2000 revealed considerable irregularities in the reported use of public funds but that more recent external financial audits reveal that local governments are more likely to comply with governmental accounting practices in the use of public funds.

Performance-based budgeting provides financial accountability (in some cases, line-item reporting) and program accountability, with expenditures tied to specific programs, activities, or cost centers. This form of accountability attempts to relate expenditures to public products in a way that allows people who are unfamiliar with government and budgeting to review the products of government. Performance audits provide assessments of the extent to which the public is getting a good return on its tax payments. They not only assess value and product quality, they also scrutinize the methodology associated with data collection and the accuracy of performance reporting (Kelly and Rivenbark 2003). Failure to conduct performance audits encourages inaccuracy in performance reporting.

Transparency and Stakeholder Engagement

Employees take their cues for acceptable behavior from leadership. If organizational leadership is actively involved in shaping performance measurement to decision-making needs, employees are more likely to follow suit. If superiors use performance measurement to guide decision making, subordinates will be more diligent in maintaining performance-measurement systems. This type of diligence and attention to details is facilitated by performance measurement that is viewed as a continuous process that regularly feeds decision making as opposed to an annual or biannual event. Kelly and Rivenbark (2003) point to Fairfax County as a model entity in this regard.

If performance measurement drives decisions, it is imperative that the information be accurate, timely, and germane. Data quality is facilitated when organizational employees are stakeholders who critically review the information they report as well as the information they receive from other agencies. Employees are stakeholders who serve as auditors by critically reviewing information in the system and reporting problems as they are discovered. This stakeholder approach also facilitates systems thinking by ensuring that stakeholders associated with a particular unit have an intimate understanding of other units with which they interact on a regular basis. Improved knowledge of how a subunit relates to the agency's broader mission reduces suboptimization. If performance measurement is actually driving decisions that influence outcomes, the information and the activities associated with performance reporting are continuously subjected to scrutiny. This process produces cleaner and more reliable data, which are continuously shaped to make them germane to resource allocation decisions.

Stakeholder processes help dislodge zero-sum behavior—intra-agency competition for limited resources in which success is defined by the ability of agencies to capture additional resources. Too often, budgetary processes encourage interdepartmental competition that is less about organizational performance and more about gaming. This zero-sum mentality promotes suboptimization and is counterproductive.

Given the propensity for zero-sum behavior, it is important to consider the logic behind performance measurement and resource allocation adjustments. In some cases, performance-based budget adjustments are driven by performance accomplishments. In this case, decisions about performance-based budgeting include resource rewards for units that meet or exceed targeted performance and penalties or resource cutbacks when a particular agency fails to meet performance targets. In other cases, performance-based budget adjustments focus on performance optimization. In this case, budget adjustments are less about rewards or penalties for performance and more about the dynamics of the organization and its environment (strategic adjustments in the use of resources). In still other cases, good performance on the part of a unit may result in the reallocation of resources away from it. That is, if a unit is able to meet targeted outputs while spending less (as a result of efficiency gains), the organizational mission might be served by shifting savings to other units. This example demonstrates the importance of linking performance measurement (the measurement of group performance) and performance appraisal (the measurement of the performance of individuals).

Connections between performance measurement and appraisal allow for individuals to be rewarded for contributing to efficiency that permits their unit to operate with fewer resources. Performance appraisal and performance measurement are often treated as independent assessments; they should be systematically linked (Glaser 1993).

Linking Performance-Based Budgeting and Performance Improvement

Performance-based budgeting must be a part of a reasoned and predictable process if it is to have a positive impact on performance (Rugumyamheto 2004). Methods used to link performance reporting and performance improvement vary considerably.

Scheps (2000) describes a continuous evaluation model employed in Dallas County, Texas, that sheds light on some of the actions necessary to secure performance improvement. First, predetermined accounting periods and progress evaluations must be in place that provide the opportunity for performance adjustment. Dallas County employs a continuous performance improvement model for evaluating performance. Second, performance evaluations must consider factors that are controllable, as well as environmental influences that are beyond the control of government but affect performance. Leaders with budgetary responsibilities are asked to critically review and describe performance expectations associated with their unit, including anticipated environmental influences on performance, and to describe and defend recommended actions in response to performance concerns. Third, the review process must be transparent, providing the opportunity for broad-based participation by stakeholders, including service recipients or program participants. Fourth, budget implications must logically flow from the review processes surrounding performance measurement.

Not every agency has the time or resources to invest in continuous performance improvement processes such as those described here. But annual or biannual assessments of performance are unlikely to bring meaningful performance improvement.

Transparency in Performance Reporting

Transparency is facilitated, and a more complete picture of government operations is presented, when line-item accountability and performance-based budgeting are combined (Kelly and Rivenbark 2003). The discussion of the Department of Community and Recreation Services in Fairfax

County provides a programmatic view of performance measurement (see tables 4.4 and 4.5). Building on these descriptions, this section explores Fairfax County's approach to transparency in performance reporting.[2]

An important requirement of performance accountability hinges on the ability to identify and hold a specific governmental agency accountable (Andrews 2003a). Consistent with this requirement, performance reporting associated with each department begins with an organizational chart. The organizational chart for Community and Recreation Services includes a breakout of departmental subdivisions, or cost centers, that allows readers to pinpoint which subagency or cost center is responsible for a particular product or service. Fairfax County's Web site provides a description of its mission, focus, and ties to the strategic agenda.

It is important that the language used to describe agencies' activities exclude or, at the very least, explain technical jargon. The narrative should be written under the assumption that the reader has limited background on budgets, performance measurement, and the activities or functions of government. Few citizens have the time or inclination to follow the full slate of performance measures. It must be easy to find items that are strategic in nature and of interest to citizens.

Consistent with the reporting format for all agencies, Community and Recreation Services provides an overview of departmental actions and activities as they relate to the strategic agenda, including "New Initiatives" and "Recent Accomplishments in Support of the Fairfax County Vision." It provides brief narratives that describe current and projected activities. These descriptions discuss the activities and help readers understand the connections between Community and Recreation Services and other Fairfax County agencies. For example, the narrative describes what appear to be seamless connections between Community and Recreation Services and the Fairfax County Public School system in connection with after-school programming. The discussion demonstrates how recreation, education, and social skills programming are combined to form a more holistic approach to the well-being of participating youths.

Financial reporting uses a variety of formats, including line-item presentations. The budget information includes line-item financial accountability for the overall agency (personnel, operating, and capital equipment), as well as cost-center breakouts. The overview of financial information includes revenue generation and identifies the net cost to the county.

Financial reporting provides the reader with a longitudinal view of budgetary changes, which allows citizens to assess budgetary trends and current year modifications to the budget. In addition to spreadsheets, the reporting identifies the amounts of the adjustments and provides an explanation of the reasoning behind funding adjustments. For readers interested primarily in general budgetary information, a pie chart provides a visual breakout of each cost center and the budgeted resources for fiscal year 2007. Cost center financial breakouts are followed by the performance information discussed earlier (see tables 4.4 and 4.5).

Tools for Engaging Citizens and Respecting Public Values

Government is responsible for actions that are consistent with the long-term well-being of community as well as responsiveness to the demands of citizens. The tension between these dimensions of performance intensifies when citizens become inordinately focused on self-interest. Although many factors contribute to the retreat into self-interest or the willingness of citizens to embrace community, the actions of government are particularly important. When government invites citizens into decision-making processes and works to improve their knowledge of government and pending concerns, citizens are more likely to support investments that are consistent with the long-term well-being of the community.

Survey research used in concert with performance-based budgeting can define and advance understanding of citizens' perceptions of performance and promote convergence between competing dimensions of performance, such as responsiveness and community. Fairfax County uses a variety of research tools, including survey research, to give citizens a voice in the decisions of government. The county reports survey research results in conjunction with performance-based budgeting to promote understanding of satisfaction or quality of service delivery. It actively encourages local government agencies to use survey research, providing an online manual that discusses research methodology related to the measurement of customer satisfaction (Fairfax County Department of Management and Budget 2005d).

While engagement vehicles such as citizen survey research hold promise, a number of considerations and limitations must be recognized. Andrews (2003b) points to the low level of citizen knowledge of government (such as knowledge of budgets) as an important barrier to meaningful citizen engagement in Sub-Saharan Africa. While these challenges are formidable, they are not insurmountable. In some parts of Sub-Saharan Africa, CBOs have laid the information foundation necessary to facilitate participation (Dolny 2001). CBOs and NBOs are potentially multifunctional vehicles that promote community improvement by laying the information foundation necessary to communicate with government, assembling the political power necessary to influence government, strengthening the civic infrastructure for collective action, and assembling resources sufficient to promote meaningful change, including collective resources associated with coproduction.

A second concern hinges on the difficulties associated with measuring citizen demand. It is not uncommon for citizens to demand more from government than they are willing to pay for. When survey research offers a smorgasbord of services without tax implications, citizens tend to support increases in most service categories. Survey research used to identify service priorities must guard against measurement error associated with inflated demand (requests for service delivery increases beyond those that citizens are actually willing to pay for, sometimes referred to as *tax-demand discontinuity*. Those using survey research to assess citizen demand are advised to use triangulation of measures, including measures that establish service delivery priorities, usage patterns, and assessments of willingness to pay increased taxes (Glaser and Bardo 1994).

The connection between demand for services and willingness to pay is not as straightforward in Sub-Saharan Africa as it is in developed countries. Revenues generated from the local tax base are one of many sources that feed service delivery and programming by local governments. Therefore, assessments of citizen demands for services may need to be adjusted to focus on opportunity costs. Deliberative processes are particularly well suited for assessing opportunity costs. Weeks (2000) makes the case for deliberative processes that promote learning through reasoned discussion of the problem and alternative solutions. He reports that these deliberative processes help citizens think less about self-interest and more about improving the long-term well-being of community and strengthening the civic infrastructure.

Coproduction is a form of citizen engagement that warrants consideration in Sub-Saharan Africa. Rebuilding the civic infrastructure is instrumental to community improvement; coproduction provides an avenue for strengthening connections among citizens and between citizens and government. For example, health care costs are driven partly by human behavior. If programming were used to facilitate citizen understanding of the health implications associated with their behavior and apply social pressure, individuals might be more willing to adjust their behavior to coproduce lower health care costs and improved health (Glaser and others 2004). Survey research and deliberative processes may be useful in laying the knowledge foundation necessary for change.

Equity is a particularly important performance concern in Sub-Saharan Africa. Government must strive to engage all classes of citizens, regardless of ethnicity and socioeconomic standing. Sampling frames associated with survey research (the list from which participants are drawn) typically underrepresent the poor. Efforts to increase access to government for those living in poverty include information-gathering techniques known as participatory poverty assessments (Norton and others 2001). Robb (2000) summarizes the logic associated with the use of participatory poverty assessments and argues that they can be particularly useful when used jointly with survey research. Like the triangulation of measures, participatory poverty assessments depend heavily on triangulation of data collection methods. Survey research is useful for identifying the demands and concerns of a broad body of citizens; participatory poverty assessments are useful for understanding the meaning of poverty and tailoring interventions to the specifics of a particular sector of the poor population. The experience of poverty presents numerous and formidable communication barriers that make the gathering of valid and reliable information challenging. Participatory poverty assessments commonly use interactive conversations between those collecting and those supplying information. Robb points out that face to face contact presents an opportunity to identify and correct conceptual misunderstandings related to questioning. It also provides an intimate understanding of the plight of the respondent, which is critical to crafting poverty policy. Interviews conducted as part of participatory poverty assessments include less structure, giving those who are conducting the interviews the option of abandoning questioning that is unfruitful and refocusing discussion on other areas. The engagement processes surrounding participatory poverty assessments also demonstrate to the poor that government cares about their plight.

Improving Government Performance in Sub-Saharan Africa

Many challenges must be overcome before performance-based budgeting can be expected to drive improved government performance in Sub-Saharan Africa. Leadership resistance to change is one of the most important barriers. Both elected and appointed officials often resist change, because the status quo serves their self-interest (Andrews and Shah 2003b). Leadership and organizational culture often interact in ways that make it difficult to promote performance improvement. In some cases, corruption drives resistance to change (Baker and others 2002; Fjeldstad 2003; Fjeldstad and others 2004). An entrenched culture of corruption is exceedingly difficult to transform. Transparency and citizen engagement can be instrumental in breaking a culture of corruption, but citizens living in poverty commonly lack the ability or the will to oversee change or successfully challenge longstanding governmental behavior. It is not difficult to understand how communities in Sub-Saharan Africa get caught in a downward spiral of hopelessness.

A number of structural and fiscal barriers make it difficult to break this cycle of hopelessness. Local control is essential if citizens are to have a hand in holding government accountable and making it responsive to the needs and concerns of the people (Andrews and Shah 2003c). A major thrust of governmental reform includes shifting control from central to local governments (Baker and others 2002). However, structural independence must be accompanied by economic independence if local governments are to have the capacity to be responsive to the needs and demands of citizens. Many governments in Sub-Saharan Africa are mired in debt and have little fiscal capacity for community improvement (Andrews and Shah 2003a). These governments usually depend on a narrow mix of revenues to fund government (Andrews and Shah 2003a).

Fiscal concerns are exacerbated by limitations in technical capacity. For example, property tax appraisal systems are commonly plagued by inaccuracy, fed in part by the weak methodology used for property valuation (Andrews and Shah 2003a). Technical problems include inaccuracy in revenue estimation, leading to frequent revenue shortfalls (Fjeldstad and others 2004). Computer systems to record, track, and analyze performance are often unavailable in Sub-Saharan Africa.

Redefining Performance through Collaborative Networks

In the long run, reversing the fortunes of Sub-Saharan Africa hinges on restoring the civic infrastructure and strengthening the bonds of trust among citizens and between citizens and government (Lange, Wallevik, and Kiondo 2000). Assuming there is a genuine interest on the part of local government leaders to engage citizens, the question becomes one of what type of citizen participation vehicle is likely to be most effective. Many of the vehicles employed by local government to involve citizens have the appearance of citizen engagement but fail to give citizens a voice in the decisions of government (Simonsen and Robbins 2000). It is also important to avoid the use of competing citizen engagement vehicles that divide the allegiance of citizens and confuse communication (Andrews and Shah 2003c; Berry, Portney, and Thomson 1993; Glaser, Yeager, and Parker 2006).

Citizen engagement must recognize the ethnic diversity in Sub-Saharan Africa, including each group's values and cultures. Citizen engagement is more effective when it is shaped to fit the unique character of diverse segments of the community (Andrews and Shah 2003b). Citizens naturally organize in neighborhoods with other citizens who have similar values and socioeconomic standing. Broad-based citizen engagement in the decisions of government through NBOs serves to protect against government capture. Issues of equity associated with government capture include situations in which the actions of government are influenced primarily by a limited number of agencies or individuals while ignoring the interests of the broader community.

NBOs can be used to organize the political voice of the community and distribute power more equitably throughout the community (Berry, Portney, and Thomson 1989). They are most effective when they simultaneously develop political, economic, and social capital. Social capital relates to the interconnectedness of individuals (Putnam 2000). When neighbors join with neighbors to strengthen their neighborhood politically and economically, they build social capital and the civic infrastructure that is desperately needed in Sub-Saharan Africa.

Neighborhood resources channeled through neighborhood-development organizations are necessary for community development, but they are not sufficient. In most cases, resources from outside the neighborhood will be required to fuel community development.

Local government in Fairfax County is providing resources to fuel community development through a variety of CBOs. The county has developed a pool of resources that leverages public dollars against community resources to enhance the capacity of CBOs to become coproducers of an improved quality of life.

In sharp contrast to Fairfax County, most local governments in Sub-Saharan Africa, and the communities they represent, lack the resources to unilaterally provide the catalyst necessary to drive community development. However, if local government resources were used in concert with external resources, such as those of NGOs, they might reach the critical mass necessary for significant community improvement. This approach depends on the formation of collaborative networks that include local governments and NGOs as core agencies in support of community improvement.

If performance-based budgeting is to guide collaborative processes in Sub-Saharan Africa, it must be fundamentally changed to provide an accounting for the investments of all core agencies as collaborators in systems solutions to the concerns of community. Transparency on the part of all collaborators is necessary to illuminate who is responsible for the various programs or components of programs identified in a community-based strategic agenda. Accordingly, performance-based budgeting must address how local government and NGO funds have been leveraged to secure investments by CBOs, including actions on the part of NBOs that are consistent with the strategic agenda of the community. This more comprehensive accounting for community resources allows citizens, acting through NBOs, to see how their investments improve organizational, neighborhood, and community well-being. This approach does not change the need for organizational financial auditing; it does affect performance auditing. Engaged citizens who understand the connection between their actions and those of core agencies, including local government, are more likely to hold these agencies accountable for the use of community resources and become meaningful stakeholders in community well-being.

Notes

1. The tables presented here reflect only a fraction of the activities and the performance measures of each agency. Readers interested in exploring performance measurement associated with a particular funtion in more detail should follow the link provided at the bottom of the tables.
2. All the information used in this chapter is posted on the county's Web site. In some cases, multiple postings for an agency reflect changes and a continuous reporting process.

References

Ammons, David N. 1995. "Overcoming the Inadequacies of Performance Measurement in Local Government: The Case of Libraries and Leisure Services." *Public Administration Review* 55 (1): 37–47.

Andrews, Matthew. 2003a. "Performance-Based Budget Reform: Progress, Problems and Pointers." In *Ensuring Accountability When There Is No Bottom Line*, ed. Anwar Shah. Washington, DC: World Bank.

———. 2003b. "Voice Mechanisms and Local Government Fiscal Outcomes: How Does Civic Pressures and Participation Influence Public Accountability?" In *Bringing Civility in Governance*, ed. Anwar Shah. Washington, DC: World Bank.

Andrews, Matthew, and Anwar Shah. 2003a. "Assessing Local Government Performance in Developing Countries." In *Measuring Government Performance in the Delivery of Public Services*, ed. Anwar Shah. Washington, DC: World Bank.

———. 2003b. "Citizen-Centered Governance: A New Approach to Public Sector Reform." In *Bringing Civility in Governance*, ed. Anwar Shah. Washington, DC: World Bank.

———. 2003c. "Towards Citizen-Centered Local-Level Budgets in Developing Countries." In *Bringing Civility in Governance*, ed. Anwar Shah. Washington, DC: World Bank.

Aristigueta, Maria Pilar. 1999. *Managing for Results in State Government.* Westport, CT: Quorum Books.

Baker, Jonathan, Hege Wallevik, James Obama, and Nazar Sola. 2002. "The Local Government Reform Process in Tanzania: Towards a Greater Interdependence between Local Government and Civil Society at the Local Level." Research and Development Report 6/2002, Agder Research, Kristiansand, Norway.

Balogun, M. J. 2003. "Performance Management and Agency Governance or African Development: The Search for Common Cause on Excellence in the Public Service." Occasional Paper 9, Development Policy Management Forum, Addis Ababa.

Behn, Robert D. 2003. "Why Measure Performance? Different Purposes Require Different Measures." *Public Administration Review* 63 (5): 586–606.

Berman, Evan, and XiaoHu Wang. 2000. "Performance Measurement in U.S. Counties: Capacity for Reform." *Public Administration Review* 60 (5): 409–20.

Berry, Jeffery M., Kent E. Portney, and Ken Thomson. 1989. "Empowering and Involving Citizens." In *Handbook of Public Administration,* ed. James L. Perry, 208–21. San Francisco: Jossey-Bass.

———. 1993. *The Rebirth of Urban Democracy.* Washington, DC: Brookings Institution.

Birdsall, Nancy. 2003. "Asymmetric Globalization: Global Markets Require Good Global Politics." *Brookings Review* 21 (2): 22–27.

Burke, John P. 1989. "Reconciling Public Administration and Democracy: The Role of the Responsible Administrator." *Public Administration Review* 49 (2): 180–84.

Denhardt, Robert, and Janet Vinzant Denhardt. 2000. "The New Public Service: Serving Rather than Steering." *Public Administration Review* 60 (6): 550–59.

Dolny, Helena. 2001. *Banking on Change.* Johannesburg: Viking.

Fairfax County Department of Management and Budget. 2005a. *A Manual for Performance Measurement: Fairfax County Measures Up.* Fairfax County, VA. http://www.fairfaxcounty.gov/dmb/Basic_Manual.pdf.

———. 2005b. *Fairfax County Manages for Results: A Guide to Advanced Performance Measurement.* Fairfax County, VA. http://www.fairfaxcounty.gov/dmb/Manages_ For_Results.pdf.

———. 2005c. *Fairfax County Manual for Data Collection for Performance Measurement.* Fairfax County, VA. http://www.fairfaxcounty.gov/dmb/Data_Collection_ Manual.pdf.

———. 2005d. *Fairfax County Manual for Surveying for Customer Satisfaction.* Fairfax County, VA. http://www.fairfaxcounty.gov/dmb/Survey_Manual.pdf.

Fairfax County Department of Systems Management for Human Services. 1999. "Consolidated Community Funding Pool." Fairfax County, VA. http://www.fairfax county.gov/service/pdf/ccfparticle.pdf.

Fjeldstad, Odd-Helge. 2003. "Fighting Fiscal Corruption: Lessons from the Tanzania Revenue Authority." *Public Administration and Development* 23 (2): 165–75.

Fjeldstad, Odd-Helge, Flordia Henjewele, Geoffrey Mwambe, Erasto Ngalewa, and Knut Nygaard. 2004. "Local Government Finances and Financial Management in Tanzania: Baseline Data from Six Councils 2000–2003." Chr. Michelsen Institute, Bergen, Norway.

Folz, David H. 2004. "Service Quality and Benchmarking the Performance of Municipal Services." *Public Administration Review* 64 (2): 209–20.

Foster, Philip. 1980. "Education and Social Inequality in Sub–Saharan Africa." *Journal of Modern African Studies* 18 (2): 201–36.

Glaser, Mark. 1991. "Tailoring Performance Measurement to Fit the Organization: From Generic to Germane." *Public Productivity and Management Review* 14 (3): 303–19.

———. 1993. "Reconciliation of Total Quality Management and Traditional Performance Improvement Tools: Program Evaluation, Performance Measurement and Performance Appraisal." *Public Productivity and Management Review* 16 (4): 379–86.

Glaser, Mark A., Maria P. Aristigueta, and David R. Miller. 2003–04. "Willingness to Pay for Capital Investments in Public Education: The Mitigating Influence of Community and Enlightened Self–Interest." *Public Integrity* 6 (1): 39–61.

Glaser, Mark A., Maria P. Aristigueta, and Stephanie Payton. 2000. "Harnessing the Resources of Community: The Ultimate Performance Agenda." *Public Productivity and Management Review* 23 (4): 428–48.

Glaser, Mark A., and John W. Bardo. 1994. "A Five-Stage Approach for Improved Use of Citizen Surveys in Public Investment Decisions." *State and Local Government Review* 26 (3): 161–72.

Glaser, Mark A., Janet Vinzant Denhardt, and Linda K. Hamilton. 2002. "Community v. Self-Interest: Citizen Perceptions of Schools as Civic Investments." *Journal of Public Administration Research and Theory* 12 (1): 103–27.

Glaser, Mark A., and Robert B. Denhardt. 1999. "When Citizen Expectations Conflict with Budgetary Reality: Discontinuity between the Public's Demand for Services and Its Willingness to Pay Taxes." *Journal of Public Budgeting, Accounting and Financial Management* 11 (2): 276–310.

Glaser, Mark A., H. Edward Flentje, Daniel J. Bryan, and Misha C. Jacob. 2004. *A Systems Approach to the Study of Community Health: Voter Concerns, Investment Priorities, and Willingness to Pay Increased Taxes.* Hugo Wall School of Urban and Public Affairs, Wichita State University, Sedgwick County, KS.

Glaser, Mark A., and W. Bartley Hildreth. 1996. "A Profile of Discontinuity between Citizen Demand and Willingness to Pay Taxes." *Public Budgeting and Finance* 16 (4): 96–113.

Glaser, Mark A., Lee E. Parker, and Stephanie Payton. 2001. "The Paradox between Community and Self-Interest: Local Government, Neighborhoods, and Media." *Journal of Urban Affairs* 23 (1): 87–102.

Glaser, Mark A., Mark D. Soskin, and Michael Smith. 1996. "Local Government Supported Community Development: Community Priorities and Issues of Autonomy." *Urban Affairs Review* 31 (6): 778–98.

Glaser, Mark A., Samuel J. Yeager, and Lee E. Parker. 2006. "Involving Citizens in the Decisions of Government and Community: Neighborhood-Based v. Government–Based Engagement." *Public Administration Quarterly* 30 (2): 177–217.

Holzer, Marc, and Kaifeng Yang. 2004. "Performance Measurement and Improvement: An Assessment of the State of the Art." *International Review of Administrative Sciences* 70 (1): 15–31.

Kelly, Janet M., and William C. Rivenbark. 2003. *Performance Budget for State and Local Government.* Armonk, NY: M. E. Sharp.

Kettl, Donald F. 2000. "The Transformation of Governance: Globalization, Devolution and the Role of Government." *Public Administration Review* 60 (6): 488–96.

Klay, William Earle. 2001. "Management through Budgetary Incentives." In *Performance-Based Budgeting,* ed. Gerald J. Miller, W. Bartley Hildreth, and Jack Rabin, 215–30. Boulder, CO: Westview Press.

Kopczynski, Mary, and Michael Lombardo. 1999. "Comparative Performance Measurement: Insights and Lessons Learned from a Consortium Effort." *Public Administration Review* 59 (2): 124–34.

Lacey, Linda, Victoria Adeyemi, and Alfred Adewuyi. 1997. "A Tool for Monitoring the Performance of Family Planning Programs in the Public and Private Sectors: An Application in Nigeria." *International Family Planning Perspectives* 23 (4): 162–67.

Lange, Siri, Hege Wallevik, and Andrew Kiondo. 2000. "Civil Society in Tanzania." Chr. Michelsen Institute, Bergen, Norway.

Logan, John R., and Gordana Rabrenovic. 1990. "Neighborhood Associations: Their Issues, Their Allies, and Their Opponents." *Urban Affairs Quarterly* 26 (1): 68–94.

Melkers, Julia, and Katherine Willoughby. 2005. "Models of Performance-Measurement Use in Local Governments: Understanding Budgeting, Communication, and Lasting Effects." *Public Administration Review* 65 (2): 180–90.

Morgan, David R., and Robert E. England. 1987. "Evaluating a Community Development Block Grant Program: Elite and Program Recipient Views." In *Policy Evaluation for Local Government*, ed. Terry Busson and Philip Coulter, 31–43. New York: Greenwood Press.

Norton, Andy, Bella Bird, Karen Brock, Margaret Kakande, and Carrie Turk. 2001. *A Rough Guide to PPAs (Participatory Poverty Assessments): An Introduction to Theory and Practice.* Overseas Development Institute, London.

Pecorella, Robert F. 1986. "Community Input and the City Budget: Geographically Based Budgeting in New York City." *Journal of Urban Affairs* 8 (1): 57–70.

Poister, Theodore H. 2003. *Measuring Performance in Public and Nonprofit Organizations.* San Francisco: Jossey-Bass.

Provan, Keith G., and H. Brinton Milward. 2001. "Do Networks Really Work? A Framework for Evaluating Public-Sector Organizational Networks." *Public Administration Review* 61 (4): 414–23.

Putnam, Robert D. 2000. *Bowling Alone.* New York: Touchstone/Simon and Schuster.

Robb, Caroline M. 2000. "How the Poor Can Have a Voice in Government Policy." *Finance and Development* 37 (4) 22–25. http://www.imf.org/external/pubs/ft/fandd/2000/12/robb.htm.

Rugumyamheto, J. A. 2004. "Innovative Approaches to Reforming Public Services in Tanzania." *Public Administration and Development* 24 (5): 437–46.

Scheps, Phillip B. 2000. "Linking Performance Measures to Resource Allocation." *Government Finance Review* 16 (3): 11–15.

Schou, Arild. 2000. "Democratic Local Government and Responsiveness: Lessons from Zimbabwe and Tanzania." *Comparative Sociology* 41 (1): 121–43.

Sharp, Elaine B. 1990. *Urban Politics and Administration: From Service Delivery to Economic Development.* New York: Longman.

Simonsen, William, and Mark D. Robbins. 2000. *Citizen Participation in Resource Allocation.* Boulder, CO: Westview Press.

Snyder, Nancy McCarthy, and H. Edward Flentje. 2000. *Enhancing the Delivery of Public Services by Nonprofit Agencies.* Hugo Wall School of Urban and Public Affairs, Wichita State University, Sedgwick County, KS.

Streib, Gregory D., and Theodore H. Poister. 1999. "Assessing the Validity, Legitimacy, and Functionality of Performance Measurement Systems in Municipal Governments." *American Review of Public Administration* 29 (2): 107–23.

Swindell, David, and Janet Kelly. 2005. "Performance Measurement versus City Service Satisfaction: Intra-City Variations in Quality?" *Social Science Quarterly* 86 (3): 704–23.

Thomas, John Clayton. 1992. "Citizen Involvement in Public Management: Lessons from Municipal Administration." In *Public Administration in Action: Readings, Profiles, and Cases*, ed. Robert B. Denhardt and Barry R. Hammond, 163–73. Pacific Grove, CA: Brooks/Cole Publishing Company.

Warren, Robert, Mark S. Rosentraub, and Louis F. Weschler. 1992 "Building Urban Governance: An Agenda for the 1990s." *Journal of Urban Affairs* 14 (3/4): 399–422.

Weeks, Edward C. 2000. "The Practice of Deliberative Democracy: The Results from Four Large-Scale Trials." *Public Administration Review* 60 (4): 360–72.

Wheatley, Margaret J., and Myron Kellner-Rogers. 1998. "The Paradox and Promise of Community." In *The Community of the Future,* ed. Frances Hesselbein, Marshall Goldsmith, Richard Beckhard, and Richard F. Shubert. San Francisco: Jossey–Bass.

Wholey, Joseph S., and Harry P. Hatry. 1992. "The Case for Performance Monitoring." *Public Administration Review* 52 (6): 604–10.

Yang, Kaifeng, and Marc Holzer. 2006. "The Performance-Trust Link: Implications for Performance Measurement." *Public Administration Review* 66 (1): 114–26.

PART Two
Strengthening Oversight and Combating Corruption

5

The Role of Political Institutions in Promoting Accountability

ROB JENKINS

This chapter reviews the various ways in which political institutions can—in theory and in practice—contribute to greater accountability of public officials to the people on whose behalf they govern. It conceives of political institutions broadly—that is, beyond merely representative bodies or the electoral arrangements through which political leaders are chosen. It does so because even "nonpolitical" institutions are often politicized, which is one of the reasons why accountability of governments to people is in such short supply. Situating political institutions within a broader understanding of political systems allows the nature of de facto relationships in which key actors are embedded to be observed.

The chapter is aimed at a nonspecialist practitioner audience, including government officials (both elected politicians and civil servants) who operate at various levels of a political system and are engaged in a range of functional roles. It does not, therefore, address the full range of theoretical concerns of interest to academic researchers. It does draw on academic research to illustrate some of the variables that appear to play roles in determining the level of accountability achieved in different settings. Brief case studies are also used to illustrate various points.

The chapter is divided into four main sections. The first section introduces and unpacks key concepts associated with the idea of accountability. These concepts are presented in order to convey the range of meanings associated with the term. The aim is to help practitioners reach a more nuanced—and context-dependent—understanding of accountability systems, one that will foster innovative approaches when conventional tools prove inadequate. These concepts are put into action in the second section, which examines the functions that particular institutions are expected to play in commonsense theories of democracy, the reasons why these functions get undermined in practice, and some of the ways in which groups have sought to overcome these problems in order to improve accountability. The third section provides an overview of a number of contemporary trends that can affect efforts to improve accountability systems. The last section outlines a procedure through which the concepts and issues raised in the first three sections can be used, in a given country context, to survey the accountability landscape in order to better understand the prospects for advancing improvements.

Key Concepts in Accountability Systems

The idea of accountability has been increasingly visible in the development field in recent years, emphasized by all actors concerned with improving governance.[1] What is meant by *accountability*?

Central to all definitions of accountability is the idea that one person or institution is obliged to give an account of his, her, or its activities to another. Generic models of accountability refer to any kind of relationship of this sort. In the field of governance, accountability refers to relationships between public and private actors. The applicability of general models to specific cases of government-citizen relations is often open to question, not least because the norms of what is considered appropriate vary from one country to another, one sphere of government activity to another, and so forth. Norms in accountability relationships also change over time.

A second general point to be borne in mind in thinking about accountability of governments to citizens is that accountability refers not to isolated relationships, or even individual institutions operating on their own, but to a system of relationships. How one institution operates can affect how others operate—and not necessarily in predictable ways. On the one hand, one poorly performing institution can undermine other specialized accountability institutions. On the other hand, when one institution fails, another can sometimes step in to fill a void.

The more talk there is of the importance of voice and accountability, the less these terms seem to mean—and the less relevance they appear to have for ordinary, and particularly poor, people. The discussion that follows seeks to define accountability and to illuminate some of the many usages of the term.

Accountability describes a relationship in which A is accountable to B if A is obliged to explain and justify his or her actions to B or if A may suffer sanctions if his or her conduct, or explanation for it, is found wanting by B (see Schedler 1999). Accountability is thus a relationship of power. But it denotes a specific variety of power: the capacity to demand that someone justify his or her behavior and the capacity to impose a penalty for poor performance.

Democratic accountability concerns the ability of the governed to exercise control over officeholders to whom power has been delegated. Achieving the consent of ordinary people is a difficult enough task on its own, and it is complicated by other factors. A consideration of the practical operation of accountability systems highlights a number of distinctions crucial to understanding how the concept of accountability is evolving in response to changes in the relationships between states and citizens, between public and private sectors, and between states and global institutions.

Structural transformations in the nature of governance—including the privatization of some state functions—have blurred lines of accountability, making it difficult to establish which actors hold ultimate responsibility for certain types of policies or services. The ongoing process of globalization has introduced a range of new power-holders—such as multinational corporations and transnational social movements—that slip through the jurisdictional cracks separating national authorities, yet whose actions have a profound impact on people's lives. The influence exercised over economic policy in poor countries by such multilateral institutions as the World Bank, the International Monetary Fund, and the World Trade Organization has also reduced the autonomy of many governments, making domestic democratic accountability even more elusive.

The Principal-Agent Conception of Accountability

The idea of accountability is most often rendered in terms of principals and agents. Principals delegate authority to agents, who are expected to act on the principals' behalf. In democracies the people (or voters) are the principals, and government officials (politicians and civil servants) are the agents. The central problem of principal-agent theory is to make sure that agents do what principals have empowered them to do, which is to promote public welfare. Agents have a tendency to promote their own interests instead, often in collusion with a specific segment of the public.

Keohane (2002: 3) states that accountability "refers to relationships in which principals have the ability to demand answers from agents to questions about their proposed or past behavior, to discern that behavior, and to impose sanctions on agents in the event that they regard the behavior as unsatisfactory." In democracies this translates into a requirement that governments account for their actions to voters and be punished at the ballot box if deemed to have failed in their public duty. Thus, an elected politician is the agent for a polity's voters, who are the collective principal. In the same way, the owner of a manufacturing firm is a principal who seeks to ensure that his or her interests are not subverted by the overseas distribution agent.

Another way of representing principals and agents—one that may be more relevant in the context of countries in which democratic political institutions are still being consolidated—is in relation to targets and seekers of accountability. The target of accountability, the one obliged to account for his or her actions and to face sanction, corresponds more or less to the agent. The seeker of accountability, the one entitled to insist on explanations or to impose punishments, is the principal.

These alternative terms can be useful, because they are more relevant to contexts in which existing relationships of power are being challenged—through political movements or the assertion of institutional independence by formerly subordinate actors. Many contemporary experiments in improving accountability aim to empower a wider range of principals to scrutinize agents more effectively; those seeking accountability may not necessarily enjoy a clear legal standing as principals. In addition, the targets they have in their sights do not always consider themselves agents of these constituencies. In short, the principal-agent framework is based on a formal contract model. It thus applies to static situations but not dynamic ones. Where power is not explicitly delegated—either to the agent or to the principal—the more direct terminology of seeker and target is more helpful.

The Answerability and Enforcement Aspects of Accountability

Two aspects of the accountability relationship are key to analyzing accountability institutions or proposing reforms to them. The first is answerability: having to provide information about one's actions and justifications for their correctness. The second is enforcement: having to suffer penalties imposed by those dissatisfied either with the actions themselves or with the rationale invoked to justify them. These aspects of accountability are sometimes viewed as weak and strong forms of accountability. (Being accountable in the sense of having to explain one's actions is less onerous than being subject to sanction.) However, in analyzing a given situation, it is helpful to disaggregate these core concepts.

Answerability consists of explanatory and informational components, the relevance of which varies from one circumstance to another. The less demanding form of answerability requires a holder of delegated power simply to furnish an explanation, or rationale, for his or her actions. For instance, when asked by a group of concerned citizens why a building permit was issued for a structure that encroaches on common lands, planning officers typically supply formulaic answers: permission was granted because all required steps under the relevant legislation were taken. Such a response provides very little of substantive value for people seeking a full, evidence-based justification of how competing considerations were weighed.

When this explanatory component to answerability is combined with an informational component—such as an obligation of full disclosure that requires the official to reveal the evidentiary basis upon which decisions were taken, such as supporting documentation and testimony from people consulted—officials find it harder to get away with explanations based on unsound logic. This hardens accountability, even when sanctions are not imposed.

Enforcement also has two components that must be distinguished when mapping the nature of accountability relationships. The first component is the adjudication of the nature of the power-holder's performance. This involves determining the persuasiveness of his or her explanation in light of available information and prevailing standards of public conduct.

The second component is sanctioning. After a pronouncement on the viability of the target's explanation, the enforcing agency must decide on the nature of the penalty to be applied. This process involves at least three components: assessing the future deterrent effect of competing sanctions, considering whether the public will believe that justice has been done, and calculating the capacity of the sanctioning authority effectively to carry out the chosen form of enforcement.

This unpacking of the main concepts is particularly important for analyzing the role of political institutions in promoting accountability, because political institutions often have quite specific mandates for particular circumstances. A representative body (such as a legislature) may be able to demand information but find it difficult to rule authoritatively on the explanation for an executive agency's decisions. The legislature may be able to withhold future funding, but determining legal compliance (whether the agency in question conformed to the obligations stipulated in law) is usually the province of the courts.

Another way of putting this is to say that accountability relationships often involve complicated divisions of labor. Those entitled to demand answers from power-holders are not necessarily the same as those put in charge of deciding on and implementing penalties. In some circumstances, information a firm provides to a regulatory agency—as part of an official state process—can, if made public, stimulate a completely different type of sanction, in the form of a consumer boycott, which operates in the space provided by the market and civil society.

The roles played by various institutions are, of course, more complicated than this very schematic picture suggests. Accountability functions are divided among different institutional actors, and certain actors play more than one role: an elected legislator is both accountable to the electorate and responsible for holding the executive to account. Courts also occupy a complex niche. They are clearly horizontal institutions of accountability (as discussed below), in that they are expected to ensure that governments comply with legal norms—not least their obligation to hold free and fair elections—and to adjudicate on conflicts between the legislative and executive branches of government. But courts also provide a forum through which citizens (principals engaged in a relationship of vertical accountability with government agents) seek to ensure that officials do not trespass on their democratic rights.

Vertical and Horizontal Forms of Accountability

Vertical channels of accountability are those that link citizens directly to government. Vertical accountability occurs when the state is held to account by nonstate actors. Elections are the formal channel of vertical accountability, but this camp also includes informal processes through which citizens organize themselves into associations capable of lobbying governments, demanding explanations, and threatening less formal sanctions, such as negative publicity.

Horizontal channels of accountability involve public institutions responsible for keeping watch on government agencies. Horizontal institutions of accountability—ombudspeople, auditors general, anticorruption bureaus—are meant to complement the role played by electoral institutions. Horizontal accountability exists when one state actor has the authority—formal or informal—to demand explanations or impose penalties on another. Executive agencies must explain their decisions to legislatures; in some cases they can be overruled or sanctioned for procedural violations. Political leaders hold civil servants to account, reviewing the bureaucracy's execution of policy decisions.

There is also an informal dimension to horizontal accountability. Civil servants collectively develop bureaucratic cultures. In some cultures, civil servants frown on colleagues who stray from the path of rule-bound governance; other cultures all but require officials to engage in actions that violate formal rules. Developing "cultures of probity" within civil services is one of the main challenges facing reformers who seek to improve the accountability of state institutions.

Many of the innovations recommended for improving the accountability of states to citizens involve breaking down the barriers separating vertical and horizontal channels of accountability. Getting citizens involved directly in horizontal (state-to-state) processes of accountability is a major preoccupation of some approaches to reform. Participation of ordinary people in the government's financial auditing functions could help government auditors do a better job, the logic goes, because citizens could augment the capacity of thinly stretched government auditing departments and exercise oversight over the way in which these agencies go about their business, rooting out collusion between official watchdogs and the executive departments they audit. Objections to such approaches to "hybrid accountability" range from self-interest on the part of corrupt audit agencies (who do not want their misdeeds exposed to scrutiny by ordinary citizens) to legitimate worries that audit agencies could have their independence undermined if, in the name of citizen engagement within oversight bodies, people with hidden agendas find themselves able to disrupt the work of auditors general, ombudspeople, and other government officials.

Capture and Bias as Sources of Accountability Failure

Political institutions that should, in theory, promote accountability of the powerful to the publics in whose name this power is exercised often fail to perform their intended functions. In developing countries, such failures are very often ascribed to corruption. But a closer look at failing accountability institutions, and the human development deprivations they allow to persist, reveals that other factors are at work. It is thus helpful to differentiate the roles of capture and bias in causing accountability failure.

The category of capture contains two types of accountability-depleting phenomena. By far the most prevalent variety of capture is corruption—the illegal use of public power for private gain. A second aspect of capture is represented by other forms of undue influence that may not, according to a strict definition, constitute corruption. In particular, accountability can be undermined when officials subvert decision-making norms as a result of intimidation (from, for instance, politicians and organized crime) rather than from an interest in direct pecuniary gain.

The category of bias refers to practices that are not illegal or motivated by the desire for private benefit but nevertheless involve allocative or regulatory decisions that benefit already advantaged groups. The literature on accountability, especially the quantitative literature, is based mainly on corruption-related nonaccountability. Bias-related failures, however, are equally important in explaining why accountability institutions have not operated in favor of ordinary people.

Corruption

In the field of corruption, the following four distinctions are worth bearing in mind:

1. *Petty versus grand corruption:* Petty corruption consists of the small-time bribes exacted by clerks and other minor officials. Grand corruption covers such transactions as commissions paid to high-level decision makers who award defense contracts.
2. *Systemic versus personalized corruption:* Systemic corruption is corruption that is all but built into official roles (in the sense that illicit income is "required" by officials in order to earn back the amounts expended in order to get themselves appointed to such lucrative posts). Personalized corruption refers to instances in which a rogue official exploits a one-off opportunity for illicit gain (Wade 1985). One reason why this distinction is important is that in local settings, systemic corruption (in which an official has little choice but to take a bribe) can become fairly legitimized when people begin to sympathize with officials who find themselves in such situations. This syndrome can make it more difficult to engage people in the process of seeking to improve the accountability of political institutions at the local level.
3. *Positive versus negative corruption:* Positive corruption occurs when an official actively seeks personal gain from his or her public position. Negative corruption occurs when an official makes biased decisions in order to avoid incurring the wrath of a powerful actor, such as a politician, an official higher up the chain of command, or a private businessperson with connections sufficient to get the official transferred, reprimanded, or even charged with a crime if he or she resists the person's demands. Positive corruption is what this chapter refers to as *corruption*. Negative corruption corresponds to the term *undue influence*.

4. *Corruption with theft versus corruption without theft:* Some cases of corruption impose a loss on the public at large ("with theft"); in other cases the illicit funds are taken from a specific individual or firm, leaving the general public no worse off ("without theft") (Shleifer and Vishny 1993). This distinction can be thought of as the difference between consensual corruption (in which, for instance, a bureaucrat and a contractor collude in the skimming of funds from a public works project) and extortionate corruption (in which someone eligible for an antipoverty benefit must pay an official in order to obtain what should be his or hers by right).

Bias

Accountability institutions also fail the poor through noncorrupt but biased official decision making. Bias-related accountability failures occur when the poor or other socially marginal groups remain disadvantaged because of built-in (or institutionalized) impediments to the reduction of the deprivations they face.

Two main varieties of bias have particularly adverse impacts on marginal groups. The first involves situations in which accountability institutions have no formal remit for addressing injustices experienced by disadvantaged people. This can occur because of inconsistent protection of rights or skewed official performance criteria.

Biases in the wording, interpretation, and enforcement of laws often allow perpetrators who violate the rights of disadvantaged people to escape punishment. The "law of provocation" in the Anglo-Saxon legal tradition, for instance, tends to absolve men who kill in self-defense while severely penalizing women who kill abusive husbands. Other laws and judgments—relating to vagrancy, land tenure, and debt collection, for example—can have built-in biases against the poor.

Many personnel procedures neither punish officials whose actions discriminate against disadvantaged people nor reward those who achieve positive outcomes for them. The accountability systems within health service bureaucracies and the medical professional bodies charged with upholding scientific and ethical standards may not take action, or at least may perceive themselves to be impotent to intervene, because staff have followed formally sanctioned procedures and met professional standards. Health services may be oriented to the needs of better-off members of society, with medical research and clinic treatment protocols privileging attention to the illnesses of the urban middle classes.

The second variety of bias involves access barriers. This type of bias takes two main forms. The first is the biased design of service delivery. Behavior that is procedurally correct may disguise aspects of policy or program design that are biased against underprivileged sections of society. Dominant social groups often find it easier to access higher levels of public services because of unexamined assumptions about their greater efficiency. Staudt's (1978) study of agricultural extension services in East Africa finds that men were favored over women in access to these services, both because men were considered more likely to increase agricultural productivity and because male extension workers found it more convenient to interact with male farmers.

The second type of access barrier has to do with institutions of redressal. A range of antipoor biases is often built into the mechanisms through which citizens are entitled to use accountability mechanisms directly, such as the access restrictions that face litigants seeking judicial remedies against powerful state or nonstate actors. Their testimony may be downgraded by biased judges and juries, or they may have difficulty mastering the skills of literacy and language required for success in these arenas.

All of these forms of bias matter when assessing the contribution of political institutions to promoting accountability. Recognizing that institutions sometimes fail to hold powerful actors to account because of biases rather than capture, policy makers might propose different reform measures, depending on the issue involved. For instance, if various forms of gender bias appear in the laws passed by legislatures that are, in theory, supposed to be accountable to women voters (and to courts charged with ensuring that women are provided equal protection under the law), one approach to institutional reform might be to develop a system of quotas that would provide greater representation for women in legislatures. A similar mechanism with respect to ethnic groups or religious minorities discriminated against (because of bias rather than capture) might also be considered. Such steps are a response to the failure of political institutions to remain accountable to particular constituencies (or accountable for their performance in upholding norms of equal treatment) when these failures are the result primarily of social bias rather than capture.

Formal versus Informal Accountability

The difference between "formal" and "informal" accountability is often invoked in discussions about why political institutions fail to produce accountability to ordinary citizens and where to focus efforts aimed at rectifying these failings.

But it is by no means always clear what is meant by the distinction. At least four meanings of "informal" accountability are currently in use.

1. *Informality as actually existing accountability:* In the real world, there is often a difference between whom one is accountable to according to law or accepted procedure (de jure accountability) and whom one is accountable to in fact, because of his or her power to impose a sanction (de facto accountability). For this reason, the stripped-down definition of accountability used in this chapter does not specify who plays the roles of targets and seekers of accountability. In principle, politicians are answerable to citizens; in practice, they are often more concerned with the sanctions wielded by corporate interests, such as the withdrawal of campaign finance. In aid-dependent developing countries, governments are often perceived to be more accountable to external donors than to domestic institutions, such as parliament, because the withdrawal of international grants and loans, or the threat of doing so if certain actions are not taken, constitutes a serious sanction. The de jure/de facto distinction is meant to differentiate between the official relationship that should exist (according to the law) and the relations that actually exist—relations that tend to subvert formal restraints on the exercise of power.
2. *Informality as a less structured (though still institutional) form of accountability:* This usage refers not to the subversion of official regulations by unofficial relations of power but rather to the less-structured mechanisms of restraint operating within vertical or horizontal accountability institutions. Within vertical institutions, voting in elections is the formal/structured mechanism of accountability used by citizens to discipline politicians. The informal/less-structured mechanism in this vertical channel is lobbying of politicians by citizen associations and the pressure exerted by investigative journalism, both of which contribute to a deeper form of answerability. Along the horizontal axis—that is, within the state—an audit office exercises formal power over the executive. The informal dimension of horizontal accountability is represented by the bureaucratic culture within which officials operate and through which their professional identities become shaped. Where an organizational ethos upholding high standards of probity exists, reputational pressures—an informal mechanism of accountability—can substitute for more formal methods.
3. *Informality as "moral" accountability claims:* This usage denotes efforts to question the very basis of formal accountability relationships that exist in law. It does not seek merely to bring de facto accountability into line with

the de jure relationships. Instead, this type of informality refers to the fact that while no formal rule might require, for instance, a pharmaceutical company to answer to the public at large—its obligations being limited to its shareholders and to regulatory authorities—the reality is that the decisions made by such firms affect the lives of ordinary people, leading many people to seek answers from firms about the long-term effects of their drugs, the biases in the types of diseases to which R&D funds are devoted, and so forth. Consumers can also impose sanctions, through boycotts, negative publicity, and pressure for regulatory change.

4. *Informality as arenas beyond the citizen-state relationship:* This usage stems from Lonsdale's observation that "it is quite possible to have accountability in . . . the high politics of the state, honest rulers and free elections, and yet profound injustice or irresponsibility in the deep politics of society, that is, the relations between rich and poor, powerful and weak" (Lonsdale 1986: 128). Accountability is often seen as irrelevant in relationships within families or ethnic communities, where authority is conferred by age, gender, or lineage rather than delegated by popular consent. Struggles by feminists, religious reformers, and human rights activists to check abuses of power in nonstate arenas are complicated by the reluctance of public authorities to intervene in "private" matters such as intrafamily relationships or religious practice. The subordinate members of these relationships, however, are increasingly subjecting the actions of power-holders to critical scrutiny. That this often involves references to human rights and shifting standards of public probity demonstrates how far the idea of accountability has seeped into institutions beyond the public arena.

Related Concepts of Governance

Accountability is closely related to other concepts of governance, not least in the context of the role of foreign assistance in building institutional capacity. Building domestic accountability is, in a sense, the underlying goal of rule-of-law programs. The rule of law refers to the primacy of fixed procedures over discretion. Ensuring that there is scrutiny of official decision making, and that enforcement action is taken to punish poor or biased decision making, is the means by which the rule of law becomes entrenched.

Accountability is also central to human rights reform and the restructuring of various types of institutional reform. It is more encompassing than the concept of rights. It has become the language of demand making, applicable even in nondemocratic systems. Whether or not human rights, the rule of law, or new aid relationships are in effect, it is essential for all relevant actors to base their programs of institutional reform on a clear analysis of the nature of various accountability relationships, from public expenditure systems to the internal workings of anticorruption agencies. Doing so can help clarify the incentives facing various institutional actors and highlight the potential relevance of methods for improving outcomes.

Accountability also needs to be distinguished from two other much-used terms: responsiveness and responsibility. Responsiveness is the desired attitude of power-holders toward citizens: officials should be responsive to the concerns and problems of ordinary people, to listen with impartiality and fairness to divergent views, and to subject all expressions of need and interest to publicly agreed rules for weighing the merits of competing claims. Conventionally, public sector actors have a duty to be responsive to the members of the public with whom they interact but to account for their actions to their managers, who in turn account to the legislature and the executive, to financial auditors, and to higher court judges (Blair 2000).

The idea of responsibility is closely related to accountability. Like accountability, it is characterized by the lack of formal compulsion. An actor may feel responsible for taking action to improve the lot of poor people but may not be obliged to account for his or her actions or nonactions. Responsibility corresponds closely to the notion of moral accountability—being accountable to other people by virtue of a shared humanity rather than because of some formally stipulated contract that can be enforced according to an agreed set of standards. That businesses speak of corporate social responsibility rather than corporate accountability is not a mere difference of terminology. It reflects a belief that measures taken to mitigate the ill effects of business activity fall into the category of voluntary action.

Another important distinction is that between the general idea of accountability and specific versions of accountability, such as financial accountability, legal accountability, and so forth. The modifiers used in such formulations are not always consistent or helpful. For instance, financial accountability refers to the domain of activity engaged in by the target of accountability rather than any particular variation in the nature of the target-seeker relationship as such. In contrast, legal accountability refers to the nature of the instruments applicable to evaluating the domain of activity. The types of accountability are not mutually exclusive categories: financial accountability is governed by the principles enshrined in legal accountability, as well as by whatever conception of moral accountability (outside the purview of legal norms) may govern the actions of the actors involved.

Similarly, a distinction is often drawn between political and administrative accountability. The World Bank uses the following definition of *political accountability*: "Political accountability refers to the constraints placed on the behavior of public officials by organizations and constituencies with the power to apply sanctions on them. As political accountability increases, the costs to public officials of taking decisions that benefit their private interests at the expense of the broader public interest also increase, thus working as a deterrent/disincentive to corrupt practices" (http://www1.worldbank.org/publicsector/anticorrupt/political accountability.htm). In this respect, political accountability is almost impossible to distinguish from accountability in general. It refers neither to the nature of the official (elected or administrative) nor to the nature of the source of accountability seeking (horizontal or vertical).

The lesson of this terminological confusion is that while context affects the nature of accountability, seeking to categorize accountability with the use of adjectival prefixes does little to enhance understanding. It is preferable to ensure that the stakeholders working to improve the effectiveness of political institutions work from a basic common understanding of what accountability is in general and the elements that go into making a functioning accountability system.

Institutions: Functions, Pitfalls, and Innovative Remedies

Applying these concepts and distinctions to specific institutions is necessary to make sense of why real accountability (tight control of principals over their agents, the ability of seekers to discipline their targets) is so often lacking in actually existing democracies. It is important to emphasize, however, that these individual institutions are embedded within a larger system. How each functions affects the others.

Elections

Democratic elections even in mature democracies, such as France or India, often fail to create incentives for representatives to promote the interests of the poor. But why? A realistic attempt to survey the accountability landscape must assess the relative role played by six factors in any given country context, as well as the viability of taking programmatic action to bring about improvements in each:

1. *Multiple issue cleavages:* Voting is a blunt instrument with which to hold principals to account for their actions. Unless every decision is to be held

to a public referendum, electorates will have to make an overall assessment of a government's performance, allowing governments (agents) to get away with a great deal of poor (or even corrupt) decision making as long as enough voters agree with their actions on matters of greatest importance to them. In the absence of a popular referendum for each policy decision—or even each policy domain—voters must select governments that take actions across a broad range of controversial issues. A voter might agree with a party on some of its policy positions but is unlikely to agree on them all.

2. *Information asymmetry:* Voters are almost by definition not fully aware of the conditions under which government decisions are made or even about what governments actually decide, to say nothing of the outcomes of these decisions. Even when governments are not especially secretive, voters do not possess the information necessary to evaluate the performance of their public representatives; there is a limit to how informed even a vigilant citizen can be.

3. *The myth of retrospective accountability:* Some scholars argue that elections are not primarily a mechanism of retrospective accountability at all (Fearon 1999). When voters exercise their franchise, they are selecting what they believe will be a good government rather than enforcing a sanction on the incumbent government. This is partly because of an implicit or explicit understanding on the part of voters that the circumstances under which government policy is made are likely to change between successive "mandates." This undermines a purist notion of democratic accountability. Voter surveys—on issues such as the levels of perceived corruption among incumbent governments—indicate that voters cast their ballots as much on what they think a government will do in the future as on what the government did in the past. Governments have considerable discretion in framing future choices in ways that make them, and not their opponents, appear the most promising alternative.

4. *Clientelism:* The ties between elite patrons and lower-status people in clientelist systems can prevent voters from punishing errant politicians at election time, for fear of losing whatever benefits they receive as loyal clients. When voters despair of ever electing a government that will be sufficiently responsive to and effective in overhauling entrenched decision-making systems, they are likely to give their vote to the party deemed most likely to provide them a discretionary benefit—an individual subsidy entitlement (such as a government-supplied house) or a collective benefit to their locality (such as a road). They do this instead of supporting the party with the most appealing program of governance reform. In such a situation, patronage politics can be said to have triumphed over

programmatic politics. Like most vicious cycles, this is a very difficult situation to escape: incentives are strongly weighted in favor of obtaining a benefit (no matter how small) in the short term rather than holding out for systemic change that will materialize only much later (if at all).

5. *History, culture, and social structure:* Social cleavages often prevent poor people from using the ballot box as a form of sanction, even where they are a majority of voters. Where voters are polarized around issues of identity (ethnicity, caste, race, religion, sect), politicians can evade accountability for their failure to deliver services and justice to the poor. This polarization is often a product of a long-term process of identity formation, abetted by state actors as well as social forces.

6. *Credibility:* In young democracies, in which few parties have a credible record of achievement on broad poverty-reduction programs, political contenders often seek electoral advantage by developing and rewarding client loyalty through targeted spending (Keefer 2002). It is difficult for voters to coordinate in assigning rewards or penalties to politicians for performance in public services, particularly primary health care and education, because these services are complex and outcomes are hard to attribute to any one representative's (or government's) term in office. As a result, voters tend to give more credit to politicians for initiating public works projects (such as construction), providing direct subsidies for essential commodities (food and fertilizer), and increasing employment in the public sector. These sorts of public resources are most easily and directly targeted to supporters.

In addition, many countries have legally permissible avenues for influence peddling that are beyond the reach of the poor, such as lax campaign finance regulations or professionalized lobbying industries. Campaign finance laws are an important way of seeking to improve the accountability of elected officials to ordinary voters by limiting the ability of wealthy individuals or special interests to fund candidates who work to advance their agendas.

Voters in many countries are right to feel cynical about reforms to electoral and campaign finance systems that seem to have no impact on the rate at which politicians accumulate illicit earnings in office. Measures requiring parliamentarians to declare their personal assets may come with confidentiality provisions that keep that information away from the ordinary citizen. Efforts by electoral commissions to proscribe parties that engage in criminal activity or violence or to prevent politicians with criminal records from taking up their parliamentary seats may be desultory, delayed by years of legal proceedings, or directly subverted by judges who have been intimidated by criminal politicians.

Once elected, representatives can easily elude citizen demands. The link between representatives and ordinary citizens is so tentative (most legislators pay far more attention to ingratiating themselves to those above them than to the people below) and representatives often seem so little concerned about voters' sanctions (ex post accountability) that much stronger ex ante controls on the quality of parties and politicians are needed to enable voters to identify scoundrels before they get into office.

Augmenting the capacity of electoral bodies as institutions of accountability is an area that has undergone significant innovation in recent years. Nongovernmental groups have shown themselves capable of filling many gaps left by government institutions that are underfunded, riddled with corruption or partisan favoritism (a form of bias), or insufficiently independent (box 5.1). The monitoring of elections can involve the use of external actors from intergovernmental organizations (such as the Organization for Security and Cooperation in Europe or the Commonwealth), an option available not just to states whose international democratic reputation is seriously tarnished but to any country seeking additional resources with which to support a poorly functioning state apparatus.

More frequently, innovations in accountability processes related to the monitoring of elections involve domestic nongovernmental actors. Nongovernmental actors can engage in a range of activities to ensure accountability in this crucial element of representative democracy. Nongovernmental organizations (NGOs) can scrutinize the documentation filed in support of candidate nominations, even if the final determination of eligibility is retained by state entities. Where electoral rules require candidates to disclose their assets and disclose whether they have ever been charged with or convicted of criminal wrongdoing, NGOs can augment a state's capacity to verify claims or prove them false or at the very least, collate and publicize the candidates' statements in order to allow voters the chance to deliberate on their likely veracity.

Nongovernmental actors working in collaboration with state agencies can also take part in monitoring campaign and postcampaign activities involving both process and content. On the process side, NGOs can be trained to monitor and report to competent authorities on campaign expenditure within geographic districts (based on agreed indicators, consultation with suppliers, and quantification of campaign inputs such as vehicles, advertising support, and so forth). With respect to content, NGOs can collate information on candidate policy statements, campaign pledges, and party manifesto commitments, publicizing this information in accessible formats. During balloting, NGOs can be empowered to remain stationed at voting

BOX 5.1 Citizen Efforts to Improve the Electoral Process in Argentina and the United States

Citizens in Argentina have taken on some of the roles of a horizontal state accountability agency, such as an electoral commission, through the Poder Ciudadano, a civil society association dedicated to fostering cleaner political competition. The Poder Ciudadano monitors campaign finance norms, disseminates information about the assets of politicians, and accumulates evidence that can be used to expose political corruption. It has "filled the vacuum left by government institutions that were supposed to bring transparency to the electoral process but failed" (Manzetti 2000: 35).

To develop mechanisms of citizen control in elections, the Poder Ciudadano first created a database of Argentine politicians, including their professional profiles and political platforms. It then launched a project aimed at "full-fledged financial disclosure of electoral campaigns for the Federal District's city council (1997 and 2000) and for presidential elections" (Manzetti 2000: 35). This kind of transparency, which included declarations of personal assets by candidates, did not in itself provide all of the elements of accountability. But it did add an increased element of answerability to complement the process by which ordinary people could exercise an enforcement mechanism—in the form of voter choice—over their elected representatives. In this sense, the project represented a substantial step toward making "politicians more accountable to public opinion by requiring them to comply with normative standards of democratic governance . . . turning what has traditionally been either a passive or partisan voter into an informed citizen" (Manzetti 2000: 35). Moreover, the data on personal assets could then serve as baseline information against which successful candidates' financial rectitude could subsequently be assessed by comparing their assets before election with those held after a term in office.

The Poder Ciudadano also created a methodology for monitoring campaign spending. This is ordinarily a job for an electoral commission, but where such institutions are not fulfilling this important function, a space is created for nonstate actors to assume these duties—sometimes in partnership with the state, sometimes in a bid to shame the relevant state institutions into performing their appointed functions more effectively (Manzetti 2000).

Voter education efforts elsewhere, such as the high-profile Project Votesmart in Oregon, in the United States, have not gone as far as the Poder Ciudadano in publicizing details of campaign financing or exposing excessive rates of asset accumulation by politicians. Project Votesmart created a database on more than 13,000 elected officials and candidates for office in the United States. This information covers officials' and candidates' backgrounds, issue positions, voting records, and campaign finance reports, as well as performance evaluations submitted by more than 100 conservative to liberal interest groups.

> Unlike Poder Ciudadano, Project Votesmart does not engage politicians directly by asking them to declare their assets or make commitments to probity. Instead, it seeks to improve political accountability by giving citizens and the media the information they need to sanction politicians for poor decision making or criminal behavior.
>
> Disappointingly, evaluations of Project Votesmart show that access to better information on the behavior of politicians had little to no short-term effect on voter mobilization among socially excluded groups (Steel, Pierce, and Lovrich 1998). Its failure to do so reflects the fact that information alone is insufficient to alter the social conditions that produce either political alienation or clientelist relationships, in which poor people vote on the basis of material inducements or social pressures exerted by powerful patrons. Indeed, research on democratic processes in developed countries shows that voters react to evidence about corruption in politics by becoming more fatalistic and apathetic about the value of political participation, increasingly refusing to vote (Pharr and Putnam 2000). Ex post controls on politicians (voting them out of office) do not necessarily operate more effectively when good information about their conduct in office is available to voters. Voter education is at best only a weak "answerability" tool, because it neither engages citizens more directly in public decision making nor reviews of spending nor ties information disclosures to investigative processes.

stations, to accompany ballot boxes to counting centers (or to keep watch over voting machines and data processing centers), and to observe counting along with political agents of the candidates and election officials.

All of these roles require the active collaboration of the civil service, a clear set of guidelines, multiple NGOs to prevent partisan favoritism, and extensive training. While there are risks to creating hybrid state-civic mechanisms for improving electoral accountability (as discussed below), there is considerable scope for such work to not only improve the conduct of elections (and therefore the accountability of elected officials) but also to energize civil society more generally, educate the public about the functions of specialized accountability institutions, and reduce the gap between people and their representatives.

The controls that voters exercise over politicians once in office are so weak, and the collusion of opposition legislators with the plans of a corrupt executive so cheaply purchased, that there are great limits to how much citizen engagement can improve political accountability. Substantial alteration of legal and constitutional frameworks is needed to produce more direct answerability of politicians to citizens, an alteration that might create formal institutional space for civil society groups in government, as is the case with corporatist constitutional arrangements. Short of such radical measures, citizens have found it possible to engage in other institutions of public oversight to considerable effect, as shown below.

Legislatures

In theory, legislatures should be the forum in which government policy is reviewed, the performance of the executive checked, and the detailed operations of key government functions—in particular, public expenditure management—put under intensive scrutiny. Legislatures are notoriously open to capture, however, through both "party discipline," which often involves subtle forms of unwarranted inducement (such as undue rewards for compliant legislators), and the buying of individual legislators by sectoral interest groups or even wealthy individuals.

Forms of bias are also evident. Institutional design often militates against deliberation on certain types of issues of concern to disadvantaged people. For example, the British House of Lords, until recently dominated by large landholders, long thwarted reform of property laws that would have given tenants greater rights in relation to property "freeholders." The U.S. Senate—to which each state, regardless of its population, elects two senators—gives disproportionate voice to agribusiness and ranching interests based in sparsely populated western states.

Accountability in parliamentary and presidential systems

Systems for representing the popular will differ in a variety of ways. Perhaps the most obvious is the difference between presidential systems, in which the chief executive is directly elected, and parliamentary systems, in which the chief executive is chosen from among the assembled elected representatives. This difference can be found not just at the national level but at the subnational (state or provincial) and even local levels, where features of institutional design are just as consequential.

In theory, a presidential system provides a primary locus of democratic accountability. A directly elected representative under whose direction a range of executive agencies operates is in a position to ensure a kind of overall accountability, making adjustments and tradeoffs, where necessary, in order to achieve results consistent with a broad understanding of the popular mandate. In a parliamentary system, executives can be "recalled" at short notice through a vote of no confidence. Whether at the village level, where elected councils in some countries have been granted and have exercised this power, or at the national level, where threats of parliamentary action can serve to channel popular outrage into direct influence on the executive, parliamentary systems of representation are able to keep governments on a short leash.

In practice, things are often different. In presidential systems the chief executive is often greatly hemmed in by an inability to forge agreement with a legislature controlled by a rival party or faction. This can lead to paralysis and the failure of government at various levels to fulfill its mandates. With each branch of government blaming the other, there is little real accountability. Chief executives in parliamentary systems are able to cow legislatures through skillful use of incentives: dangling the prospect of an important executive posting, supporting spending in the parliamentarian's home constituency. A prime minister can also wield threats of his or her own.

Rule-making and oversight functions

Legislatures make laws. They codify the rules concerning what constitutes an acceptable standard of accountability. They do so by crafting the content of the rules and by establishing the means by which rules are developed. Laws that are vague, full of loopholes, or lacking in fully specified penalties (or remedies obtainable by citizens who suffer executive abuses) provide avenues of discretion for officials. The result is often corruption and the subversion of accountability.

Representative bodies are expected to debate the advisability of rule changes in ways that not only provide a forum for interest groups to pursue their interests but also frame issues in ways that indicate what is considered minimally acceptable behavior in the conduct of official business. In theory, this should help evolve collective norms against which citizens can hold their representatives accountable, through elections or other means.

Keohane (2002) notes the need for agents to account to their principals for "proposed or past behavior." This can be thought of as the distinction between ex ante and ex post accountability. Most understandings of accountability refer only to ex post, or retrospective, accountability—the need for agents to answer questions from principals about their past actions. When this notion is expanded to include ex ante, or prospective, accountability, the possibility of keeping officials more firmly tied to the needs and wishes of citizens emerges. It is through constant engagement on public issues that legislatures can shift accountability seeking toward the ex ante end of the spectrum. Doing so is critical, because once a decision has done its damage, it is often too late to provide restorative justice.

Committee systems: information, capacity, and participation

Support from donor agencies for parliamentary institutions has a long history in the development field. Such support has taken place both through official donor agencies and the party-linked "endowments" found in, for instance, German and U.S. aid programs. The idea is to increase the capacity of microinstitutions within legislatures to perform their tasks more effectively. The assumption often is that bodies such as parliamentary clerks' offices, party caucuses, ethics panels, and sectoral committee systems are underresourced. Another view is that they lack the systematic access to relevant information necessary to effective deliberation. There is also a concern that the rules governing appointments to committees (which often leave party managers with enormous discretion to transfer particularly inquisitive parliamentarians out of committees) are stacked against those who would use such appointments to provide accountability of the executive.

Formal efforts to improve the accountability functions of political institutions such as parliaments focus on enabling elected politicians to hold the executive to account. Conventional reforms in these areas include finance and audit acts that focus on strengthening the hand of the legislature through access to detailed monthly reports on actual expenditure, capacity building to aid the deciphering of budgets, or mechanisms to restrain off-budget expenditure. Citizen efforts to participate in processes designed to cast light on departmental operations or off-the-books spending can strengthen the hand of crusading legislators by demonstrating popular demand for probity (box 5.2).

> **BOX 5.2 Civil Society Achievements in Mexico, South Africa, and Zambia**
>
> The sleuthing and publicizing work of the Mexican civil society group FUNDAR, within a broad-based network called the Civic Alliance, helped bring an end to the use of a presidential secret account that operated independently of congressional approval (Krafchik 2001). After a sustained campaign, the group was able to have the secret fund abolished and other measures to improve budget transparency put in place.
>
> South Africa's parliamentary committees are transparent and accessible to the public, going so far as to hold hearings in remote locations in order to overcome the mobility and time constraints of poor people. While these steps are positive, the right to make submissions to parliamentary committees keeps civil society in a weak "information-provision" role; no submission is guaranteed a full hearing or investigation, and civil society groups are not guaranteed full access to the information on which legislators make their decisions.
>
> Civil society groups have also been active in Zambia. In 2000 they provoked unprecedented moves by parliament to lift the president's immunity from prosecution, freeze the presidential discretionary fund, and publicize the assets of members of parliament (www.state.gov/e/eb/ifd/2005/42202.htm).

In addition, there has been an increasing tendency in recent years to develop new institutional means of exercising oversight over legislative activities. These include direct participation of citizens and their associations. One of the most well known is the participatory budget process in various municipalities in Brazil (box 5.3).

> **BOX 5.3** Does Participatory Budgeting Increase Accountability in Brazil?
>
> In Brazil the Workers Party has been promoting participatory budgeting at the municipal level since 1988. The process gives groups of citizens a direct say in how local funds are spent and institutionalizes their role in monitoring the execution of public works and reviewing actual spending. It has tended to be most effective where the Workers Party has been in charge of city government, particularly in Porto Alegre and Belo Horizonte.
>
> Participatory budgeting is a multistep annual exercise involving city residents both directly and through neighborhood representatives in a cascading system of public assemblies and sectoral committees. These bodies establish spending priorities for basic capital investments (paved roads, drainage and sewage, school construction) in their own neighborhoods.
>
> Citizen engagement in monitoring public works has led to much higher levels of efficiency in executing physical projects (Navarro 1998). Whether this system endows participants with the legal and technical capacity to audit past expenditures remains unclear from published accounts. While "reviews" of previous budgets are conducted at the beginning of each planning year, the process is undertaken at huge assembly meetings and therefore does not permit the degree of disaggregation necessary to audit the many spending decisions involved in capital projects. Also unclear is how far spending information is broken down, whether participants have a right to demand spending details for every project, and the extent to which the monitoring of public works involves close inspection of the quality of the inputs, their technical appropriateness, and other relevant factors by members of the Participatory Budget Council, which is responsible for assembling the municipal budget.
>
> Recent research has found additional problems with augmenting formal institutional accountability with these kinds of methods. While expanding citizens' roles in participatory decision making can bring them more directly into key processes, "these institutions could also undermine municipal councils' ability to curb the prerogatives of mayors" (Wampler 2004: 79), hindering the capacity of an elected representative body to undertake key accountability functions. "Mayors have differing capacities to implement their policy preferences, and this greatly affects how accountability may be extended" (Wampler 2004: 82).

Political Parties

The impact of electoral rules

It is very difficult to pin down the influence of specific institutional differences on the patterns of accountability generated by political institutions, because there are many possible combinations of different variables. A presidential system, for example, can use a single-member simple-plurality system or any one of several proportional representation voting systems. Different party structures can exist within each of these various permutations. Moreover, relations with other kinds of accountability actors (such as civil society and the judiciary) can have a significant impact on the ultimate outcomes achieved.

Bowen and Rose-Ackerman (2002: 202) find that "if party discipline is relatively high in a presidential system and if courts and civil society are weak, then executive oversight will be relatively more politicized"—that is, more likely to operate along party lines. The downside of this outcome is that efforts to produce accountability—including specific charges of malfeasance—can be more easily dismissed as motivated by political gain. This proposition is supported by the experience of Argentina, a presidential system with closed-list proportional representation, where corruption investigations are easily branded partisan. In contrast, oversight of the executive tends to be significantly less partisan in Brazil, which has a presidential system with open-list proportional representation; in Germany, which has a parliamentary system; and in the United States, which has a presidential system and single-member simple-plurality system. Investigation into the qualitative dimensions of politics in these kinds of countries would be required to derive more sensitive conclusions of relevance to other national contexts.

The importance of the larger civil society context

Conceptually, political parties are usually located outside of civil society, in a domain sometimes referred to as "political society" (the distinction resting on the fact that parties, while nonstate entities, seek direct control over state institutions). But the nature of the civil society context within which they operate is of fundamental importance to their ability to act as political institutions capable of securing democratic accountability.

In some places many of the largest "civic groups" are in fact functional associations affiliated with major political parties. These groups have been a major feature of India's civil society, for instance. The ability of these groups to act independently is often constrained: the numerous organizations connected to almost every political party—the women's wings, student federations, trade unions, farmers associations—have usually lacked autonomy.[2] In this respect, ironically, India resembled authoritarian regimes such as Indonesia and Vietnam. When NGOs were legalized in these countries in the early 1990s, one of the main challenges they faced was to pry themselves loose "from the state-controlled mass organizations to which they are loosely affiliated" (Clarke 1996: 6).

The ability of civil society organizations to contribute to the accountability function played by political institutions such as parties depends on various structural features of civil society. Scholte (2004) identifies six features that influence the ability of civil society to make this kind of contribution:

1. Resources, including but not limited to financial backing
2. The social and political networks within which civic groups are embedded
3. The attitudes of official institutions with which they must interact
4. The nature and composition of the media on which groups rely for amplifying their messages and exposing any misdeeds their research and investigations may identify
5. The prevailing political culture ("the established ways that questions concerning the acquisition, allocation and exercise of power are handled in a given social context")
6. The accountability of civil society itself.

While Scholte focuses on the processes of global governance, these features are applicable to domestic policy domains as well. It is not difficult to grasp the importance of the relation between political parties and civil society in determining the ability of civil society to undertake the four roles that Scholte sees as possible for civil society in promoting accountability: increasing public transparency of governance operations, monitoring and reviewing policies, seeking redress for mistakes and harms attributable to public authorities, and advancing the creation of formal accountability mechanisms.

Specialized Accountability Institutions

In theory, specialized accountability institutions are meant to be separate and distinct from political institutions—indeed, this is supposed to be one of their great advantages in promoting greater accountability. In practice, they are often captured by partisan elites. For this reason they are a necessary element in this chapter's discussion of the role of political institutions in improving accountability.

The autonomy of investigative agencies

There are as many difficulties with horizontal channels of accountability as there are with vertical channels: institutions of oversight are as ineffective in producing real accountability as elections are. While many of these difficulties stem from the peculiarities of institutional design, the central problem is that horizontal institutions of accountability are themselves agents working on behalf of principals (ordinary people), who have difficulty keeping track of them. It is therefore not surprising that the same principal-agent problems that afflict the relationship between people and their governments are found in the relationship between people and the oversight institutions allegedly working to keep political and bureaucratic agents in check.

There are considerable incentives for auditors charged with keeping tabs on government doctors, for instance, to collude with those over whom they are supposed to exercise oversight: in exchange for allowing abuses to go unpunished, auditors can obtain a share of the rewards enjoyed by doctors who abuse their authority (by charging patients for treatment that should be free, by stealing medicines and selling them on the black market). Horizontal institutions, while a necessary element in a democratic political system, end up begging the perennial question "who will watch the watchdog?"

Australia, Hong Kong (China), South Africa, Sweden, and Uganda have had varying degrees of success using dedicated horizontal channels of accountability provision (Coldham 1995). Countries in the early stages of the transition to a more liberal form of politics, especially those emerging from civil conflict, face additional hurdles to making such institutions work effectively.

El Salvador and Guatemala are among the countries in this category that have sought to build institutions to support the rule of law (Dodson and Jackson 2004). The judicial branch of government in both countries was widely seen as riddled with corruption and open to political influence along partisan lines. This undermined one of the key institutions responsible for checking the abuse of power by executive bodies and the legislature (including the legislature's own specialized accountability agencies, such as the public accounts committee).

To pick up the slack, a new agency, the Human Rights Ombudsman (HRO), was created in each of the two countries. Partly as a result of the way in which the agencies were created, they were likely to be undermined by many of the same ills that caused existing bodies in El Salvador and Guatemala to fail (Dodson and Jackson 2004). The reasons for failure varied. In El Salvador rather than lacking independence (a frequent institutional shortcoming of such bodies), the HRO may have been too isolated: "the ombudsman's office drifted towards becoming an island within the Public Ministry" (Dodson and Jackson 2004: 2). In Guatemala the main problem appeared to be the indifference of key players rather than outright hostility. This indifference emerged in a context in which organized and sporadic violence was on the rise after a number of years of relative calm.

Despite their differences, the structure of government in both El Salvador and Guatemala shared two common problems. The first was the "legacy of centralized, compartmentalized bureaucratic authority [which] remains an obstacle to creating horizontal accountability" (Dodson and Jackson 2004: 15). The second was, ironically, the weakness of the judiciary itself: without courts to back up the HROs' constitutional authority when prosecuting cases, there was little chance of these bodies fulfilling their mandate to fill the accountability void left by compromised judiciaries.

The politicization of specialized agencies

Oversight or regulatory agencies often fail to take action to investigate abuses of power in the public or private bodies over which they exercise jurisdiction, for reasons of both capture and bias. Audit offices, environmental protection agencies, electoral commissions, equal opportunities bodies, labor standards offices, and even anticorruption commissions can underperform in response to capture by political leaders or interest groups. The nominal independence of these specialized accountability institutions is undermined in practice when governments fill them with people who will turn a blind eye to official malpractice, either because the people in question are themselves biased or because they seek undue rewards. Oversight bodies designed to preserve professional standards, such as medical or teaching associations, may fail to demand answers of public authorities (including those in their profession acting in a public capacity) because of internalized and largely unremarked biases that prevent detection of certain types of abuses, such as abuses of the rights of subordinated groups.

Judiciaries suffer from capture when court officials subvert official operating procedures to benefit bribe-payers or when judges lack autonomy from the political executive and respond to political agendas. Biases are built into judicial proceedings. Their formal impartiality offers little protection for the poor when access is limited by their inability to purchase legal representation, travel to court locations, or understand the language spoken in judicial proceedings. More insidious and less obvious biases are also common: courts routinely discount the testimony of certain categories of plaintiff, such as women or the poor, especially when they press charges against powerful social actors. Elite biases are reflected when crimes committed

> **BOX 5.4** Political Interference in Prosecuting Corruption in Malawi
>
> Fairly clear-cut cases of corruption were put on hold in Malawi in 2001–02 because of executive intervention. The partisan behavior of the Speaker of Parliament, who hailed from the ruling party, further undermined confidence in legislative oversight as a tool of accountability. The Public Accounts Committee of Parliament compiled its first serious reports on the misuse of government funds. Its findings were not acted upon by the relevant enforcement agencies.
>
> This syndrome is not confined to Malawi. When aid-dependent countries are pushed to crack down on corruption, it is often those who are out of political favor that become scapegoats. This hardly reinforces the idea of the impartial rule of law.
>
> *Source:* Jenkins and Tsoka 2003.

largely by the poor, such as petty theft, are investigated with more alacrity than are elite crimes, such as tax evasion. More important, the work of these state accountability agencies is still very much constrained by political interference from the executive (box 5.4).

Civil Service Accountability and the Political Process

Reporting and management systems in the civil service make subordinates accountable to their superiors. The result is often capture. Under pressure to please their bosses, lower-level officials—regardless of their inclinations—are often obliged to collude in the abuse of public office in order to retain their jobs, to avoid punishment transfers, or even to ensure that they are not themselves charged with corruption. Classic abuses include buying and selling positions in bureaucratic hierarchies, obtaining undeserved promotions, and subverting competitive procurement procedures. All of the mechanisms provide officials with illicit income.

Antipoor biases pervade various aspects of accountability systems within public bureaucracies. Without a direct or explicit mandate to serve the poor, even well-intentioned officials who seek to do so may find it impossible to work against the grain of official incentives (as opposed to political pressures, which would constitute capture) that compel them to focus on other, better-connected constituencies.

The consequence of these forms of bias and capture is that putatively public goods, even those as basic as the maintenance of law and order, can be dispensed as favors rather than as entitlements, making citizens not rights-holders but supplicants. Public expenditure management systems that make only notional connections between the spending proposals of line ministries and actual spending patterns, that fail to prevent extrabudgetary spending on the military or perks for top politicians, and that lack adequate auditing mechanisms to expose these deviations are examples of the capture of public resources. While outright capture can itself cause ex ante resource scarcities, elite biases in decisions about how to allocate limited resources can also be the cause of antipoor distortions in public spending. Decisions about taxation and the mobilization of resources may favor the wealthy but result in inadequate revenue for the polity in general. These kinds of biases in the management of public finances may go entirely unchecked in formal audits because they represent sanctioned expenditure, not theft.

One way of overcoming some of these problems is through results-oriented management schemes, in which promotion and pay increases are linked to specific outcomes. These programs can also be abused, through favoritism or a failure to fund them sufficiently.

It should, in theory, be possible to overcome the subversion of performance-contract and results-based-management-type systems by instituting additional layers of oversight.[3] Civil service commissions are one example of a mechanism for counteracting the political subversion of performance-based management reforms. The idea is that decisions about how civil servants are assessed should be left to a completely independent commission composed of people who are immunized from political pressure. This model is followed in many countries, with the extent of the civil service commission's powers varying enormously. In some cases they are responsible mainly for recruitment to the civil service, setting norms and implementing examinations. Occasionally, they play a role in determining terms and conditions of employment, in which case they help determine what constitutes acceptable performance.

In the past several years, efforts have been undertaken to endow some civil service commissions with a more prominent role. In the process of seeking to create an institutional environment within which its Poverty Reduction Strategy could effectively be implemented, the government of Malawi (with assistance from the World Bank and other donors) began to examine additional means of improving its system of public expenditure management. By 2001–02 public expenditure management reform had been in process for several years, with very mixed results. The government's own Medium-Term Expenditure Framework review identified a range of problems (Government of Malawi 2000). The most important of these was that patterns of actual expenditure often bore little resemblance to the budget. Shifting spending between budget heads was a frequent occurrence.

Expenditure ceilings were violated with impunity and on a regular basis by line ministries and other government agencies.

Reforms that delve deep into the institutional substructure of financial management were proposed in Malawi's 2001 Public Expenditure Review. These included performance contracts for senior civil servants linking personal emoluments to their ability to adhere to proper financial management practices. But policy makers recognized that this would not go far enough. Another World Bank proposal was to expand the role of the Malawi Public Service Commission, as a way of insulating senior officials from political pressures exerted by powerful forces in the ruling party and cabinet. Government officials, including the finance minister, openly embraced the need for such changes (though not always agreeing with the details of specific World Bank proposals) and agreed to implement some of them as part of Bank and International Monetary Fund lending arrangements. The results require further analysis.

While these innovations represent an attempt to bring fresh thinking to a chronic problem, they encounter an intractable obstacle: it is very difficult to devise a mechanism to ensure that public service commissioners will be as independent as is necessary. If the powers of the commissioners to override political decisions are substantial, politicians will naturally seek to fill these posts with pliable people—perhaps even people who are themselves corrupt and therefore easily manipulated by threats of exposure.

Economic Liberalization and the Reduction in Clientelism

Liberal economic reform is commonly considered a key ingredient in any recipe to undermine clientelism. Market-based reform is supposed to strike at the heart of the political machines through which electoral support is cultivated. By this logic, clientelist relationships—in which the government machinery is used to reward those who supported (or are likely to support) the winning party—are undermined by the relative decline in the state's involvement in economic decision making and the concomitant rise of market forces.

To understand how clientelism may or may not be affected by shifts in the economic policy regime in ways that improve accountability, it is necessary to devise a more complex model of patron-client relations than is often used, one that considers a much wider array of influences. Although, as Waterbury (1977: 329) argues, "one cannot advance irrefutable, generally accepted criteria by which to establish what patronage is and when (not to mention how) it becomes something else," it is nevertheless important to identify as many facets of the phenomenon as possible. At a minimum, a model of how clientelism is changing in response to liberal economic reforms should incorporate, and therefore reflect an appreciation of, the five factors outlined below.

Expenditure and nonexpenditure forms of patronage

Discussions of the relative opportunities for patrons to engage clients in reciprocal political relationships tend to focus on the delivery of material benefits, usually in the form of access to goods and services distributed through large government programs, such as employment-generation schemes, house-building subsidies, and credit programs. Because these are measurable goods, they offer a useful proxy for the degree of discretionary control available to state officials and their political bosses. There are also rules for how these schemes are implemented, which indicate the number and type of individuals involved, the period over which expenditures are made, and even the location and profile of beneficiaries. Government jobs are a classic form of patronage, routinely steered toward supporters of the politicians with a say over who gets hired.

Other types of discretionary decision making can be as important, if not more so, to the maintenance of patron-client ties between politicians and voters. At the local level, for example, the police can be used to favor political followers. The use of this kind of nonexpenditure form of patronage goes well beyond the police, however, to include the larger set of institutions required to administer the law and resolve disputes. The management of labor disputes, for instance, is an extremely important service that patrons can provide on behalf of their clients. To the extent that economic reforms create frictions that require adjudication—formal or informal—between competing claimants for resources, opportunities for mediation arise that may help substitute for some of what is lost in terms of the capacity to direct state patronage in biased ways to political followers.

The changing role of intermediaries in patron-client relationships

The nature of patron-client relationships can vary, and it can be influenced by various factors. Khan notes the numbers of potential clients, which can affect their success in organizing collective action in bargaining with patrons, as well as the homogeneity of clients. Relatively heterogeneous client groups may present higher transaction costs for patrons, leading to a preference for more homogeneous groups, "even if others may notionally have been willing to pay more" (Khan 1998: 25). He also cites the institutions through which patrons and clients interact and the relative power of patrons and clients.

Better understanding of the crucial link political fixers play in subverting accountability can provide clues to the way clientelism may be changing as a result of economic reform. Krishna's (2002) research on India is potentially useful in fleshing out what are often rather stripped-down models of clientelist politics. More complex models should also make it easier to appreciate changes in the operation of clientelist politics and links between any such changes and wider shifts in economic policy.

Political intermediaries play two different roles. They work as "administrative fixers" (dealing with government business on behalf of individuals) and "political brokers" (extracting promises from politicians in exchange for a group's collective vote). These roles can also be seen as functions relating to retail and wholesale politics. Rather than asking, in any given country context, whether clientelism is on the decline, one can ask whether shifts are evident in one or the other of these two roles for clientelism's intermediaries.

It could be hypothesized, for instance, that if economic reform reduces the discretionary power of elected and bureaucratic officials, the two roles will change in tandem. For example, the relationship between a local intermediary (as political broker) and the elected representative will influence the intermediary's access to the state bureaucracy and therefore his or her performance as an administrative fixer. Other intervening variables may also affect the degree to which such a relation between the two roles might hold true.

A second issue is the extent to which traditional elites monopolize both the administrative fixer and political broker sectors and nonelites face high barriers to entry. While ridding a political system of fixers entirely is optimal, opening up the market for "fixer" services to nontraditional players may be a step in the right direction. Indeed, this commonly happens when societies are democratized and access to education and social mobility spreads. The resultant liberalization of the market for fixers can come as a boon to consumers of these services, who now have a choice of providers.

When it comes to the political broker role, increasing the supply of intermediaries may have more ambiguous implications. More intermediaries could increase the number of political entrepreneurs offering party leaders their services as wholesale vote brokers for their localities. Paradoxically, this proliferation of middlemen may undermine this variety of clientelism, because any increase in the number of political brokers claiming the ability to deliver a preponderance of a locality's vote could be expected to reduce the mean level of broker credibility. It could thus be hypothesized that the less politicians trust their ability to correctly select the most credible broker, the less stock they will place in the value of clientelist politics. Over the longer term, then, wider participation by a broader array of political brokers (while not the textbook solution to nonaccountability) can undermine the basis of clientelist politics by reducing the expected return (to politicians) from vote-brokering transactions.

What counts as reform?

Because of the rhetorical claims of liberalizers, it is often assumed that reformist energies are put in the service of increasing the exposure of economic activity to market forces. Many "market" reforms are, in fact, riddled with patronage. (This is distinct from the argument that under-the-table payoffs are used to compensate powerful economic interest groups who object to reform.)

What do voters consider "policy"? When incumbents are voted out of office after a spell of reform, are voters voting against neoliberal economic policy reform or something else, such as the many other administrative and institutional reforms undertaken by governments? Some initiatives are introduced in the name of supporting market-oriented reform, but many are justified on the general need to improve the citizen-government interface. Indeed, many reforms that draw the ire of voters are in fact governance reforms (such as the creation of participatory development committees to manage rural development schemes) and not necessarily of a market-leaning sort. Political influence is often brought to bear to steer key posts in these complex undertakings to party loyalists or unaffiliated groups whose loyalty can be purchased.

A major problem in the study of the impact of economic reforms on clientelism is that there is more than a fair bit of analytical bait-and-switch going on. In addition to inviting private sector investment from domestic and foreign firms in a large range of sectors and undertaking a number of other generally market-friendly economic reforms, many ostensibly reformist politicians pursue a large number of administrative and other organizational reforms. Some of these reforms focus on internal government procedures; others involve large-scale changes in program design and the structures through which high-profile government initiatives were implemented. For many voters who might be assumed to be interested in undermining clientelist politics (in the name of enhancing the accountability of elected representatives to ordinary people), these types of reforms (which have little direct connection with "liberalization") would likely have been the most visible manifestation of government policy change, although they might nevertheless be reported in election survey results as disaffection with "neoliberal" reforms.

Why does this matter? It may be that what causes reforming governments to lose power is not market-oriented policies but various governance reforms that are viewed as a strategy by which a reformer seeks to maintain control over the political instruments necessary to operate within the confines of what Chandra (2004a) has labeled a "patronage democracy." If this is the case, a different set of analytical vistas opens up. As Chandra argues:

> a "patronage-democracy" [is one] in which elections have become auctions for the sale of government services. The most minimal goods that a government should provide—security of life and property, access to education, provision of public health facilities, a minimum standard of living—have become, for large numbers of people, market goods rather than entitlements. This is a violation of modern norms of governance. Worse, this violation affects citizens unequally. And worst of all, this violation has become routinized in everyday imagination, so that it is now no longer perceived as illegitimate.

The fact that political favoritism can exist on such a massive scale and that fairly naked clientelist politics is a pervasive feature of political life in many developing countries surely has an impact on both the willingness and capacity of individual political actors (presidents of aid-dependent countries contemplating various reform-inflected policy mixes, for instance) to effect a transition to a "programmatic" form of political competition (in contrast to a clientelistic form), to use Kitschelt and Wilkinson's (2006) terminology.

The reasons why such leaders sometimes find it hard to translate these approaches into durable electoral support (and hence turn toward more authoritarian methods) may be that they are unsuccessful in devising a party instrument sufficiently disciplined and sensitive to deliver patronage in politically efficient ways. When such leaders take steps to liberalize their economies and then lose political support, it is often assumed that they have strayed too far into programmatic politics. However, it is also possible that they were simply incapable of building an organization with which to play the game of clientelism effectively—that is, to offer rewards and dole out punishments in a politically optimal fashion. This is in some ways not surprising, as parties in nonconsolidated democracies are notorious for being highly centralized, which means that the information flowing up the system to party leaders is severely impeded. The lesson of electorally unsuccessful liberalizers in the developing world may be that intraparty democracy could have helped create parties more efficient at distributing patronage.

The effect of a jagged reform trajectory

A jagged reform trajectory, such as that which has characterized many liberalization programs in developing countries, may make it difficult to classify policy decisions as either patronage or public goods. The talent shown by many developing country leaders for infiltrating every corner of the state with party followers is both loudly deplored and (sotto voce) grudgingly admired by their political enemies. Rewarding followers in clientelist fashion—rather than remaining accountable to voters at large—is even possible when pursuing such classically liberalizing reforms as commercializing key infrastructure sectors.

Reforming the power sector, for instance, often involves breaking up a state monopoly into commercialized generation, transmission, and distribution units and introducing a phased program of metering usage and increasing prices across all user categories. Moving toward remunerative pricing does not always (perhaps not even usually) take place on an impartial basis. Some users are exposed to the market, while others are effectively shielded, with officials often targeting those associated with opposition parties who refuse to defect to the ruling group. Political opponents and their clients may find their properties getting metered before others do and can be subjected to more insistent demands for payment of flat-rate fees. Cost recovery on upgrading equipment can also be passed on to these customers, while the more politically compliant get treated far more leniently.

This kind of "market clientelism" is consistent with what one would expect of clientelist politics in a patronage democracy. A key analytical problem is that clientelist politics is often miscataloged as programmatic politics, because in many cases market-based liberalization is the continuation of clientelist politics by other means.

Ironically, were an opposition party to seek electoral support by promising to do away with user charges if elected to power, it might be charged by foreign donors as engaging in populism, but it would not (technically speaking) be engaged in a return to clientelist politics. In fact, it would be undertaking a programmatic gesture, albeit of a nonmarket variety. Free electricity (if promised by a party in power as a reversal of a user-charge policy) would be a nonexcludable good that would, in theory, apply to all users, regardless of the party they supported. This example reveals the difficulty of relying on familiar categories to analyze the way in which policy change may or may not lay the basis for reducing clientelism and increasing accountability to voters.

Principal-agent difficulties in patronage distribution

Some politicians may find clientelism unreliable as a political strategy and therefore avoid it, increasing accountability to the electorate. They may perceive the strategy as unreliable, because political parties are too centralized or because the bureaucracy is imposing corrupt charges that make voters feel they have to pay for government favors twice—once with their votes and once with cash. If one views political leaders as principals and bureaucrats as agents, politicians are faced with a potentially fatal agency dilemma: is what threatens clientelism as a vote-winning formula the shift away from jobs for supporters and toward a cash economy for corrupt favors? If it is, it would represent a delicious irony, insofar as the most potent form of marketization to have taken place during the era of structural adjustment in many countries may well have been in the area of corruption.

It is plausible—based on anecdotal evidence from a range of countries—that it is the capture of resources by (bureaucratic) agents that thwarts the (political) principal's aim of buying over vote-bearing individuals. It is tempting to see this as a hopeful harbinger of change—indeed, a much deserved comeuppance for both the politicians and bureaucrats who have long benefited from the system of discretionary control on which clientelism rests. But this may be wishful thinking. If capture by bureaucratic agents is indeed viewed by political principals as one of the key constraints on the effectiveness of clientelism as a political strategy, politicians may invest in new systems for keeping tabs on these agents—which arguably is what politicians in many countries are doing in seeking to "professionalize" their parties, without necessarily democratizing them—rather than in new policies that reduce discretion and deliver public goods.

In other words, the more a politician regards an electoral defeat as mainly a flaw in the principal-agent wiring of his or her political machine rather than a reflection of tectonic shifts in the conduct of electoral politics—toward demands for greater accountability, more programmatic politics, or the provision of more public goods—the less likely he or she is to invest in policies and organizational structures that declientelize politics. While there is a market orientation to many policies that seek to reduce the prospects for official discretion in the allocation of resources, not all such declientelizing policies are about the spread of markets.

Key Trends Affecting Efforts to Improve Accountability Systems

Many trends can affect the nature of accountability relations. This section addresses trends that seem to have the most direct bearing on the prospects for reform of accountability institutions in low-income countries in which democratic institutions are in the process of being consolidated.

Changes in the Roles Played by Key Actors in Accountability Relationships

The roles played by various actors in accountability relationships are in a state of flux: ordinary people are less and less inclined to rely on oversight institutions to carry out accountability functions; they want to get involved directly. Ordinary citizens want to monitor the monitors, in some cases playing a formal role in such processes as auditing expenditure, reviewing proposed legislation, and assessing the environmental impact of government and corporate projects.

When this formal role is not open to them (because of legal prohibitions or practical constraints), civic groups often seek to perform this watchdog function in a quasi-formal manner—by holding informal public hearings, issuing reports, calling press conferences, and seeking to canvass voters' views. The ability to get involved in these ways has been facilitated by increasing demand (partly a function of spreading democratic culture) as well as increasing supply (most notably in the form of access to official information, obtained either legally, through freedom of information provisions, or through other means, such as leaks by sympathetic civil servants). The ability of such groups to disseminate their findings through nonconventional media (particularly e-mail lists, Internet discussion groups, and Web sites) has also contributed to this process.

Because of this increased role for civic groups in monitoring the monitors, or substituting for ill-performing official watchdog agencies in some cases, it is not surprising that civic groups themselves have become targets of accountability seeking by a range of constituencies, including public officials. Public officials may have genuine concerns about the accountability and motives of nongovernmental watchdog groups, or they may seek to deflect attention away from their own misdeeds. Either way, who plays the role of target and who the seeker is much less predictable than it once was. Ad hoc arrangements, with overlapping mandates and duplicated efforts, rather than a formal integrated system of checks and balances conforming to a master design, are increasingly the norm.

Changes in the Methods Used to Hold Power-Holders Accountable

The methods of holding power-holders accountable have also changed. This trend is related to the first insofar as the new roles of actors in accountability relationships—particularly the increased profile of nongovernmental actors in official processes—tend to influence the methods used to promote accountability. For instance, the practice of issuing nonofficial survey-based report cards, not only on public service delivery agencies but on the performance of individual elected officials as well, is designed to contribute to several different accountability processes. Report cards help educate voters about the performance of politicians, in theory influencing the way in which voters cast their ballots at the next election. They also provide an incentive for legislatures to demand accountability (in the form of holding legislative hearings, for instance) from executive agencies whose scores on such ranking exercises are below par. Report cards can even help spur public interest litigation by other private groups.

Similarly, the changing legal and institutional landscape can provide new methods of holding powerful actors accountable. These may or may not be more effective than earlier methods, but their existence changes the pattern of activity among accountability seekers while altering the incentives facing the targets of accountability. For instance, regulatory bodies to manage private sector activity have emerged in certain sectors across the developing world. The specific provisions in these bodies that allow (or disallow) members of the public to make representations about the performance of firms operating in a sector within the regulator's remit can provide opportunities for accountability seeking. To the extent that the regulator possesses the power to enforce sanctions on firms that have not upheld their public service mandates, such processes are potentially promising avenues for greater accountability, especially where the regulator is more independent than the government department that had previously managed (or indeed provided services itself to) the sector concerned.

Changes in the Standards to Which Power-Holders Are Held Accountable

Implicit in any discussion of accountability is the question, "What is the actor—public or private—being held accountable for?" That is, what is the relevant standard of accountability? This question is difficult to disentangle in practice from the earlier two trends, which involve changing actor roles and changing methods. If the method involves grievances submitted to an independent regulatory body, the relevant standard is likely to be defined restrictively by the legislation under which the regulator operates. It might, for example, concern only monopolistic practices rather than the quality of service provision, if the guiding legislation assumes that service quality is a matter for the market to determine through the mechanism of consumer choice.

There are two aspects to the issue of standards. The first concerns the level of performance: how well accountable actors must perform in order to avoid sanction. There appears to be a trend of more minutely calibrating performance measures, through benchmarking, targets, and other management tools. Whether or not these measures are appropriate or sufficiently linked to enforcement processes, taken together they represent an interlinked set of concerns relating to standards.

The second aspect of standards that is undergoing profound change is the actions the target should be held accountable for. The most important development is the increasing emphasis on outcomes as opposed to processes. Adherence to a set of procedural norms was once considered sufficient to demonstrate that an accountable actor operated in conformity with his or her remit. Actual outcomes are now increasingly seen as the relevant measure by accountability seekers. This shift in the standard employed cannot be separated from the question of the methods used (which can be more or less geared to outcome measures, depending on preference) and the changing nature of actors: when a wider array of accountability seekers is involved, including ordinary people who care more about outcomes, standards are likely to shift.

The Impact of Changing Aid Modalities and Donor-Government Relations

The relationship between donor and recipient governments has undergone important shifts since the late 1990s. The "new aid modalities" are the centerpiece of this shift, manifested most visibly in the proliferation of national poverty-reduction strategies.

The Paris Declaration of March 2005, issued under the auspices of the Development Assistance Committee (DAC) of the Organisation of Economic Co-operation and Development, committed donor governments and multilateral institutions to increasing the proportion of resources channeled through the national budgets of aid-recipient governments.[4] The objective was to reverse two longstanding aid trends: the conditioning of aid on the implementation of reform measures prioritized by donors rather than recipient governments and the emphasis on shrinking developing country states instead of augmenting their capacities. These are worthwhile aims, which reveal refreshing candor about the ruinous impact of more than 20 years of externally imposed market reform. That government-to-government arm-twisting seldom yields the desired developmental results[5] and that it is possible to reduce the scope of state activity while still increasing the state's ability to undertake essential tasks[6] are important insights.

The new aid consensus focuses on improving policy and governance in aid-recipient countries on the state as a unitary entity—that is, on a state as a whole rather than on parts of a state (such as an executive department, a region, or a semiautonomous institution). It is especially fixated on developing countries' national budgets (and associated antipoverty plans) as the key instruments for effecting lasting change. The laudable intention is to shore up state capacities in developing countries, to instill a sense of national ownership over their development strategies, and to reduce the transaction costs (and policy conflicts) that arise when aid-recipient governments must answer to a large number of donor agencies, each with its own priorities and reporting procedures.

There are accountability implications to the new aid consensus. Most notable is the idea—noted in the Paris Declaration—that donors should also be accountable for fulfilling their commitments with regard to the predictability of finance, the alignment of priorities with national poverty plans, the reduction of conditionality, and so forth. This is the idea of mutual accountability. Allied to this notion—and in a sense a logical corollary to it—is the idea that responsibility for holding aid-dependent governments accountable would be shifted away from external actors toward domestic constituencies and institutions.

The long-term impacts of this paradigm for accountability are very difficult to gauge. The reaction of civil society in many countries that have developed poverty reduction strategies (and worked with donors to increase budget support and reduce conditionalities) has been encouraging, in that it has formed structures for engaging in both policy dialogue and coordinated protest on issues of substance and process. But there is an element of wishful thinking in assuming that the new aid relationship will result in the emergence of domestic political leverage sufficient to hold government (or donors) accountable for their commitments. Civil society remains extremely weak and fragmented in many aid-dependent countries, and government remains highly suspicious of the more vocal elements within its ranks.

The connection between improved governance and the process of developing national poverty strategies in the formal arena—that is, state accountability institutions—has varied from country to country. In many countries the preparation of such plans provided an opportunity for a small group of parliamentarians to become involved in substantive questions of oversight, but the number of legislators committed and capable enough to engage in these sorts of processes over the longer term is tiny. Budgets for parliamentary committees often remain miniscule.

Resources for other state accountability institutions have increased in some countries, but their work is frequently constrained by political interference from agencies controlled by the executive. Moreover, arrangements for monitoring commitments made under the new aid modalities emphasize the need to involve civil society in a central role—either officially (in a partnership with government machinery) or unofficially (through a parallel process independent of the state-operated system for tracking progress on antipoverty indicators). Given the current weakness of civil society in many aid-dependent countries, unofficial arrangements will likely prove the more effective mechanisms over the long term, given civil society's need to develop independence from the state. Civil society groups would nevertheless continue to rely on substantial external assistance for a large proportion of the funds required to carry out such monitoring. In light of the likely political and institutional inadequacies of whatever arrangements for monitoring the implementation of antipoverty strategies and the outcomes produced by them are adopted, donors will need to continue their own monitoring and financial oversight mechanisms over the medium term.

Opposition to Innovation

Attempting to improve accountability by innovative means leads to various problems. These can take the form of principled objections to efforts to reform institutions, on the basis of hypothetical arguments as well as empirical evidence. They can also take the form of political backlashes from actors whose access to power or resources is threatened by reform. The more difficult problems faced by those seeking to reengineer accountability relationships are those that arise when vested interests ally with principled opponents of reform efforts on the basis of theoretically plausible but empirically untested criticisms. Two such points of convergence have given rise to backlashes that innovators need to anticipate—both because there may be substance to the claims advanced and because even if they are motivated by privilege rather than principle, it is necessary to develop a reasoned rebuttal.

Constant reinvention of accountability is costly

The first criticism of efforts to reengineer accountability systems is that accountability is costly: designing systems of oversight and staffing them with competent people, engaging in continuous ex ante consultation, supplying information to a wide array of constituencies, and assessing claims of malfeasance all require considerable resources. These are the direct (transaction) costs of accountability innovations.

Indirect costs include the inefficiencies that arise from delayed decision making, the introduction of veto points that stymie efforts to bring about important policy shifts, and the uncertainty that arises in the minds of economic agents (investors, employers, consumers) when oversight introduces additional levels of clearance for what otherwise may have been straightforward decisions. This is not the same thing as arguing that corruption is efficient, an argument that has fallen out of favor in recent years. The argument here is that there is a point at which efforts to combat corruption (or indeed bias) can prove counterproductive.

A variation of this argument concerns the process of reform: if accountability seeking is expensive, the constant reinvention of accountability institutions is even more so. Reengineering oversight processes, recalibrating performance contracts, reconstructing reporting relationships all come with a price tag, in both designing these new systems and teaching targets and seekers of accountability to operate within them. Some civic organizations believe that reinvention may help the corrupt more than those seeking to hold them accountable if the constant changing of norms and procedures means that officials can plausibly claim that they were unaware of the new rules and thus find a convenient way of justifying their abuses of power.

Parallel systems undermine state development

Opponents of innovative ways of increasing accountability often argue that efforts to improve accountability often put nongovernment actors in prominent roles, which can undermine the proper development of state capacity. Substituting nonstate actors when state capacity is weak may be tempting, but it is shortsighted: bypassing poorly functioning state institutions can lead to further atrophy of official organs.

There may be some merit to this claim at certain times and in certain places, especially when efforts are not made to build up state institutions through other means. However, it is just as plausible that alternative methods and channels of promoting accountability can act as a spur to state institutions, injecting an element of interinstitutional competition that can increase overall accountability performance. This is an empirical question, not one that can be determined by appeals to the general principle that innovative alternatives automatically disempower the state.

Diagnosing Accountability Failures in Political Institutions

The following four-step procedure may be useful in diagnosing what is preventing political institutions from playing a more constructive role in securing accountability, identifying ongoing obstacles to change, and specifying potential catalysts of improved accountability.

Step One: Describing the Problem in Outcome-Oriented Terms

What is the accountability problem under investigation? That is, what is the problem that program interventions are not able to tackle?

Step Two: Establishing the Institutional Failure

Which set of accountability institutions should have prevented this adverse outcome or punished those responsible after the fact (the de jure accountability system)? Were they primarily institutions of internal scrutiny (horizontal accountability), or were they open to public influence (vertical accountability)? At what level of the institution in question did the problem occur—at the interface between the institution and citizens or at the top level?

Step Three: Identifying the Reasons for Accountability Failure

To what degree was the failure of this set of institutions attributable to capture or bias? If capture is involved, is it corruption or intimidation? If it is corruption, is it corruption with theft or corruption without theft? If it is bias, is it the no-remit version of bias or the unintended form of bias that obstructs poor people's capacity to activate accountability systems? To what extent did the institutions fail because of an inability to provide ex ante answerability or ex post enforcement/sanction?

Step Four: Evaluating Programmatic Remedies

In evaluating the suitability of potential programmatic remedies for the institutional shortcomings identified, five considerations are worth bearing in mind. First, consider sector-specific factors, such as geographical concentration, frequency of contact with providers, and the technical intensity of the service, that will shape the degree to which reforms can appeal to citizen power or to the oversight powers of accountability systems. Different types of reforms tend to produce better results in some kinds of sectors than others.

Second, tailor remedies to problems of bias. Problems of bias are deep seated and tend to shift only after long-term attitudinal and social change, but some immediate actions can be taken to address the no-remit and access-constraint versions of bias. No-remit forms of bias can be addressed through policy and legal change to ensure that group-specific forms of disadvantage are recognized as such in law or addressed in policy. Biases embedded in access conditions, operating procedures, and payment requirements that exclude certain groups of people can be removed through simple measures to make accountability institutions more accessible to these groups.

The good governance agenda addresses problems of sheer corruption, often through remedies involving privatization. Research indicates that focusing first on corruption without theft produces the benefit of a quick win—a constituency of people that benefit from the reform will support the more challenging problems of addressing corruption with theft (Jenkins 2004).

Third, assess the prospects for creating accountability hybrids. Can steps be taken to institutionalize citizen participation and oversight on the functioning of the accountability institutions in question? Can this citizen engagement be made more than notional—that is, can citizens be given a formally sanctioned position in an oversight panel; access to official documentation; the right to issue dissenting reports to other accountability institutions, including the media; and the right to have complaints formally investigated?

Fourth, identify the appropriate stage of the accountability cycle. If the accountability failure stems from inadequate ex ante deliberation (for instance, regarding industrial development schemes and their impact on the environment), mechanisms for consultation may need to be widened.

Fifth, identify nascent accountability innovations that may be generating new accountability seekers or raising public debate about the standards against which the actions of power-holders should be judged. The following questions may be useful in identifying catalysts for accountability:

- Who is seeking accountability?
- From whom (or what) is accountability sought?
- Where (in which forums and over what extent of geographic coverage) is accountability being sought?
- How (through what means) are the powerful being held to account?
- For what (which actions and against which norms) is accountability being sought?
- When (at what stage in the policy-making/implementing/reviewing process) are accountability mechanisms triggered?

Notes

This chapter draws extensively on earlier collaborative work with Anne Marie Goetz.
1. One indicator of the increasing salience of accountability is that the number of USAID publications with the word *accountability* in the title increased every year between 1995 and 2002. There were 4 such publications in 1995, 7 in 1996, 14 in 1997, 16 in 1998, 17 in 1999, 21 in 2000, 27 in 2001, and 40 in 2002. The author is grateful to Andrea Cornwall for bringing this piece of information to his attention.
2. Rudolph and Rudolph (1987) argue, however, that some of these organizations were nevertheless able to function as effective demand groups.
3. Performance contracts are themselves devised as methods for overcoming two kinds of subversion of civil service rules, the use of political pressure to prevent dedicated officials from performing their jobs effectively and impartially and the use of political pressure to protect officials who do not perform their jobs effectively and impartially.
4. The 2005 Paris Declaration was an outcome of the High-Level Forum on Aid Effectiveness, which included representatives of donor and recipient countries, multilateral institutions, and civil society organizations. The forum was the culmination of a deliberative process undertaken by the Working Party on Aid Effectiveness and Donor Practices, established in 2003 by the OECD's Development Assistance Committee. The text is available at http://www1.worldbank.org/harmonization/Paris/finalpari declaration.pdf.
5. The failure of conditionality-based development programs became an increasingly prominent theme during the 1990s. It is carefully documented and analyzed in Burnside and Dollar (1997); Mosely, Harrigan, and Toye (1991); and van de Walle and Johnston (1996).
6. Fukuyama (2004) elaborates this notion with considerable elegance.

References

Blair, Harry. 2000. "Participation and Accountability at the Periphery: Democratic Local Governance in Six Countries." *World Development* 28 (1): 24.

Bowen, Jeff, and Susan Rose-Ackerman. 2002. "Partisan Politics and Executive Accountability: Argentina in Comparative Perspective." *Supreme Court Economic Review* 10 (1): 157–210.

Burnside, Craig, and David Dollar. 1997. "Aid, Policies, and Growth." Policy Research Working Paper 1777, World Bank, Development Research Group, Washington, DC.

Chandra, Kanchan. 2004a. "Elections as Auctions." *Seminar* 539. www.india-seminar.com/2004/539/539%20kanchan%20chandra.htm.

———. 2004b. *Why Ethnic Parties Succeed: Patronage and Ethnic Head Counts in India.* Cambridge: Cambridge University Press.

Clarke, Gerard. 1996. "Non-Governmental Organisations (NGOs) and Politics in the Developing World." Papers in International Development 20, Centre for Development Studies, University of Wales, Swansea.

Coldham, Simon. 1995. "Legal Responses to State Corruption in Commonwealth Africa." *Journal of African Law* 39 (2): 115–26.

Dodson, M., and Donald Jackson. 2004. "Horizontal Accountability in Transitional Democracies: The Human Rights Ombudsman in El Salvador and Guatemala." *Latin American Politics & Society* 46 (4): 1–27.

Fearon, James D. 1999. "Electoral Accountability and the Control of Politicians: Selecting Good Types versus Sanctioning Poor Performance." In *Democracy, Accountability and Representation*, ed. Adam Przeworski, Susan C. Stokes, and Bernard Manin, 55–97. Cambridge: Cambridge University Press.

Fukuyama, Francis. 2004. *State-Building: Governance and World Order in the 21st Century*. Ithaca, NY: Cornell University Press.

Government of Malawi. 2000. "MTEF Phase Two: Consolidation Revitalisation. Overview and Plan of Action." October. Lilongwe.

———. 2001. "Malawi 2000 Public Expenditure Review." August. Ministry of Finance and Economic Planning, Lilongwe.

Jenkins, Rob. 2004. "In Varying States of Decay: The Politics of Anti-Corruption in Maharashtra and Rajasthan." In Regional Reflections: Comparing Politics across India's States, ed. Rob Jenkins, 219–52. Oxford: Oxford University Press.

Jenkins, Rob, and Maxton Tsoka. 2003. "Institutionalization and Malawi's PRSP." *Development Policy Review* 21 (3): 197–215.

Keefer, Philip. 2002. "Clientelism, Credibility, and Democracy." Background paper to the *World Development Report 2004*, World Bank, Washington, DC.

Keohane, Robert. 2002. "Global Governance and Democratic Accountability." Working Paper, Department of Political Science, Duke University, Durham, NC.

Khan, Mushtaq. 1998. "Patron-Client Networks and the Economic Effects of Corruption in Asia." In *Corruption and Development*, ed. Mark Robinson. London: F. Cass.

Kitschelt, H., and S. Wilkinson, eds. 2006. *Patrons or Policies*. Durham, NC: Duke University Press.

Krafchik, Warren. 2001. "Can Civil Society Add Value to Budget Decision-Making? A Description of Civil Society Budget Work." Background paper for the Exploratory Dialogue on Applied Budget Analysis as a Tool for the Advancement of Economic, Social and Cultural Rights, International Budget Project, World Bank, Washington, DC.

Krishna, Anirudh. 2002. *Active Social Capital: Tracing the Roots of Development and Democracy*. New York: Columbia University Press.

Lonsdale, John. 1986. "Political Accountability in African History." In *Political Domination in Africa: Reflections on the Limits of Power*, ed. Patrick Chabal, 126–87. Cambridge: Cambridge University Press.

Manzetti, Luigi. 2000. "Keeping Accounts: A Case Study of Civic Initiatives and Campaign Finance Oversight in Argentina." Working Paper 248, Centre for Institutional Reform and the Informal Sector, University of Maryland, College Park, MD.

Mosely, Paul, Jane Harrigan, and John Toye. 1991. *Aid and Power: The World Bank and Policy-Based Lending*. London: Routledge.

Navarro, Zander. 1998. "Participation, Democratizing Practices and the Formation of a Modern Polity: The Case of Participatory Budgeting in Porto Alegre, Brazil (1989–1998)." Federal University of Rio Grande do Sul, Brazil.

Pharr, S., and R. Putnam. 2000. *Disaffected Democracies: What's Troubling the Trilateral Countries*. Princeton, NJ: Princeton University Press.

Rudolph, Lloyd, and Susanne Hoeber Rudolph. 1987. *In Pursuit of Lakshmi: The Political Economy of the Indian State.* Chicago: University of Chicago Press.

Schedler, Andreas. 1999. "Conceptualizing Accountability." In *The Self-Restraining State: Power and Accountability in New Democracies*, ed. A. Schedler, Larry Diamond, and Marc F. Plattner, 14–17. Boulder, CO: Lynne Rienner.

Scholte, Jan Aart. 2004. "Civil Society and Democratically Accountable Global Governance." *Government & Opposition* 39 (2): 211–33.

Shleifer, A., and R. Vishny. 1993. "Corruption." *Quarterly Journal of Economics* 108: 599–612.

Staudt, Kathleen. 1978. "Agricultural Productivity Gaps: A Case Study of Male Preference in Government Policy Implementation." *Development and Change* 9 (3): 439–58.

Steel, B. S., J. C. Pierce, and N. P. Lovrich. 1998. "Public Information Campaigns and 'At Risk' Voters." *Political Communication* 15 (1): 117–33.

van de Walle, Nicolas, and Timothy A. Johnston. 1996. "Improving Aid to Africa." Policy Essay 21, Overseas Development Council, Washington, DC.

Wade, Robert. 1985. "The Market for Public Office: Why the Indian State Is Not Better at Development." *World Development* 13 (4): 467–97.

Wampler, Brian. 2004. "Expanding Accountability through Participatory Institutions: Mayors, Citizens, and Budgeting in Three Brazilian Municipalities." *Latin American Politics & Society* 46 (2): 73–99.

Waterbury, John. 1977. "An Attempt to Put Patrons and Clients in Their Place." In *Patrons and Clients in Mediterranean Societies*, ed. John Waterbury. London: Duckworth.

6

Legal and Institutional Frameworks Supporting Accountability in Budgeting and Service Delivery Performance

MALCOLM RUSSELL-EINHORN

Throughout the developing world, citizens are demanding greater government accountability and responsiveness as well as better delivery of public services. Economic inequalities accentuated by globalization, lagging public sector reform efforts, entrenched corruption, and persistent concerns about the overall legitimacy of government decision making at all levels have fueled such demands, creating a deeper sense of urgency about budgeting and service delivery shortcomings.

A consensus among development specialists favors the creation of more effective and participatory policy-making mechanisms to exert greater control over service delivery design and operation, but implementing such mechanisms has proven difficult. Stronger citizen "voice"—demand-side pressures for reform—should result in better incentives for public officials to budget and deliver services of the type and amount desired by the public.

Appropriate legal and institutional frameworks can create significant participatory "spaces" and opportunities—often grounded in individual and collective rights—for the public to exert such agency and make meaningful choices about service delivery quality, access, accountability, efficiency, and equity. A wide range of contextual factors, however, complicates straightforward emphasis on these formal interactive organizational arrangements—factors that include background politics and power relations, sociocultural norms, and government and civil society organization (CSO) capacity. Reformers need to both incorporate the influence of such factors into legal and institutional designs and acknowledge important limitations—at least in the short run—in the ability to mitigate many of these conditions.

This chapter provides an overview of global trends and experience with legal and institutional arrangements that support greater citizen voice in budgeting and the delivery of public services. The emphasis is on relatively direct, grassroots, demand-side mechanisms, particularly at the local level, rather than indirect, higher-level mechanisms (such as courts, supreme audit institutions, and national legislatures), which are harder for citizens to access or influence and are often more readily captured by special interests. The chapter extracts lessons learned about what kinds of demand-side mechanisms (and what kinds of attributes of such mechanisms) appear to be necessary—though by no means sufficient—for citizen voice to operate effectively. Without making any claims that they can or should be replicated everywhere, the chapter examines the broader role that legal and institutional frameworks can play in allowing citizen-oriented accountability dynamics to take root, especially at the local level. These legal and institutional frameworks include both direct and indirect facilitative mechanisms (such as laws on participatory budgeting and independent media). The emphasis, however, is on direct provisions, principally those concerned with participation in and oversight of local representative government (legislative functions) and those concerned with bureaucratic transparency and accountability at all levels of government (executive functions).

The chapter examines whether formal legal and institutional mechanisms per se can sometimes not only fail to promote vibrant participatory spaces but actually restrict them by cutting off opportunities for more spontaneous and innovative informal practices. It therefore investigates what kinds of other process improvements, some informal, might strengthen existing accountability mechanisms. It also identifies a wide range of other facilitating activities or initiatives—involving media, public education, and capacity building (particularly cross-training)—that may need to be undertaken to enable participants to make more effective use of citizen voice accountability tools. At all times, the discussion is cognizant of the variable nature of citizen "participation"—the degree to which its attributes are heavily contingent on the different interests and statuses of the individuals and groups involved, the specific types of issues in question (producing differential costs and benefits), and various embedded social norms. The discussion also recognizes the formidable challenges (in terms of political economy) of introducing and implementing effective voice mechanisms.

The chapter is organized as follows. The first section reviews the literature tying better theoretical and actual budget and service delivery outcomes to increased opportunities for citizen voice to be heard. The second section examines the main kinds of citizen voice mechanisms that currently exist, including the main legal and institutional structures that embody or affect their operation. The third section presents an empirically grounded framework for assessing the potential or actual impact of various voice mechanisms, while also identifying institutional design and process considerations that should inform policy makers' thinking. The fourth section presents case studies (from Bolivia, the Philippines, and South Africa) of relatively well-developed legal and institutional frameworks for citizen participation in planning and decision making at the local level. It also identifies ways in which their promise has not been realized because of various legal, institutional, and enabling environment shortcomings. The concluding section describes the ways political economy factors can best be managed to maximize the utility of otherwise useful legal and institutional mechanisms.

The Importance of Effective Citizen Voice to Budgeting and Service Delivery Performance

Over the past few decades, the concept of participation has increasingly moved from the arena of community or development projects to the broader universe of democratic governance, in which citizen voice is viewed as an indispensable element of government accountability and the effective delivery of public services. Ensuring adequate civil society engagement in democratic governance and service delivery is seen as helping articulate and aggregate societal demands, build consensus for broader-based political and economic reforms, and refine or improve public policy proposals. This process involves simultaneously moving government toward civil society and beyond mere social and project participation toward a broader conception of citizenship (UNECA 2004). Citizen participation in various dimensions of governance is viewed as a potential source of discipline, guidance, and demand (Andrews 2005).

To a great extent, these shifts are mirrored in the evolution, under World Bank auspices, of Poverty Reduction Strategy Papers (PRSPs), which reflect the aspiration for broader societal engagement of civil society in the development of pro-poor policies (Eberlei 2003). In its 2004 *World Development Report*, the World Bank highlighted the extent to which enlargement of citizens' choice and participation in budgeting and service delivery can help them monitor providers and make them more responsive to public needs. This is part of a broader interest of the World Bank and others in "social accountability," whereby citizens and CSOs can create new vertical mechanisms of accountability and strengthen existing horizontal ones (Malena 2004).

A consensus has emerged as to how such accountability of the public sector through citizen voice should operate. Voice mechanisms should ideally allow the public to "influence the final outcome of a service through some form of participation or articulation of protest/feedback" (Paul 1992: 1048). Such mechanisms are crucial to performance-based government, in which citizens, as end users, are able to relay information back to governments on the fit between delivered services and particular community requirements and preferences (Gopakumar 1997). Voice mechanisms embrace a variety of legal and institutional avenues through which citizens can regularly make their views known to governments.

These mechanisms can take many forms, depending on their specific function and country- and locality-specific manifestations. They share a common reform logic, however, whereby they can lead to enhanced voice "expression," which in turn can lead to enhanced public sector accountability (Andrews 2005). These expected impacts, though framed in developing-country contexts, generally parallel those set forth by the Organisation for Economic Co-operation and Development (OECD 2001b) and others (such as Fung and Wright 2003), who see a worldwide need for strengthened citizen consultation and participation in order to promote (a) better public policies and their implementation as demanded by society and markets, (b) more transparency and accountability for delivery of government services, (c) greater trust in government and more legitimate decision making, and (d) more active citizenship and engagement (to counter increasing "democracy deficits").

Decades of experience with conventional top-down, supply-side approaches to public sector reform—featuring administrative, civil service, and capacity-building reforms; results- or performance-oriented management; and decentralization (particularly of the delegative or deconcentration type)—have not improved governance. In view of this failure, Andrews and Shah (2005a) posit an alternative "citizen-centered governance" approach, aimed at local and regional government. Their approach includes the following elements:

- Communication and participation through implicit social and explicit political contracts between citizens and their representatives (with contracts built on both the social, political, and legal pressures citizens can exert on public servants and the creative political and economic pressures that can be institutionalized through devices like citizens' charters)
- Results-oriented relationships and performance contracts within the government, with executives responsible for ensuring that administrators use total quality management (TQM) and similar methods to develop productive interaction between administration and citizens, as well as management-for-results approaches (performance-based budgeting, benchmarking, regular reporting, activity-based costing) to meet citizen demands
- Internal and external impact and process evaluations by the government, as well as citizen evaluations, scorecarding, and other publicizing of government service delivery performance by civil society organizations so as to provide feedback on how well demands were met.[1]

In each of these three dimensions, the incentive structures for citizens, local elected representatives, and administrators have been changed and made mutually reinforcing.

This model for citizen-centered governance is highly persuasive and intuitively appealing. Some empirical evidence supports the positive impact of these elements on budgeting and service delivery outcomes.[2] Anecdotal case studies also attest to the positive effects of opening up formal and informal channels for citizen participation and evaluation. Given the overwhelming importance of empowered citizen participation to this general model (particularly in a world dominated by top-down imperatives, patronage, corruption, and lack of capacity of the poor), the challenge is to identify what specific kinds of participation need to be cultivated and how. Given the very strong background factors above, which militate against meaningful citizen participation in developing countries, what kinds of characteristics should such participation embody? How should participation be structured and protected? To answer these questions, existing laws, policies, and institutions designed to promote greater citizen voice can be surveyed and analyzed.

Cross-Country Experience with Legal and Institutional Frameworks That Support Citizen Voice Mechanisms

In response to the need for, and perceived benefits of, greater public participation in policy making, governments in developed countries—and to a lesser extent, developing countries, where systems of accountability and public pressures are often much weaker—have embraced a wide variety of citizen voice mechanisms. A broad array of laws, policies, and institutions can embody or undergird such mechanisms (table 6.1).

Some governments have formally established such mechanisms; and many of these have uncritically transplanted laws and institutions from developed countries. Where formal laws and institutions are nonexistent or inadequate, informal, ad hoc institutions have arisen in response to public needs and demands.[3]

There are many ways to conceptualize how these various mechanisms or constituent parts can be classified and how they are supposed to operate. Arnstein (1969), an early theorist, takes a citizen-activist stance, proposing a unitary participatory "ladder" that runs from the most degraded form of participation—manipulation—up through informing, consulting, and placating (characterized as degrees of tokenism) to partnership, delegated power, and citizen control. She views only the last three forms as providing meaningful participation. Paul (1987) envisions a continuum of increasing citizen participation intensity, spanning information sharing, consultation, decision making, and initiation of policy proposals. The OECD (2001a: 23) posits an ascending scale involving information (a one-way relationship in which government provides information to citizens), consultation (a two-way relationship in which citizens provide feedback to the government), and active participation (a relationship based on partnership, in which citizens "actively engage in defining the process and content of policymaking").

Looking at participation from the vantage point of public officials, Thomas (1990) identifies discrete needs for participation, the modes of which vary by problem type and societal resources.[4] Bishop and Davis (2002) paint a more nuanced, discontinuous picture of participation—derived in part from OECD surveys on national approaches to public consultation—that does not make normative judgments but emphasizes five distinct meanings or styles of participation that can be used in the public policy process in complementary ways: (a) participation as consultation; (b) participation as partnership; (c) participation as legal standing; (d) participation as consumer choice; and (e) participation as control (most notably through referendums). They note that extensive participation may "make

TABLE 6.1 Key Laws, Policies, and Institutions Supporting Voice Mechanisms

Category	Legislation	Policy	Institutions	Tools
Information				
Passive	Freedom of information laws	Response times and fees/charges	Implementation: all public units. Enforcement: ombudsmen, courts	Information registers. Information management systems. Government Web sites and portals
Active	Freedom of information laws; sectoral legislation	Government communications and transparency policies	Government information offices	TV, radio, print media, official gazettes, annual reports, brochures. Internet broadcasting
Consultation and feedback				
Unsolicited	Administrative procedure laws. Notice and comment periods	Management and analysis of complaints	Implementation: offices for relations with the public. Enforcement: ombudsmen, courts	Data analysis software. E-mail addresses for contact people
Solicited	Environmental impact assessment laws	Regulatory impact assessments. Policies on consultation (with social partners, for example)	Government ministries and agencies. Central strategy and support units	Surveys, opinion polls. Public hearings, focus groups, citizen panels. Consultation guidelines. Online chat events

(*continued*)

TABLE 6.1 (*continued*)

Category	Legislation	Policy	Institutions	Tools
Active participation				
Government led	Referendums	Policies on engaging citizens Public-private partnerships	Government ministries and agencies Central strategy and support units	Consensus conferences Citizen juries Public dialogue sessions Online discussion groups
Citizen led	Popular legislative initiative	Development of alternative policy proposals Self-regulation	CSOs Academic centers Think tanks	Discussion meetings Independent Web sites, online chat rooms, e-mail lists

Source: Adapted from OECD 2001a.

policy resolution more difficult by raising expectations, or introduce a power of veto that allows some to block a project of benefit to others" (Bishop and Davis 2002: 26). In general, these conceptual frames can help show whether particular mechanisms, especially in combination, actually result in broad-based citizen impact on government transparency and service delivery performance.

Before examining examples of participatory mechanisms and analyzing their effectiveness, it is useful to acknowledge two important preliminary considerations. The first concerns the characteristics and advantages of using laws and formal institutions versus informal norms and institutions in developing countries. The second is the extent to which institutions and institutional design are only one of many critical factors that may impinge on the ultimate effectiveness of given voice mechanisms.

Advantages of Formal versus Informal Institutions in Channeling Citizen Voice

Although it is difficult to find rigorous empirical studies showing that legally grounded citizen voice mechanisms produce superior service delivery or accountability outcomes, Andrews' (2002) in-depth study of decentralization and South African municipalities lends indirect support to the notion.[5] Andrews' (2005) study of a larger sample of citizen voice mechanisms suggests that broader, more influential citizen voice was registered in local planning processes where citizen views were incorporated directly into formal decision-making processes rather than kept separate from actual planning decisions.

The large number of contextual, confounding factors at play—many relating to local politics and sociocultural traditions—makes it difficult to render categorical judgments on this matter. At the same time, it is intuitively compelling that legally entrenched participation norms—particularly those built into local government legislative rules of procedure, including both national and local bureaucratic norms of administrative procedure—would provide legislators and administrators with more powerful incentives than would informal custom or practice to adopt a citizen service orientation. Many possible reasons may support this thesis, such as the following:

- *Practical and rhetorical impact.* Legal provisions mandating public participation may be harder for public officials to ignore than informal or discretionary processes. Rights conferred by legislation may also provide practical and rhetorical weapons to citizens and CSOs seeking to have their voices heard in the policy-making process.

- *Greater precision and attention to procedural detail.* Grounding practices in legal requirements and legal culture may result in more precision and less ambiguity about government and civil society rights and responsibilities, which is often crucial to providing depth and weight to the various dimensions of the policy-making process.
- *Legitimacy.* Adopting and using effective voice mechanisms within existing formal institutions—particularly representative government institutions, such as municipal councils—potentially carries greater weight and legitimacy with government officials and the public alike, unless such institutions are substantially compromised, in which case new institutions may provide important advantages (Ackerman 2004).
- *Political dynamics.* As a matter of political economy, legislators and bureaucrats may resent or avoid new participation mechanisms that not only seek to make government decision making more transparent and less discretionary but may appear to end-run or run parallel to formal legal processes. This may be true even in the case of quasi-formal or hybrid mechanisms. As a result, such separate or partially integrated mechanisms may be treated less seriously by officials or be consciously marginalized.
- *Administrative culture and social capital.* Simply as a matter of influencing administrative culture and bureaucratic routine, it may be easier to introduce voice mechanisms into existing legal frameworks and representative processes instead of creating new structures and procedures outside government channels.
- *Cost and effort.* Regardless of its financial cost, the creation of new participatory mechanisms may require considerable investment of time and energy by citizens and officials, as well as social capital that exceeds that possessed by a given community. At the very least, these channels may be somewhat duplicative and "stretch civic interest and time," which may be in short supply on the part of government officials and citizens alike (Andrews and Shah 2005b: 193).

Quite apart from the question of current effectiveness, it would seem preferable, where feasible, to invest in the longer-term improvement of legal frameworks and formal representative institutions than to establish a separate participatory infrastructure that does not address the root of the problem.[6] Whether reliance on formal institutions and legal provisions is feasible in particular countries, however, must be determined on a case-by-case basis. Reliance on formal accountability channels where neither vertical nor horizontal accountability mechanisms function as advertised is often futile. Where these traditional forms of accountability are ineffective due to patronage, weak parliamentary or municipal council oversight, poor internal controls over civil servants, excessive executive control over appointments and agendas (in strong presidential or other executive systems, for example), or basic lack of civil society capacity or experience, it is unsurprising that informal voice mechanisms may be the only political recourse.

Where political economies are only somewhat unfavorable, hybrid (or so-called diagonal) accountability mechanisms may still take root, whereby the public (as vertical actors) holds public officials accountable through horizontal institutions characteristic of administrative law. These include the use of consultative or public oversight bodies, ombudspeople, and administrative litigation (Ackerman 2004; Goetz and Jenkins 2001). Indeed, "social accountability" often takes root where such civic engagement is positively fostered by the state (Ackerman 2005).

Where political economies are much less favorable, voice mechanisms may function largely or wholly outside formal state-sanctioned channels (for example, NGO-organized scorecarding of services, media exposés, ad hoc public meetings). These dynamics must be kept in mind when gauging the effectiveness of formal participatory mechanisms. Indeed, the development landscape is littered with ineffective legislation that remains under- or unutilized because of the lack of supportive political, economic, or sociocultural environments, not to mention inadequate bureaucratic and public education, training, and capacity building.[7] Some East Asian countries, for example, have vibrant, participatory local governance and effective delivery of social services without complex legal mandates (which could conceivably limit further development and creativity).[8]

Other Critical Background Constraints

Whether formal or informal institutions are involved, a wide range of factors other than institutional design are necessary for, if not indispensable to, the success of citizen voice mechanisms. Since this chapter emphasizes legal and institutional tools, a discussion of other variables affecting the impact of citizen voice must necessarily be abbreviated. Reformers should keep these variables in mind, however, as they contemplate whether and how to introduce or strengthen various voice processes.

At least six key groups of factors can limit the effectiveness of participatory mechanisms in achieving democratic and development goals (figure 6.1). These dimensions can be further grouped into two broad categories. The first consists of sociocultural, political, and legal administrative traditions

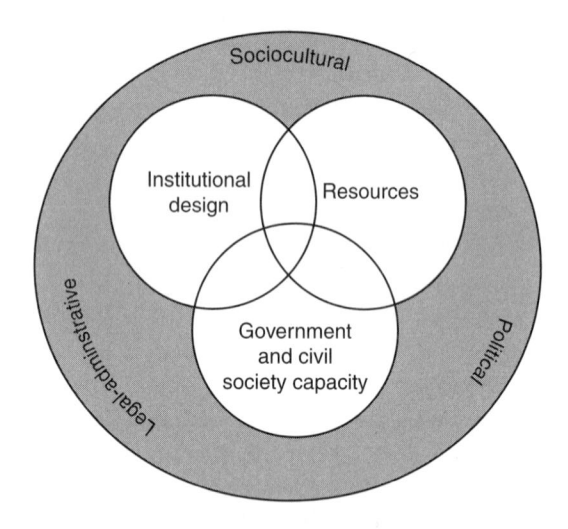

Source: Author.

FIGURE 6.1 Six Dimensions of Background Constraints

and legacies. The second addresses institutional design, resource availability, and the capacities of key government and civil society actors. These factors overlap with those used by the Participation and Civic Engagement Team of the World Bank under the ARVIN (association, resources, voice, information, negotiation) framework (Thindwa, Monico, and Reuben 2003). ARVIN presents a more detailed methodology for assessing civic engagement enabling environments (see annex table 6A.1).

Embedded cultural limitations—such as traditions of deference to hierarchy and formal authority (which, at the very least, can result in co-optation of the disadvantaged), deep-seated distrust and social conflict, weak social structures and civil society capacity, gender discrimination, and illiteracy—need to be factored into any institutional design plans and cost-benefit calculations about near-term use of particular voice machanisms. The same is true of political traditions and the degree to which parties are institutionalized and politics are genuinely democratic and contested (as opposed to being based on personalism and clientelism).[9] For example, politics in the Philippines have traditionally been more vibrant and democratic than those in Indonesia. This has produced somewhat greater accountability effects in the former. The nature of state administration adds further complications related to whether the state is developmental in orientation, whether there is a reasonably professional civil service, whether there is any degree of decentralized governance, and whether the bureaucracy represents a largely or wholly closed culture. All of these factors have a profound impact on the potential scope of civil society influence.

The second category of constraints may prove somewhat more susceptible to near- or medium-term reform influence, at least at the level of particular projects or jurisdictions. Significant infusions of financial and technical assistance, technology, mentoring (on matters ranging from legal literacy to internal organization and transparency), and training (especially cross-training) may be required to strengthen government and CSO capacity—to allow relevant government and civil society policy-making participants to strengthen mutual trust and working relationships and use voice mechanisms for their intended purpose.[10] According to a cross-country survey of citizen voice mechanisms, resource issues relating to the establishment and maintenance of functional interfaces with citizens are consistently overlooked (McGhee 2003). Public officials and CSO representatives must frequently be encouraged and trained to communicate in a more empirically informed, persuasive manner that bridges divides based on entrenched views. CSO representatives must be trained to be communicative and transparent with their own members and sensitive to the need to represent more encompassing interests in society and build alliances and coalitions. Such process strengthening must go hand in hand with institutional innovation. These considerations echo those of an in-depth assessment of constraints on local participation in Tanzania (Cooksey and Kikula 2005).

These perspectives serve as a potent reminder of the limitations of pursuing "empowerment as a technique" or seeking "optimal institutional arrangements" (Li 2006: 34) without implicitly, if not explicitly, addressing embedded social norms and structures as well as contingent power relations that are "historically tied to the outcome of struggles of social forces and interests . . . the product of grinding social change over centuries" (Hadiz 2004: 702). A focus on institutions can turn into "oversimplistic evolutionism," in which informal norms and understandings regrettably carry little or minimal weight in development strategies (Cleaver 1999).

Examples of Legal and Institutional Frameworks Supportive of Citizen Voice Mechanisms

Many different legal, policy, and institutional frameworks can support effective citizen voice mechanisms, which, in turn, can improve service delivery performance. Seldom, however, do they cohere in perfectly logical, complementary fashion in developing countries. As befits their adoption through successive, incremental layers of reform initiatives, many of which reflect compromise and half-measures (and many of which predate a societal interest in citizen participation per se), these frameworks and instruments often leave significant gaps and ambiguities.

This section provides a highly impressionistic overview of some of the most important legal, policy, and institutional elements underpinning citizen voice mechanisms currently in use around the world, beginning at the national level and working downward to the local government context. Where these formal institutions do not exist or are dysfunctional, certain relevant informal mechanisms are surveyed, mostly at the local level.

Direct and indirect national-level legal frameworks and institutions

Four main types of national-level legal framework have an important bearing on the effectiveness of citizen voice mechanisms: constitutional provisions, laws on local government, administrative procedure laws and their legislation concerning public input on draft laws and regulations, and freedom of information legislation, plus other national legislation indirectly affecting civil society's ability to organize itself and advocate effectively on behalf of citizens.

CONSTITUTIONAL PROVISIONS. The constitutions of many countries include direct and indirect provisions that bear on the degree to which citizens can influence the quality and accountability of service delivery at the national, provincial, or local level. Constitutions address such important issues as freedom of speech, conscience, assembly, and association, as well as other civil and social rights (including rights to information, which may provide an important foundation for civic organizing and advocacy). More directly, many constitutions provide for referendums and plebiscites, elections and electoral representation, and the role of civil society in development planning and policy formulation. Uganda's constitution, for example, provides for direct democracy through referendums (including through resolutions passed by a majority in at least half of the country's district councils), as well as minority representation at the national level (the constitution guarantees one parliamentary seat per district for women; parliament may provide representation for youth, people with disabilities, and other disadvantaged groups).

Legal, institutional, capacity, and resource constraints make enforcement of these rights difficult in developing countries. The Philippines Constitution of 1987 contains progressive provisions on constitutional amendment by popular initiative and special affirmative representation of marginalized groups in local legislative councils. Implementing legislation is still lacking, however, which means that such provisions carry largely rhetorical weight. In Tanzania the constitution includes broad declarations of civil rights, but they are undercut by a number of carefully worded exceptions that restrict their application. The Indian Constitution, through Amendments 73 (1992) and 74 (1993), created new tiers of local governance (municipalities and *panchayats*) and devolved significant economic development and social service provision responsibilities from federal states to municipalities and urban councils. But Indian states have interpreted these mandates differently in their own constitutions, resulting in highly uneven shifts of responsibility to local levels of government. Uganda is emblematic of a number of countries whose constitutions proclaim a wide range of economic, civil, and political rights that are seldom realized because of political and resource pressures.

In general, constitutional provisions offer a strong rhetorical basis for advancing effective citizen voice mechanisms, but they often fail to generate practical results—even where some legislative elaboration exists—as a result of problems with enforcement mechanisms and the legal and political culture. Without effective political and economic competition, as well as effective and accountable judicial, audit, and law enforcement institutions, constitutional provisions alone are of limited value.

LAWS ON LOCAL GOVERNMENT. A number of national laws dealing with local government and decentralization may have an impact on the extent and quality of citizen participation in local government. At a minimum, both kinds of legislation are important to the extent that they do, or do not, create a mandate for local fiscal responsibilities, legislative initiative, and citizen participation, the details of which are often left to municipalities. In some cases national legislation is relatively uniform and prescriptive as to how budgeting, planning, and overall decision making (including its participatory quality) are to occur. Such is the case with so-called big bang (comprehensive) decentralization initiatives, such as those adopted in Bolivia, the Philippines, and to some extent Indonesia during the past decade and a half. In other countries, such as Brazil and India, there is greater de jure (not to mention de facto) heterogeneity in the extent and nature of responsibilities transferred to states and localities and the planning and budget systems of each (Bardhan and Mookherjee 2006; Rocamora 2003).

In some countries, such as Thailand and Uganda, local government laws are relatively uniform and prescriptive, but they are also vague, contradictory, or restrictive as to the form that institutionalized participation should take

(Gaventa 2002; Orlandini 2003; Rocamora 2003). By contrast, statutory frameworks for public participation at the local level in Bolivia and the Philippines are quite progressive and relatively specific in design. In Bolivia the 1994 Law of Popular Participation created 311 municipal governments; allocated 20 percent of the national budget to these municipalities (supplemented by local taxes on land, cars, and other subjects); and devolved responsibilities to them for economic development, social services, and infrastructure investment and maintenance. Alongside these changes, it created mechanisms and conditions for indigenous, peasant, and neighborhood organizations to participate with legal rights in local government as territorial grassroots organizations (OTBs). Specifically, municipalities are enjoined to involve OTBs in the Annual Operation Plan (POA) of the municipality, as well as the Municipal Development Plan (PDM)—a five-year plan that is supposed to inform the POAs. National and local guidelines have sprung up to inform the participation processes. At the same time, the Law of Popular Participation created *comites de vigiliancia* (oversight committees) made up of OTB representatives that became a mechanism for rudimentary civil society participation in budgeting, as well as for ensuring local government accountability. The oversight committees are specifically empowered to oversee and monitor POA (budget) implementation and can even freeze the budget under certain circumstances and help reformulate the POA (Faguet 2006; Saule, Velasco, and Arashiro 2002). The Uruguayan national framework for local government participation is also quite expansive (box 6.1).

BOX 6.1 Local Government Participation under the Uruguay National Agreement of 1992

Montevideo embarked on an impressive decentralization effort within its administrative department in 1990. Inspired by that model, the country as a whole adopted a national agreement in 1992 that created formal spaces for popular participation at the municipal level, including neighborhood councils with consultative and control functions over local councils and the administrative departments of the state. The agreement also required representation of different political parties in the local councils. Neighborhood councils later obtained the right to propose citizen initiatives. Further evolution of participatory planning and decision making has extended beyond the local councils and neighborhood councils to specialized commissions on health and social programs comanaged by local government and civil society representatives.

Source: Saule, Velasco, and Arashiro 2002.

National-level laws and institutions established for local governments (as opposed to locally generated laws and institutions) have produced highly variable results in terms of participation. Such laws often include insufficient elaboration of rights and responsibilities, not to mention inadequate training and information for citizen and CSO participants. Co-optation of citizen representatives is also a frequent problem (Antlov 2003; Beneria-Surkin 2005; Iszatt 2002; Rocamora 2003; Saule, Velasco, and Arashiro 2002). In some cases, prescriptive forms of participation clash with, or limit, local traditions and creativity (Goudsmit and Blackburn 2001; Iszatt 2002; Li 2006). Another frequent problem affecting participation is conflicting legislative mandates between levels of government as to fiscal and service delivery responsibilities and a lack of proper institutional coordination (Beneria-Surkin 2005; Goudsmit and Blackburn 2001; Iszatt 2002). These problems are often slow to resolve.

ADMINISTRATIVE PROCEDURE–RELATED LEGISLATION AND INSTITUTIONS. National laws on administrative procedure and other key matters of public law may provide significant direct support for public participation—in the context of decisions (or appeals of decisions) by administrative bodies (to higher bodies within the administration or to judicial bodies) or rules for open regulation drafting or policy making.

This type of legislation, which is often well developed on paper (but often drastically less so in practice), provides individuals and groups with the basic right to be informed about the process of administrative decision making, to have access to information held by the state relating to their case, to have an opportunity to present relevant information to administrative decision makers before a decision is made, to know the reasons and legal basis for a decision, and to have a clear understanding of how and when to appeal such a decision. Where, as is common, civil society capacity and advocacy skills are low and bureaucratic culture is both closed and of poor quality, compliance with these administrative procedure principles at the national agency level or municipal level (municipal administrative bodies are usually subject to such laws) is likely to be weak. Administrative impunity is likely to be even greater where judicial independence and effectiveness are also lacking.

Legislation on open regulatory drafting procedures is rare even in many established democracies. It is usually adopted only on a sectoral or ministry-by-ministry basis (with environmental rule making and policy making often the most progressive, because of a long history of civil society pressure). In these contexts, some kind of notice and comment mechanism may exist, requiring public authorities to circulate drafts of proposed regulations or decrees in advance of parliamentary consideration and to solicit comments or engage in mandatory consultations with civil society representatives and occasionally the general public (through public hearings or town meetings). Occasionally, such procedures are accompanied by regulatory impact analysis—procedures that may require, at a minimum, that the proposing agency qualitatively document that it has considered the potential costs and benefits of the proposed regulations through public consultations.

Three other administrative law–related types of legislation and accompanying institutions that may facilitate public participation are those governing ombudsman functions, open meeting procedures, and advisory councils or committees. The ombudsman is often a creation of parliament, charged with reviewing questions of "maladministration" or illegality by administrative agencies. Despite their lack of enforcement powers, ombudsmen have been effective in some countries (box 6.2). Open meeting laws (which are more common in countries with a common-law heritage) can be important tools for enhancing the accountability of local government councils, boards, or other multimember bodies: they may be required, with narrow stated exceptions, to conduct their deliberations in public at accessible locations. Legislation on advisory groups or councils (rare in the developing world, even for individual ministries) can help

---

BOX 6.2 The Everyday Effectiveness of the Peruvian Ombudsman

Although best known for its work investigating human rights violations, the Peruvian Ombudsman's Office (*Defensor*) also deals with everyday complaints lodged by ordinary citizens about maladministration. Enshrined in the 1993 Constitution, the Defensor operates through eight regional offices, handling roughly 3,000 cases a year, many of them dealing with complaints about municipal housing and utilities. Defensor officials use a strategic mix of education, investigation, and advocacy to obtain their objectives. Whereas formal administrative and court challenges to administrative actions may take months or even years to resolve, the Defensor typically obtains at least some kind of resolution within a week, with an overall resolution rate of nearly 85 percent. The regional offices have also issued report cards on local and regional public administration, which have gained significant media attention and shamed public authorities into compliance on many issues.

Source: CIDA n.d.

make public the membership and work of such groups, aiding overall government transparency.

FREEDOM OF INFORMATION LAWS AND INSTITUTIONS. Freedom of, or access to, government-held or -generated information is a fundamental precondition for governmental transparency, accountability, and citizen engagement in policy making and decision making. Most freedom of information legislation also contains affirmative obligations that require governments to make publicly available a wide range of information about their most important policies and practices, including organization and budgets (where such requirements refer to more issue-specific information, they may also be contained in specialized or sectoral legislation or regulations). Not only are such affirmative provisions relating to key kinds of information much more effective in reaching and empowering citizens, they may also be much more efficient for governments, obviating the need for individual, case-by-case applications for the vast majority of the most commonly requested data. This may also simplify governments' information management and organizational requirements (especially those of local governments), allowing them to focus on the most publicly relevant and commonly needed information.

Freedom of information laws usually presume disclosure: the state may restrict access to information only in limited circumstances, such as national security, or with regard to confidential personal or commercial information. If the state is going to deny information, it must give a legally sanctioned reason and the party must have the right to appeal (initially to an agency or ombudsman, then to the courts). These national laws provide a compelling framework for information disclosure at all levels of government. However, because most freedom of information legislation in developing and developed countries is predominantly responsive in nature, it is critical for public participation in sectoral or local governance that there coexist specialized legislation or regulations prescribing affirmative disclosure of key kinds of information (for example, relating to budgets, planning documentation, contracts, procurement, and key government organization and operations). These affirmative provision systems can be tied to one-stop-shop information and application windows, such as that in Sindudhurg, Maharashtra, India, where citizens can interact with public officials and obtain a clear understanding of their rights regarding licenses, permits, and the delivery of services, potentially avoiding the need to pay bribes (Goetz and Gaventa 2001). Even where such affirmative information provision is modest, responsive systems with few restrictions can be enormously effective (box 6.3). Where

> **BOX 6.3** Goa's Right to Information Act
>
> In 1998 the Indian state of Goa introduced a Right to Information Act whose liberal disclosure provisions are among the most progressive in the world. Among its provisions are those permitting citizens the right to photocopy files pertaining to virtually all government operations, including certain kinds of informal notes made by administrators and politicians. Hundreds of citizens have used the act to investigate government decision making and service delivery problems in the health, education, banking, environment, and foreign investment sectors. Such investigations have aided efforts by citizens and CSOs to seek court redress for their grievances.
>
> *Source:* Goetz and Gaventa 2001.

government information is hard to come by, CSOs like those undertaking citizen report cards in Bangalore can collect and disseminate important information about the quality of public services (Goetz and Gaventa 2001).

OTHER NATIONAL LEGISLATION AND INSTITUTIONS. A wide range of other national laws and institutions may have important direct and indirect effects on the extent and quality of citizen voice mechanisms, whether they involve central, provincial, or local governments. Electoral laws providing for maximum citizen and party participation, as well as diverse and representative government, are critical for a functioning democracy and political competition—but so are laws that govern referendums and citizen initiatives. Laws governing the registration and taxation of for-profit and especially not-for-profit organizations can have a profound impact on the health of the Third Sector and the vibrancy of civic engagement, as can laws governing media ownership and operation, defamation, speech, and assembly. Public security and antiterror laws can shut down or chill many kinds of civic organizing and information dissemination if improperly applied.

National legislation may provide for special kinds of citizen participation. The Bolivian National Dialogue Law of 2001 institutionalizes a consultative mechanism between the government and civil society every three years in order to define priorities in the fight against poverty. The same is true of the Brazilian Statute of the City, also adopted in 2001, which sets forth a means of institutionalizing participation in urban areas through local participatory planning and budgeting. National legislation or initiatives can also spur special monitoring or consultation processes. Uganda, for example, has used

Participatory Poverty Assessments to conduct national consultations on people's perceptions of poverty and priorities for poverty reduction, as well as to increase citizen capacity for poverty monitoring. It has also used a comprehensive service delivery survey to provide longitudinal data on the efficiency and responsiveness of key services (Gaventa 2002). National-level frameworks can also provide a foundation for joint management of sectoral programs. In India, for example, national guidelines on watershed development set forth legal and organizational parameters for community mobilization and management of local watersheds in cooperation with government agencies and NGOs (Goetz and Gaventa 2001).

A number of important, reasonably functional national institutions are usually needed to help create meaningful accountability frameworks at multiple levels of government. These include well-staffed and resourced electoral commissions, legislatures, staffs, courts, audit bodies, and a generally professional civil service. Based on the public goods they provide, it is difficult for good governance and accountability to take root and improve in the absence of these institutions.

Local-level legislative and administrative frameworks

In many countries, national laws prescribe the basic jurisdiction of local representative bodies and public participation avenues; in other countries these mechanisms arise largely from provincial and local legislation and policies. In Brazil and India, for example, there is wide local variation in how states and localities arrange their legislative and administrative affairs and use participatory policy-making, planning, and decision-making vehicles. In Brazil state-level constitutions determine the mechanisms for participation in state management and metropolitan administration. Organic municipal laws regulate popular participation at the local level, establishing *subprefeituras* (subprefectures) as neighborhood management entities with rights of community representative participation (Saule, Velasco, and Arashiro 2002).

Perhaps the best-known feature of local participatory mechanisms in Brazil are the numerous participatory budgeting processes that have evolved over the past decade and a half, including the much-studied original Porto Alegre model. Using special local assemblies with citizens and civil society representatives on an annual cycle, and a Participatory Budget Council composed of delegates elected from local meetings, neighborhood associations, special interest groups, municipal unions, and local governments, the process entails deliberations on projects for specific districts as well as overall municipal investment priorities. As many as 103 Brazilian cities carried out participatory budget processes between 1997 and 2000 (Baiocchi 2006).

In India, where states have significant planning and budgeting autonomy, the State of Kerala launched a planning initiative to empower local councils to draw up development plans to prioritize projects (receiving up to 40 percent of the state budget for this purpose) based on a highly participatory, village-based planning process involving neighborhood groups, resource experts, and retired teachers and government officials (Goetz and Gaventa 2001).

Where government-initiated or -led community participatory planning or review processes are weak or compromised at the state, district, or municipal level, there may be greater recourse to submunicipal structures, such as village assemblies, for public input into matters of local significance. In Indonesia, for example, erratic efforts toward genuine decentralization resulted in greater participatory engagement in village councils, which have legislative and budgetary decision-making autonomy over village affairs and to which the village head is answerable (Rocamora 2003). If municipal and village assemblies are captive to special or elite interests, CSOs may have to independently collect information and investigate government spending practices (box 6.4).

In a less adversarial vein, CSOs and foreign donors may step in to lead or assist with participatory planning, budgeting processes, or service delivery

---

BOX 6.4 Promise and Pitfalls of Noninstitutionalized Participation: Mumbai's Action Committee for Rationing

India has suffered from rampant corruption in public works projects and leakage from the Indian Public Distribution System, wherein ration shops sell basic food items and household goods for personal profit. Because official vigilance committees and village assemblies have often been captured by corrupt actors and many ration shop owners are politicians, in the 1990s the Mumbai Action Committee for Rationing (RKS) stepped in to develop its own parallel oversight system. Using clients of the ration shops to monitor and evaluate the quality and prices of the goods sold, as well as publicity campaigns to oblige shopowners to publicly display prices and samples of goods, the RKS presented comprehensive reports on the situation to both users and officials of the Public Distribution System in Mumbai.

The initiative was successful as long as a key progressive bureaucrat held the position of Regional Rationing Controller; it achieved limited success after he or she left. Although an institutionalized role for this state–civil society partnership might not have been possible at the beginning, its absence later proved damaging.

Source: Goetz and Jenkins 2001.

review that are incipient or fragile. In Indonesia tenuous decentralization and tenacious local elites led the World Bank to support a $1 billion Kecamatan (subdistrict) Development Program aimed at meeting local social development needs in tens of thousands of villages. The program involved the creation of new or reformed participatory processes that employed innovative forums and stakeholder committees to guide investment choices (Li 2006).

In Nicaragua, which began a process of decentralizing the national system of public investment in 2003 and subsequently passed a law on municipal transfers that required greater budget allocations to localities, CSOs such as Grupo Fundemos worked with municipalities and their local development committees to develop priorities for public spending through participatory processes. In one municipality, Fundemos applied deliberative processes in 29 rural communities to achieve consensus on budgetary priorities and strengthen the role of the local development committee as a liaison between communities and the local government. The elaboration of the process was not formalized, but it did give rise to potentially institutionalized practices (Partners of the Americas' Center for Civil Society 2005).

State–civil society synergy is also apparent in local sectoral contexts. In Brazil, for example, decentralization has spawned a large array of comanaged sectoral councils concerned with implementation of social policies. Health councils are a particularly vibrant area of citizen participation and monitoring.

What Kinds of Mechanisms and Conditions Create Effective Citizen Voice?

This brief overview of legal and institutional frameworks for citizen voice mechanisms raises a number of key questions about effectiveness. What general kinds of processes and conditions yield the most (and least) effective results? How should effectiveness be defined? What kinds of functional processes are required to overcome common impediments to citizen voice mechanism effectiveness? Should these functional processes be grounded in formal, legal institutions or in informal, possibly ad hoc institutions? Notwithstanding the importance of institutional design, what other conditions, including participant capacities, must be in place or taken into consideration in deciding whether to create or strengthen such institutions?

What Tends to Creates Effective Citizen Voice?

In order for reformers to determine which mechanisms to use, they must first understand the functions and expected impact of these mechanisms, as well as common impediments that may stand in the way of their effective functioning. They must then consider specific impediments that may affect particular voice mechanisms, based in part on the foregoing areas of concern.

There is anecdotal reason for skepticism about whether greater provision of such mechanisms at the local level has broad-based impact (Charlick 2001; Manor and Crook 1998; Mohan and Stokke 2000; Souza 2001). Conducting a meta-analysis of more than 50 literature-based cases as well as an in-depth quantitative analysis of the adoption of participation and voice mechanisms in 273 South African municipalities between 1995 and 2000, Andrews (2005) examines whether the adoption and use of voice mechanisms had a measurable effect on accountability, defined in terms of indicators such as changes in the quality of resource responsibility, government responsiveness and performance, transparency, corruption, and political and administrative accountability.

He finds three types of potential outcomes: (a) no effect (or even a negative effect) on accountability; (b) a narrow effect, reflecting the use (or in some cases, capture) of such mechanisms by selected social groups, influential NGOs, academics, or leading business interests; and (c) a broad effect, reflecting an increase in responsibility, transparency, or responsiveness of public organizations to society in general. According to Andrews, these results are explained by the combined impact and interaction of voice *influence* (the degree to which voice, expressed through a voice mechanism, actually affects who governs, how they govern, the content of the governance agenda, and governance outcomes) and voice *focus* (that is, *whose* voice is expressed through a given voice mechanism). This impact and interaction can be portrayed in a matrix, in which the ideal accountability impacts (touted in much of the participation literature) can be found in the upper-right-hand quadrant (figure 6.2).

Voice influence		Narrow	Broad
	High	Narrow accountability effect (risk of capture) — Narrow focus, high influence	Broad accountability effect (representative) — Broad focus, high influence
	Low	No accountability effect — Narrow focus, low influence	No accountability effect — Broad focus, low influence

Voice focus

Source: Andrews 2005.

FIGURE 6.2 Voice Expression and Accountability Effects

Andrews offers several explanations as to how and why such accountability effects emerge, many of which point to general obstacles to the successful functioning of voice mechanisms:

- Voices expressed in budget planning and other participatory planning and review contexts tend to be influential if they are incorporated into the actual planning exercises and decision-making processes rather than conducted in separate forums.
- Voice focus is narrowed when mechanism design limits voice access—when participation is by invitation only or highly dependent on particular meeting place accessibility, for example.
- Highly technical processes yield low voice influence and narrow voice focus, whereas mechanisms designed to improve citizen access to and understanding of the issues facilitate high voice influence and broad voice focus.
- Monitoring and evaluation devices that are built into or accompany a voice mechanism stimulate voice influence.
- Voice influence is low where there is no medium for voice transmission to carry criticism and feedback directly to decision makers.
- Centralizing political and fiscal structures limit voice influence and narrow voice focus, so that if there is no true delegation of power and responsibility downward to regional or local governments, hierarchical pressures and higher-level political and budget priorities will tilt power and influence toward central political leaders and technical administrators.
- Closed administrative systems limit voice influence and narrow voice focus. They often go hand in hand with bureaucratic inertia and ordinary professional technical culture.
- Voices of the poor are muted or silenced by the higher cost of participation for them and their relative lack of sophistication, as well as weak social structures and disorganized communities. Alliances with better-situated groups may facilitate voice influence but still not deliver the advantages associated with broad voice focus.

What Types of Functional Processes Maximize the Impact of Citizen Voice?

Even if general mechanisms exist to incorporate citizen voice into budgeting and policy making regarding service delivery, they often fail to deliver results, usually as a result of an intentional or inadvertent lack of attention to procedural details. Without such details—which concretely and precisely answer the basic who, what, where, why, and how questions about citizen participation—many ostensibly progressive mechanisms or mandates are destined to fall short of expectations.

Andrews and Shah (2005b) identify some of the more important design details associated with establishing a functional, effective arena for citizen participation in the context of public budgeting—arguably the broadest and most important arena in which public service delivery issues can be addressed by citizens and CSOs. Breaking down the budget process into five common stages (budget target development, bid and draft formulation, bid selection, bid implementation, and evaluation and control), they delve more deeply into impediments to participation, noting that even where legislation mandates some form of participatory budgeting, citizens are hampered by lack of notice, insufficient background information and documentation, overly complex budget documents, forums that are detached from the actual budgeting process, and the lack of a systematic way of capturing and transmitting the evidence or products of public participation. Thus, even where citizens are involved in developing budget proposals, they frequently lack access to influence administrators in acting upon their suggestions, monitor implementation of budget decisions, or evaluate the impact of those decisions (Andrews and Shah 2005b).

These common impediments can be mitigated by breaking down the practical needs of citizens into discrete functions or stages and then identifying and mapping particular kinds of procedures to enable minimally effective participation. An overarching requirement, of course, is that citizens be treated as integral participants in budgeting and service delivery policy making to begin with. Ensuring this requires formal or informal arrangements by which citizen voice is incorporated into one or more stages of the policy cycle. This core mandate is often expressed vaguely or rhetorically in a constitution or in framework laws on local government (and occasionally in sectoral legislation and regulations); it is rarely brought down to earth in terms of concrete procedures. The crucial question of which citizens or citizens groups will be incorporated into decision-making processes is either left unaddressed or tilted toward minimizing participation. The challenge is to determine what these concrete participation rules and procedures should be and how they can best be structured. Such processes should acknowledge the utility of all of the principal levels and forms of participation intensity—information sharing, consultation, and active participation—commonly cited in the literature to characterize an ascending scale of citizen voice effectiveness (Andrews and Shah 2005b).[11]

Borrowing from Andrews and Shah but going beyond the specific context of budgeting to citizen participation into the broader arena of shaping,

Temporal (stages)	Voice elicitation ➡	Deliberation and ➡ decision making	Reporting, feedback, ➡ and evaluation	Complaint and ➡ redress
Foundational (cross-cutting, at <u>each</u> stage)	⬆	⬆	⬆	
	⊚ Affirmative/balanced representation ⊚ Notification and agenda setting ⊚ Affirmative information provision ⊚ Transparency and documentation			

Source: Author.

FIGURE 6.3 Key Functional Institutions Necessary for Effective Stakeholder Participation/Consultation

monitoring, evaluating, and seeking redress for various kinds of service delivery, eight institutional processes can be identified to facilitate citizen needs (figure 6.3).[12] Some of these processes temporally focus on the stages of the policy-making cycle. Others are cross-cutting and serve as *preconditions* for other processes.

Affirmative/balanced representation institutions

Citizens, as constituents, should have at least some balanced representation in local governments through reasonably equitable local government electoral laws or rules and, where necessary—depending on documented need—special legislation that affirmatively endows underrepresented segments of society with some kind of supplemental participatory or voting status in municipal or provincial councils. These provisions could range from a small number of reserved seats for women or minorities on municipal or district councils to special issue- or constituency-oriented group representation on particular sectoral or subject matter boards or committees. While other voice elicitation procedures can be used to collect a wider range of citizen voice (see below), an effective participatory scheme must first address questions of who rather than what or how, by considering the need for some kind of equitable representation rules and institutions.

Notification and agenda-setting institutions

Citizens must have accurate, timely advance notice that public deliberations or decisions requiring or inviting their input are scheduled, so that they have time to prepare for such events. Media—ranging from radio, newspaper, and TV announcements to posted notices on public buildings—should be used (depending on the circumstances) to ensure that such information is transmitted. Citizens should also have access to planned agendas and be provided with the opportunity to comment on and influence them. These agendas should be easy to read and include useful background reading or documentation where necessary.

Affirmative information provision institutions

Governments should be required or informally pressured to provide the public (free of charge, in specified quantities, at designated locations) with certain kinds of information and documentation for purposes of study, deliberation, comment, decision making, monitoring, and evaluation. Such information should include laws, regulations, and budgets; budget planning, implementation, and evaluation documents; major program documents; annual reports; transcripts and summaries of public meetings; survey results; audits; organizational charts; and information directories. This affirmative approach—with the onus on government—contrasts with many freedom of information regimes, which rely largely or wholly on so-called "responsive" information access systems, where disclosure is triggered only by individualized, carefully identified information requests, often for a fee.

Transparency and documentation institutions

Governments should be required or pressured to hold legislative council or official advisory committee meetings that are open to the public and the media. Rules should require that all proceedings be recorded in some fashion, summarized, reported to participants, and made available to the public in specified quantities at designated locations. It is critical that citizen views and demands—and public representatives and officials' response to them—be recorded and captured in order to create effective incentives for the public sector to take civic interests seriously.

Affirmative voice elicitation institutions

Governments should have rules and processes—or, failing that, customs or practices—that require them to elicit information on citizen concerns, demands, and priorities. This can be done in different ways, depending on local circumstances, traditions, and needs. Where possible, rules and processes should be mandatory rather than discretionary and require affirmative, systematic processes on the part of elected representatives (council members), administrators, or both, whereby they respond to the advocacy efforts of a handful of well-situated and well-organized CSOs (which may advance a narrow set of views). These elicitation methods can range from collection of written information submissions to the holding of specialized public hearings by council members and bureaucrats. The products of these information collection avenues should also be summarized, recorded, and disseminated through particular media.

Deliberation and decision-making institutions

At the stage of policy-making deliberations or decision making, which may or may not necessitate the involvement of smaller groups of citizens or specially designated citizen representatives, procedures should be in place that require affirmative steps by government bodies to present policy proposals, spending targets, or proposed legal or regulatory changes in easy-to-comprehend formats (with appropriate background documentation and due consideration by the recognized participants).[13] Depending on who is accredited to vote, voting could take the form of council votes informed by advisory opinions or advisory voting by consultative groups or the public at large; alternatively, binding referendums on budgets or specific proposals could be held. If information of greatest interest and comprehensibility to citizens is properly organized, citizens can make informed decisions about the types, methods, cost, and past impact of particular service delivery programs and spending streams, including over multiyear periods.

Reporting, feedback, and evaluation institutions

Regardless of their degree of involvement in the policy or budget planning and decision stages, citizens are often denied opportunities to monitor policy and budget execution—that is, the actual delivery of services. As Andrews and Shah observe, administrators are then left to their own devices, without oversight or incentives to adhere to agreed upon parameters. Accordingly, "administrators are often criticized for spending more than budgeted, producing goods and services other than those requested, ... using production and provision techniques that guarantee neither competitive production nor acceptable quality levels, or losing a great deal of money to corruption" (Andrews and Shah 2005b: 203). Governments should have formal, systemic procedures for disseminating implementation data, service results, and customer feedback (including both service delivery quality and timeliness), or they should move in this direction informally with the assistance of various business, community, and nongovernmental organizations. Similarly, there should be formal or informal incentives for governments, assisted by civil society partners, to conduct meaningful evaluations that are widely disseminated, shared, and discussed with legislators and administrators, including front-line service providers.

Complaint and redress institutions

Public input should ideally be institutionalized, so that opportunities to lodge individual or collective complaints are systematically available to citizens (through complaint windows, ombudsmen offices, or when applicable, administrative courts or other special court departments). In addition, agencies should be required to disseminate the resulting data to auditors and the public in readily comprehensible formats, in order to facilitate review by legislators, special advisory groups, and other oversight bodies. Mechanisms designed to facilitate redress and justice in individual cases should be complemented by policy-level responses that are required to be taken, particularly when service delivery reports evidence poor systemic performance. These could range from simple reporting by auditors, legislators, or both to mandatory budget reductions or disciplinary measures against responsible administrators.

The foregoing discussion not only identifies specific processes and procedures to ameliorate the worst problems resulting from poorly designed citizen participation schemes (many of which may have been adopted for purely rhetorical purposes), it also provides a framework for evaluating the effectiveness of existing citizen voice mechanisms—including their implementation and the capacity, resources, and political relationships of the actors responsible therefor. The importance of many of these institutionalized functions was underscored by a recent World Bank study examining outcomes of service delivery projects in several municipalities in Indonesia (Leisher and Nachuk 2006).[14] There has also been a rise in interest in, and practical guidance on, the procedural details of structuring and managing various kinds of effective citizen participation mechanisms, ranging from implementation handbooks (RTI 2003; Sera 2004) to model strategies (ICPS 2006; Tikare and others 2001).

Case Studies on Strengthening Citizen Voice Mechanisms to Improve Service Delivery

The functional analytical framework discussed above derives much of its practical strength from the successful experiences of participatory budget processes in Latin America, particularly in Brazil. Those experiences reflected a willingness on the part of government and civil society activists to pay attention to the details of the process, to stay engaged, to make the costs of participation low for the ordinary citizen, and to make the overall system truly deliberative and a learning experience. This framework can result in real improvements in pro-poor investments and in the quantity and quality of service delivery to average citizens (Baiocchi 2006).

There is ample evidence that such a framework is a necessary but not sufficient condition for citizen voice effectiveness and measurable accountability results. A wide range of contextual factors were critical to the outcomes—from the political economies in Brazil that originally favored Workers' Party electoral success in the cities that later adopted participatory budget systems to the skills and capacity of the civic organizers who organically developed the experiments in partnership with civic and grassroots organizations.

To understand better how such citizen voice mechanisms might be strengthened under different circumstances, this chapter now turns to case studies of Bolivia, the Philippines, and South Africa. The Bolivian case study is extracted from a small number of qualitative studies chronicling experience with implementation of the Law of Popular Participation in a handful of Bolivian municipalities. The case studies on the Philippines and South Africa reinforce many of the lessons from Bolivia.

The case studies were selected based on the availability of secondary literature and the fact that all three local government laws in question were adopted with high hopes when central government reformers and key legislators in each country sought to increase opportunities of the disadvantaged to influence government policy at the local level. Each case reflects mixed outcomes (only low-to-moderate focus and voice influence) and permits an examination as to whether applying elements of the functional analytical framework presented above might result in broader voice focus and higher voice influence. All of the case studies reveal the critical relevance of a host of contextual factors, only some of which may be susceptible to direct improvements in the near term.

The case studies serve a dual purpose. First, they highlight common weaknesses in legal and institutional frameworks—weaknesses that one or more elements of the functional analytical framework might ameliorate. Second, they highlight many of the challenges that such technical fixes face in stimulating participation in highly embedded social, political, and administrative environments. By considering these factors in relatively well-institutionalized environments, they raise a cautionary note about the more daunting challenges that may accompany reform initiatives in countries and regions with fewer institutional endowments and weaker civil societies.

Implementation of Bolivia's Law of Popular Participation

Several anecdotal studies have examined the Bolivian experience implementing the 1994 Law of Popular Participation (Beneria-Surkin 2005; Faguet 2004, 2006; Goudsmit and Blackburn 2001). Many of these studies examine the process of implementation up close, from a political economy and ethnographic perspective, in a handful of Bolivian communities, including several that did not have significant institutional endowments at the time the law was adopted.

The law had several key elements:

- It created 198 new municipalities (for a total of 311).
- It devolved 20 percent of all national tax revenue to municipalities, on a strict per capita basis.
- It transferred ownership of local infrastructure in education, health, irrigation, roads, sports, and culture to municipalities, along with responsibility for maintaining, administering, and investing in such infrastructure.
- It created participatory mechanisms and conditions for indigenous, peasant, and neighborhood organizations to participate in local government planning and budgeting as territorial grassroots organizations (OTBs with legal rights).
- It created oversight committees composed of elected representatives from districts within municipalities (usually drawn from the ranks of OTBs), to provide a focused, alternative channel for popular demand in the policy-making process, to audit government budgets and operations, and to seek redress (including budget reformulation and suspension of disbursements from central to local authorities) if they determine that funds are being misused.

Oversight committees carry significant moral authority based on their corporatist approach and grassroots constituencies. They are led by an elected president whose legal status is comparable to that of the municipal mayor (Faguet 2006). As a result of adoption of the 2001 National Dialogue Law, municipalities were eligible to receive Heavily Indebted Poor Country (HIPC II) funds from the central government, with up to 60 percent going to the poorest rural municipalities. Oversight committees were charged with watching over disbursement of these funds as well.[15]

The most important role for the OTBs and oversight committees is helping shape the Annual Operation Plan (POA) of the municipality, as well as the Municipal Development Plan (PDM)—a five-year plan intended to undergird the POAs. In addition to national and local guidelines that have been developed to inform the mechanics of the participation processes, many municipalities have formally engaged NGOs to help implement such processes.

Vallegrande, a recently studied municipality of some 16,000 inhabitants and with significantly higher levels of human capital than existed in many similarly situated municipalities, allowed a leading NGO, Grupo Nacional de Trabajo para la Participacion (GNTP), to mobilize 23 local organizations to implement the PDM and POA processes in 2003/04 in a more methodical manner than previously. The initiative involved several other NGOs, the municipal government, other government agencies, and the local university. The initial planning process was highly participatory. Several institutions took responsibility for researching, educating, and mobilizing the populations of eight zones within the municipality and training representatives in participatory methods. Following such consciousness raising and information sharing, GNTP and its partners undertook dozens of community appraisals through participatory workshops and then shared the results with local communities for revision and validation. To prepare for the drafting of the PDM, GNTP held preparatory workshops with participants from 61 communities, a municipal sector strategy workshop with 249 representatives of civil society, as well as an institutional fair that consolidated the views and needs of large numbers of CSOs and associations on the mix and type of specific projects. The fair featured a brief, easy-to-read document on the PDM that was disseminated to the public. The 2003 budget was also displayed at municipal offices, and officials were available to answer questions about it (Beneria-Surkin 2005).

The 2004 POA process, meanwhile, was underpinned by circulation of 74 community appraisals, a workshop attended by 122 representatives of OTBs, producer associations, neighborhood groups, water committees, and school groups, as well as 42 community assemblies to offer feedback on the proposed municipal budget. All of these led up to a municipal participatory budget workshop, in which participants finalized the vision for each of the municipality's eight zones and reviewed information on municipal expenditures since 1998. For each zone, participants defined the key objectives, strategies, projects, and programs for the budget and elected three representatives for the participatory budget commission, which included municipal government and NGO representatives and was responsible for approving the budget. Once approved, the budget was circulated widely to the public (Beneria-Surkin 2005).

The aftermath of this 2003/04 budget process produced mixed results. Earlier trends since 1994 toward steady poverty reduction and increased per capita consumption and revenue collection ostensibly continued and appear correlated with higher rates of citizen participation. Levels of participation and perceptions of social accountability and local government management capacity improved significantly in 2003/04 and 96 percent of participants surveyed in the process felt they had good opportunities to participate and make their views known (97 percent of participants, meanwhile, stated that they had not previously participated in the PDM and POA processes). There was also, however, widespread dissatisfaction with the legitimacy, transparency, and activism (or lack thereof) of many OTB and oversight committee representatives.[16] Local elites, working through the municipal government, subsequently controlled budgetary implementation priorities (by reformulating the budget without intervention by the oversight committees), leaving many 2004 POA commitments unfulfilled. The oversight committee apparently also overreached, alienating some municipal officials. Oversight committee members appear to have had inadequate training, skills, and resources to do their jobs properly. Partly for these reasons, and partly as a result of possible co-optation, they failed to solicit continuing input from community representatives. Meanwhile, key government information on past budget decisions and program documents were missing or difficult to access. Possibly as a result of the foregoing, interest in and commitment to the participatory processes tailed off shortly thereafter (Beneria-Surkin 2005).[17] Although Vallegrande's municipal government and civil society were quite well developed and progressive and the participatory budgeting processes relatively well established, they still fell subject to powerful political influences and capacity constraints.

These contextual factors are mirrored in two other recently studied municipalities—Baures and Guayaramerin (Faguet 2006). Baures, which manifested significant competition, balance, and trust among economic, political, and civil society interests, engendered successful PDM and POA processes and pro-poor investment decisions. In contrast, Guayaramerin was dominated by powerful, concentrated economic elites who had captured the major political parties. Moreover, civil society in Guayaramerin was distrustful and balkanized, with many migratory newcomers who found it hard to gain acceptance from other ethnic and social groups and the community at large. Planning procedures were dominated by municipal staff and closed to popular input. Community ideas had little influence in project planning or execution. As one public official noted, "We reformulate the [annual budget] as we see fit. We don't consult grassroots organizations because they bitch too much. We know we should, but we don't" (Faguet 2006: 76).

Based on the experience of the indigenous NGO community in Bolivia, Goudsmit and Blackburn (2001) find implementation problems widespread. They fault the origins of the Law of Popular Participation as a technocratic invention drafted behind closed doors and criticize its tendency to be rigidly applied based on the recommendations of the National Secretariat of Popular Participation. Rather than exploring a wide variety of experimental participatory methodologies, those responsible for the law's implementation often carry out its provisions according to a prescribed recipe—one that sometimes conflicts with indigenous forms of community participation. Facilitators and activists may or may not be adequately trained in sociocultural sensitivity skills or substantive issues (such as land tenure), resulting in inadequate trust in participatory encounters. At the same time, Goudsmit and Blackburn see the PDM process as having to fit with preconceived national and departmental plans and spending priorities, so that substantive experimentation is also frequently squelched. They suggest that community activists, OTB leaders, oversight committee members, and others circulate more widely in the community, acknowledge their role as negotiators rather than disinterested interpreters, and make more of an effort to let participants speak for themselves in workshops and assemblies (rather than having facilitators summarize or characterize their views for them).

The major design features of the law are set up to encourage broad voice focus and high voice influence. There is official guidance, as well as significant room (in theory) for local adaptation, encouraging the establishment of mechanisms designed to reach out to the broader population and diverse communities; there are also effective forums to elicit and transmit various concerns and priorities. The costs of participation have been made quite low. When generally well implemented, the participatory budgeting process in Bolivia can involve relatively diverse participation and representation, reasonably effective collection and documentation of citizen views, and a number of spaces for fair and thorough deliberation.

Even where well implemented, however, it appears that both the framework of the law and guidance and supporting institutions are inadequate to ensure that many other key functional processes necessary for effective citizen voice influence can operate. Based on the case studies cited above, it is not clear how participatory the agenda setting has been—either for the initial participatory appraisals or for the budget preparation workshops and assemblies. Official guidance on the law should require or encourage greater attention to participatory agenda setting at virtually all forums. While time is often of the essence, much of the participatory budgeting process seems highly instrumental and rushed, in order to meet deadlines. This has resulted in missed opportunities to elaborate or consolidate views more thoroughly or thoughtfully. In some cases it has also dissipated trust and engendered cynicism.

Availability of information also appears to be a significant problem. Information, particularly background documentation necessary for putting decisions, planning, and monitoring in context, is often highly controlled or unavailable. Key representatives from the municipal government, OTBs, and oversight committees may need more training and monitoring to share more information, particularly after the views of civil society have been collected. Such representatives may also need to be rotated more frequently to prevent capture and promote more encompassing interests. More broadly, the Law of Popular Participation itself, National Secretariat guidance, and municipal implementing bylaws may need amending in order to provide for affirmative provision and wide public availability of key kinds of information, including past budgets, key supporting budget documents, sectoral plans, and the results of the participatory information-gathering forums themselves.

Overall, based especially on the experience in Vallegrande, it appears that the greatest potential functional weaknesses with the design of the law, and certainly its implementation, relate to ongoing feedback to the population and to monitoring, evaluation, and complaint/redress processes. Persistent complaints were expressed in Vallegrande about the lack of feedback from organizers, oversight committees, and the municipal government about the results of their information gathering and drafting of the PDM—even though the PDM was available in particular locations and particular times. This argues for still better integration of the law's participatory features into the regular budget process, and for more aggressive information dissemination through print media, radio, and TV.

Despite the involvement of a wide range of civil society partners, there appears to be very little ongoing monitoring and evaluation of the budget by oversight committee and OTB representatives or by broader civil society constituencies. While academic surveys were performed about participation and overall investment levels, little or no scorecarding or other monitoring was performed about specific prioritized projects or sectoral service delivery. Perhaps a revised law, or regulations or guidance regarding the law, should require that certain kinds of monitoring or data collection be conducted and the results made publicly available.

To ensure proper accountability, better complaint and redress institutions are also needed. It is unclear what kinds of channels are actually available to citizens to register complaints about budget or service gaps or poor service performance (for example, ombudsmen, municipal complaint desks, official administrative procedures, lawsuits brought by NGO representatives). It may prove useful to explore ways of facilitating citizen initiatives to request budget reformulation based on certain criteria, including significant deviation from multiple POA priorities or spending categories.

Oversight committee members appear to be unable or unwilling to exercise their legal rights and duties to seek reformulation of the budget consistent with original POA and PDM priorities and commitments. It is unclear what the most effective recourse against recalcitrant or neglectful oversight committee members might be. Certainly, the public might be empowered to engage in some form of recall of such individuals based on municipal council initiative or a public petition mechanism. Shorter terms for oversight committee members might also make sense. Another avenue might be to strengthen the legal recourse of oversight committees to suspend central government transfers. As it now stands, such suspension is not a right but rather requires that a request or complaint be brought to the attention of central government authorities, some of whom may have institutional or political incentives to side with municipal governments and local elites.

At a deeper level, all of these potential legal and institutional improvements require a conducive political economy, a relatively committed municipal government leadership, and an open administrative culture. Each—not to mention the original provisions of the Law of Popular Participation—depends on critical capacities and skills among all key participants, most notably municipal government officials and oversight committee representatives. In a given locality, this may necessitate significant training in substantive and process-oriented skills, including active listening, negotiation, and budget analysis. More training manuals and guidance based on in-depth case studies may also be needed.

In turn, such process improvements and capacity building may require significant budgetary outlays that may not fit within the 15 percent cap on municipal operating costs permitted under the Law of Popular Participation (which may be all that most municipalities with modest resources can afford). Perhaps more discouraging, even if ostensibly targeted at the right individuals for the right purposes, improved implementing activities may take considerable time to change behaviors, particularly information hoarding, instances of which are less visible, harder to monitor, and more subject to neglect and manipulation than simple poor performance (see, for example, Azfar, Livingston, and Meagher 2006).

Beyond matters of institutional design, skills and capacity, and resources lie the harder-to-influence realms of culture and politics. Still, bureaucratic and societal culture, at least in the less remote parts of Bolivia, is changing more rapidly than ever; public education efforts and actual experiences in participatory processes can have a profound impact on individual and collective attitudes, making it easier to mobilize constituencies and strengthen diverse sources of demand-side pressures for accountability. In the political arena, the initiation and maintenance of robust participatory mechanisms may depend to a significant degree on particular parties or coalitions being in power, as in Brazil (Baiocchi 2006). As society becomes more familiar with participatory mechanisms as a fixture on the local governance landscape, such mechanisms will become objects of political solicitation and competition by different parties, assuming politics remain relatively contested. At the same time, however, the quality of such processes will continue to depend on elite support for their effective implementation. As suggested by Andrews (2004) and supported by implication by the examples of Baures and Guayaramerin in Faguet's (2006) study, participatory mechanisms take root as a matter of both elite and popular support based on public choice calculations. These will always need to be taken into account in reformers' calculations as to where and how to support these important channels for citizen voice in service delivery.

The Philippines' Experience with the Local Government Code of 1991

The experience of the Philippines with the landmark Local Government Code of 1991 reinforces the notion that an otherwise progressive piece of legislation can achieve relatively little if structural disadvantages of the poor are not addressed and provisions supporting public participation in decision making are not made specific and concrete. After the fall of the Marcos regime in the mid-1980s, the constitution of 1987 was adopted with a provision (Article XIII, Section 16) that established the right of the people and their organizations to effective and reasonable participation at all levels of social, political, and economic decision making. The provision also mandated establishment of consultation mechanisms. Based on this foundation, the Philippines passed a Local Government Code in 1991 that was designed to break the self-perpetuating nature of centralized power. The code has several notable features, including the rights of initiative and referendum; public hearings for key decisions (for example, reclassification of agricultural lands, enactment of local tax ordinances, siting of public facilities, and closure of public streets and parks); and creation of village development councils, intended to mobilize citizen participation in local development planning, implementation, and service delivery efforts (Iszatt 2002).

Despite a vibrant civil society and the activity of a large number of well-organized and respected NGOs, the code has not met its promise of empowering the disadvantaged or key people's organizations and NGOs at the local or provincial level. The code is unnecessarily vague about how public hearings are to be conducted, and it includes no provisions for notifying the public in advance about their occurrence. Local governments are not required to make available certain information or documentation to support the public's participatory role. No mandatory public evaluation and monitoring functions or opportunities are spelled out, and there are no sanctions for public officials who deprive citizens of their right to participate. The code does provide for special local bodies that serve as critical advisory groups on particular issues, including those dealing with health, public safety, education, infrastructure procurement, or local development (through Local Development Councils, where no less than one-quarter of the council consists of representatives of NGOs or people's organizations). These groups can propose; they cannot approve or monitor initiatives nor can they compel information. Neither public budgeting per se nor review of service delivery performance is subject to mandatory public hearings and public participation.

In addition to the lack of specificity and empowerment in the Local Government Code, a host of other, deeper issues prevent it from being used to greatest advantage in monitoring public service delivery. Participation often depends on the skilled and dedicated leadership of NGOs or people's organizations, which in many communities are inexperienced and easily co-opted by local politicians or business elites.[18] Resources are hard to come by, and the prevailing social and political culture may be indifferent or hostile to genuine input from disadvantaged or marginalized groups.[19]

Where the code is silent, overly vague or generic, or poorly implemented, other participatory mechanisms have grown up at the sectoral or individual municipality level, many of them involving highly tangible issues and more specific formal or informal practices. Many concern environmental protection and agrarian reform, where participatory norms have often been incorporated into various assistance programs. A small number of progressive municipalities and cities have adopted legal norms that entrench participatory processes in various arenas. The best known of these, the Naga City Empowerment Ordinance, consciously compensates for gaps left by the Local Government Code. Enacted in 1995, the ordinance provides for local accreditation of NGOs and people's organizations and creates a single people's council made up of accredited organizations. The council elects or appoints representatives to all city government bodies, boards, councils, committees, and task forces, as well as representatives to observe, vote, and participate in the conceptualization, implementation, and evaluation of city programs; propose legislation; and vote at the committee level of the city council. The ordinance also specifically provides for affirmative representation of marginalized or disadvantaged groups on the city's boards, committees, and special bodies, and includes provisions governing public hearings, consultation, information boards, and suggestion boxes, all of which can influence the quality of service delivery (Iszatt 2002).

The contrast between the Local Government Code and the Naga City Ordinance highlights the degree to which participation mandates must be made concrete and specific in order to have a chance of being put to practical use. In particular, it reinforces the need for the cross-cutting, functional institutions discussed in the previous section to be well conceived and applied. It is very important to make sure that a truly diverse and capable group of citizen and government representatives participates in the process, that there is adequate notice of upcoming meetings or hearings, that sufficient relevant background information is made available to such representatives during such processes, and that key deliberations and other forms of participation are adequately documented and disseminated to create a proper public record. An appropriate legal and institutional framework for public participation should also feature a complaint and sanctions regime that creates incentives for public officials to honor their commitment to such participation. Moreover, while these legal and institutional features are critical, they will have little impact without the additional vigilant involvement of the mass media, key advocacy groups, and a significant number of citizens willing to shed traditional deference to authority.

South Africa's Implementation of the Local Government Transition Act

To lay down a new foundation for local governance, in 1996 South Africa adopted a Local Government Transition Act (LGTA) that mandated transparent mechanisms for robust public participation in policy making. The law required municipalities to establish consultative mechanisms soliciting community organizations' views on service needs, feedback mechanisms allowing citizen input on service delivery performance, help desks to register citizen complaints, and procedures for responding to complaints on budget implementation and service delivery (Andrews 2002). Although these provisions had a democratizing thrust, they also had a pragmatic purpose: to better permit municipalities to understand and respond to unmet public demands.

Andrews (2005) identifies a number of situations in which formally adopted participation norms fell short of their promise. In many cases, effective implementation of the LGTA was undermined by conscious or inadvertent neglect of practical procedural details, rendering participation essentially meaningless and having no effect on accountability. In some municipalities, participants in consultative forums were isolated from decision-making processes and were not provided with feedback on their own compartmentalized interactions with public officials. This was especially characteristic of public involvement in the planning and budgeting initiative known as the Integrated Development Plan, where technical experts involved the public only in immaterial parts of the process. In other cases, women, youth, and the poor were inadequately represented in workshops seeking input on budgeting and spending priorities, and the workshops themselves lacked a transparent methodology (Andrews 2005). In the Uthungula municipality, the selection of and poor publicity about meeting locations limited the number and diversity of attendees (in contrast, in the Thabanchu municipality, public planning meetings and workshops were announced in the media and broader participation was observed). In a number of instances, views that did surface were ignored: "Where individuals articulate issues that don't fit in with the process consultant's definition of the session, the information (mostly useful) becomes lost in the process" (DCD-GTZ 1999, cited in Andrews 2002: 27). In the towns of Nelspruit and Cradock, public hearing results were not systematically processed, interpreted, translated, or transmitted to decision makers (Andrews 2005).

In the Howick municipality, attendance at community meetings was by invitation only and business leaders dominated, resulting in a significant expansion of the tourism-related infrastructure and a decline in direct services to the poor. In Thabanchu many citizens were unable to participate because of language barriers and their lack of understanding of key concepts. In Bothaville community participants showed little interest in providing input, because of "poor understanding of government," and withdrew their voices from the planning process as a result of their limited ability (DCD-GTZ 1999, cited in Andrews 2005: 28).

Andrews (2002) finds no evidence of a broad voice focus in these processes. The lack of broad voice seems to reflect the inability of implementers or facilitators of the LGTA to pay careful attention, to the kind of procedural details and representativeness found in Vallegrande, Bolivia, or Naga City, Philippines. Little attention is paid in South Africa to making participatory forums accessible (in terms of location, scheduling, and languages used) or collecting and transmitting their contents to decision makers. The South African case studies demonstrate the tenacity of problems concerning poor community organization, particularly in isolated rural villages. And like Bolivia and the Philippines—and a host of other developing countries around the world—South Africa has enormous resource and capacity-building needs that must be addressed even if progressive, effective legal and institutional participation frameworks are put into place.

Conclusions

Citizen participation, and the processes of decentralization and democratization that are usually presumed to enlarge it, are the products of a given political and social environment. As such, they are susceptible to both positive and negative outcomes, most notably elite capture and manipulation. As Fung and Wright (2003: 263) perceptively argue, different governance modes—as the product of the intersection of adversarial or collaborative approaches as well as top-down or participatory processes—suffer from the "characteristic danger that some interests and parties may be improperly subordinated for the sake of more powerful interests and groups." Moreover, "collaborative governance without an appropriate form of countervailing power is likely to fail"—to degenerate into more adversarial modes, entrench powerful preexisting interests, or simply allow those interests (even with institutional rules for collaboration in place) to advance their causes more ably and effectively. Consequently, "*the problem of generating countervailing power suitable for collaborative governance is not easily solved through clever public policies and institutional designs*" (emphasis in original) (Fung and Wright 2003: 267).

The problem is not solved through the activities of either purportedly neutral technocrats or high-level NGOs or other organizations steeped in special advocacy skills and adversarial modes of exercising power. The strongest forms of collaborative countervailing power come from the ranks of locally organized adversarial entities and politicians seeking populist opportunities. Locally organized groups have deep local knowledge and "are already organized for action at the levels of government and society most appropriate for decentralized problem-solving" (Fung and Wright 2003: 283). Many already engage in local service delivery and are often willing and able to collaborate and experiment rather than engage in abstract policy discussions. Politicians seeking populist opportunities view participatory collaboration as not only good policy but good politics.

These two groups— reform-minded politicians and civil society organizations with adversarial and grassroots ties and credibility—need to be in alignment in order for resources to be released and implementation and capacity-building activities undertaken that can support good institutional designs (and the functional processes discussed in this chapter) embodying effective citizen voice mechanisms. This is certainly the lesson of the widely studied experience of participatory budgeting in Brazil,[20] and it conforms to the experience with implementation of the Law of Popular Participation in Bolivia and the success of the Naga City Empowerment Ordinance. Only if these two players engage in constructive dialogue and work in tandem can the promise of effective institutional designs for service delivery accountability be realized.

Annex: The ARVIN Framework

TABLE 6A.1 The ARVIN Framework: A Way to Assess the Enabling Environment for Civic Engagement

Item	Legal and regulatory framework	Political and governance context	Sociocultural characteristics	Economic conditions
Association	Freedom of association	Recognition and accreditation policies and procedures	Social capital, gender barriers, illiteracy	Cost of legal registrations and accreditations, cost of convening meetings and forums
Resources	Tax systems; fund-raising and procurement regulations	Government grants, private funds, contracting, and other transfers	Social philanthropy (the culture of giving), history of associational life, self-help and gap-filling	Size of and stresses in the economy, unemployment, impact of economy on contribution by members, infrastructure and cost of communications
Voice	Freedom of expression, media, and information and communication technology–related laws	Political control of public media	Communication practices (use of media by different social groups)	Fees associated with expressing views in media (advertisements versus op-eds); costs to present, publish, and distribute views (petitions, newsletters, radio announcements)
Information	Freedom of information; rights to access to and provision of public information	Information disclosure policies and practices, ability to demystify public policy and budgets	Information networks, illiteracy, word of mouth	Costs/fees for access to information

(continued)

TABLE 6A.1 (continued)

Item	Legal and regulatory framework	Political and governance context	Sociocultural characteristics	Economic conditions
Negotiation	Legally established dialogue spaces (referendums, lobby regulations, public forums, and so forth)	Political will, institutionalized dialogues and social accountability mechanisms, capacity of parliament and national government to engage	Social values and hierarchies that establish who can speak on what subject in what context and when	Bargaining power, impact of economic constraints on autonomy and advocacy

Source: Thindwa, Monico, and Reuben 2003.

Notes

1. Andrews and Shah also note the tendency for most public sector reforms to have substantial centralizing effects based on the way in which reforms are initiated and the preferences of central governments and external reform partners for centralized hierarchical systems that reduce transactions costs for assistance and facilitate the monitoring of how funds are used.
2. There is evidence suggesting that certain forms of "voice" (such as transparency and participation-enhancing mechanisms) have a greater impact on government accountability than do the quality of internal administrative rules, meritocratic personnel standards, or higher public sector wages (see, for example, Kaufmann, Mehrez, and Gurgur 2002). Research based on the participatory budget experience in Brazil suggests that such practices have targeted poorer residents and needier areas better than ordinary budget practices. Participatory budget reforms across Brazil between 1997 and 2000 were associated with increased municipal spending on health services, improved fiscal status, and certain improvements in service delivery (such as drinking water) and some human development outcomes, including poverty and educational enrollment rates (Baiocchi 2006). A World Bank study of 121 rural water supply projects in 49 developing countries finds a strong correlation between project success and beneficiary participation: only 8 percent of the 49 projects with low levels of participation were successful, while 42 percent of the 64 projects with high levels of participation were deemed successful (Narayan 1995). A study of the use of citizen report cards in Bangalore, India, also finds some impact on service delivery outcomes (Ravindra 2004). In Bolivia there appears to be some correlation between increasing levels of decentralized public participation and higher investment in human capital and social services, including in the poorest municipalities (Faguet 2004).
3. In this chapter, *institutions* is used primarily to denote organizational forms or processes rather than its broader New Institutional Economics meaning that includes a wide spectrum of rules, norms, and practices.
4. These modes include, on a rough continuum, autonomous managerial decision (no participation), modified autonomous managerial decision (a decision that may or may not reflect group influence), segmented public consultation (a decision based on separate consultations—ranging from interviews to meetings to surveys—that does reflect group influence), unitary public consultation (shared deliberation with a unified public group through advisory groups or public meetings), and public decision (shared deliberation and decision making with broader segments of the public, also via advisory groups or public meetings) (Thomas 1990).
5. This study shows that South African municipalities that adopted legislation in the 1990s requiring new budget planning, information reporting, auditing, participatory governance, and administrative procedure rules had better fiscal outcomes than those that did not.
6. According to Ackerman (2004), such institutionalization can take three forms, depending on the level at which such institutions are formalized. First, they can be built into the strategic plans of government agencies, and rules and procedures can be required that obligate front-line officials to consult or otherwise engage with societal actors. Second, specific agencies can be created that have the goal of ensuring societal participation in government activities (that is, serve as a liaison between government

and civil society). Third, participatory mechanism can be inscribed in law, requiring agencies or the government as a whole to involve societal actors at various points in the public policy cycle.
7. Many countries seek to "legislate progress" in public participation, relying on legal mandates to prescribe the major contours of citizen voice transmission. This may initially appear to be a rational approach in countries where excessive bureaucratic discretion and corruption seem to suggest the need for rigid and detailed legal prescriptions. Such a legalistic approach does not guarantee compliance with, or use of, voice mechanisms, however.
8. Top-down, highly formal mandates may privilege elite, central government interpretations of how local democracy should operate; at worst, they may create ceilings rather than floors, cutting off local understandings and bottom-up innovation that endow local actors with greater social capital and give them a greater investment in seeing that voice mechanisms operate effectively. The best solution to these dilemmas in many developing countries may be to have a national law on local self-government mandate certain minimal standards for citizen participation—many of which might track the functional requirements described in the previous section—while leaving it to local authorities and CSOs to determine how these rules and institutions—or a variety of informal processes—might best be structured consistent with local values and norms.
9. According to Goetz and Gaventa (2001:11), "where there is robust multiparty competition, with well-institutionalized and ideologically diverse parties, civil society groups may pursue confrontational, high-visibility strategies to promote group interests or challenge state behavior, in the hope of interesting opposition parties in taking up their concerns in the legislature."
10. Gaventa and Valderrama (1999) survey common constraints and suggestions for alleviating such impediments, based on a review of seven multicountry studies.
11. Both the OECD (2001b) and the Institute of Development Studies at the University of Sussex (McGee 2003) employ variations of this three-tiered framework to describe increasing intensities of citizen participation.
12. In the budgeting context, Andrews and Shah (2005b) list different institutional processes, but they share most of the same functions: the right to information institutions, revelation institutions, reflection and resolution institutions, reporting institutions, and response and redress institutions. These opportunity structures overlap with those offered by Goetz and Gaventa (2001), who posit processes that facilitate consultation, presence, and influence (roughly corresponding to opportunities to offer views, participate to a limited degree in decision making, and help shape actual policy and financial decisions relating to service delivery).
13. Andrews and Shah (2005b) propose budget formats that are written in a clear, easy-to-read, and understandable style and that cluster and focus attention on the budget information of the greatest interest to citizens. They propose that all agencies and departments make budget bids that focus on producing specific outputs. They also suggest that departments make alternative proposals as to how outputs can be produced and disclose the specific performance criteria they would be willing to commit to (based on the specific output projected to be generated, according to quantity, location, and date) and associated benchmarked targets (based on total cost, cost per unit, and quality).

14. Leisher and Nachuk (2006) find that a favorable decentralization legal framework, formal local laws and regulations, robust information dissemination systems, and solid monitoring and data collection plans were critical to local success in delivering better services to the public. They also note the importance of noninstitutional factors, such as local political leadership and financial sustainability.
15. The government can spend only 15 percent of coparticipation funds on operational costs. In some cases, this has been inadequate to support the work of the oversight committees in participatory budgeting processes (Beneria-Surkin 2005).
16. In Brazil some participatory representatives are reportedly cynically referred to as "professional citizens," who often monopolize and control access to information (Beneria-Surkin 2005).
17. Nearly 40 percent of civil society participants in the 2003/04 processes said they still had little or no knowledge of how participatory planning functions operate and what the rules were for the municipal budget (Beneria-Surkin 2005).
18. To counter these impediments somewhat, the Local Government Code establishes village development councils, which are tasked with mobilizing citizen participation in local development efforts, including development planning. The public also receives significant organizational and legal help from the more than 250 village legal resource centers around the country, which provide redress and accountability regarding resource tenure and access to justice (Iszatt 2002).
19. The constitution mandates sectoral representation on legislative councils at all levels. Three seats are reserved for women, labor groups, and the urban poor, indigenous cultural communities, or disabled. After nearly two decades, however, implementation is spotty, partly because of the lack of sufficient support for implementing legislation that would establish greater specificity on the selection of these representatives.
20. There is ample evidence that the initial success of participatory budgeting in Porto Alegre and its successful replication in several other cities are directly traceable to the efforts of these two players. Not only was participatory budgeting championed by Workers' Party politicians, it was carefully designed by citizen activists with long experience in community organizing. These social actors led the process and modeled it on previously existing practices and demands. For example, the Porto Alegre experiment originated as an initiative proposed by the Union of Residents' Association (Ackerman 2004; Baiocchi 2006).

References

Ackerman, John. 2004. "State-Society Synergy for Accountability." Working Paper 30, World Bank, Washington, DC.

———. 2005. "Social Accountability in the Public Sector: A Conceptual Discussion." Social Development Paper 82, World Bank, Participation and Civic Engagement, Washington, DC.

Andrews, Matthew. 2002. "Fiscal Institutions Adoption in South African Municipalities." Paper presented at the Center for Science and Industrial Research, Pretoria, South Africa, March 15.

———. 2004. "Selecting and Sustaining Community Programs in Developing Countries." *Public Administration Quarterly* 28 (1/2): 12–46.

———. 2005. "Voice Mechanisms and Local Government Fiscal Outcomes: How Does Civil Pressure and Participation Influence Public Accountability?" In *Public Expenditure Analysis*, ed. Anwar Shah. Washington, DC: World Bank.

Andrews, Matthew, and Anwar Shah. 2005a. "Citizen-Centered Governance: A New Approach to Public Sector Reform." In *Public Expenditure Analysis*, ed. Anwar Shah. Washington, DC: World Bank.

———. 2005b. "Toward Citizen-Centered Local-Level Budgets in Developing Countries." In *Public Expenditure Analysis*, ed. Anwar Shah. Washington, DC: World Bank.

Antlov, Hans. 2003. *Civic Engagement in Local Government Renewal in Indonesia*. LogoLink report, Institute of Development Studies, Brighton, United Kingdom.

Arnstein, Sherry, 1969. "A Ladder of Citizen Participation," *Journal of the American Planning Association* 35 (4): 216–24.

Azfar, Omar, Jeffrey Livingston, and Patrick Meagher. 2006. "Decentralization in Uganda." In *Decentralization and Local Governance in Developing Countries: A Comparative Perspective*, ed. Pranab Bardhan and Dilip Mookherjee. Cambridge, MA: MIT Press.

Baiocchi, Gianpaolo. 2006. "Inequality and Innovation: Decentralization as an Opportunity Structure in Brazil." In *Decentralization and Local Governance in Developing Countries: A Comparative Perspective*, ed. Pranab Bardhan and Dilip Mookherjee. Cambridge, MA: MIT Press.

Bardhan, Pranab, and Dilip Mookherjee, eds. 2006. *Decentralization and Local Governance in Developing Countries: A Comparative Perspective*. Cambridge, MA: MIT Press.

Beneria-Surkin, Jordi. 2005. "The Struggle for Resources: Citizen Engagement and Democratic Governance in the Municipality of Vallegrande, Bolivia." Paper presented at the workshop proceedings for the "International Conference on Resources, Citizen Engagement, and Democratic Local Governance," December 6–9. http://www.ids.ac.uk/logolink/resources/ReciteConfpapers.htm#Bolivia.

Bishop, Patrick, and Glyn Davis. 2002. "Mapping Public Participation in Policy Choices." *Australian Journal of Public Administration* 61 (1): 14–29.

CIDA (Canadian International Development Agency). n.d. "All I Want Is Justice." www.acdi-cida.gc.ca/CIDAWEB/acdi.cida.nsf/En/EMA-218121723-PL4.

Charlick, Robert. 2001. "Popular Participation and Local Government Reform." *Public Administration and Development* 21: 149–57.

Cleaver, Frances. 1999. "Paradoxes of Participation: Questioning Participatory Approaches to Development." *Journal of International Development* 11: 597–612.

Cooksey, Brian, and Idris Kikula. 2005. "When Bottom-Up Meets Top-Down: The Limits of Local Participation in Local Government Planning in Tanzania." Special Paper 17, Research on Poverty Alleviation, Dar es Salaam.

DCD-GTZ (Department of Constitutional Development and German Technical Corporation). 1999. *Integrated Development Planning Pilot Projects Assessment Study*. South African Department of Constitutional Development, Pretoria.

Eberlei, Walter. 2003. "Institutionalizing Participation in the PRSP Implementation, Monitoring, and Review Process." Paper presented at the "International Forum for Sharing of Experiences on PRSP Monitoring and Implementation: The Involvement of Civil Society," Lusaka, Zambia, June.

Faguet, Jean-Paul. 2004. "Does Decentralization Increase Government Responsiveness to Local Needs? Evidence from Bolivia." *Journal of Public Economics* 88 (3): 867–93.

———. 2006. "Decentralizing Bolivia: Local Government in the Jungle." In *Decentralization and Local Governance in Developing Countries: A Comparative Perspective*, ed. Pranab Bardhan and Dilip Mookherjee. Cambridge, MA: MIT Press.

Fung, Archon, and Erik Wright. 2003. *Deepening Democracy: Institutional Innovations in Empowered Participatory Governance*. London: Verso.

Gaventa, Jonathan. 2002. "Legal and Policy Frameworks for Citizen Participation in Local Governance in East Africa: A Regional Report." LogoLink report, Institute of Development Studies, Brighton, United Kingdom.

Gaventa, Jonathan, and Camilo Valderrama. 1999. "Participation, Citizenship, and Local Governance." Background paper for workshop on "Strengthening Participation in Local Governance," Institute of Development Studies, Brighton, United Kingdom, June 21–24.

Goetz, Anne Marie, and Jonathan Gaventa. 2001. "Bringing Citizen Voice and Client Focus into Service Delivery." Working Paper 138, Institute of Development Studies, Brighton, United Kingdom.

Goetz, Anne Marie, and Rob Jenkins. 2001. "Hybrid Forms of Accountability: Citizen Engagement in Institutions of Public-Sector Oversight in India." *Public Management Review* 3 (3): 363–83.

Gopakumar, Krishnan. 1997. "Public Feedback as an Aid to Public Accountability: Reflections on an Alternate Approach." *Public Administration and Development* 17 (2): 281–82.

Goudsmit, Into, and James Blackburn. 2001. "Participatory Municipal Planning in Bolivia: An Ambiguous Experience." *Development in Practice* 11 (5): 587–96.

Hadiz, Vedi. 2004. "Decentralization and Democracy in Indonesia: A Critique of Neo-institutional Perspectives." *Development and Change* 35 (4): 697–718.

ICPS (International Centre for Policy Studies). 2006. *Model for Public Watch over Healthcare Spending*. Kiev.

Iszatt, Nina. 2002. *Legislating for Citizens' Participation in the Philippines*. LogoLink report, Institute of Development Studies, Brighton, United Kingdom.

Kaufmann, Daniel, Gil Mehrez, and Tugrul Gurgur. 2002. "Voice or Public Sector Management? An Empirical Investigation of the Determinants of Public Sector Performance Based on a Survey of Public Officials in Bolivia." Draft. World Bank Institute, Washington, DC.

Leisher, Stefan, and Susannah Nachuk. 2006. *Making Services Work for the Poor: A Synthesis of Nine Case Studies from Indonesia*. Washington, DC: World Bank.

Li, Tania. 2006. "Neo-liberal Strategies of Government through Community: The Social Development Program of the World Bank in Indonesia." International Law and Justice Working Paper 2006/2, Global Administrative Law Series, New York University Law School, New York.

Malena, Carmen. 2004. "Social Accountability: An Introduction to the Concept and Emerging Practice." Social Development Papers, Participation and Civic Engagement Paper 76, World Bank, Washington, DC.

Manor, James, and Richard Crook. 1998. *Democracy and Decentralization in South Asia and West Africa: Participation, Accountability and Performance*. Cambridge: Cambridge University Press.

McGee, Rosemary. 2003. *Legal Frameworks for Citizen Participation: Synthesis Report.* LogoLink report, Institute of Development Studies, Brighton, United Kingdom.

Mohan, Giles, and Kristian Stokke. 2000. "Participatory Development and Empowerment: The Dangers of Localism." *Third World Quarterly* 21 (2): 247–68.

Narayan, Deepa. 1995. "The Contribution of People's Participation: Evidence from 121 Rural Water Supply Projects." Environmentally Sustainable Development Occasional Paper 1, World Bank, Washington, DC.

OECD (Organisation for Economic Co-operation and Development). 2001a. *Citizens as Partners: Information, Consultation, and Public Participation in Policy-Making.* Paris: OECD.

———. 2001b. *Citizens as Partners: OECD Handbook on Information, Consultation and Public Participation in Policy-Making.* Paris: OECD.

Orlandini, Barbara. 2003. *Civic Engagement in Local Governance: The Case of Thailand.* LogoLink report, Institute of Development Studies, Brighton, United Kingdom.

Partners of the Americas' Center for Civil Society. 2005. *Involving Citizens in Public Budgets: Mechanisms for Transparent and Participatory Budgeting.* Washington, DC: U.S. Agency for International Development.

Paul, Samuel. 1987. *Community Development in Development Projects: World Bank Experience.* World Bank Development Paper 6, Washington, DC.

———. 1992. "Accountability in Public Services: Exit, Voice and Control." *World Development* 20 (7): 1047–60.

Ravindra, Adikeshavalu. 2004. *An Assessment of the Impact of Bangalore Citizen Report Cards on the Performance of Public Agencies.* Evaluation Capacity Development Working Paper Series 12, World Bank, Operations Evaluation Department, Washington, DC.

Rocamora, Joel. 2003. *Legal and Policy Frameworks for Participation in Thailand, Indonesia and the Philippines.* LogoLink Regional Report, Institute of Development Studies, Brighton, United Kingdom.

RTI (Research Triangle Institute International). 2003. *A Practical Guide to Citizen Participation.* RTI-USAID Local Government Assistance Program, Bucharest.

Saule, Nelson, Alejandra Velasco, and Zuleika Arashiro. 2002. *Legal Frameworks for Citizen Participation: Latin American Regional Report.* LogoLink Regional Report, Institute for Development Studies, Brighton, United Kingdom.

Sera, Yumi. 2004. *Consultations with Civil Society: A Sourcebook.* Working Document, World Bank, NGO and Civil Society Unit, Washington, DC.

Souza, Celina. 2001. "Participatory Budgeting in Brazilian Cities: Limits and Possibilities in Building Democratic Institutions, Urban Governance, Partnership and Poverty." Working Paper 28, University of Birmingham, United Kingdom.

Thindwa, Jeff, Carmen Monico, and William Reuben. 2003. *Enabling Environments for Civic Engagement in PRSP Countries.* Social Development Note 82, World Bank, Washington, DC.

Thomas, John C. 1990. "Public Involvement in Public Management: Adapting and Testing a Borrowed Theory." *Public Administration Review* 50 (4): 435–45.

Tikare, Seema, Deborah Youssef, Paula Donnelly-Roark, and Parmesh Shah. 2001. "Organizing Participatory Processes in the PRSP." World Bank, Washington, DC.

UNECA (United Nations Economic Commission for Africa). 2004. *Best Practices in the Participatory Approach to Delivery of Social Services.* Addis Ababa.

7

Tailoring the Fight against Corruption to Country Circumstances

ANWAR SHAH

Although statistics on corruption are often questionable, the data suggest that corruption accounts for a significant proportion of economic activity. In Kenya "questionable" public expenditures noted by the controller and auditor general in 1997 amounted to 7.6 percent of GDP. In Latvia a recent World Bank survey found that more than 40 percent of households and enterprises agreed that "corruption is a natural part of our lives and helps solve many problems" (Shah and Schacter 2004: 40). In Tanzania service delivery survey data suggest that bribes paid to officials in the police, courts, tax services, and land offices amounted to 62 percent of official public expenditures in these areas. In the Philippines the Commission on Audit estimates that $4 billion is diverted annually because of public sector corruption (Tapales 2001).

A 2004 World Bank study of the ramifications of corruption for service delivery concludes that an improvement of one standard deviation in the International Country Risk Guide corruption index leads to a 29 percent decrease in infant mortality rates, a 52 percent increase in satisfaction among recipients of public health care, and a 30–60 percent increase in public satisfaction stemming from improved road conditions. Studies also show that corruption slows growth, impairs capital accumulation, reduces the effectiveness of development aid, and increases income inequality and poverty (Gupta, Davoodi, and Alonso-Terme 1998; Hall and Jones 1999; World Bank 2004).

Not surprisingly, there has been a growing global movement to condemn corrupt practices—a movement that has resulted in the removal of some national leaders. In addition, many governments and development agencies have devoted substantial resources and energy to fighting corruption in recent years. Despite these efforts, however, it is not clear that the incidence of corruption has declined perceptibly, especially in highly corrupt countries.

This chapter argues that the lack of significant progress can be attributed to the fact that many programs are simply folk remedies or one-size-fits-all approaches that offer little chance of success. For programs to work, they must identify the type of corruption they are targeting and tackle the underlying, country-specific causes, or "drivers," of dysfunctional governance.

This chapter examines the conceptual and empirical basis of these concerns. The next section defines *corruption* and *governance* and discusses the importance of current concerns about corruption. The second section describes some theoretical models of the drivers of corruption and summarizes lessons drawn from country case studies. The third section examines how government policy makers can approach anticorruption, depending on specific circumstances in their countries. The last section presents some conclusions.

What Is Corruption?

Corruption is defined as the exercise of official powers against public interest or the abuse of public office for private gains.[1] Public sector corruption is a symptom of failed governance. *Governance* is defined as the norms, traditions, and institutions by which power and authority in a country are exercised. These norms, traditions, and institutions include the institutions of participation and accountability in governance, mechanisms of citizen voice and exit, and norms and networks of civic engagement; the constitutional-legal framework and the nature of accountability relationships between citizens and government; the process by which governments are selected, monitored, held accountable, and renewed or replaced; and the legitimacy, credibility, and efficacy of the institutions that govern political, economic, cultural, and social interactions among citizens and between citizens and their governments.

Concern about corruption is as old as the history of government. In 350 BCE, Aristotle suggested in *The Politics*, "To protect the treasury from being defrauded, let all money be issued openly in front of the whole city, and let copies of the accounts be deposited in various wards."

Concerns about corruption have mounted in recent years, in tandem with growing evidence of its detrimental impact on development (see World Bank 2004). Corruption slows GDP growth (Abed and Davoodi 2000; Mauro 1995) and adversely affects capital accumulation (Lambsdorff 1999a, 1999b). It lowers the quality of education (Gupta, Davoodi, and Tiongson 2000); public infrastructure (Tanzi and Davoodi 1997); and health services (Tomaszewska and Shah 2000; Treisman 1999b). It reduces the effectiveness of development aid and increases income inequality and poverty (Gupta, Davoodi, and Alonso-Terme 1998). Bribery, often the most visible manifestation of public sector corruption, harms the reputation of and erodes trust in the state. Poor governance and corruption make it more difficult for the poor and other disadvantaged groups, such as women and minorities, to obtain public services. Corruption may also affect macroeconomic stability, when, for example, the allocation of debt guarantees based on cronyism or fraud in financial institutions leads to a loss of confidence by savers, investors, and foreign exchange markets. The Bank of Credit and Commerce International (BCCI) scandal, uncovered in 1991, for example, led to the financial ruin of Gabon's pension system; the corrupt practices at Mehran Bank in the Sindh Province of Pakistan in the mid-1990s led to a loss of confidence in that country's national banking system.

Corruption is not manifested in one single form. It typically takes at least four broad forms:

1. *Petty, administrative, or bureaucratic corruption.* Many corrupt acts are isolated transactions by individual public officials who abuse their office by demanding bribes and kickbacks, diverting public funds, or awarding favors in return for personal considerations. Such acts are often referred to as petty corruption, even though, in the aggregate, a substantial amount of public resources may be involved.
2. *Grand corruption.* The theft or misuse of vast amounts of public resources by state officials—usually members of, or people associated with, the political or administrative elite—constitutes grand corruption.
3. *State or regulatory capture and influence peddling.* State capture is the collusion by private actors with public officials or politicians for their mutual, private benefit. In this form of corruption, the private sector "captures" the state legislative, executive, and judicial apparatus for its own purposes. State capture coexists with the conventional (and opposite) view of corruption, in which public officials extort or otherwise exploit the private sector for private ends.

4. *Patronage, paternalism, clientelism, and being a "team player."* Corruption occurs when officials use their official position to provide assistance to clients or colleagues with the same geographic, ethnic, or cultural origin so that they receive preferential treatment in their dealings with the public sector, including public sector employment.

What Drives Corruption?

The factors that cause corruption are country specific. Approaches that apply common policies and tools (that is, one-size-fits-all approaches) to countries in which acts of corruption and the quality of governance vary widely are likely to fail. Policy makers need to understand the local circumstances that encourage or permit public and private actors to be corrupt. Efforts to combat corruption also demand strong local leadership and ownership if they are to be successful and sustainable.

Public sector corruption, as a symptom of failed governance, depends on a multitude of factors, such as the quality of public sector management, the nature of accountability relations between the government and citizens, the legal framework, and the degree to which public sector processes are accompanied by transparency and dissemination of information. Efforts to address corruption that fail to adequately account for these underlying drivers are unlikely to generate profound and sustainable results.

To understand these drivers, a conceptual and empirical perspective is needed to understand why corruption persists and what can be done to stop it. At the conceptual level, a number of interesting ideas have been put forward.[2] These ideas can be broadly grouped into three categories: principal-agent models, New Public Management perspectives, and neoinstitutional economics frameworks.

Principal-Agent Models

The most widely used modeling strategy is the principal-agent model. A common thread in these models is that the government is led by a benevolent dictator (the principal), who aims to motivate government officials (agents) to act with integrity in the use of public resources (see Banfield 1975; Becker 1968, 1983; Becker and Stigler 1974; Klitgaard 1988, 1997; Rose-Ackerman 1975, 1978).

One such view, the "crime and punishment" model of Gary Becker (1968), states that self-interested public officials seek out or accept bribes as long as the expected gains from corruption exceed the expected costs (detection and punishment) associated with corrupt acts. According to this view, corruption could be mitigated by reducing the number of transactions over which public officials have discretion, reducing the scope of gains from each transaction, increasing the probability for detection, or increasing the penalty for corrupt activities.

Klitgaard (1988) restates this model to emphasize the unrestrained monopoly power and discretionary authority of government officials. According to him, corruption equals monopoly plus discretion minus accountability. Under this framework, corruption is curtailed by establishing a rules-driven government that includes strong internal controls and leaves little room for discretion by public officials. This model gained wide acceptance in public policy circles and served as a foundation for empirical research and policy design to combat administrative, bureaucratic, and petty corruption. Such an approach is not appropriate in highly corrupt countries, however, where the rules enforcers themselves add an extra burden of corruption and lack of discretion is thwarted by collusive behavior by corruptors. In fact, lack of discretion is often cited as a defense by corrupt officials who partake in corruption as part of a vertically well-knit network enjoying immunity from prosecution.

Another variant of the principal-agent model integrates the role of legislators and elected officials in the analysis. In this variant, high-level government officials—represented by legislators or elected public officials—institute or manipulate policy and legislation in favor of particular interest groups (representing private sector interests and entities or individual units of public bureaucracy competing for higher budgets) in exchange for rents or side payments. Legislators weigh the personal monetary gains from corrupt practices and improved chances of reelection against the chance of being caught, punished, and losing an election with a tarnished reputation. Factors affecting this decision include campaign financing mechanisms, information access by voters, the ability of citizens to vote out corrupt legislators, the degree of political contestability, the type of electoral system, the democratic institutions and traditions in place, and the institutions of accountability in governance (see Acconcia, D'Amato, and Martina 2003; Andvig and Moene 1990; Chand and Moene 1997; Flatters and Macleod 1995; Grossman and Helpman 1994; Rose-Ackerman 1978; and Van Rijckeghem and Weder 2001). This conceptual framework is useful in analyzing political corruption or state capture.

A fine line divides theoretical models that focus on the effects of localization on corruption and those that analyze the decentralization of corruption within a multitier hierarchy from an industrial organization of corruption type of framework. In the multitier hierarchy approach, a distinction is made between top-down corruption (in which corrupt high-level officials buy lower-level officials by sharing a portion of their gains) and bottom-up corruption (in which low-level officials share the bribes they collect with higher-level officials in order to avoid detection or punishment). Top-down corruption is more likely to exist in a federal system of governance, where power may be shared by various orders of government. Bottom-up corruption is more likely to prevail in unitary or centralized forms of governance or in dictatorial regimes.

The impact of governance on corruption networks is an interesting topic that has not been studied adequately. Tirole (1986) analyzes one aspect of this network by means of a three-tier principal-supervisor-agent model (see also Guriev 1999). This extension of a conventional principal-agent model helps draw inferences about the type of corrupt relations that could evolve under a three-tier unitary government structure. These inferences are highly sensitive to underlying assumptions about principal-agent relationships under a multitiered system of governance.[3] In Guriev's three-tier hierarchy model, the mid-level bureaucrat supervises the agent and reports to the principal. Guriev (1999: 2) concludes that top-level corruption "is not efficient, as it redistributes rents in favor of agents, and therefore makes it more attractive for potential entrants," thereby leading to higher total corruption.

Shleifer and Vishny (1993) use a conventional industrial organization model to analyze corruption. They conclude that decentralization is likely to increase corruption. In their model government bureaucracies and agencies act as monopolists selling complementary government-produced goods that are legally required for private sector activity. The main idea behind the model is that under centralized corruption, bureaucracies act like a joint monopoly, whereas under decentralized corruption bureaucracies behave as independent monopolies. When bureaucracies act as independent monopolies, they ignore the effects of higher prices on the overall demand for a good and hence drive up the cumulative bribe burden.

Waller, Verdier, and Gardner (2002) define decentralized corruption as a system in which higher-level officials collect a fixed amount of bribe income from each bureaucrat who takes bribes, without mandating the bribe size the bureaucrats charge. In a centralized system, in contrast, bribe size is determined by the higher level of government, which collects the bribes from bureaucrats and redistributes them after keeping a share. Waller, Verdier, and Gardner posit that decentralized corruption leads to lower levels of total corruption in the economy (lower spread), higher levels of bribe per entrepreneur (higher depth), and a smaller formal sector than does a centralized corruption equilibrium. These results vary widely for specific "regimes" in the model, however: if, for example, wages are high enough and monitoring systems effective enough, centralized corruption may reduce total corruption and expand the formal economy.

Ahlin (2001) focuses on the effects of different types of decentralization, from a horizontal, as opposed to a hierarchical, perspective. In his model a country is divided into regions, each with a given number of independent power groups. Bureaucratic decentralization affects the political organization in a region by increasing the number of power groups or bureaucracies; the number of jurisdictions captures the degree of regional decentralization. Ahlin's theoretical results suggest that corruption is determined by mobility of economic agents across regions. Under the assumption of no interregional mobility, corruption increases with the degree of bureaucratic decentralization but is independent of the degree of regional decentralization. For perfect interregional mobility, corruption decreases with regional decentralization and is independent of bureaucratic decentralization. A key intuition of the model is that corrupt bureaucrats fail to internalize the costs of increases in bribes imposed on other bureaucrats.

Arikan (2004) uses a tax competition framework to examine localization-corruption links. In his model corruption is measured as the proportion of tax revenue appropriated by bureaucrats; decentralization is captured by the number of jurisdictions competing for a mobile tax base. Local governments decide on the levels of tax rates and corrupt earnings in order to maximize a weighted sum of corrupt earnings and citizens' utility. A higher degree of decentralization is expected to lead to lower levels of corruption.

Bardhan and Mookherjee (2005) shed light on the determinants of capture of the democratic process. They conclude that the extent of capture is ambiguous and context specific: the extent of capture at the local level depends on the degree of voter awareness, interest group cohesiveness, electoral uncertainty, electoral competition, and the heterogeneity of interdistrict income inequality. A key assumption of this model is that the degree of political awareness is correlated to education and socioeconomic position. In particular, the model assumes that the fraction of informed voters in the middle income class is lower than or equal to the fraction of rich voters and higher than the fraction of poor voters. Uninformed voters are swayed by campaign financing, whereas informed voters favor the party platform that maximizes the utility of their class. The outcome of local and national elections in terms of policy platforms will coincide under four assumptions: (a) all districts have the same socioeconomic composition, and swings among districts (district-specific preferences for one of two political parties) are perfectly correlated; (b) national elections are majoritarian; (c) there is an equal proportion of informed voters in local and national elections; and (d) the proportion of the rich who contribute to their lobby is equal at the national and local levels (that is, the rich are as well organized nationally as they are locally). Capture will be higher at the local level if the proportion of informed voters is lower at the national level and the rich are less organized nationally than they are locally. Greater electoral uncertainty at the local level as a result of differences in electoral competition implies less capture at the local level. If, for example, swing voters are not identical but are drawn from the same distribution across districts (assuming this distribution satisfies a regularity condition), heterogeneity of swing voters will favor different parties, implying less capture of the nationally dominant party.

No definitive conclusions can be drawn about corruption and the centralization-decentralization nexus from agency-type conceptual models. These models simply reaffirm that the incidence of corruption is context dependent and therefore cannot be uncovered by generalized models.

New Public Management Frameworks

The New Public Management (NPM) literature points to a more fundamental discordance among the public sector mandate, its authorizing environment, and the operational culture and capacity. This discordance contributes to government acting like a runaway train and government officials indulging in rent-seeking behaviors, with little opportunity for citizens to constrain government behavior. This viewpoint calls for fundamental civil service and political reforms to create a government that is under contract and accountable for results. Under these reforms, public officials would no longer have permanent rotating appointments but instead would keep their jobs as long as they fulfilled their contractual obligations (Shah 1999, 2005).

The NPM paradigm has clear implications for the study of localization and corruption, as it argues for contractual arrangements in the provision of public services. Such a contractual framework may encourage competitive service delivery through outsourcing, strengthening the role of local government as a purchaser but not necessarily a provider of local services. The NPM goals are harmonious with localization, as greater accountability for results reinforces government accountability to citizens through voice and exit mechanisms. Conceptually, therefore, NPM is expected to reduce opportunities for corruption (see Shah 1999, 2005; Von Maravic 2003).

Andrews and Shah (2005a) integrate these ideas in a common framework of citizen-centered governance. They argue that citizen empowerment holds the key to enhanced accountability and reduced opportunities for corruption. Others disagree with such conclusions and argue that NPM could lead to higher corruption rather than greater accountability, because the tendering for service delivery and separation of purchasers from providers may lead to increased rent-seeking behaviors and enhanced possibilities for corruption (Batley 1999; Von Maravic 2003). Some argue that decentralized management leads to weaker vertical supervision from higher levels and the inadequacy of mechanisms to exert controls over decentralized agencies (Scharpf 1997). This loss in vertical accountability is seen as a source of enhanced opportunities for corruption. Of course, this viewpoint neglects potential gains from greater horizontal accountability.

Neoinstitutional Economics Frameworks

Neoinstitutional economics presents a refreshing perspective on the causes and cures of corruption. This approach argues that corruption results from the opportunistic behavior of public officials, as citizens either are not empowered to hold public officials accountable for their corrupt acts or face high transaction costs in doing so. Neoinstitutional economics treats citizens as principals and public officials as agents. Principals have bounded rationality—they act rationally based on the incomplete information they have. They face high transaction costs in acquiring and processing more information. In contrast, agents (public officials) are better informed. This asymmetry of information allows agents to indulge in opportunistic behavior that goes unchecked because of the high transaction costs faced by principals and the lack of adequate countervailing institutions to enforce accountable governance.[4]

Corrupt countries have inadequate mechanisms for contract enforcement and public safety and weak judicial systems. These deficits raise the transaction costs in the economy, increasing the cost of private capital as well as the cost of public service provision. The problem is compounded by path dependency (the fact that a major break with the past is difficult to achieve, because major reforms are likely to be blocked by influential interest groups); cultural and historical factors; and attitudes, in which those who are victimized by corruption feel that attempts to deal with corruption will lead to further victimization, with little hope of corrupt actors being brought to justice. These considerations lead principals to the conclusion that any attempt on their part to constrain corrupt behaviors will invite strong retaliation from powerful interests. Therefore, citizen empowerment (through devolution, citizens' charters, bills of rights, elections, and other forms of civic engagement) assumes critical importance in combating corruption, because it may have a significant impact on the incentives faced by public officials to be responsive to public interest.

Lessons from Country Case Studies

The empirical literature on corruption lends support to the neoinstitutional economics perspective. It identifies key drivers based on in-depth country studies (including a 2004 World Bank look at Guatemala, Kenya, Latvia, Pakistan, the Philippines, and Tanzania) and econometric studies of developing, transition, and industrial countries (see Gurgur and Shah 2002; Huther and Shah 2000; Tomaszewska and Shah 2000).

The six country case studies by the World Bank examined the root causes of corruption and evaluated the impact of Bank efforts to reduce corruption in each country. These studies identified the following drivers of corruption:

- *The legitimacy of the state as the guardian of the "public interest" is contested.* In highly corrupt countries, there is little public acceptance of the notion that the role of the state is to rise above private interests to protect the broader public interest. "Clientelism"—public officeholders focusing on serving particular client groups linked to them by ethnic, geographic, or other ties—shapes the public landscape, creating conditions that are ripe for corruption. The line between what is public and what is private is blurred, so that abuse of public office for private gain is a routine occurrence.
- *The rule of law is weakly embedded.* Public sector corruption thrives where laws apply to some but not others and where enforcement of the law is often used as a device for furthering private interests rather than protecting the public interest. A common symbol of the breakdown of the rule of law in highly corrupt countries is the police acting as lawbreakers rather than law enforcers (stopping motorists for invented traffic violations as an excuse for extracting bribes, for example). The independence of the judiciary—a pillar of the rule of law—is also usually deeply compromised in highly corrupt countries.
- *Institutions of participation and accountability are ineffective.* Societies in which the level of public sector corruption is relatively low usually have strong institutions of participation and accountability that control abuses of power by public officials. These institutions are either created by the state itself (for example, electoral process, citizens' charter, bills of rights,

auditors general, the judiciary, the legislature) or arise outside of formal state structures (for example, the news media and organized civic groups). In highly corrupt countries, weaknesses in institutions of participation and accountability are glaring.
- *The commitment of national leaders to combating corruption is weak.* Widespread corruption endures in the public sector when national authorities are either unwilling or unable to address it forcefully. In societies in which public sector corruption is endemic, it is reasonable to suspect that it touches the highest levels of government and that many senior officeholders will not be motivated to work against it.

What Can Policy Makers Do to Combat Corruption?

Experience strongly suggests that combating corruption requires an indirect approach that starts with its root causes. To understand why, it is helpful to look at a model that divides developing countries into three broad categories—high, medium, and low—reflecting the incidence of corruption. The model assumes that countries with high corruption have a low quality of governance, those with medium corruption have fair governance, and those with low corruption have good governance (table 7.1).

What this model reveals is that because corruption is itself a symptom of fundamental governance failure, the higher the incidence of corruption, the less an anticorruption strategy should include tactics that narrowly target corrupt behaviors and the more it should focus on the broad underlying features of the governance environment. For example, support for anticorruption

TABLE 7.1 Priorities for Anticorruption Reforms Given Level of Corruption and Quality of Governance

Incidence of corruption/ quality of governance	Priorities for anticorruption efforts
High/poor	Establish rule of law, strengthen institutions of participation and accountability, establish citizens' charter, limit government intervention, implement economic policy reforms
Medium/fair	Decentralize and reform economic policies and public management; introduce accountability for results
Low/good	Establish anticorruption agencies, strengthen financial accountability, raise public and official awareness, require antibribery pledges, conduct high-profile prosecutions

Source: Huther and Shah 2000.

agencies and public awareness campaigns is likely to meet with limited success in environments in which corruption is rampant and the governance environment deeply flawed. In fact, in environments where governance is weak, anticorruption agencies are prone to being misused as tools of political victimization. These types of interventions are more appropriate in a "low" corruption setting, where governance fundamentals are reasonably sound and corruption is a relatively marginal phenomenon.

The model also suggests that where corruption is high (and the quality of governance correspondingly low), it makes more sense to focus on the underlying drivers of malfeasance in the public sector—by building the rule of law and strengthening institutions of accountability, for example. Indeed, a lack of democratic institutions (a key component of accountability) has been shown to be one of the most important determinants of corruption (Gurgur and Shah 2002). Malaysia's adoption of a "clients' charter" in the early 1990s that specified service standards and citizen recourse in the event of noncompliance by government agencies helped reorient the public sector toward service delivery and transform the culture of governance (Shah 1999, 2005).

In societies in which the level of corruption is moderate, it may be advisable to attempt reforms that assume a modicum of governance capacity. Such reforms include trying to make civil servants more accountable for results, bringing government decision making closer to citizens through decentralization, simplifying administrative procedures, and reducing discretion for simple government tasks, such as the distribution of licenses and permits.

With this model in mind, it is not hard to understand why so many anticorruption initiatives have met with so little success (table 7.2). Media awareness campaigns and workshops on corruption targeted to government officials, parliamentarians, and journalists have almost universally failed. As the model shows, this outcome would be expected in countries with weak governance, where corruption is openly practiced but neither the general public nor honest public officials feel empowered to take a stand against it and even fear being victimized. In contrast, awareness campaigns would be expected to have a positive impact in countries where governance is fair or good and the incidence of corruption is low.

Decentralization illustrates the importance of understanding the circumstances in which corruption occurs. There is evidence that decentralization can be an effective antidote to corruption, because it increases the accountability of public authorities to citizens (see Gurgur and Shah 2002; Shah, Thompson, and Zou 2004). But decentralization creates hundreds of new public authorities, each having powers to tax, spend, and regulate that

TABLE 7.2 Empirical Evidence on Success of Selected Anticorruption Programs

Program	Empirical evidence
Anticorruption agencies	Anticorruption agencies have been successful in Australia, Chile, Hong Kong (China), New South Wales, and Singapore (Klitgaard 1997; Segal 1999). Developing country officials, however, do not view such agencies as effective anticorruption tools in countries with endemic corruption (Kaufmann 1997; Shah and Schacter 2004).
Public opinion surveys	Public opinion surveys have served as a useful tool in articulating citizen concerns (examples are the scorecard used in Bangalore, India, and the "corruptometer" used by an Argentine NGO). Transparency International surveys, such as those compiled by International, highlight countries in which corruption is perceived to be endemic.
Higher public sector wages	Van Rijckeghem and Weder (2001) find no short-run impact of raising public sector wages, as the income from bribery dominates total income. Gurgur and Shah (1999, 2002) find a negative but insignificant effect; Treisman (1999b) and Swamy and others (2001) find no relationship. The Swiss Agency for Development and Co-operation (SDC) finds no relationship between wage increases and corruption in the forestry sector in Pakistan (Personal communications with the SDC). In corrupt societies, public positions are often purchased by borrowing money from family and friends. Raising public sector wages simply raises the purchase price and subsequent corruption efforts needed to repay the loans. Where public sector wages are so low that officials cannot live on their wages, raising salaries is likely to reduce petty corruption (Gurgur and Shah 1999).
Smaller public sector size	LaPalombara (1994), La Porta and others (1997), and Tanzi and Davoodi (1998) find that reducing the size of the public sector reduces corruption. Gurgur and Shah (1999) find that this result holds only when important variables such as the judiciary, democratic institutions, colonial heritage, decentralization, and bureaucratic culture are omitted. Elliot (1997) finds an inverse relationship between budget size and corruption. Privatization in some countries (such as the Russian Federation) has led to increased corruption and exploitation.
Media independence	Freedom of the press is negatively correlated with the level of corruption (Brunetti and Weder 1998).
Judicial independence	Judicial independence reduces corruption, according to Ades and Di Tella (1996), Goel and Nelson (1998), and Gurgur and Shah (1999, 2002).

(continued)

TABLE 7.2 (continued)

Program	Empirical evidence
Citizen participation	Citizen participation leads to reduced corruption, according to Gurgur and Shah (1999, 2002) and Kaufman and Sachs (1998).
Decentralization	Decentralization and corruption are negatively correlated, according to Fisman and Gatti (2002), Gurgur and Shah (2002), and Huther and Shah (1998).
Bureaucratic culture	Gurgur and Shah (1999, 2002) find a positive relationship between command-and-control–type civil service orientation and corruption.

Source: Huther and Shah 2000.

are liable to abuse in environments where governance is weak. As the World Bank's analysis of the Philippines in the 1990s shows (Tapales 2001), decentralization may multiply rather than limit opportunities for corruption if it is implemented under the wrong circumstances.

The model provides some insights into the effect of raising civil service salaries and reducing wage compression (the ratio between the salaries of the highest- and lowest-paid civil servants in a given country). The evidence suggests that in environments where governance is weak, wage-based strategies are not likely to have a significant impact on civil service corruption (see Huther and Shah 2000 for references). Reducing wage compression may even encourage corruption, if public sector positions are viewed as a lucrative career option. In corrupt societies public positions are often purchased by borrowing money from family and friends. Raising public sector wages simply raises the purchase price and subsequent corruption efforts to repay loans.

The effectiveness of "watchdog" agencies with a mandate to detect and prosecute corrupt acts —which most developing countries have established— also depends on the governance-corruption nexus. Watchdog agencies have achieved success only in countries where governance is generally good, such as Australia and Chile. In weak governance environments, these agencies often lack credibility and may even extort rents. In Kenya, Malawi, Nigeria, Sierra Leone, Tanzania, and Uganda, for example, anticorruption agencies have been ineffective. In Tanzania the government's Prevention of Corruption Bureau produces only about six convictions a year, mostly against low-level functionaries, in a public sector environment rife with corruption. In Pakistan the National Accountability Bureau lacks a mandate to investigate corruption in the powerful and influential military. Ethics offices and ombudsmen have had

TABLE 7.3 Relevance of Anticorruption Programs Given Country Circumstances

Program	Weak	Fair	Good	Comments
Public awareness raising of corruption through seminars	Not relevant	Low	Medium	In countries with weak governance, corrupt practices and agents are generally well known.
Awareness raising of public officials through seminars	Not relevant	Low	Medium	Public officials may be aware of corruption but unwilling or unable to take action because of incentive problems in countries with weak governance.
Anticorruption agencies/ ombudsmen	Not relevant	Low	Medium	With endemic corruption, anticorruption agencies or ombudsmen may extort rents. Their influence is likely to be positive if preconditions for good governance exist.
Ethics office	Not relevant	Low	Medium	Positive influence may be limited to societies with good governance.
Increase in public sector wages	Negligible	Low	Medium	Little impact on grand corruption; may have a positive impact on petty corruption. Impact will be negative if part of the problem is excessive public employment.
Reduction in wage compression	Negligible	Negligible	Negligible	More relevant as an incentive mechanism for career development than for reducing corruption. May increase corruption if greedy elements of society view the public sector as a lucrative career.
Merit-based civil service	Low	Medium	High	May be derailed by bureaucratic processes in highly corrupt societies.

(continued)

TABLE 7.3 (continued)

Program	Relevance of program when governance is			Comments
	Weak	Fair	Good	
Public opinion surveys	Low	Medium	Medium	Have served as useful tools in articulating citizens' concerns (in Bangalore, India, for example).
Financial accountability	Low	Low	Medium	Appropriate when democratic accountability and a substantial accounting/bookkeeping infrastructure with some integrity are in place.
Parliamentary oversight	Low	Medium	Medium	Can be helpful, but parliamentary micromanagement is not an effective form of governance.
Reduction in public sector employment	Medium	Low	Low	May reduce opportunities for corruption.
Decentralization	Medium	Low	Low	May improve accountability and increase a sense of social purpose for public officials.
Client-based civil service/bureaucratic culture	Medium	Medium	Low	Success depends on the service delivery orientation of public service, reinforced by accountability for results.
Economic policy reform	High	Medium	Low	Reduces potential corruption by shifting decision making to the private sector.
Media and judicial independence, citizen participation	High	Medium	Low	Allows for detection, followed by accountability.
Reduction in size of public sector	High	Medium	Low	Allows officials to focus on primary objectives of the state.
Rule of law	High	Medium	Low	Essential for any progress.

Source: Huther and Shah 2000.

no more success than anticorruption agencies in countries where governance is poor (Huther and Shah 2000; Shah and Schacter 2004).

This discussion confirms the policy conclusion that due recognition of the initial conditions is critical for the effectiveness of anticorruption policies. Anticorruption strategies are unlikely to succeed unless they recognize the pecking order of reforms in poor governance environments (table 7.3).

Conclusions: Don't Use the "C" Word

Policy makers too often use the "C" word and focus directly on dealing with the symptoms of corruption while ignoring the broader disease of dysfunctional governance. Only by focusing on governance is the fight against corruption likely to be successful in the long run. The following considerations may be helpful in designing and implementing anticorruption strategies:

- *Recognize the pecking order of reforms.* Because corruption reflects a system of failed governance, the higher the incidence of corruption, the less an anticorruption strategy should include tactics that are narrowly targeted to corrupt behaviors and the more it should focus on the broad underlying features of the governance environment. This suggests a pecking order of reforms in highly corrupt countries. The first order of priorities in these countries should be establishing the rule of law, strengthening institutions of participation and accountability, and establishing a citizens' charter defining basic legal rights, including access to defined public services standards. Limiting government interventions and implementing economic policy reforms should be part of this package. The second order of priority should be clarifying the roles and responsibilities of various orders of government and introducing performance-based accountability to hold government to account for service delivery performance. The third order of priority should be implementing policies dealing with detection and punishment of corrupt acts.
- *Assess service delivery performance.* Any serious effort by domestic and external stakeholders to hold governments to service delivery standards will eventually compel those governments to address the causes and consequences of corruption. Given the difficulty of detecting corruption through financial audits, corruption may be more easily detected through observation of public service delivery performance. Malaysia's clients' charter represents an important innovation to empower citizens to hold government to account for delivery of defined service standards (Shah 2005).

- *Empower citizens by supporting bottom-up reforms.* In many countries in which corruption is entrenched, governments lack either the will or the capability to mount effective anticorruption programs. Internal and external stakeholders may choose to amplify citizen voice and strengthen exit mechanisms in order to enhance transparency, accountability, and the rule of law. Strengthening local governance and establishing home rule may be important tools in this regard.
- *Disseminate information.* Letting the sun shine on government operations is a powerful antidote to corruption. The more influence donors can exert on strengthening citizens' right to know and governments' obligation to release timely, complete, and accurate information about government operations, the better the prospects for reducing corruption. Information about how governments spend money and manage programs and what these programs deliver in services to people is a key ingredient of accountability, which in turn may be an important brake on corruption.
- *Support economic policy reform.* Trade and financial liberalization can reduce opportunities for corruption by limiting the situations in which officials can exercise unaccountable discretionary powers, introducing transparency, and limiting public sector monopoly powers.

Notes

1. This section draws on Shah and Schacter (2004).
2. For comprehensive surveys on corruption, see Aidt (2003) and Jain (2001).
3. Bac and Bag (1998) and Carillo (2000) model four-tier hierarchies.
4. Following this line of thought, Lambsdorff, Taube, and Schramm (2005: 14) note that in fighting corruption from a neoinstitutional perspective, policy makers should aim to "encourage betrayal among corrupt parties, to destabilize corrupt agreements, to disallow corrupt contracts to be legally enforced, to hinder the operation of corrupt middlemen and to find clearer ways of regulating conflicts of interest."

References

Abed, George T., and Hamid R. Davoodi. 2000. "Corruption, Structural Reforms, and Economic Performance in the Transition Economies." IMF Working Paper 00/132, International Monetary Fund, Washington, DC.

Acconcia, Antonio, Marcello D'Amato, and Riccardo Martina. 2003. "Corruption and Tax Evasion with Competitive Bribes." CSEF Working Paper 112, Centre for Studies in Economics and Finance, University of Salerno, Italy.

Ades, Alberto, and Rafael Di Tella. 1996. "The Causes and Consequences of Competition: A Review of Recent Empirical Contributions." *Institute for Development Studies Bulletin* 27 (2): 6–11.

Ahlin, Christian. 2001. "Corruption: Political Determinants and Macroeconomic Effects." Working Paper 01–W26, Department of Economics, Vanderbilt University, Nashville, TN.

Aidt, Toke S. 2003. "Economic Analysis of Corruption: A Survey." *Economic Journal* 113 (491): F632–52.

Andrews, Matthew, and Anwar Shah. 2005a. "Citizen-Centered Governance: A New Approach to Public Sector Reform." In *Public Expenditure Analysis*, ed. Anwar Shah, 152–82. Washington, DC: World Bank.

———. 2005b. "Towards Citizen-Centered Local Budgets in Developing Countries." In *Public Expenditure Analysis*, ed. Anwar Shah, 183–216. Washington, DC: World Bank.

Andvig, Jens C., and Karl O. Moene. 1990. "How Corruption May Corrupt." *Journal of Economic Behavior and Organization* 13 (1): 63–76.

Arikan, Gulsun. 2000. "Fiscal Decentralization: A Remedy for Corruption?" Department of Economics, University of Illinois, Urbana-Champaign.

———. 2004. "Fiscal Decentralization: A Remedy for Corruption?" *International Tax and Public Finance* 11(2): 175–95.

Bac, Mehmet, and Parimal K. Bag. 1998. "Corruption, Collusion and Implementation: A Hierarchical Design." Department of Economics, University of Liverpool, United Kingdom.

Banfield, Edward. 1975. "Corruption as Feature of Government Organization." *Journal of Law and Economics* 18 (3): 587–695.

Bardhan, Pranab. 1997. "Corruption and Development: A Review of Issues." *Journal of Economic Literature* 35 (3): 1320–46.

Bardhan, Pranab, and Dilip Mookherjee. 2005. "Decentralizing Anti-Poverty Program Delivery in Developing Countries." *Journal of Public Economics* 89 (4): 675–704.

Batley, Richard. 1999. "The Role of Government in Adjusting Economies: An Overview of Findings." International Development Department, University of Birmingham, AL.

Becker, Gary. 1968. "Crime and Punishment: An Economic Approach." *Journal of Political Economy* 76 (2): 169–217.

———. 1983. "A Theory of Competition among Pressure Groups for Political Influence." *Quarterly Journal of Economics* 97 (3): 371–400.

Becker, Gary, and George Stigler. 1974. "Law Enforcement, Malfeasance and the Compensation of Enforcers." *Journal of Legal Studies* 3 (1): 1–18.

Brunetti, Aymo, and Beatrice Weder. 1998. "A Free Press Is Bad News for Corruption." Discussion Paper 9809, Wirtschaftswissenschaftliches Zentrum der Universitat Basel.

Carrillo, Juan D. 2000. "Corruption in Hierarchies." *Annales d'Economie et de Statistique* 59 (3): 37–61.

Chand, Sheetal K., and Karl O. Moene. 1997. "Controlling Fiscal Corruption." IMF Working Paper 97/100, International Monetary Fund, Washington, DC.

Elliott, Kimberly Ann. 1997. "Corruption as an International Policy Problem: Overview and Recommendations." In *Corruption and the Global Economy*, ed. Kimberly Ann Elliott. Washington, DC: Institute for International Economics.

Fisman, Raymond, and Roberta Gatti. 2002. "Decentralization and Corruption: Evidence across Countries." *Journal of Public Economics* 83 (3): 325–45.

Flatters, Frank, and W. Bentley Macleod. 1995. "Administrative Corruption and Taxation." *International Tax and Public Finance* 2 (3): 397–417.

Goel, Rajeev K., and Michael A. Nelson. 1998. "Corruption and Government Size: A Disaggregated Analysis." *Public Choice* 97 (1–2): 107–20.

Grossman, Gene M., and Elhanan Helpman. 1994. "Protection for Sale." *American Economic Review* 84 (4): 833–50.

Gupta, Sanjeev, Hamid Davoodi, and Rosa Alonso-Terme. 1998. "Does Corruption Affect Income Inequality and Poverty?" Working Paper 98/76, International Monetary Fund, Washington, DC.

Gupta, Sanjeev, Hamid Davoodi, and Erwin Tiongson. 2000. "Corruption and the Provision of Health Care and Education Services." Working Paper 00/116, International Monetary Fund, Washington, DC.

Gurgur, Tugrul, and Anwar Shah. 1999. "The Causes of Corruption." Background paper for Study on Anti-corruption and Governance, World Bank, Operations Evaluation Department Washington, DC.

———. 2002. "Localization and Corruption: Panacea or Pandora's Box?" In *Managing Fiscal Decentralization*, ed. Ehtisham Ahmad and Vito Tanzi, 46–67. London: Routledge.

Guriev, Sergei. 1999. "A Theory of Informative Red Tape with an Application to Top-Level Corruption." Working Paper 99/007, New Economic School, Moscow.

Hall, Robert E., and Charles I. Jones. 1999. "Why Do Some Countries Do Much More Output per Worker Than Others?" *Quarterly Journal of Economics* 114 (1): 83–116.

Huther, Jeff, and Anwar Shah. 1998. "Applying a Simple Measure of Good Governance to the Debate on Fiscal Decentralization." Policy Research Working Paper 1894, World Bank, Washington, DC.

———. 2000. "Anticorruption Policies and Programs: A Framework for Evaluation." Policy Research Working Paper 2501, World Bank, Washington, DC.

Jain, Arvind K. 2001. "Corruption: A Review." *Journal of Economic Surveys* 15 (1): 71–121.

Kaufmann, Daniel. 1997. "Listening to Stakeholders' Views about Their Development Challenges and World Bank Instruments." World Bank Institute, Global Programs, Washington, DC.

Kaufmann, Daniel, and Jeffrey Sachs. 1998. *Determinants of Corruption*. Cambridge, MA: Harvard University Press.

Klitgaard, Robert E. 1988. *Controlling Corruption*. Berkeley: University of California Press.

———. 1997. "Cleaning Up and Invigorating the Civil Service." *Public Administration and Development* 17 (5): 487–509.

Lambsdorff, Johann Graf. 1999a. "Corruption in Empirical Research: A Review." Paper presented at the Ninth International Anti-corruption Conference, Durban, South Africa.

———. 1999b. "The Impact of Corruption on Capital Accumulation." Department of Economics, Gottingen University, Germany.

Lambsdorff, Johann Graf, Markus Taube, and Matthias Schramm, eds. 2005. *The New Institutional Economics of Corruption*. London: Routledge.

LaPalombara, Joseph. 1994. "Structural and Institutional Aspects of Corruption." *Social Research* 61 (2): 325–50.

La Porta, Rafael, Florenicio Lopez-De-Silanes, Andrei Shleifer, and Robert W. Vishny. 1997. "Trust in Large Organizations." *American Economic Review, Papers and Proceedings* 137 (2): 333–38.

Rose-Ackerman, Susan. 1975. "The Economics of Corruption." *Journal of Public Economics* 4 (2): 187–203.

———. 1978. *Corruption: A Study in Political Economy.* New York: Academic Press.

Sanjeev, Hamid Davoodi, and Rosa Alonso-Terme. 1998. "Does Corruption Affect Income Inequality and Poverty?" Working Paper 98/76, International Monetary Fund, Washington, DC.

Scharpf, Fritz W. 1997. *Games Real Actors Play: Actor-Centered Institutionalism in Policy Research.* Boulder, CO: Westview Press.

Segal, Philip. 1999. "Dealing with the Devil: The Hell of Corruption." International Finance Corporation, Washington, DC.

Shah, Anwar. 1999. "Governing for Results in a Globalized and Localized World." *Pakistan Development Review* 38 (4): 385–431.

———. 2005. "On Getting the Giant to Kneel: Approaches to a Change in the Bureaucratic Culture." In *Fiscal Management,* ed. Anwar Shah, 211–29. Washington, DC: World Bank.

Shah, Anwar, and Mark Schacter. 2004. "Combating Corruption: Look before You Leap." *Finance and Development* (International Monetary Fund) 41 (4): 40–43.

Shah, Anwar, Theresa Thompson, and Heng-Fu Zou. 2004. "The Impact of Decentralization on Service Delivery, Corruption, Fiscal Management and Growth in Developing and Emerging Market Economies: A Synthesis of Empirical Evidence." Cesifo Dice Report. *Journal for Institutional Comparisons* 2 (1): 10–14.

Shleifer, Andrei, and Robert W. Vishny. 1993. "Corruption." *Quarterly Journal of Economics* 108 (3): 599–617.

Swamy, Anand, Stephen Knack, Young Lee, and Ozmar Azfar. 2001. "Gender and Corruption." *Journal of Development Economics* 64 (1): 25–55.

Tanzi, Vito, and Hamid Davoodi. 1997. "Corruption, Public Investment, and Growth." IMF Working Paper 97/139, International Monetary Fund, Washington, DC.

———. 1998. "Roads to Nowhere: How Corruption in Public Investment Hurts Growth." In *New Perspectives on Combating Corruption,* ed. Daniel Kaufman. Washington, DC: Transparency International and the World Bank.

Tapales, Prosperpina. 2001. "An Evaluation of Anti-corruption Programs in Philippines." World Bank, Operations Evaluation Department, Washington, DC.

Tirole, Jean. 1986. "Hierarchies and Bureaucracies: On the Role of Collusion in Organizations. " *Journal of Law Economics and Organization* 2 (2): 181–214.

Tomaszewska, Ewa, and Anwar Shah. 2000. "Phantom Hospitals, Ghost Schools, and Roads to Nowhere: The Impact of Corruption on Public Service Delivery Performance in Developing Countries." Working Paper, World Bank, Operations Evaluation Department, Washington, DC.

Treisman, Daniel S. 1999a. *After the Deluge: Regional Crises and Political Consolidation in Russia.* Ann Arbor: University of Michigan Press.

———. 1999b. "The Causes of Corruption: A Cross National Study." Department of Political Science, University of California, Los Angeles.

Van Rijckeghem, Caroline, and Beatrice Weder. 2001. "Bureaucratic Corruption and the Rate of Temptation: Do Low Wages in Civil Service Cause Corruption?" *Journal of Development Economics* 65 (2): 307–31.

Von Maravic, Patrick. 2003. "How to Analyse Corruption in the Context of Public Management Reform." Paper presented at the first meeting of the "Study Group on

Ethics and Integrity of Governance European Group of Public Administration Conference," Oeiras, Portugal, September 3–6.

Waller, Christopher J., Thierry A. Verdier, and Roy Gardner. 2002. "Corruption: Top-Down or Bottom-Up." *Economic Inquiry* 40 (4): 688–703.

World Bank. 2004. *Mainstreaming Anticorruption Activities in World Bank Assistance: A Review of Progress since 1997.* Washington, DC: World Bank.

8

Disrupting Corruption

OMAR AZFAR

During the 1990s, Vladimir Montesinos, the chief of Peru's secret police under Alberto Fujimori, bought off the media, the opposition, the judiciary, and the armed forces, extracting large rents for himself and possibly Fujimori.[1] Such systems of rent extraction are not rare. In fact, hybrid regimes that are democratic but lack genuine political competition represent a significant and rising proportion of the world's governments (Diamond 2002). While in some cases the goals of such regimes may simply be power itself, in most cases at least a secondary purpose is rent extraction.

This chapter examines how these systems can be disrupted. The first part of the chapter analyzes how an honest principal can deal with incidental corruption. It compares two strains of the literature on corruption—the economics of crime (prevention) and principal-agent theory—and proposes some concrete policies and reforms that could help alter incentives in incidentally corrupt systems. The second part addresses the problem—widespread in developing countries—of the sale of jobs and the effect the practice has on mechanisms of accountability. The third part analyzes corruption that involves the principal (systemic corruption). The fourth part draws on evidence from case studies of Belarus, Brazil, Kenya, and Turkey to show how systems of corruption can be exposed, disrupted, and eliminated. The chapter closes with recommendations about what various actors—citizens, the media, activists, nongovernmental organizations (NGOs), universities, foreign governments, aid agencies, the World Bank, and local governments—can do to prevent and expose systemic corruption.

Dealing with Incidental Corruption: Principal-Agent Theory versus the Economics of Crime

Two strains of microeconomic theory relate to the control of incidental corruption: principal-agent theory and the economics of crime. (The term *incidental* is meant to convey that the various acts of corruption are not part of the same system. The term is not meant to denote rarity: incidental corruption can be rare or widespread.) Each suggests a different approach to fighting corruption (table 8.1).

The fundamental insight of principal-agent theory is that a principal can induce an agent to undertake actions optimal for the principal even if the principal can observe only outcomes and outcomes are affected by unobserved factors in addition to the agent's actions. The archetypical case is the owner of a firm who gives managers or workers incentives to exert effort by sharing some of the firm's profits with them, where profits depend on many variables other than effort.

The economics of crime focuses on how potential criminals can be dissuaded from committing crimes by punishments based on observable and verifiable behavior. The fundamental insight of the economic theory of crime is that as the verifiability of punishments decreases, the severity of the punishment should rise.

Application of the economic theory of crime to corruption may involve setting very high penalties, because the probability of detecting a corrupt transaction is low. For many acts of corruption that are tolerated in various societies, this may lead to reluctance to report the crime, even on the part of people who would like corruption to be eliminated. Consider the example of a schoolteacher who sells grades. Even upstanding, socially responsible people in many societies would not report the teacher to the police if the consequence involved sending the teacher to jail. They are more likely to report a teacher if the likely consequence is termination of employment. Proving that the schoolteacher actually took bribes is, however, very difficult. Hence the likely consequence is that reforms based solely on incontrovertible evidence of criminal wrongdoing are unlikely to be effective.

Principal-agent theory would advise that rather than look for evidence of actual bribery, exams should occasionally be rechecked. If a teacher is found to veer too far from reasonable grading, he or she should be gently punished—by having to take a salary cut, for example, or attend a summer course on grading. Such a reform would not eliminate corruption; a teacher who favored a few students by giving marginally better grades would be difficult to detect. The reform could, however, lead to improvements in grading even among honest teachers.

TABLE 8.1 Examples of Anticorruption Efforts Suggested by the Economics of Crime and by Principal-Agent Theory

	Economics of crime solution		Principal-agent theory solution	
Form of corruption	Remedy	Evidence required	Remedy	Evidence required
Doctors dilute vaccines.	Try doctors for diluting vaccines.	Evidence of actual dilution	Provide doctors with kits to check if vaccines are at required strength, and punish doctors (with fines or suspensions) found giving substandard vaccines.	Substandard vaccines
Loans in microfinance programs meant for poor farmers are given to the nonpoor or to nonfarmers in exchange for bribes.	Try loan officers for taking bribes and misallocating funds.	Bribes	Punish loan officers (with fines, suspensions, or dismissals) found giving loans to nonpoor and nonfarmers.	Names of nonpoor, nonfarmer loan recipients
Regulatory officials create deliberate delays to extract ransoms.	Try officials caught taking bribes.	Bribes	Punish officials (with fines, suspensions, or dismissals) for not registering companies on time.	Delays in registration

Source: Author.

To take another example, consider two reforms for dealing with the problem of civil servants who systematically miss work. In the first reform, severe punishments are handed out for unjustified absences. This may lead to a more diligent pursuit of collecting the proper—if false—justifications for absences. It is easy to obtain fraudulent doctor's notes in many countries (it is also often difficult for a genuinely sick person to obtain one). A set of reforms in Venezuelan hospitals that punished nurses for unjustified absences did not reduce absences but did lead to a reduction in unjustified absences offset by an increase in justified absences (Jaen and Paravisini 2001).

The second reform, suggested by principal-agent theory, would set a limit on total absences. Some absences are caused by factors outside the agent's control. But as long as punishments are not draconian and rewards significant but not extravagant, there is no great injustice in providing incentives for attendance. Deducting 2 percent of teachers' monthly salary for each day of absence, for example, regardless of the reason would motivate teachers to show up without creating an undue burden. (Exceptions could be made in the case of severe chronic illnesses, in which case the illness would have to be observed by a supervisor.)

In many cases, principal-agent theory, rather than the economics of crime, suggests a more realistic set of reforms for controlling corruption. It is important to keep in mind, however, that principal-agent theory is a poorly understood tool. Agents respond to the incentives they are given, not to the reason why the principal gives them the incentive. Give a teacher incentives for better student performance, for example, and grades will often improve. The result may reflect teaching for the test or even teacher-induced cheating, however (Jacob and Levitt [2003] find that this happens even in U.S. public schools). Incentives must be given in such a way that agents can reap higher payoffs only by actually improving performance on factors that the principal really cares about. Azfar and Zinnes (2005) find that giving trainers incentives based on students' performance on 80 questions improved performance (measured by satisfaction ratings, not test performance), but giving incentives based on 20 questions did not, perhaps because trainers were teaching for the test. Incentives should be given on the basis of broad measures of performance, and exams should be proctored and set by people other than those who teach the class.

In summary, by using a combination of incentives for good behavior, civil penalties for corruption-related instances where neglect and mismanagement can be proved, and criminal penalties when evidence of the most harmful kinds of corruption can be proved, a committed principal can significantly reduce corruption by agents (box 8.1). A more difficult problem is faced when the principals themselves are corrupt and complicit in the acts of incidental corruption that most people experience.

The Sale of Jobs and Its Effect on Mechanisms of Accountability

In many corrupt systems, jobs are systematically sold by senior officials in exchange for both up-front payments to purchase the position and bribe-sharing arrangements. The practice has a long and distinguished history. The Catholic Church sold jobs in the late Middle Ages (Noonan 1984). The East India Company sold customs posts, and many European armies sold military

> **BOX 8.1** Experimental Evidence on Controlling Corruption
>
> Azfar and Nelson (2007) designed an experiment to examine the impact of three factors on corruption: the likelihood that effort by a prosecutor would succeed in exposing corruption of the executive, the wages of the potentially corrupt executive and the prosecutor, and the political independence of the prosecutor. They model the mechanism of exposing the executive in a way that is much simpler than obtaining a criminal conviction; the executive faces no punishment other than losing the stolen funds and (often) not being elected in the next round. This is closer to a highly publicized civil trial, except for the requirement that the investigation be carried out by a public prosecutor. The experiment involves eight players who play 12 rounds of a corruption game. In each round, three players are selected as candidates and can get elected as president and in some variations elected as attorney general (in other variations the president appoints the attorney general). The president can then steal public funds, and the attorney general can expose the wrongdoing to the voters. Then the next round is played with a new election—the previous round's president, attorney general, and a randomly selected third player are candidates. The experimental variations are wages, transparency, and whether the attorney general is elected or appointed. Their results indicate that both an increase in the ease of exposure and an increase in wages reduce corruption. Barr, Lindelow, and Serneels (2004) find similar effects in a sample of Ethiopian nurses.
>
> Olken (2005) conducted a field experiment in which he randomly increased the probability of auditing the funds of Indonesian local governments in World Bank–financed projects. He found that credible threats to increase the probability of audits did reduce corruption. Criminal charges were seldom filed following the audits. Instead, corrupt local officials faced social and political costs.

positions. The exchange of prestigious ambassadorial positions for campaign contributions continues to the present day, even in developed countries.

In developing countries, low-level positions such as posts as customs officers and tax collectors are sold in exchange for explicit payments to senior officials. These sales are often packaged with job protections, so the officials who buy their jobs also buy some protection from being fired. Sometimes regular civil service protections suffice; at other times extra protection is offered. These arrangements also often include bribe-sharing agreements in which low-level officials share their bribe receipts with the senior officials who hired them. Not all sales of jobs are intended to result in bribe farming. The jobs of schoolteachers and "ghost workers" are sold not primarily for the purpose of selling the right to demand bribes but simply in return for the right to collect a paycheck.

What happens if the microeconomic remedies suggested by principal-agent theory or the economics of crime in a system are applied where jobs are sold? An increase in wages would lead to a higher price for the jobs. Such an increase in the price of the job would either constrict employability in the public sector to the elite or lead to officials having to borrow money to buy their appointments. Those who go into debt may be compelled to take bribes, even if they would otherwise not have done so. The increase in wages would also increase the value of patronage networks and may increase the proportion of people who join them. Raising public sector wages is a good preventive measure for reducing the likelihood that corruption emerges and becomes entrenched, but once systemic corruption is in place, raising salaries itself is unlikely to be effective unless combined with various other accountability measures.

The use of microeconomic incentives by increasing the likelihood of being fined, suspended, fired, or imprisoned would not be enforced. Such laws would be stillborn, rarely used, and possibly used selectively to punish those who step out of line in the system of corruption. One of the reasons why Montesinos may have videotaped the bribe payments may have been that he wanted evidence with which to blackmail anyone who stepped out of line in his system of corruption.

Dealing with Systemic Corruption

Many countries in the world suffer from systemic corruption. This type of corruption is analogous to organized crime: participants act not independently but in concert with one another, maintaining the system that allows them to extract rents and taking their own share of the rents. Systems of corruption can involve the sale of jobs, the sharing of rents from bribery or theft, and the compromising of systems of integrity that could control corruption.

Governments use several mechanisms to deal with corruption, including the judiciary, ombudsmen and inspectors general, anticorruption commissions, and legislative accountability committees. In many countries, however, these mechanisms of accountability do not work, because they are captured by a systemically corrupt government. Cases are assigned to complicit judges, or public prosecutors decline to charge officials with corruption. Ombudsmen, inspectors general, and anticorruption commissioners may target only members of the opposition or rival politicians in the ruling coalition. If they are given extraordinary powers, they might use them to punish those who deviate from the system.[2] These mechanisms may therefore be ineffective or even counterproductive in reducing corruption.

Vladimir Montesinos and Alberto Fujimori compromised the systems of integrity in Peru by buying the judiciary, the legislature, the press, and the broadcast media, reducing Peruvian democracy to a set of electoral formalities. This section offers a set of rules that, if implemented in conjunction with a system of regular multiparty elections, might prevent the emergence of the kind of systemic corruption that existed in Peru (table 8.2).

Elections and Recalls of Politicians

Elections offer a mechanism for the orderly removal of corrupt governments from power. They form the bedrock of accountability in the framework presented here. The basic presumption is that various mechanisms listed in this chapter will expose corruption, which will lead to the government being voted out of office.

Nondemocracies may remove corrupt governments from power by revolution, but the costs of revolution are much higher than the costs of elections and the likelihood of their occurring is much lower. Elections also offer a focal point for citizen protest if they are rigged or canceled. Ultimately, electoral systems rely on protest as a final sanction. To constrain the most corrupt regimes, there may have to be a reasonable chance of a revolution if an election is canceled or rigged. Rigged elections precipitated protests in Chile, Ecuador, Georgia, the Kyrgyz Republic, Nicaragua, the Philippines, and Ukraine; in many instances corruption was one of the major precipitating factors of the protests (Karatnycky and Ackerman 2005).

Several arguments have been made about the advantages of democracies. This chapter focuses on the notion that democracies are likely to have less corruption than other types of regimes (Treisman 2000). The literature shows a strong (negative) relationship between democracy and corruption. Persson and Tabellini (2005) examine the impact of various details of electoral systems on corruption. They find that presidential systems, more independent legislators, and larger electoral districts are associated with lower levels of corruption.

Both single-member districts and proportional representation have advantages in fighting systemic corruption. Single-member districts have the advantage that voters can vote against any person they consider corrupt. However, such districts encourage political monopolies and duopolies that can leave voters with a restricted set of choices—sometimes with no option other than voting for a corrupt party. Single-member districts also reduce

TABLE 8.2 Alternatives to Traditional Mechanisms of Accountability in Countries with Systemic Corruption

Traditional mechanism of accountability	Why mechanism does not work in systemically corrupt countries	Alternative mechanisms
Justice system in which public prosecutors bring cases and the government assigns judges to cases	Public prosecutors will not charge public officials; the government assigns corrupt judges to cases.	■ Allow private citizens to charge public officials with civil charges related to corruption, or criminal charges (*qui tam*). ■ Elect or have local governments appoint prosecutors. ■ Randomly assign judges to cases.
Legislative accountability committees selected by a majority	Committee will be complicit with the executive.	■ Establish opposition-led accountability committees (although these too can be captured). ■ Allow parliamentary questions, where any member of the legislature can question members of the executive branch every week, and broadcast the question and answer session live.
State-owned or -regulated media	Media are pressured to not expose corruption.	■ Allow privately owned and international media, including Web sites.
Impeachment	Legislators who would conduct impeachment may be complicit.	■ Survey citizens at regular intervals or hold citizen councils to decide on recalls.
Legislative committees or ombudsmen with the right to question public officials	Committees and ombudsmen can become complicit.	■ Pass freedom of information acts that allow any citizen to demand information.

Source: Author.

the number of independent legislators. There are also significant advantages to incumbency. In the United States, many legislative seats are simply not contested, especially in state elections.

Proportional representation has a significant advantage in terms of allowing a greater number of parties into the legislature. This increases the likelihood that some vigorously anticorruption legislators are elected, who, if facilitated by institutions such as parliamentary question time, could reduce systemic corruption. Proportional representation has a significant disadvantage, however, because it is difficult for the electorate to exclude corrupt politicians who buy themselves slots high on a party list.

Systems of indirect election are susceptible to corruption and capture.[3] In general, therefore, direct elections may be preferable for reducing corruption (this may explain the effect that Persson and Tabellini find for presidentialism, as presidents are typically elected in direct elections, unlike prime ministers who are generally indirectly elected via the legislature or sometimes appointed by the president). Systems of indirect elections of the upper houses of parliaments could be replaced with systems of direct elections. Accountability could also be increased by holding elections for upper and lower houses at different times. There is significant inertia in political systems, because those it selects typically have a comparative advantage in being selected by that system. External pressures can lead to reform, however. U.S. senators resisted changing the system of elections to direct elections until members of the House—who used to select them—vowed to follow popular referendums in their own voting for senators.

Electoral systems could also be designed that take advantage of both the benefits of proportional representation (that is, greater variety of parties in the legislature) and the ability to exclude corrupt politicians. For instance, there could be a requirement for primaries, which would allow citizens to exclude corrupt politicians at the primary stage. Alternatively, a two-stage election could be held for parliamentary seats, in which the top two vote-getters would compete in a run-off. Such a system would minimize strategic voting in the first stage and allow the entry of third parties. Citizens could also have the option of crossing out the names of candidates on a party list whom they do not want to be elected on the party slate (voters would be allowed to do so only if they voted for that party).

Citizens could also be given the right to remove corrupt elected officials through recalls. A system of recalls, whereby the electorate can call a new election by, say, collecting enough signatures, is one mechanism for getting rid of corrupt politicians. To prevent frivolous recalls, a large number of signatures could be required or a randomized survey of a representative sample of people could be conducted in which a high threshold (say, 60 percent or two standard deviations above 50 percent) would have to support the recall.

Participation and Surveys

The primary purpose of participatory governance is improved preference matching; improved accountability is a by-product. A survey-based system of governance, in which preferences are elicited by surveys and communicated to public officials, could have such an effect, albeit without the benefits of discussion. One example of participatory governance, Deliberative Democracy, designed by James Fishkin of Stanford University, involves collecting a set of randomly selected people and asking them to discuss issues and vote on them (bostonreview.net/BR31.2/fishkin.html). The meetings are often televised. In some instances, they may change popular opinion about reforms.

How can participation be used to target corruption? Suppose a set of randomly selected people is asked to discuss campaign finance reforms. The result may be a franker discussion and stronger proposals for reform than in a legislature, where each member has some need for financing.

Another option would be to empower each member of the randomly selected group to identify a public official for investigation. The person could also identify who would investigate the official. This mechanism would have the benefit of having a selection system for investigation that cannot easily be completely captured and does not waste too many resources on investigating obviously honest officials (as random selection of officials for investigation would).

The World Bank could use such an institution to finesse the issue of compromising sovereignty in its efforts at increasing accountability. If a randomly selected set of citizens—rather than World Bank staff—is asked whom to audit and who should audit, no reasonable notion of sovereignty is compromised. Organizations such as the Open Society Institute could sponsor these accountability councils, which could be televised, generating considerable interest. If the country had a freedom of information act, citizens could watch a citizens' council decide which congressperson's finances to audit or investigate.

Civil Charges

Changes in the law that allow private parties to bring civil charges in cases of neglect or mismanagement could be an effective remedy against forms of corruption in which the victims know they are being victimized. Another option is instituting a rule that allows private persons to file criminal charges on their own—a process known as *qui tam*. The adoption of *qui tam* could lead to a significant improvement in integrity in many systemically corrupt countries where the prosecutor's office has been compromised.

Allowing civil charges of neglect and mismanagement to be filed in corruption-related cases in which corruption itself is difficult to prove may reduce corruption (box 8.1). Corruption itself—and its most typical manifestation, bribery—is very easy to hide. However, the consequences of corruption are not always so easy to hide, especially in the case of the more harmful forms of corruption. It is very difficult to expose the corrupt behavior of a judge who, after accepting the same bribe from both parties, then makes a fair decision; a judge who makes a large number of unfair decisions is more easily identifiable.

Direct evidence of corruption is not always necessary to fight corruption in the courts. Even though no direct evidence may exist of corrupt collusion, there may be clear evidence for neglect and mismanagement (box 8.2). It would be wrong to charge, convict, and jail an official for corruption on the basis of such evidence, but such evidence should be enough to suspend or even fire an official on charges of neglect or mismanagement. This in itself would provide some deterrence to official corruption, especially in the most visibly harmful cases.

Random Assignment of Judges and Prosecutors

In many developed countries, judges are randomly assigned to cases. The process of assignment can be highly visible (a ball, a roulette wheel, or a pack of cards could be used in clear view of everyone). If there are even a few

---

BOX 8.2 Fighting Corruption Indirectly in Indonesia

Indonesian law in 2001 made it difficult for officials to pursue corruption charges. Photocopies were inadmissible as evidence, the legal definition of *corruption* included only embezzlement, and a case became moot if the money was paid back.

Several cases in Indonesia suggest the usefulness of an indirect legal approach that relies on charges of official neglect rather than corruption. In Malang, East Java, corrupt businessmen who had purchased a stamp of approval from the relevant government officials were producing substandard motor oil. When Malang Corruption Watch investigated the motor oil factory, following complaints to a consumer rights association, they found that the oil was substandard. This constituted enough evidence to charge the manager of the company, who was indicted and had to shut down operations. It was not feasible to file charges of corruption against the government officials who approved the oil for sale, although charges of neglect could have been brought against them.

The Café Corporation in North Sulawesi was supposed to channel small loans to farmers. In fact, only half of all recipients were farmers—and only half of those farmers actually received their loans. When farmers who did not receive loans complained, a government agency investigated the case. Prosecutors were able to get a conviction on charges of mismanagement.

Source: Author.

honest and diligent judges, random assignment of cases will ensure that at least some cases will receive fair hearings in court.

Criminal law systems generally require that charges be brought by a public prosecutor. Public prosecutors are typically appointed by the executive branch of government and assigned to particular cases by some higher authority. Each of these steps is liable to be captured by those running a system of corruption.

A remedy for the second problem—assignment to cases—is the random assignment of prosecutors to corruption cases. Assuming that there are some honest judges and prosecutors, and that judges are assigned to cases randomly, this would at least occasionally lead to a situation in which both the judge and the prosecutor were honest. A conviction of a low-level official could be used to gather evidence that could lead to the conviction of senior officers and other members of the system. Even if the conviction of other people is outside the jurisdiction of the case, a judicial process in which facts are found and publicized can create legal and political momentum that becomes difficult to stop.

Dealing with systemic corruption is difficult in that many of those who are counted on to expose corruption cannot or will not do so. But one or two cases may be enough to expose a system; each case does not have to be tried independently. A single exposure can cause the entire system to unravel.

Random assignment of judges and prosecutors is probably not the most efficient way of dealing with incidental corruption. It is a good way of dealing with the far more pernicious practice of systemic corruption, however. Given the far greater costs of systemic corruption, and the likelihood that it will emerge if given the chance, all countries would be well advised to adopt rules on randomized assignment of judges, even if they think they do not have systemic corruption.

Election of Prosecutors

One way of dealing with the risk that the executive branch may appoint lazy or complicit prosecutors to protect corrupt politicians is to involve citizens in their selection. One argument against electing rather than appointing too many officials is that elections tax the civic virtue of the citizenry, who may not really want to decide who should be elected to various unglamorous posts (Cooter 2003). The office of prosecutor, however, is one that does interest the citizenry, particularly in places where corruption is rife.

A possible objection to election of prosecutors is that it favors people who like—or at least can tolerate—running for office. This may be a virtue, however, because the love of attention and power that comes with an affinity for politics may lead to a greater enthusiasm for the diligent prosecution of high-profile cases.

In some federal systems, prosecutors are appointed by the state or provincial governments. In Pakistan, for example, Nawaz Sharif, the chief minister of the Punjab, appointed the public prosecutor who indicted Asif Zardari, the husband of Prime Minister Benazir Bhutto, for corruption. The indictment would have been unlikely had the federal government appointed all prosecutors.

An alternative to election of prosecutors would be the appointment of some prosecutors by the legislature or even by opposition parties. While possibly an improvement on selection by the executive, the process may not always be as good as direct elections, as the opposition itself may be captured (as was the case in Peru under Fujimori).

Randomized Audits and the Public Declaration of Assets

The public declaration of assets makes wrongdoing more difficult to hide. Ill-gotten gains can be hidden in the accounts of relatives, friends, and associates, but this makes them complicit and increases the likelihood of identification when systemic corruption unravels.

Requirements for public declarations of assets of public officials need to be matched with randomized audits of public officials. These audits should include the audits of relatives, friends, and associates. Audits that show how people game the system should be used to adapt the system.

Auditors should be randomly selected. Alternatively, a random selection of people could decide whom to audit and who should audit. Another option would be to allow private auditors to audit whomever they want and to offer rewards for the identification of corrupt officials.

Public Expenditure Tracking Systems and Randomized Audits of Governmental Finances

Examination of the finances of public sector entities can reveal certain kinds of corruption. Public expenditure tracking systems (PETS) that require each level of government to state how much it receives from and sends to every other level can reveal corruption. Reinikka and Svensson (2002) introduced a PETS in Uganda and reduced reported leakages from about 80 percent to about 20 percent. Whether actual leakages fell by quite that much is unclear, as some leakages can be hidden from PETS by determined officials who collude. If, however, the PETS were followed by a deep audit of some randomly selected points, such collusive reporting could be spotted.

Accountability Committees and Question Time

The legislature can play a significant role in exposing corruption in the executive branch if empowered to do so. Accountability committees should be headed by the party in opposition to the executive. These committees should be given significant powers to investigate members of the executive branch and to question them in the legislature. Such committees cannot prevent corruption (Montesinos had compromised the opposition), but they may reduce it.

Other reforms, such as question time, in which any legislator can ask questions of the executive in a widely broadcast regular proceeding, may be more effective at revealing corruption. The executive branch should be regularly questioned by the committee and other legislators, and the proceedings should be televised live and rebroadcast in the evening. In the British Parliament, the prime minister is questioned every week, and his senior ministers are questioned every day except Friday. Each legislator can pose up to two questions. Questions are shuffled, virtually guaranteeing that opposition members will get to ask several questions every day. Questions not answered in the oral period receive written answers, which are made public. This process ensures that any attempt to pack the proceedings with innocuous questions by the majority party is visible to the electorate. There tends to be significant interest in these proceedings, making it worthwhile for networks to carry them. The information revealed can have significant political consequences.

In Croatia parliamentarians can ask 30 questions of the executive branch every month. One such set of questions on a bribe allegedly accepted by Foreign Minister Miomir Zuzul led to his resignation. President Stjepan Mesic easily won reelection soon after, suggesting that political fallout from a corruption scandal can be limited (The Associated Press 2005).

Whether to allow the legislature itself to dismiss the government following the revelation of corruption in question time is not clear. On the one hand, it would make the legislature look like an impotent debating society if it could not dismiss the government following such a demonstration. On the other hand, allowing the legislature to dismiss the government runs counter to presidential systems, which appear to reduce corruption. One possibility is to authorize the legislature to call for a large nationwide survey about a recall, calling a new election only if a supermajority asks for a recall. The survey could explicitly ask whether people thought the government was corrupt, rather than whether voters wanted the government recalled. This would not prevent citizens from opportunistically responding that the government was corrupt simply to get a chance to change it, but with a modicum of civic virtue among a proportion of the citizenry, asking specifically about corruption may reduce recalls for other reasons.

There should be a political mechanism to dismiss a government that appears to be corrupt even in the absence of incontrovertible evidence of corruption. Elections are supposed to dismiss governments that are incompetent or establish priorities that are not consistent with the people's will. In the case of corruption, however, the electorate should not be required to wait for a scheduled election to change government.

The political and judicial mechanisms for dismissal are not mutually exclusive. The system could allow for both; depending on the complexity of the case or the sophistication of the form of corruption, the judicial mechanism may be more effective. The two mechanisms may even be complementary. The facts found in a judicial investigation may help bolster a political ouster. The advantage of the political process is that it allows a corrupt government to be dismissed even in the absence of incontrovertible evidence, without compromising the rule of law—which for very good reasons is based on the need for incontrovertible evidence in criminal cases. It makes sense to have high standards of proof before subjecting people to severe criminal punishment; there is no need to have the same standards of proof to dismiss a government.

The question of parliamentary immunity is a difficult one. It is needed to prevent legislators from being intimidated by governments, but it offers refuge to criminals. The freedom of a few criminals is often a small price to pay for the benefits of an independent legislature. There does not need to be immunity from investigation, however. In fact, a few members of parliament should be randomly selected for investigation every year. Random selection will prevent the government from using the investigations for retaliation, and occasional selection for an investigation will create some incentives for legislators to be honest.

The Media

The media play a crucial role in both investigating and publicizing systemic corruption. Two reporters, Carl Bernstein and Bob Woodward, exposed the Watergate scandal; Montesinos and Fujimori were eventually brought down by the airing of a video of Montesinos paying a bribe; and the media led the investigations that resulted in the resignations of senior politicians in Brazil in 2005.

Systemically corrupt governments spend a lot of money, effort, and political capital corrupting the media. Indeed, Montesinos spent most of his bribe money bribing the media. He used bribery, intimidation, defamation, and state ownership of media to control the content provided to the public. Many other electoral dictatorships use similar tactics. The Committee to Protect Journalists (www.cpj.org) and Reporters without Borders (www.rsf.org) both document the ways the press is intimidated and suppressed in many countries.

A variety of verifiable rules can be implemented that make it likely that there will be at least some inquisitive, independent, and diligent journalists who will expose corruption if systemic corruption exists. An advantage in fighting systemic corruption is that only some instances need to be exposed for the system to unravel. Another advantage is that a system of corruption creates a lot of evidence, even if it is all private knowledge. Montesinos bribed hundreds of people. Even small systems of systemic corruption generally involve dozens of people. A diligent investigator could uncover parts of such a system, leading to the unraveling of the system. But such investigators can be threatened or neutralized: Reporters without Borders reports that 63 journalists were killed, 800 arrested, and 1,300 physically attacked or threatened in 2005. In addition, 1,000 media outlets were censored in 2005.

To prevent such intimidation, policy makers can take several steps:

- Prohibit censorship. Prohibiting censorship will not prevent subtle forms of censorship, including inducements for self-censorship by, for example, withholding advertising revenue from newspapers, but it can prevent the most obvious forms of corruption.
- Commit to allowing an international investigation into the death of any journalist, and allow all imprisoned journalists to appeal in an international court.
- Allow private television channels and ban state-owned newspapers. State ownership of the media is correlated with worse governance across countries (Djankov and others 2001). While there are anomalies, such as National Public Radio in the United States and the British Broadcasting Company, which provide excellent coverage, in general allowing the government to own the media creates space for systemic corruption.[4]
- Allow foreign journalists to cover domestic stories. In many small developing countries, too few journalists have the training and independence to cover stories. Allowing foreign journalists to cover stories would increase the likelihood of exposing corruption. Foreign journalists also have the benefit of protection from their embassies.

- Allow foreign transmissions of radio and television broadcasts and Web sites of foreign newspapers. With increased access to the Internet and the improvement of computer translations, allowing foreign media into a country could significantly increase the ability of activists to obtain news.

Freedom of Information Acts

A freedom of information act allows the general public to access information by filing requests. Supplementary legislation that requires local governments, political parties, and public officials to disclose their finances makes freedom of information acts a useful anticorruption tool.

Many freedom of information acts have been adopted in the past few years. In some developing countries and transition economies, these acts have actually leapfrogged over similar laws of developed countries. An example is India's recent law, under which all government documents not specifically classified as secret are accessible by the public (sadly, the act explicitly omits Kashmir from its purview) (Ministry of Personnel, Public Grievances and Pensions 2005).

The effectiveness of freedom of information acts can easily be verified. Civil society organizations and even private citizens can file requests for information and record how quickly and how well public servants respond to their request. Freedom of information acts can be used both for the initial exposure of corruption and in the process of unraveling systemic corruption, by starting independent investigations of officials who may be implicated in a scandal.

Freedom of information acts are typically limited by concerns about privacy and national security. The appeals process that decides whether some requests for information should be denied should include members of the opposition, and a unanimous vote should be required to classify a document as secret. Doing so would make it less likely that information that could expose corruption would opportunistically be labeled as a national security secret.

The Role of Local Governments

The existence of multiple layers of government creates the opportunity for the separation of powers, in which different levels of government can discipline one another. Increasing the likelihood of audits by a central government agency reduced corruption in local governments in Indonesia (Olken 2005). If, however, the central government agency is itself corrupt, the system of audits can end up being used to cement rather than disrupt a rent-extraction system. The logic of disruption dictates that a second round of audits, in which any private firm or NGO can reaudit the central government's audit, be instated to prevent systemic corruption involving the central government's auditing agency.

One problem with fighting systemic corruption is the limited contestability of political markets. In some democratic but highly corrupt countries, such as Bangladesh, all credible leaders are tainted by corruption. Local governments provide an excellent training ground for politicians to learn both the process of governing and the process of campaigning. They thus increase the contestability of political markets. The existence of local governments can increase the choices voters have, allowing them to throw the rascals out rather than just choose among rascals.

Local governments also allow ideas to be tested in some places and then tried elsewhere if they work. They can be used to conduct a scientific analysis based on the randomized assignment of localities to treatment and control groups.

Many of the reforms suggested here could be legislated by a majority in a local council in many countries. Where reforms succeed in reducing corruption, neighboring localities could come under pressure to implement similar reforms. A university or NGO could arrange for a high-publicity competition in which localities compete for the adoption of anticorruption legislation. A recent project in Romania created such a competition for the adoption of deregulatory reforms; eventually, the central government adopted some of the deregulation reforms as well (Timisoara City Hall 2007). If reforms are effective, the process may even create a dynamic that induces the central government to adopt some of these reforms—though resistance to adopting anticorruption reforms may be higher.

Case Study Evidence on Systemic Corruption

Four case study examples yield lessons on dealing with systemic corruption. This section discusses Belarus, Brazil, Kenya, and Turkey and then briefly the role of revolution sparked by electoral (or other) fraud in disrupting systemic corruption.

Belarus

Between the mid-1990s and 2005, the government of Alyaksander Lukashenka subverted democracy while maintaining the facade of multiparty elections

(Silitski 2004). Lukashenka used physical intimidation and constitutional reform to ensure electoral victories and remain in power. Several lessons can be learned from his rule about how to prevent democracy from being preempted (table 8.3).

Brazil

A recent set of corruption scandals in Brazil reveals how the interconnectedness of systemic corruption can be used to make the system unravel (Saibro 2006). Reporters from the weekly magazine *Veja* recorded the head of procurement at the post office taking a kickback. The opposition parties called for a parliamentary investigation, which the government first resisted but then agreed to. The resulting investigation implicated Roberto Jefferson of the PTB (Partido Trabalhista Brasileiro), a party allied with the government. Jefferson was also implicated in another scandal when Lidio Duarate, the head of the Brazilian Reinsursers Institute, reported to the media that Jefferson demanded kickbacks for giving Duarate his job and that Duarate hired Jefferson's associates.

Jefferson, in turn, accused the ruling party, which had only a minority in parliament, of bribing legislators to obtain a majority. Two leaders of opposition parties, Severino Cavalcanti of a conservative party and Waldemar Costa Neto of a liberal party, were implicated, and Costa Neto resigned; the president's chief of staff, Jose Dirceu, also resigned. The crisis led to pressures for reforms that would combat corruption. It has been politically costly for the ruling party.

What lessons can be learned from the experience? First, the media play a critical role in investigating and publicly exposing corruption. Second, parliamentary investigations are vital. Empowering the parliamentary opposition to launch an investigation without the assent of the majority increases accountability. Third, systems of corruption that are based on the sale of jobs, can unravel as soon as someone starts talking.

Kenya

President Mwai Kibaki came to power in 2002, after winning an election against the corrupt Daniel Arap Moi. Moi had tried to rig the elections, but a combination of international observers and domestic activists foiled his attempt. The new government, beholden to the forces of integrity, appointed John Githongo as head of the Kenyan Anti-Corruption Commission.

TABLE 8.3 Rules That Might Have Prevented Democracy from Being Subverted in Belarus

Action by Lukashenka	Rules to prevent subversion of democracy
Killed or imprisoned journalists	Government allows independent inquiry into the death of any journalist (with the family of the journalist choosing the investigator). Imprisoned journalists have the right to appeal to an international court. Broadcast the reports of the inquiries into deaths and the judgment from the appeals process.
Denied accreditation to election observers	Accreditation is given by a panel that includes an equal number of members of the opposition. There is a simple accreditation process that can be approved in the first instance by any member of the accreditation committee. A supermajority or even a unanimous vote is required to deny accreditation.
Stuffed election commission with cronies	An equal number of members of the election commission is nominated by any significant party in the legislature (say, with more than 10 percent of the members of parliament). Smaller parties also get to nominate members of the election commission. Each member of the commission writes an independent report on the election that is broadcast, published in newspapers, and circulated over the Internet. The broadcast of the reports of commission members is followed by a question-and-answer session with the press.
Disallowed exit polls	Multiple organizations are allowed to conduct exit polls, so that pollsters can flag statistically significant differences between their polls and other polls and between the polls and the election results as evidence of rigging. Such a system may not detect minor rigging, but it will detect major vote fraud.
Shut down universities	Either ban the closure of or require a majority of the opposition to shut down a university.
Used firearms against protesters	Ban the use of live ammunition against unarmed protesters.
Changed constitution to appoint heads of regional administrations	Require election—preferably direct election—of leaders of provinces and the capital city. These alternative power centers are important for a credible opposition.
Censored mass media	Disallow censorship in all circumstances. Allow opposition oversight of advertising budgets of state-owned companies so that critical newspapers cannot be punished by withholding advertising revenues.

Source: Author and Silitski 2004.

The primary case of grand corruption Githongo investigated involved the sale of "services" by Anglo Leasing, an apparently fictitious company, to the Kenyan government. The sale required the signatures of the secretary of interior and the secretary of the treasury. Githongo uncovered evidence that at least 10 senior officials or legislators were involved in the multimillion dollar scheme and that many other similar schemes existed (Githongo 2005).

Githongo's efforts to reverse the sale and remove the secretaries from office met with significant pressures from many senior officials. These included threats to kill him and to use the legal system against his family. His dogged pursuit of the issue did bear some fruit—some of the money was returned to the Kenyan government—but eventually he was forced to resign. After his resignation, the parliamentary public accounts committee, led by an opposition leader, interviewed Githongo in Great Britain, where he was living in exile. The interview led to the resignation of two ministers.

A number of aspects of this story are worth highlighting. First, there may have been a moment of extraordinary politics at the end of the Moi regime when reforms not normally politically feasible may have become possible. It led to the appointment of Githongo. Had the forces of integrity had a set of integrity-enhancing rules, such as those discussed in this chapter, some of them may have been adopted. Second, systemic corruption involves many people, and the system can unravel. Third, the system will fight back. The rules must therefore include protections for key players on the side of integrity. Fourth, details of constitutional form or political tradition, such as opposition leadership of the public accounts committee, matter.

Turkey

On November 3, 1996, a car carrying a police chief, a prominent member of parliament, a criminal, and his mistress crashed into a truck in the roadside town of Susurluk in western Turkey, killing everyone but the member of parliament. The criminal, Mehmet Ozbay (also known as Abdullah Catl), a notorious smuggler and blackmailer wanted by Interpol, possessed an identification card personally signed by the interior minister, Mehmet Agar. The car contained a bag full of dollars and a trunk full of weapons; the passengers' pockets were full of cocaine. The incident led to a change of government in Turkey (Akay 2003).

Immediately after the crash, student protests broke out in response to this evidence of grand corruption; they were repressed. Then a group of activists and NGOs began a nonviolent campaign by asking people to turn off their lights for one minute every evening at 9:00 p.m. The media, initially reluctant, joined the campaign, playing an important role in the dynamics of the protest. These protests became widespread: millions of Turks began turning off their lights in protest of the government's corruption. The government initially resisted the campaign and tried to discredit it, but eventually the momentum created by this campaign led the National Security Council to ask the government to resign.[5] An accident that revealed corruption and a sustained campaign brought down a government.[6]

Several lessons can be drawn from this experience. First, exposure of corruption needs to be followed by a sustained campaign to create genuine political costs. Governments will try to suppress these campaigns, but in a country like Turkey, which cares about its international image, the ability to suppress a nonviolent campaign is limited. Second, the role of the media is important. Even if initially reluctant, the media will often join a campaign once it gets going. Third, having an external source of accountability that can call a government to resign is critical. In Turkey this body is the National Security Council, which may have asked the government to resign only because its members did not like the government in the first place. In other countries, a supreme court or constitutional court may play such a role—it was such a court that eventually asked Slobodan Milosevic to hand over power to the elected government after several days of protest in Serbia. Another option would be an explicit constitutional provision under which a group of citizens can ask for a recall.

According to the Center for Global Integrity, integrity systems in Turkey are very weak (www.globalintegrity.org). The Turkish government objected to the report, but the objectivity and specificity of the center's methodology allowed it to respond to the Turkish government's criticisms. The hope is that the Turkish government will reform its integrity system to improve its scores on the "Global integrity" matrix.

Elections and Revolutions

Popular protests and new elections have occurred in Georgia, Indonesia, Lebanon, the Philippines, Serbia, and Ukraine. Some of these revolutions were inspired by corruption; all were driven at least in part by dissatisfaction with the constitutional mechanisms of changing a government, either because an election had been rigged or because the constitutional process of impeachment was compromised (Karatnycky and Ackerman 2005). In the Philippines after the Senate refused to impeach Joseph Estrada in 2000–01, "people power" brought a change of government. In Ecuador, President Luizo Gutierrez's attempt to pack the courts with his cronies led to protests that brought down the government in 2005.

One should not overestimate the power of parchment; the constitution of integrity is ultimately written on the hearts of men and women who must ultimately demand their rights when they are denied them. The role of parchment is to provide a set of clear rules, so that brave people can coordinate their demands and protests in a way that disrupts systems of corruption. Elections are one such set of rules. Holding elections regularly and often—and having a population that can be relied on to change a government by protest if an election is massively rigged or canceled—is an important mechanism for controlling grand corruption, especially if combined with other mechanisms.

Recommendations

What can different members of society do to fight corruption? National governments in partially democratic, partially dysfunctional states cannot be expected to adopt reforms to combat systemic corruption. The recommendations provided below, therefore, focus on what steps other groups—ordinary citizens, the media, NGOs, international organizations, foreign governments, and local governments—can take to fight corruption.

The Role of Citizens

Citizens should pay attention to the information provided by the media and by activists on corruption and related matters. They should vote, and they should protest vociferously if elections are rigged or canceled or the government undertakes significant anti-integrity measures, such as replacing the entire judiciary with its cronies. Citizens should also pay attention to efforts by activists to mobilize them in mass anticorruption campaigns when systemically corruption is exposed, as they did in Turkey, even if no election is scheduled. Such mobilizations can lead to recalls even if there is no such provision in the constitution.

The Role of the Media

The media have a vital role to play in preventing systemic corruption by exposing corruption, causing it to unravel, and mobilizing the citizenry into action. If citizens are the jury in the court of public opinion, the media are the prosecutors. Journalists and columnists should courageously investigate corruption cases; report threats and intimidation to the Committee to Protect Journalists, Reporters without Borders, or Transparency International; publicize cases of corruption; follow leads to other involved parties; and communicate to the public the efforts of activists to mobilize them into action.

Much of the media will be co-opted into the system of corruption, but it takes only a few independent journalists to expose systemic corruption. Once exposure starts, the rest of the media may defect into the integrity camp to demonstrate they were not complicit—or at least that they are no longer complicit. In Peru after the first video of corruption was aired, even the television stations in Montesinos' pocket felt compelled to air them. In Turkey, after initial reluctance, the media started publishing stories and even publicizing the protests.

The international media also have a role to play. International journalists should work to expose corruption and to train their local counterparts if they trust them not to be complicit in systemic corruption. Foreign journalists have much greater protection afforded to them by their governments than local journalists enjoy. Foreign media should also broadcast into systemically corrupt countries. Foreign media sources should maintain their independence from their own governments and not become or appear to become mouthpieces for their governments.

In some cases the foreign media have not done enough to expose systemic corruption. In Peru, for example, it seems unlikely that a vigorous effort to expose Montesinos, who had bribed 1,600 people, would not have produced some evidence.

The Role of Activists, NGOs, and Universities

The role of activists is to find evidence of pieces of the corrupt system and to use this to start protests, to urge the media to pursue these cases and to publicize them, to press for parliamentary inquiries, and to create greater domestic and international pressure for reform. Use of the Internet to spread information can be effective. Activists should also keep up pressure by exposing related cases all the way to the next election, so there is real political bite to exposure of corruption.

NGOs should keep their activism and service delivery wings separate; ideally, NGOs should do one or the other, not both. Activism requires a certain arm's length and adversarial relationship with the government; working on service delivery sometimes requires close coordination. Activist NGOs can work with foreign donors, but they should be careful to resist pressures to become their mouthpieces and should not get involved with donors that intensify such pressures. Doing so would quickly rob them of their credibility. Local NGOs and universities can also organize competition among local governments on the adoption of the reforms described in this chapter. Universities could also study the impacts of reforms.

International NGOs and universities can help in two important ways. First, they can collect and publicize information on these bright line rules. Given the importance the European Union and the United States place on reform, publicizing these rules can create an important dynamic toward reform. Second, they can help NGOs learn from the experiences of other countries that have created a successful dynamic for reform.

The Role of Foreign Governments, Aid Agencies, and the World Bank

Developed country governments can make an issue of corruption by asking on visa application forms whether the applicant has ever taken a bribe. Because lying on the visa application form is a crime in the country being visited, charges can be brought in the visa-issuing country if the applicant lies. Penalties may be light, but the production of evidence will have political costs.

The World Bank can add questions about bribes to its job application forms. Because lying on these forms can lead to termination of employment, adding such questions will increase the cost of being corrupt to the many civil servants who aspire to jobs in international organizations. Civil charges against human rights violators have created significant costs, even though the civil penalties—typically fines—are much milder than their crimes warrant (Coliver and Feeney 2005).

The World Bank and aid agencies can insist that accountability committees be formed and their audits attached to projects they fund, thus creating expertise and examples of how such a process should occur. The Kecamatan Development Program in Indonesia is one example of such an effort. By insisting on community oversight, the World Bank was able to sidestep a notoriously corrupt Indonesian government, without compromising sovereignty, because it was Indonesians themselves who were empowered (Guggenheim 2007).

Aid agencies and international financial institutions can establish clear conditionalities based on the measures proposed here. Loans and aid could be granted only to countries that have parliamentary debate with significant public input—including televised town hall meetings—and adopt the following rules:

- The legislature should be allowed to question the executive branch every week and the chief executive at least once a month. These proceedings should be broadcast live on radio and television.
- Cases of corruption—at least cases involving public officials—should be randomly assigned to judges.
- The murder or imprisonment of a journalist should be investigated by an international panel. Unless the government is completely exonerated, aid will be withdrawn entirely.
- Foreign journalists and foreign broadcasts should be allowed. Foreign Web sites should be allowed, local organizations should be free to create their own Web sites, and access should not be tampered with.
- Public officials should be required to declare their assets and incomes.
- Private auditors should be allowed to audit public officials.
- In cases of neglect and mismanagement, even when corruption may be involved, private parties should be allowed to file civil lawsuits.
- Elections should be monitored by domestic and international observers.

These agencies can also set rules, such as that of the Millennium Challenge Account (MCA) allocating aid on the basis of performance on governance ratings. (The MCA allocates U.S. aid to developing countries on the basis of several indicators of governance, human development, and economic freedom. The countries themselves are supposed to have greater flexibility in the use of funds than they typically have over other development aid.) These ratings may have induced considerable reform in areas based on actionable indicators, such as the number of days to start a business, and the hope is that they would also lead to reforms on governance if actionable governance indicators were used for allocating MCA funds.

The Role of Local Governments

An honest local government can combat corruption by leading by example. It can pass local laws mandating that all public officials in the locality should declare their assets publicly; that the local executive will answer questions in the local council, which will be broadcast; that the council itself will be overseen by an accountability committee of randomly selected citizens, who will be provided with a lawyer and an accountant they can instruct to investigate financial and legal matters. Once some local governments start doing this, NGOs and universities could organize a nationwide competition among local governments. The leaders of local governments that do well could be well placed to compete on the national political stage. The World Bank could reward these communities with more development projects.

Local governments can also use the mechanisms described above to discipline national governments by, say, questioning the relatives of national politicians who are in the local council (in systemically corrupt countries, several members of a family are often in politics; some may serve in local councils). Citizens could ask lawyers and accountants to investigate central government issues.

Demonstrating That a Government Is Not Systemically Corrupt

To establish its innocence, a government that claims to have been falsely accused of being systemically corrupt and hence denied funding or a loan could hold a referendum on adopting some of the reform measures suggested in this chapter. If a government is on the margins of eligibility on other measures of performance and conducts parliamentary debate on adopting these rules, it should be given a chance to compete for the loan or aid; if it does not hold such a debate, then it should not be given the chance.

The rules in this chapter are also useful to have when a new government comes into power on an anticorruption platform after the dismissal of a corrupt regime. Efforts often dissolve into a mix of noble pronouncements and toothless or even counterproductive actions, such as the creation of ineffective or even politicized anticorruption commissions. The rules outlined here would give activists and honest politicians something to make the government focus on.

Notes

The author is extremely grateful to Melissa Thomas and Anwar Shah for their inspiration and ideas and to Bilal Siddiqi and Ruth Coffman for their comments and advice. None of the aforementioned are responsible for any of the shortcomings of this chapter.

1. The system is vividly documented in a series of videos and described by McMillan and Zoido (2004).
2. One of the best-known systems of corruption was created in Peru, where the government of Fujimori had given extraordinary powers to law enforcement agencies because of the struggle with the Shining Path guerrillas.
3. In Indonesia, for example, corrupt politicians bought their places on party lists after the elections were held and then sold their votes for the indirect election of the mayor. Most citizens and journalists thought the system was corrupt (Azfar 2002). The system was eventually replaced with direct election of mayors.

4. Private ownership of the media can also be problematic, especially if private owners achieve monopolies. There is no easy solution to this problem, as authorizing the government to tighten antitrust regulations against media monopolies could strengthen its hand against the media.
5. Per Article 118 of the Turkish Constitution, the National Security Council (the Milli Güvenlik Kurulu [MGK]) is set up as an advisory organ. The council, chaired by the president of Turkey, is made up of the chief of the General Staff, the four main commanders of the Turkish Armed Forces, and select members of the Council of Ministers. Like the national security councils of other countries, it develops the "national security policy of the state" of the Turkish republic.
6. Since the incident, Turkey has had two elections. The two parliamentarians implicated in the incident—Sedat Bucak, who was in the car, and Mehmet Agar, the interior minister who signed Ozbay's identification card—won their seats and remain in parliament.

References

Akay, Ezel. 2003. "A Call to End Corruption: One Minute of Darkness for Constant Light: New Tactics in Human Rights." www.newtactics.org.

The Associated Press, Reuters. 2005. "Croatia Minister Quits Amid Bribery Scandal." *International Herald Tribune*, January 5.

Azfar, Omar. 2002. "Direct Elections of the Bupati." IRIS Center, University of Maryland, College Park.

Azfar, Omar, and William Robert Nelson. 2007. "Transparency, Wages, and the Separation of Powers: An Experimental Analysis of Corruption." *Public Choice* 130 (3): 471–93.

Azfar, Omar, and Clifford Zinnes. 2006. "Which Incentives Work? An Experimental Analysis of Incentives for Trainers." IRIS Center, University of Maryland, College Park.

Banisar, David. 2004. "The Freedom Info.Org Global Survey: Freedom of Information Acts around the World." www.freedominfo.org/survey.htm.

Barr, Abigail, Magnus Lindelow, and Pieter Serneels. 2004. "To Serve One's Community or Oneself: The Public Servant's Dilemma." Policy Research Working Paper 3187, World Bank, Washington, DC.

Coliver, Sandra, and Moira Feeney. 2005. "Reparations: Using Civil Law Suits to Obtain Reparation for Survivors of Human Rights Abuses and Challenge the Impunity of Human Rights Abusers." www.newtactics.org/Symposium/Presentations/WK411/WK411SCpresentationoutline.doc.

Cooter, Robert. 2003. "The Optimal Number of Governments for Economic Development." In *Market-Augmenting Government*, ed. Omar Azfar and Charles Cadwell. Ann Arbor: University of Michigan Press.

Diamond, Larry. 2002. "Elections without Democracy: Thinking about Hybrid Regimes." *Journal of Democracy* 13 (2): 21–35.

Djankov, Simeon, Caralee Mcliesh, Tatiana Nenova, and Andrei Shleifer. 2001. "Who Owns the Media?" Working Paper 8288, World Bank, Washington, DC.

Githongo, John. 2005. "Report to the President on Graft in Kenya." http://news.bbc.co.uk/1/shared/bsp/hi/pdfs/09_02_06_kenya_report.pdf.

Guggenheim, Scott. 2007. "The Kecamatan Development Program, Indonesia." In *The Search for Empowerment: Social Capital as Idea and Practice at the World Bank*, ed. Anthony Bebbington, Scott E. Guggenheim, Elisabeth Olson, and Michael Woolcock. Bloomfield, CT: Kumarian Press.

Jacob, Brian A., and Steven D. Levitt. 2003. "Rotten Apples: An Investigation into the Prevalence and Predictors of Teachers' Cheating." *Quarterly Journal of Economics* 118 (3): 843–77.

Jaen, Maria, and Daniel Paravisini. 2001. "Wages, Capture and Penalties in Venezuela's Public Hospitals." In *Diagnosis Corruption: Fraud in Latin America's Public Hospitals*, ed. Raphael Di Tella and William Savedoff, 57–94. Washington, DC: Inter-American Development Bank.

Karatnycky, Adrian, and Peter Ackerman. 2005. "How Freedom Is Won: From Civic Resistance to Durable Democracy." Freedom House, Washington, DC. www.freedomhouse.org.

Klitgaard, Robert. 1988. *Controlling Corruption*. Berkeley: University of California Press.

McMillan, John, and Pablo Zoido. 2004. "How to Subvert Democracy: The Case of Montesinos in Peru." *Journal of Economic Perspectives* 18 (4): 69–82.

Ministry of Personnel, Public Grievances and Pensions, Government of India. 2005. "Right to Information Act." New Delhi.

Noonan, John T. 1984. *Bribes*. New York: Macmillan.

Olken, Ben. 2005. "Monitoring Corruption: Evidence from a Field Experiment in Indonesia." NBER Working Paper 11753, National Bureau of Economic Research, Cambridge, MA.

Persson, Torsten, and Guido Tabellini. 2005. *The Economic Effect of Constitutions*. Cambridge, MA: MIT Press.

Reinikka, Ritva, and Jakob Svensson. 2002. "Assessing Frontline Service Delivery." World Bank, Public Services Research Group, Washington, DC.

Saibro, Ana Luisa Fleck. 2006. *Brazil: Global Corruption Report*. Transparency International. London: Pluto Press.

Silitski, Viyali. 2004. "Preempting Democracy: The Case of Belarus." *Journal of Democracy* 16 (4): 83–97.

Timisoara City Hall. 2007. "Timisoara: A Five Star City." Timisoara, Romania. www.primariatm.ro/index.php?meniuId=17&viewCat=608&viewItem=657.

Treisman, Daniel. 2000. "The Causes of Corruption: A Cross-National Study." *Journal of Public Economics* 76 (3): 399–457.

9

Corruption in Tax Administration

MAHESH C. PUROHIT

Corruption has always been in existence, in one form or another. As far back as the fourth century BCE, Kautiliya, a Sanskirt scholar, wrote, "Just as it is not possible not to taste honey (or poison) placed on the surface of the tongue, even so it is not possible for one dealing with the money of the king not to taste the money in however small a quantity. Just as fish moving inside water cannot be known when drinking water, even so officers appointed for carrying out works cannot be known when appropriating money" (Kangle 1972: 91). Kautiliya points out the ways in which employees can be involved in corruption and prescribes the modus operandi to be adopted by the king to deal with corruption and make appointments.

Broadly speaking, corruption can be classified into five categories: political corruption, administrative corruption, grand corruption, petty corruption, and patronage/paternalism and being a "team player." In this chapter the term is defined to include pecuniary or nonpecuniary considerations given to government officials for the use of public office for private gains.[1] Activities that lead to personal benefit that do not involve the government or a quid pro quo are not examined here.

The scope of this chapter is confined to corruption in tax administration. The chapter is divided into five sections. The first section focuses on the main causes of corruption in tax administration. The second section presents issues related to corruption in tax administration and analyzes the role of procedures for administering custom duties, excise duties, and value added tax (VAT). The third section reviews the impact of corruption on the economy. The fourth section suggests policy measures for combating corruption in tax administration. It highlights how the design of the tax structure and procedures of tax administration can reduce the risk of corruption. The last section summarizes the chapter's conclusions and recommendations.

Causes of Corruption in Tax Administration

A variety of factors contribute to corruption in tax administration (box 9.1). These include the complexity of tax laws and procedures, the monopoly power and degree of discretion of tax officials, the lack of adequate monitoring and supervision, the commitment of political leadership, and the overall environment in the public sector.

Complexity of Tax Laws

The complexity of tax laws and procedures increases the magnitude of corruption in the tax system. Tax evasion is more likely to occur in a highly corrupt environment. Lack of requisite information makes taxpayers unaware of their rights and more exposed to discretionary treatment and exploitation.

BOX 9.1 Causes of Corruption in Tax Administration in Bulgaria

A survey in Bulgaria reveals that the main drivers of tax corruption are low pay, lack of professional ethics, legal loopholes, conflicts of interest, get-rich-quick ambitions, and bureaucratic red tape. The less satisfied tax officers are with their pay scales or with the fairness of career development and financial incentive schemes, the more inclined they are to engage in corrupt behavior. If their wages are comparable to the wages for a similar job in the private sector, they may not take the risk of engaging in corruption. However, if their wages are too low to support themselves and their dependents, the incentives for corruption rise. Tax officers' attitudes to corruption are also conditioned by the severity of the punishment for corrupt behavior and the likelihood of being punished when detected. Taxpayers do not play a significant role in determining corrupt practices.

Source: Pashev 2005.

Monopoly Power and the Discretionary Power of Tax Officials

Tax officers are allotted a particular geographical area of operations. For a particular taxpayer, the tax officer is the tax department. This monopoly power gives tax officers the opportunity to create circumstances that entice taxpayers into corrupt practices.

A lack of clearly defined roles, functions, and duties of public officials creates an environment ripe for abusive behavior (Pashev 2005). A high degree of discretionary power and the lack of adequate monitoring and reporting mechanisms are vital in providing opportunities for corruption. The greater the discretion, the greater the opportunity tax officials have to provide "favorable" interpretations of government rules and regulations to businesses in exchange for illegal payments.

Lack of Monitoring and Supervision

Because of asymmetrical information, it is difficult to monitor officers and hold them accountable for their actions. The absence of supervision and accountability gives workers an opportunity to refrain from performing public duties. The absence of measures designed to maintain the integrity of staff—such as the promotion and enforcement of ethical standards, merit-based recruitment and promotion procedures, and regular staff rotation schemes to prevent the creation of lucrative networks—increases the likelihood of staff indulging in corrupt practices.

Unwillingness of Taxpayers to Pay Taxes

In some developing countries, such as India, the extreme unwillingness of taxpayers to comply with the law—and hence their readiness to bribe tax collectors in order to reduce their tax liability—are important causes of corruption. Many taxpayers are willing to abet tax collectors if there is clear gain. This phenomenon is common in many middle-income countries.

Political Leadership

Political leadership sustains and often creates and protects corruption. Corrupt political leadership makes the spread of corruption at lower levels relatively easy. A hierarchy of administrative levels is typically associated with different corrupt transactions. In the case of fiscal incentives, for example, relatively high-level officials and politicians are more likely to be involved in corrupt practices. In the case of foreign trade taxes and other routine activities, lower-level officials are also likely to be involved, sharing their illegal gains with those higher up in the chain of authority. It is these routine cases of lower-level corrupt tax practices that ultimately erode public confidence in governmental institutions. For this reason, these practices are often seen as more corrosive than abuse of power at higher levels (Asher n.d.) As the power of a leader evolves into the political management of a service, the independence of officials is rapidly eroded by the interference of political leaders, and the risk of corruption increases. Political appointments not only reduce work efficiency, they also facilitate corruption, as they did in Tanzania, where entrance into the police or the legal profession required joining the party (Sedigh and Muganda 1999).

Overall Government Environment

The level of corruption in tax administration generally parallels that in the administrative environment as a whole. Liberal economic systems offer fewer opportunities for corruption than socialist systems. The greater the administrative controls over the economy, the greater the problems of monitoring and accountability, because a greater share of economic planning decisions depend on bureaucrats.[2]

Administering Tax Policy

The objectives of a tax policy can be achieved only when the policy is properly administered. Most developing countries face various organizational and operational constraints to effective tax administration (box 9.2). In these countries, tax administration plays a crucial role in determining the real (or effective) tax system: tax administration is tax policy (Casanegra de Jantscher 1990). Failure to properly administer the tax, therefore, defeats its purpose and threatens the canon of equity. It allows the government to collect taxes only from easy-to-tax sectors and people who cannot avoid paying.

According to the business process model, the main factor causing corruption in tax administration is procedures. The greater the procedural interaction with the taxpayer, the greater the possibility of corruption.

Customs Duty

Corruption in customs administration is a major problem in many developing countries. Case studies of Mali and Senegal, for example, indicate that

> **BOX 9.2** The Nature of Tax Fraud in India
>
> An empirical study based on fieldwork conducted in 1994–95 indicates that tax evasion in India occurs partly through collusion between taxpayers and tax officers. Of 5,840 offenses detected, 87 percent were procedural. These offenses included incomplete or insufficient documentation, inappropriate use of credit on capital goods, inadmissible deduction of inputs, taking of credit before the commencement of production, use of undeclared inputs, faulty interpretation of notification issued by the department, use of unregistered dealer's invoices, extension of credit on endorsed invoices, declaration of invoices with incorrect address, and submission of invoices that were not in the name of the unit.
>
> "Substantial" violations accounted for 7 percent of total revenue loss. These violations included irregular use of deemed credit, extension of credit on exempted final products, rejected inputs sent back without reversal of credit, extension of credit on basic customs duty, misuse of the facility of "job work," excess credit taken, and the use of the CenVAT (the federal VAT) credit by small-scale units that had opted out of the system.
>
> Fraudulent violations accounted for 6 percent of total revenue lost. These violations included extension of credit without producing the required documents, extension of credit on invoices without physical movement, duplicate extension credit on the same invoice, extension of credit without payment of duty, and use of fraudulent documents. These violations show a deliberate attempt on the part of the taxpayer to defraud the government.
>
> *Source:* Shome, Mukhopadhyay, and Saleem 1997.

these countries have faced serious problems of customs fraud in recent years (Stasavage and Daubree 1998).

Customs administration in India has been reformed over time. Some problems remain, however. One relates to the valuation of cargo. Taxpayers are often harassed on the grounds that the valuation is not correct; on this pretext, goods are detained. Importers usually compromise on the assessment in order to free the goods from detention. The imported cargo of regular importers is allowed to pass through a green channel, but the cargo of casual traders is subjected to a full check.

Domestic Trade Taxes

The system of domestic trade taxes in India is unique. Under India's constitution, the union government has the authority to impose a broad spectrum of excise duties on production or manufacture, while the states are assigned the power to levy sales tax on consumption.

As a result of this dichotomy of authority, India has adopted a dual (federal and state) VAT system. The federal VAT, known as CenVAT, has effectively replaced the system of union excise duty. CenVAT allows instant credit for taxes paid on inputs. Empirical studies of its impact show that it has reduced the transaction cost of business (NIPFP 1989).

All Indian states except Uttar Pradesh have adopted the VAT, replacing their age-old sales tax system. Most of the procedures prescribed for sales tax administration continue under the state VAT. Checkposts at the borders of each state continue to monitor the flow of goods into the state through the main arteries of interstate trade. The use of road permits for administering the tax also continues. Under this system, the importing dealer receives these permits from the tax department of the importing state and sends them to his counterpart in another state before importing the goods. The trucks bringing the specified goods into the state are expected to carry back these permits for scrutiny and verification at the checkposts. One copy of the road permit is then sent to the checkpost to the concerned assessing officer. All imports are accounted for and therefore taxed.

Although these checkposts play an important role, the system does not work as effectively and smoothly as it was intended to. The checkposts interfere with the flow of trade and traffic within the state and harass a large number of dealers, the majority of whom are not liable for tax. The procedures allow for many points of interaction between taxpayers and officials, some of which could be eliminated.

Impact of Corruption

Corruption drastically reduces tax revenues, forcing governments to find other avenues for financing government expenditure, including borrowing. Future fiscal flexibility is reduced, because servicing of debt has to be given priority over other expenditures. This creates a vicious circle endangering fiscal sustainability.

Corruption is particularly alarming because it breeds further corruption—"corruption may corrupt," as stated by Andvig and Moene (1990). Collusion between corrupt taxpayers and corrupt tax officials puts honest taxpayers at a disadvantage, encouraging them to evade taxes. If they do not, their profit margins are low, especially for small businesses.[3]

The effect on tax officials is also important. Corrupt colleagues and friends weaken the will of honest officers and reduce the probability of being detected or losing one's reputation. As the number of corrupt tax collectors increases, the guilt feeling of indulging in wrongdoing decreases.

As Fjeldstad (2005) notes, when networks of corruption exist, firing some corrupt officials does not improve the situation, as the fired officials become consultants and add to the network.

Corruption affects the quality of governance. It forces officials to make decisions that do not serve the public interest but promote the interests of corrupt individuals. Administrative efficiency is at a low level because patronage and nepotism tend to encourage the recruitment of incompetent people.

Corruption adversely affects investment and growth (Mauro 1995). When growth is weak, the returns to entrepreneurship fall relative to those to rent seeking; the ensuing increase in the pace of rent-seeking activities further slows growth. Higher bribes imply declining profitability on productive investments relative to rent-seeking investments, crowding out productive investments. Innovators are particularly at the mercy of corrupt public officials, because new producers need government-supplied goods, such as permits and licenses, more than established producers (Murphy, Shleifer, and Vishny 1993).

Widespread corruption reduces both foreign and domestic investment, as investors look for locales in which there is less corruption, less red tape, simpler laws and procedures, and transparent administration, all of which provide greater opportunities to grow. Corruption leads to economic waste and inefficiency, because it adversely affects the optimal allocation of funds, productivity, and consumption. When public resources meant for setting up productivity-enhancing infrastructure are diverted to politicians' private consumption, growth falls.[4] Pervasive corruption can also result in refusal by the donor community to grant aid.[5]

The cost of corruption to the society (in terms of both tangible and intangible costs) is extremely high. Intangible costs include the loss of trust in democracy, in leaders, in institutions, and in fellow citizens. Tangible costs include the impact on trade and investments, administrative efficiency, good governance, and equality of citizens.

Corruption has the potential to undermine the political stability of a country, by provoking social unrest and civil war that can threaten macroeconomic stabilization. In Tanzania corruption contributed to political instability and increased ethnic tension when a leader, for his own political purpose, claimed that some wealthy businesspeople from Asia, in collaboration with African leaders, were transferring the country's wealth abroad and impoverishing ordinary Tanzanians (Sedigh and Muganda 1999). He also insisted that the government was selling the country to Arabs and Zanzibaris. His comments not only intensified racial tensions, which a number of politicians sought to exploit, they also caused enormous capital flight from Tanzania.

Combating Corruption in Tax Administration

Which policy measures need to be adopted to combat corruption in tax administration depends on the social environment and the attitude about corruption held in the society—the factors that account for the degree of corruption in a country. What is regarded as corrupt practice in one country may be regarded as part of a routine transaction in another country. Social norms may be such that allegiance to their ethnic or religious group supersedes individuals' responsibility to act as honest bureaucrats.

Each country has to evolve the measures best suited to its own local requirements. Some policies that could be adopted by all developing countries plagued with corruption are described below.

Rationalize the Design of Tax Laws

One of the most important policy prescriptions for curbing corruption is establishing a rational tax system with simplified tax laws. The number of tax rates should be as low as possible and the number of tax exemptions as small as possible (if they cannot be eliminated altogether). In addition, the tax system should be integrated, with different taxes levied by all tiers of government. For taxes on commodities and services, it is important to avoid end-use exemptions, a major source of corruption.

The design of the tax structure should be as broad based as possible. The goal should be to have as many taxpayers as possible in the tax net, depending on the administrative capability of the country. If the number of taxpayers is well below its potential, the burden on each taxpayer will be too heavy.

A survey in India revealed that 89 percent of potential income taxpayers did not file (Aggarwal 1991). To expand its tax base, India adopted the "one-in-six scheme," under which an individual satisfying one out of six criteria has to file an individual income tax return, irrespective of his or her level of income.[6] This measure significantly increased the number of individual income taxpayers.

Designate Corruption a National Crime

The problem of corruption needs to be addressed at both the national and international levels. National political leaders must make a commitment to eradicate this menace. A holistic approach, including prevention and enforcement, will have a much better chance of success than a simple focus on individuals. The problem of corruption needs to be checked at the international level as well. Particularly given the fact that multinational companies bribe officials of developing countries to procure orders and contracts, a coordinated approach by bilateral donors and international organizations is useful. An important step in this direction would be blacklisting by multinational organizations of multinational corporations that engage in corrupt practices to obtain international contracts and encourage corruption in developing countries.

Reduce Monopoly Power

Since the monopoly power of tax officials encourages them to indulge in wrongdoing, the first step in combating corruption has to be to curb the monopoly power of these officials. Two steps have to be taken. First, tax departments must be reengineered in countries where all activities of administration and assessment are performed by the same unit. It would be useful to assign the role of administration and audit to different units, as many developed countries do.

Second, tax officials should not be assigned to particular jurisdictions. Random assignment would not only take away the opportunity of tax officers to misuse their monopoly powers, it would also free taxpayers from the clutches of tax officials. For the selection of cases for audit, a separate unit should look into all available information and apply principles of risk management. This would eliminate contact between tax officers and taxpayers, reducing opportunities for corruption.

Another way to reduce the monopoly power of tax officials is to give them competing jurisdictions. Since collusion among several officials is difficult, competition tends to reduce the level of bribes substantially. Competition in the provision of government services must also be accompanied by more intensive monitoring and auditing to prevent corruption.

Make Civil Servants Accountable and Salaries Competitive

The system of recruitment of officers should be streamlined and a competitive examination system introduced. In addition, training must make tax officials committed to achieving clearly identified objectives. It should be made clear to officials that they are fully responsible and accountable for their assigned duties.

Civil servants' salaries should be high enough to allow them to resist the temptation to use their office for private gain. The incentives for corruption are considerably greater where salaries do not allow civil servants to live above the poverty level.[7]

In many African countries, civil servants' salaries and conditions of service have continuously deteriorated over the years, in most cases failing to keep pace with inflation (Kpundeh 1992). In such circumstances, employees may look for other ways to generate additional income. Departments such as customs and VAT, which have large numbers of low-paid workers who are in direct contact with the public, are especially ripe for corrupt behavior. In pre–civil war Somalia, salaries were so low that officials had to hold more than one job. Such a situation encourages bureaucrats to fall prey to corrupt practices (Klitgaard 1988).

An attempt should be made to reduce the overall number of employees in the public sector.[8] It would also be useful to adopt an incentive-based wage policy for public officials, as Singapore and Hong Kong (China) have done (Mookerjee 1995). In Singapore salaries in the public sector are higher than those in the private sector, discouraging corruption (Mookerjee 1995). It is also important to adopt a broad range of human resources measures, including development of performance indicators and performance-based incentive and promotion schemes.

Restructure Tax Administration Agencies

Tax administration agencies could be restructured functionally. The duties of various functionaries within the VAT department should be streamlined, with an eye to minimizing personal interactions with taxpayers (Purohit 2001a). Internal audits must also be strengthened. The selection of an audit must be based on risk assessment based on information from local offices, the results of audits conducted in the past, and the results of the computer assessment of returns received in the department. It is equally important to establish a wing of auditors specially trained to examine the accounts of vendors. Checkposts must be abolished and enforcement strengthened.

Severely Punish Corrupt Officials

Punitive action against corrupt officials can have an important deterrent effect. The role of the media is important in publicizing the punishment of corrupt officials. Pecuniary penalties for corrupt behavior should be harsh enough to discourage officials from engaging in wrongdoing.

In addition to pecuniary penalties, in some severe cases of corruption, tax evaders need to be publicly denounced or imprisoned. Stringent laws for punishment of corrupt officials, along with the confiscation of property amassed through bribery, will help reduce corruption. Such laws must apply to domestic offenders and foreigners alike.

Use Information Technology to Combat Corruption

Many countries around the world, at all income levels, are attempting to use information technology to combat administrative corruption (box 9.3). The use of such technology reduces the discretionary power of local officials, cuts transaction costs, and increases transparency. Most important, it reduces the interaction between taxpayers and tax officials, thereby reducing the opportunity to engage in corrupt practices.

The use of information technology automates government actions and procedures, reducing delays and face-to-face contact. It builds transparency

> **BOX 9.3** Using Information Technology to Streamline Services and Reduce Corruption in India
>
> The Indian state of Andhra Pradesh has used information technology to reduce corruption in several tax areas. The Computer-Aided Administration of Registration Department (CARD) replaces manual procedures that lacked transparency in property valuation and resulted in a flourishing business for brokers and middlemen, who exploited citizens buying or selling property. The CARD system replaces the manual services with computerized services and introduces several new services. It eliminates interaction with tax officers. It completes registration formalities within an hour, through electronic delivery of all registration services. It improves the quality of services offered by providing a computer interface between citizens and the government.
>
> Eseva Kendra provides a one-stop venue for services of the state and central government departments and private businesses. It provides online transaction processing of various payments to government agencies and issues certificates needed by citizens and businesses. It connects citizens to departments and agencies such as the state VAT and other state taxes; the electricity, water, and telephone utilities; the passport office; municipal corporations; and the departments of transport, tourism, and health.
>
> All offices of India's commercial tax department, including checkposts, have been computerized. Databases contain details regarding registered dealers, which can be analyzed and used for investigating evasion of the state VAT.
>
> Land records have also been revolutionized by computer technology. Until recently, obtaining land record documents was difficult and almost always required the help of middlemen. With the digitization of land records, farmers can now obtain land ownership certificates in 5–30 minutes from a Citizen Information Centre (CIC) at the Revenue Office. Computerization of this function has ensured transparency in the system and made the life of ordinary citizens easier. Farmers can now apply for mutation either at the CIC or over the Internet. They can also check the status of their request online and present documentary evidence to authorities if their request is not processed within the stipulated time period.
>
> *Source:* Author.

and trust by sharing information with the public and making them more aware of their rights and privileges. It encourages greater accountability by officials, as it creates disincentives for corruption by creating fear of exposure.

Before introducing information technology, it is important to have a completely integrated system of taxes. Data from tax returns of individuals and corporations should be collected from the time of registration, continuing up to the payment of tax and the processing of returns. Information from the mainframe and data warehouse should be used to select cases for audit. Results of investigations should also be recorded, and other agencies should provide all necessary information. Such a system should maintain very tight security and confidentiality, without which the information could be abused.

Set Up an Independent Anticorruption Organization

Many countries have set up anticorruption commissions (box 9.4). Some are constitutionally independent of the executive branch; others are set up by the executive branch to serve either in an advisory role or with the

> **BOX 9.4** Using an Independent Agency to Combat Corruption
>
> The wide variety of anticorruption management structures suggests the diverse approaches for combating corruption in different countries. Hong Kong (China) established an Independent Commission against Corruption, which carries out investigative, preventive, and communications functions. It has enjoyed resounding success in fighting corruption: Hong Kong now ranks as one of the least corrupt jurisdictions in East Asia (www.transparency.org).
>
> India and Singapore established bodies devoted entirely to investigating corrupt acts and preparing evidence for prosecution. These bodies have also been successful in reducing corruption (Heilbrunn 2004; Vittal 2003).
>
> In New South Wales, commissions report to parliamentary committees; they are independent from the executive and judicial branches of state. These commissions have changed the norms of how business is conducted, preventing corruption from occurring (Heilbrunn 2004). The United States implemented a multiagency model that includes offices that are individually distinct but together form a web of agencies that fight corruption (Heilbrunn 2004).
>
> The success of such organizations has encouraged governments elsewhere (in Argentina, Bosnia-Herzegovina, Guinea, the Republic of Korea, and Mauritius, for example) to create similar organizations. Mounting evidence suggests, however, that commissions have not been successful in countries where low levels of political commitment, lack of articulation among branches of state, and severe budgetary constraints have prevented the establishment of large and expensive anticorruption commissions (Heilbrunn 2004).

authority to investigate and help prosecute public officials at all levels. Countries also use presidential commissions, multisectoral advisory groups, institutions to administer ethical codes of conduct, special authorities or commissions to handle or investigate specific corruption allegations, and other bodies.

Decentralize Government

Experience and theory suggest that an organization is most vulnerable to corruption when bureaucrats enjoy a monopoly over taxpayers and take actions that are difficult to monitor. The relation between the executive branch and other participants in government, such as the legislature, the judiciary, local jurisdictions, political parties, the media, the private sector, and nongovernmental organizations, needs to be broadly articulated.

Democratic systems offer a mechanism to minimize corruption by introducing greater accountability and transparency in governance. When local governments have some real power, they not only address local interests more authentically and confidently, they also exercise a check on the operations of higher levels of authority. However, the effectiveness of decentralized service delivery depends on the design of decentralization and the institutional arrangement governing its implementation. An institutional environment should provide political, administrative, and financial authority to local governments, along with effective channels of local accountability and central purview.

Two key ingredients are needed for the potential gain to outweigh the costs. First, decentralization must involve real delegation of authority, including the authority to generate and reserve a portion of local revenues. Second, local authorities must themselves be accountable to higher levels and local groups. Abuse of authority and public corruption are less likely to occur if the rules governing local officials are at least in part defined by local norms (Charlick 1993).

Establish a Code of Ethics

At the national level, every country should have a comprehensive code of ethics that spells out appropriate and inappropriate behavior for politicians as well as bureaucrats. A leadership code of conduct is important, because the country's future prospects depend, to a very large extent, on the quality and honesty of its leaders. The leadership code should describe the expected and prohibited forms of conduct by government leaders (Kpundeh 1999; Ruzindanda and Sedigh 1999). It should outline a broad concept of what constitutes leadership, emphasize the role of leaders in setting an example, and identify principles of good leadership. It should include provisions that check the misuse of state property through annual disclosure of leaders' income, assets, and liabilities. At the same time, it should ban certain activities, such as seeking or accepting gifts or benefits relating to official duties and personal interests; abusing government property; and misusing official information not available to the public.

Provide Tax Officers with Ethics Training

Intensive training of officers in ethical conduct is of paramount importance, even in countries that lack good governance (Huther and Shah 2001). Course contents should include the laws and rules of the tax being administered and emphasize ethical values such as integrity, honesty, public service, justice, transparency, accountability, and the rule of law. Training should be repetitive in nature, followed up with refresher courses. Officers should be aware of existing anticorruption measures, as well as their responsibilities and the liability involved.

A public ethics program can be carried out in several ways. Ethics management guidance can be offered by training tax officials. Ethics audit research and inquiry can be conducted to assess their strengths and weaknesses. The objective of ethics maintenance is to make the ethical gains of the agency sustainable. Assistance from anticorruption bodies, civil society organizations, and private firms can be used to sustain best practices, as well as to improve and monitor the effectiveness of public ethics programs. Taxpayer education programs could be strengthened through interactive television and radio programs and pamphlets.

Inform Taxpayers of Their Rights

Access to accurate information should be a right that is publicized adequately so that taxpayers are aware of it. All tax rules, rates, and procedures should be available on the Internet. Lack of access to information about rules and regulations makes taxpayers unaware of their rights and exposes them to discretionary treatment by corrupt officers.

Conclusions and Policy Recommendations

An irrational tax structure, monopoly and discretionary power in the hands of government officials, a low degree of accountability or transparency in administration, and interference by political leadership are the main causes of corruption in tax administration. Low pay, the lack of severity of punishment for corrupt behavior, poor-quality service, and greater politicization of government also encourage corruption.

The desired objectives of tax policy can be achieved only when it is properly administered. In most developing countries, tax administration is tax policy. Failure to properly administer the tax, therefore, defeats its very purpose and threatens equity. Involved procedures cause deficiencies in tax operations, reduce overall tax collection, and cause corruption in tax administration.

When corruption becomes a way of life, it has far-reaching implications. It undercuts efficiency and equity, as well as the macroeconomic and institutional functions of government. It reduces revenue to government, endangering fiscal sustainability, and adversely affects investment and growth. The presence of corrupt officials encourages other officials to engage in corruption, because the probability of being detected or losing one's reputation declines. Likewise, the presence of corrupt taxpayers encourages other taxpayers to cheat.

Fighting corruption takes time. Power groups whose interests are threatened can scuttle efforts. But letting corruption fester can be even more dangerous. Which policy measures need to be adopted depends on the overall social environment and the attitude about corruption held by society.

One of the most important policy prescriptions for curbing corruption is creating a tax system that is rational, equitable, and simple. Reducing the monopoly and discretionary power of tax officials is also very important. The tax structure should be as broad as possible in order to maximize equity. Bureaucrats should be given competing jurisdictions, so that competition among officers will drive the level of bribes to zero. Monitoring and auditing must be increased to prevent corruption. The system of recruitment of officers should be streamlined, and officers should be given intensive and repetitive training for promoting a code of conduct, with emphasis on ethical values, such as integrity, honesty, public service, justice, transparency, accountability, and rule of law. Salaries should be high enough that officials are able to support themselves and their dependents without accepting bribes. An anticorruption commission can be set up that maintains transparency in the system and makes political leaders and officers accountable for their actions. Decentralization can also help curb corruption. Its effectiveness depends on the design of decentralization and the institutional arrangements governing its implementation.

Notes

The author is grateful to R. J. Chelliah, Richard Bird, Tuan Minh Le, Pawan Aggarwal, B. V. Kumar, T. R. Rustagi, Vivek Johari, Sudhir Krishna, Arun Kumar, D. N. Rao, and V. K. Purohit for their very useful comments on the original draft of the chapter. Thanks are also due to Madhulika Purohit for her competent research assistance in the course of the preparation of this material. The author alone, however, remains responsible for the errors, if any.

1. Corruption is, of course, prevalent in the private sector, too.
2. In Sierra Leone the All People's Congress, the only political party from 1978 to 1992, totally controlled civil servants' political views and associations. From the inception of the one-party system, neopatrimonial politics dictated that civil servants be party members. In return for their loyalty, civil servants were often shielded, pampered, and allowed to increase the range of their powers and pursue opportunities for self-enrichment (Kpundeh 1999).
3. A 1999 survey conducted by the European Bank for Reconstruction and Development of some 3,000 enterprises in 20 transition economies revealed that "bribes" (a category that includes corrupt tax practices) act like a regressive tax. The bribe paid by smaller firms amounted to 5 percent of their annual revenue; bribes paid by medium-size firms amounted to 4 percent of their annual revenue, while those paid by larger firms amounted to slightly less than 3 percent of their annual revenue. The study reveals that smaller firms paid bribes more frequently than medium-size or larger firms (Asher n.d).
4. The diversion of public resources, services, and assets to private use in Uganda resulted in deteriorating roads, poor medical facilities, dilapidated and ill-equipped schools, and falling educational standards (Ruzindana and Sedigh 1999).
5. The international donor community jointly suspended aid to Tanzania in 1994, largely in response to massive irregularities in the tax system. Donors declared that they would not resume assistance until the government took steps to collect evaded tax, recover exempted tax, and initiate legal proceedings against corrupt tax officials (Sedigh and Muganda 1999).
6. This scheme was introduced to identify potential taxpayers. It stipulated that a person having a credit card, owning a house, possessing a vehicle, paying an electricity bill of more than Rs. 50,000 a month, leaving the country during the year, or belonging to a club is obligated to file an income tax return (Aggarwal 1991). The scheme was eliminated in 2006–07.
7. A more workable solution for making civil service salary competitive would be to focus on the performance-based component of gross pay, reflecting and rewarding each tax officer's contribution to the success of anticorruption policies and higher collection rates (Pashev 2005).
8. Uganda reduced the number of employees through a variety of measures. "Overdue leavers" (workers past retirement age, irregular entrants, and those identified through performance assessment as incompetent) and "ghost workers" (deceased workers, fictitious workers, or former employees who remained on the government payroll) were identified and eliminated. The "group employees' scheme," which allowed senior managers to recruit their own casual, short-term workers without reference to established job grades, was abolished. Surplus workers who were competent, bona fide workers but could not be deployed elsewhere in

the government received severance packages. These measures helped Uganda replace a large number of public sector employees with a smaller number of higher-quality staff.

References

Aggarwal, Pawan K. 1991. "Identification of Non-Filer Potential Income Tax Payers." *Asia Pacific Tax and Investment Research Centre Bulletin* 9 (6): 217–24.

Andvig, J., and K. O. Moene. 1990. "How Corruption May Corrupt." *Journal of Economic Behaviour and Organization* 3 (1): 63–76.

Asher, Mukul G. n.d. "The Design of Tax Systems and Corruption." Public Policy Programme, National University of Singapore.

Bardhan, Pranab. 1997. "Corruption and Development: A Review of Issues." *Journal of Economic Literature* 35 (September): 1320–46.

Casanegra de Jantscher, Milka. 1990. "Administering the VAT." In *Value Added Tax in Developing Countries*, ed. Malcolm Gillis, Carl S. Shoup, and Gerardo P. Sicat. Washington, DC: World Bank.

Charlick, Robert. 1993. "Corruption and Political Transition: A Governance Perspective." *Corruption and Reform* 7 (3): 177–88.

De Dios, Emmanuel S., and Ricardo D. Ferrer. 2001. "Corruption in the Philippines: Framework and Context." *Public Policy* 5 (1): 1–42.

Fjeldstad, Odd-Helge. 2005. "Revenue Administration and Corruption." U4 Utstein Anti-Corruption Resource Centre, Chr. Michaelson Institute, Bergen, Norway. http://partner.u4.no.

Goudie, A.W., and D. Stasavage. 1997. "Corruption: The Issues." Working Paper 122, OECD Development Centre, Organisation for Economic Co-operation and Development, Paris.

Heilbrunn, John R. 2004. *Anti-corruption Commissions: Panacea or Real Medicine to Fight Corruption?* World Bank Institute, Washington, DC.

Huther, Jeff, and Anwar Shah. 2001. "Anticorruption Policies and Programs: A Framework for Evaluation." Policy Research Working Paper, World Bank, Washington, DC.

Kangle, R. P. 1972. *The Kautiliya Arthasastra*. Part II. Bombay University, Mumbai.

Klitgaard, R. 1988. *Controlling Corruption*. Berkeley: University of California Press.

———. 1991. "Strategies for Reform." *Journal of Democracy* 2 (4): 86–100.

Kpundeh, S. J. 1992. *Democratization in Africa: Africa Views, African Voices*. Washington, DC: National Academy Press.

———. 1999. "The Fight against Corruption in Sierra Leone." In *Curbing Corruption: Toward a Model for Building National Integrity*, ed. Rick Stapenhurst and Sahr J. Kpundeh. Washington, DC: World Bank.

Kumar, B.V. 2000. "Corruption: An Indian Perspective." *Journal of Money Laundering Control* 3 (3): 266–79.

Mauro, Paolo. 1995. "Corruption and Growth. " *Quarterly Journal of Economics* 110 (3): 681–712.

Mendoza, Amado M., Jr. 2001. "The Industrial Anatomy of Corruption: Government Procurement, Bidding, and Award of Contracts." *Public Policy* 5 (1): 43–71.

Mookerjee, Dilip. 1995. "Reforms in Income Tax Enforcement in Mexico." India Working Paper 6, IRIS Center, University of Maryland, College Park.

Murphy, Kevin, Andrei Shleifer, and Robert W. Vishny. 1993. "Why Is Rent Seeking So Costly to Growth?" *American Economic Review* 83 (2): 409–14.

NIPFP (National Institute of Public Finance and Policy). 1989. *The Operation of MODVAT.* New Delhi: NIPFP.

Pashev, Konstantin. 2005. *Corruption and Tax Compliance: Challenges to Tax Policy and Administration.* Centre for the Study of Democracy, Sofia, Bulgaria.

Purohit, Mahesh C. 2001a. *Sales Tax and Value Added Tax in India.* Delhi: Gayatri Publications.

———. 2001b. "Structure and Administration of VAT in Canada: Lessons for India." *International VAT Monitor* 12 (6): 311–23.

———. 2006a. *State Value Added Tax in India: An Analysis of Revenue Implications.* Delhi: Gayatri Publications.

———. 2006b. *Value Added Tax: Experiences of India and Other Countries.* Delhi: Gayatri Publications.

Ruzindana, Augustine, and Shahrzad Sedigh. 1999. "The Fight against Corruption in Uganda." In *Curbing Corruption: Toward a Model for Building National Integrity,* ed. Rick Stapenhurst and Sahr J. Kpundeh. Washington, DC: World Bank.

Sedigh, Shahrzad, and Alex Muganda. 1999. "The Fight against Corruption in Tanzania." In *Curbing Corruption: Towards a Model for Building National Integrity,* ed. Rick Stapenhurst and Sahr J. Kpundeh. Washington, DC: World Bank.

Shah, Anwar. 2006. "Corruption and Decentralized Public Governance." Policy Research Working Paper 3824, World Bank, Washington, DC.

Shleifer, Andrei, and Robert W. Vishny. 1993. "Corruption." *Quarterly Journal of Economics* 108 (3): 599–617.

Shome, Parthasarathi, S. Mukhopadhyay, and H. N. Saleem. 1997. "Modvat Administration." In *Value Added Tax in India: A Progress Report,* ed. Parthasarathi Shome. New Delhi: Centax Publications.

Stasavage, D., and C. Daubree. 1998. "Determinants of Customs Fraud and Corruption: Evidence from Two African Countries." Working Paper 138, OECD Development Centre, Organisation for Economic Co-operation and Development, Paris.

Tanzi, Vito. 1994. "Corruption, Governmental Activities, and Markets." IMF Working Paper 94/99, International Monetary Fund, Washington, DC.

Tirole, Jean. 1996. "A Theory of Collective Reputations." *Review of Economic Studies* 63 (1): 1–22.

Vitosha Research. 2004. "Corruption Monitoring System (Business Sector)." April. Sofia, Bulgaria.

Vittal, N. 2003. *Corruption in India.* Academic Foundation, New Delhi.

10

Corruption and Fraud Detection by Supreme Audit Institutions

KENNETH M. DYE

This chapter examines the fraud and corruption issues confronting supreme audit institutions (SAIs) and offers some strategies and ideas for improving SAI performance in detecting fraud and corruption. Some SAIs have already tested some of these strategies, with considerable success. For other SAIs they may be new ideas that can help them contain fraud and corruption in their countries.

The chapter is written for SAIs, with the hope that it will generate debate at the International Congress of Supreme Audit Institutions and cause a change in auditing emphases by SAIs—sooner rather than later. It is also written for government officials and legislators concerned about good governance, accountability, transparency, and probity, particularly in countries where fraud and corruption are well embedded in the local culture. The ideas and strategies expressed in this chapter could be the subject of donor support to countries where fraud and corruption interfere with good governance.

The Rise in Fraud and Corruption

Fraud and corruption have devastating effects, especially on the poorest citizens of developing countries. Corruption has no borders and has spread worldwide, even to countries once considered "clean." Public sector bribery, fraud, and corruption have become leading concerns for legislators around the globe, as the diversion of public funds undermines parliamentary control of the public purse. This diversion of public monies robs public policies of resources to do the good they were intended to finance.

Corruption makes no economic distinctions and infects all forms of government. No country can afford to sustain the social, political, or economic costs that corruption entails. Corruption erodes public confidence in political institutions and leads to contempt for the rule of law, it distorts the allocation of resources and undermines competition in the marketplace, and it has a devastating effect on investment, growth, and development. It also exacts a disproportionately high price on the poor by denying them access to vital basic services.

Detailed rules and norms of behavior govern the behavior of civil servants in developing countries. But the process of corruption is so invisible that it leaves little documentary evidence. Despite knowledge of the fact that there is widespread corruption in government departments, state audit has not played any effective role to forestall it, except in a few developing countries, notably China. The cases of corruption that come to light are hardly ever taken serious note of. Partly for this reason, society has gradually become more tolerant of corruption. Responsibility is borne by small fries, with the big fish remaining untouched. This has a demoralizing effect on auditors, who believe that it is pointless to detect or report corruption in a society in which accountability is weak.

In developing countries it is common for SAIs to report unauthorized expenditures, waste of public funds, abuse of procedures resulting in losses to the public treasury, and so forth. These institutions are well respected for their independence and even feared, curbing initiative and encouraging avoidance of decisions. However, audit staff often tend to take a clerical approach, demanding strict compliance with procedures while often missing the objective of the procedures. Minor aberrations and misuse of funds are highlighted, while major systemic failures resulting in large losses to the public treasury go unidentified. Audit officers and staff need training to determine what is significant enough to warrant reporting and training for government officials and staff on public procurement concepts, objectives, processes, and their rationale.

There is an increasing desire among legislators to take the initiative in controlling bribery, fraud, and corruption. This is a difficult challenge, particularly for legislators who lack the institutional support, knowledge, and experience to achieve the conditions necessary to hold their governments to account. The supreme audit community cannot remain indifferent to the special difficulties faced by legislators laboring within the context of corrupt, and often ruthless, regimes.

In recent years major donors have concluded that strengthening the governance capacity of weak nations is a good strategy to support improved accountability, transparency, and probity. Good governance is a strong antidote to corruption and fraud. Donors can bolster good governance by promoting acceptance of international accounting and auditing standards. Legislators and SAIs should unite in support of international standards for accounting and auditing. These standards, promulgated by the International Accounting Standards Board and the International Federation of Accountants, are now available for the public sector as well as the private sector. The International Organization of Supreme Audit Institutions also provides useful audit and internal control guidance to SAIs.

The Need for a Change in Audit Emphasis

Public sector fraud and corruption thrive when accountability and transparency are absent. Good financial reporting and auditing help reduce the misrepresentation that hides fraudulent operations and misleads the reader. Auditing provides the desirable assurance that audited financial statements can be trusted to represent the economic activities they are intended to portray. SAIs can make a constructive difference by auditing the financial statements of governments and government agencies and making their audit opinions available to legislatures on a timely basis.

There is a gap between stakeholder expectations and audit mandates for SAIs. Traditionally, SAIs have agreed that the primary responsibility for preventing and detecting corruption rests with the administrative authorities, such as the police or anticorruption agencies. SAIs have not seen fraud and corruption busting as their main goal; the approach has been to prevent corruption in the field rather than detecting illegal activities. The public, however, believes that SAIs seek to detect fraud and corruption.

This gap needs to be addressed by the SAIs, which should put more emphasis on detecting fraud and corruption to shrink the expectation gap. They should continue to play an active role in raising awareness of the risks of fraud and corruption and fostering good governance and standards of conduct, but they should go further and focus more on detecting fraud and corruption. This can be done by combining controls audit procedures with financial attest audit procedures.

It is easier to prevent fraud and corruption than to detect it. SAIs have been creating and fostering a preventive environment against fraud and corruption, including strengthening financial management systems, evaluating internal control systems, and identifying and correcting weaknesses. Today there is widespread growth in white-collar crime, including both fraudulent financial reporting and misappropriation of asset schemes. Racketeering and terrorist groups often rely on money laundering schemes to finance and disguise their activities. It is time to consider shifting audit emphasis to audit techniques designed to detect fraud and corruption, as well as prevent this scourge on society. This chapter is not recommending that SAIs go so far as to usurp the role of anticorruption agencies. Within the scope of their audit work, however, they should be more vigilant and capable of detecting fraud and corruption.

When giving an audit opinion on financial statements, it is the custom of SAI auditors to ask the reader of the opinion to assume that all the internal controls are functioning appropriately if nothing specific about controls is mentioned by the auditor. In recent years, auditors have been confronted with new technologies with which to select samples to examine, as well as new rules and regulations on appropriate accounting methods. These requirements have drawn their attention away from the basics of evaluating and testing the functionality of internal controls. Moreover, because there is no requirement in financial attest audit standards to report specifically on the internal controls present, the auditor remains silent and places less emphasis on this important audit area.

It is time for public sector auditors to consider giving an opinion on whether or not the internal controls present are appropriate and sufficient to ensure that the systems support the accuracy and fairness of the financial systems and that fraud and corruption opportunities are minimized. In the conduct of a financial attest audit, public sector auditors could now be providing

- an evaluation of the effectiveness of internal control over financial reporting against a suitable control framework;
- evidence providing reasonable support for the evaluation of the effectiveness of internal control over financial reporting;
- reports of material weaknesses in internal control over financial reporting; and
- an audit of internal control over financial reporting.

Doing so requires a change in the public sector auditors' standard opinion to include a statement that the auditors have examined the internal controls and found them sufficient and functioning appropriately to support the accuracy of the figures stated in the financial statements and to safeguard the assets of the enterprise. Public sector auditors could opine on matters of internal control present in the enterprise that

- pertain to the maintenance of records that in reasonable detail accurately and fairly reflect the transactions and dispositions of the assets of the entity;
- provide reasonable assurance that transactions are recorded as necessary to permit preparation of financial statements in accordance with the entity's Generally Acceptable Accounting Principles and that receipts and expenditures of the issuer are being made only in accordance with government rules and regulations; and
- provide reasonable assurance regarding prevention or timely detection of unauthorized acquisition, use, or disposition of the issuer's assets that could have a material effect on the annual financial statements or interim financial statements.

SAIs could reasonably take the position that these requirements are those of management, not the external auditor, but that would probably not satisfy the needs of a Public Accounts Committee. (In the private sector, it is up to management to ensure that internal controls are effective.) Some SAIs may resist adding this responsibility to their financial audit reports, as it is not yet required by national or international standard setters. Another reason for not embracing this responsibility is the additional cost. There is no cost to stumbling upon breakdowns; detecting them is time consuming. Very few jurisdictions require an opinion on the state of controls. The United States is one of them.

What Are Fraud and Corruption?

No precise international legal definition of *fraud* exists because these events are covered by national country acts; no international act exists. The term is used to describe deception, bribery, forgery, extortion, corruption, theft, conspiracy, embezzlement, misappropriation, false representation, concealment of material facts, and collusion. For practical purposes, and for this discussion, fraud may be defined as the use of deception with the intention of obtaining an advantage, avoiding an obligation, or causing loss to another party.

Fraud refers to a deliberate act that usually involves the use of deception to obtain some form of financial benefit or advantage from a position of authority or trust that often results in some form of loss to the organization defrauded. It refers to dishonesty in the form of an intentional deception or a willful misrepresentation of a material fact.

The word *corruption* comes from the Latin verb *corruptus* (to break); it means "broken object." Conceptually, corruption is a form of behavior that departs from ethics, morality, tradition, law, and civic virtue. The World Bank and Transparency International treat corruption as the use of one's public position for illegitimate private gains. Abuse of power and personal gain, however, can occur in both the public and private domains, often through collusion by individuals from both sectors. The Lebanese, therefore, define *corruption* as the "behavior of private individuals or public officials who deviate from set responsibilities and use their position of power in order to serve private ends and secure private gains" (Kulluna Massoul 1999). The United Nations Global Programme against Corruption defines *corruption* as the "abuse of power for private gain" and includes both the public and private sectors.

Although perceived differently from country to country, corruption tends to include fraud, bribery, political corruption, conflict of interest, embezzlement, nepotism, and extortion. Examples of government operations particularly vulnerable to corruption are travel claims; collection of taxes and customs revenues; administration of procurement contracts; concessions of subsidies, permits, and licenses; hiring, administration of personnel, and payroll systems; privatization processes; petty cash abuse; and e-commerce and Internet credit card transactions. Some of the most common forms of corruption include misappropriation of assets, patronage, influence peddling, and bribery.

Transparency International attempts to measure corruption in a country by using an index called the Transparency International Annual Bribe Payers and Corruption Perception Index. This index has some shortcomings in that the number of intelligence-gathering points is not large in some countries. However, it does provide some way of comparing corruption across countries, which can identify countries that should take action sooner rather than later.

The causes of corruption vary from one country to the next. Among the contributing factors are faulty government and development policies, programs that are poorly conceived and managed, failing institutions, inadequate checks and balances, an undeveloped civil society, a weak (corrupt) criminal justice system, inadequate remuneration of civil servants, and a lack of accountability and transparency.

A serious impediment to the success of any anticorruption strategy is a corrupt judiciary. A corrupt judiciary means that the legal and institutional mechanisms designed to curb corruption, however well targeted, efficient, or honest, remain crippled. Mounting evidence is surfacing of widespread judicial corruption in many parts of the world, a trend that poses a major challenge for SAIs in the future.

The International Organization of Supreme Audit Institutions' Interest in Fraud and Corruption

The International Organization of Supreme Audit Institutions (INTOSAI) is the worldwide federation of SAIs. It hosts an international conference every three years called the International Congress of Supreme Audit Institutions (INCOSAI). The 16th INCOSAI, held in Montevideo, Uruguay, in 1998 was devoted partly to preventing and detecting fraud and corruption. The conference looked at (a) the role and experiences of SAIs in preventing and detecting fraud and corruption and (b) methods and techniques for preventing and detecting fraud and corruption.

The Uruguay INCOSAI agreed that corruption in government wastes resources, reduces economic growth and the quality of life, undermines the credibility of state institutions, and reduces their effectiveness. It noted the strong correlation between corruption and the weakening of state institutions. An understanding emerged that corruption is often linked to the socioeconomic environment of the population (social injustice, poverty, violence) and that a country's traditions, principles, and values influence the nature of corruption. While registering the gravity of the challenge posed by corruption, the INTOSAI community also observed that it is difficult to detect many acts of corruption and to estimate their financial impact, which does not necessarily get reported in financial statements.

The Uruguay INCOSAI adopted the following accords:

> SAIs agree that fraud and corruption are significant problems affecting all countries in varying degrees and that the SAIs can and should endeavor to create an environment that is unfavorable to fraud and corruption. As provided in the Lima Declaration adopted by INTOSAI in 1977, SAIs agreed that they should be independent and have adequate mandates that enable them to effectively contribute to the fight against fraud and corruption. It was also agreed that, where possible, SAIs should:
>
> 1. seek an adequate level of financial and operative independence and breadth of audit coverage;
> 2. take a more active role in evaluating the efficiency and effectiveness of financial and internal control systems and aggressively follow up on SAIs recommendations;

3. focus audit strategy more on areas and operations prone to fraud and corruption by developing effective high risk indicators for fraud;
4. establish an effective means for the public dissemination of audit reports and relevant information including establishing a good relationship with the media;
5. produce relevant audit reports that are understandable and user friendly;
6. consider a closer cooperation and appropriate exchange of information with other national and international bodies fighting corruption;
7. intensify the exchange of experiences on fraud and corruption with other SAIs;
8. encourage the establishment of personnel management procedures for the public service that select, retain, and motivate honest, competent employees;
9. encourage the establishment of guidance for financial disclosure by public servants, and monitor compliance as part of the ongoing audit process;
10. use the INTOSAI Code of Ethics to promote higher ethical standards and a code of ethics for the public service;
11. consider the establishment of a well-publicized means to receive and process information from the public on perceived irregularities; and
12. continue work regarding fraud and corruption through INTOSAI's existing committees and working groups; for example, the Auditing Standards Committee will consider these issues as part of developing implementation guidance as part of a broader standard framework (INTOSAI 1998).

While these recommendations may have been appropriate in 1998, it is becoming apparent that more could and should be done to detect fraud and corruption and that SAIs are well positioned to do so, including by opining explicitly on the state of internal controls.

Anticorruption Policies

Exposure to fraud and corruption can be mitigated if a government has a set of relevant anticorruption policies. SAIs should encourage adoption of anticorruption policies for government and assist in the development of antifraud programs.

SAIs can audit the implementation of the policy. Such a policy might include features such as the following:

- All losses of money and allegations of offenses, illegal acts against the government, and other improprieties must be fully investigated.
- Suspected offenses should be reported to the responsible law enforcement agency.
- Departments should ensure that employees are aware of and periodically reminded of their personal responsibility to report any knowledge of a

contravention of government laws or its regulations, a contravention of any revenue law, or any fraud against the government.
- Departments should take reasonable measures to protect the identity and reputations of both the people reporting offenses and improprieties and the people against whom allegations are made.
- Departments should establish and ensure that employees are aware of procedures to deal with tips about alleged losses, offenses, improprieties, and improper practices, however obtained or received and whether anonymous or otherwise.
- Managers who fail to take appropriate action or directly or indirectly tolerate or condone improper activity should be personally held to account.

SAIs can test compliance with policies such as these to determine if the government has enabled an appropriate anticorruption and antifraud regime to be set up throughout government and audited by the SAIs.

Types of Audits

All audits begin with objectives, which determine the type of work to be performed and the auditing standards to be followed. The types of work, as defined by their objectives, are financial audits, compliance audits, controls audits, performance audits, forensic audits, and computer audits.

Audit engagements may have a combination of objectives, which may include more than one type of work or have objectives limited to only some aspects of one type of work. International standards for audit work have been developed by INTOSAI and the International Federation of Accountants (IFAC) and are being rationalized into a common set of standards. Many countries have their own auditing standards, but most are moving toward the IFAC standards, known as the International Standards on Auditing. Public sector auditors should follow the standards that are applicable to the individual objectives of the audit and to the jurisdiction.

Financial Audits

While financial audits sometimes reveal frauds, they often do not, because they are not designed to do so. It is possible to stumble upon fraud and corruption while examining the financial records for purposes of providing an attest opinion. If auditors find fraud or corruption, they are bound to report on the circumstances, albeit not necessarily in the audit opinion, which might be a clean opinion. The purpose of financial audits is to give assurance that the financial statements are not misleading and fairly present the economic transactions of the enterprise in accordance with an accounting framework. Detection of fraud is not a primary objective of financial auditing.

Compliance Audits

Fraud and corruption are often identified though compliance audits, which are designed to ensure that laws, rules, and regulations are observed. Compliance audit objectives relate to compliance criteria established by laws, regulations, contract provisions, grant agreements, and other requirements that could affect the acquisition, protection, and use of the entity's resources and the quantity, quality, timeliness, and cost of services the entity produces and delivers.

Nonobservance may indicate a fraudulent transaction, although not all cases of nonobservance are fraudulent. Some transactions identified could reflect breakdowns in internal controls, not fraudulent transactions. Such findings would be reported to management. Tests can be designed to ensure that enterprise financial policies are implemented in accordance with expectations. Deviations would be reported to management. Where a transaction or a series of transactions is revealed to be contrary to the law, such transactions are reported to management and possibly to an enforcement authority.

A Priori Audits

A form of compliance audit popular in Latin countries is the a priori audit, which focuses on the legality of a transaction. Expenditures cannot be processed until an a priori auditor signs off on each document as to its legitimacy, legality, and completeness. In recent years a priori auditing has become synonymous with real-time auditing, in which transactions are examined in real time offline for legitimacy, legality, and completeness. The focus is on transactions, not systems.

Controls Audits

Controls audits are designed to ensure that appropriate controls over systems and software are in place to ensure that internal controls and internal checks are functioning as designed. Controls audits can have features built into them to ensure that fraudulent truncations are flagged or made difficult, if not impossible, to transact. Controls audits provide assurance that controls are working, but they do not necessarily detect fraud or corruption.

Internal controls audit objectives relate to management's plans, methods, and procedures used to meet the organization's mission, goals, and objectives. Internal control includes planning, organizing, directing, and controlling program operations and the systems put in place to measure, report, and monitor program performance.

Performance Audits

Performance audits aim to provide information and assurance about the quality of the management of public resources. They assess the economy, efficiency, and effectiveness of the management of public sector entities by examining resource use, information systems, delivery of outputs, and outcomes, including performance indicators, monitoring systems, and legal and ethical compliance.

Performance audits are designed to compare operational performance against norms and predetermined criteria. They can therefore be designed to include some references to laws and regulations and to assist in identifying fraud and corruption. Because performance audits focus on operational issues, especially in high-risk areas, it is not uncommon for auditors to notice some activities that are not in accordance with rules and regulations. Thus, although performance audits are not designed to identify fraud and corruption, these issues sometimes surface.

Forensic Audits

Forensic auditing and accounting include providing investigation and litigation support to corporations, government, and law enforcement agencies. They are relatively new in the public sector.

The increased use of computer technology to conduct criminal activities presents new challenges to the forensic accountant. Forensic auditors design their audits to gather evidence to prove the existence of fraud and corruption. The skills required to do this exceed the audit skills necessary to conduct a financial or compliance audit.

Under some circumstances, laws, regulations, or policies require auditors to report indications of certain types of fraud to law enforcement or investigatory authorities before extending audit steps and procedures. Auditors may also be required to withdraw from or defer further work on the engagement or a portion of the engagement in order not to interfere with an investigation. The follow-on audit work is known as forensic auditing.

Computer Audits

Computer audits are designed to provide assurance that computer-generated financial records are correctly entered so as to comply with the accounting policies and standards of an enterprise. Computer audits explore the risks associated with equipment malfunction, system design errors, calculation correctness, and human error to provide assurance that the computer systems will deliver accurate information. The audits can be designed to test whether laws, rules, and regulations are observed correctly, making a computer audit potentially useful in detecting fraud and corruption.

Fraud Audit Standards

Encouraging auditors to shift emphasis to detecting fraud and corruption does not change the audit standards. Fraud audit standards are very similar to financial attest audit standards, in that they are segregated into general standards of independence: qualifications, due professional care, and professional skepticism. Field standards include planning, knowledge of the entity, management representations, and audit risk. However, fraud audit standards differ when it comes to communications with management and reporting.

Detecting Fraud

Fraud is usually difficult to detect, because collusion occurs and transactions are not recorded. Well-designed internal controls help prevent fraud. Auditors need considerable training to recognize fraud when it does occur.

Internal Auditors in Government

Internal audit is not well developed in many countries in the world; where it is part of the culture, it is often underfunded in government. Internal auditing has thus not played the important role it should have in helping government managers manage better and improve systems of accountability. Seldom do SAIs rely on the work of government internal auditors, whose work has rarely been sufficiently reliable and whose activities are not focused on the same areas as SAI audits.

SAIs can foster the development of internal auditing in government by sharing their training capacity with the internal audit community in government. The SAI can become the intellectual leader for internal auditors, even though they report directly to government departments. SAIs typically have better audit methodologies than internal auditors, which could be shared with the internal audit community.

It would be very desirable to have the internal audit community in government recognized for their expertise in financial management systems and their valuable contributions to management. In Canada the government has recognized that internal audit capacity has not been well maintained. Despite some weakness, internal auditors in the Department of National Defence found a Can$100 million contract fraud in which services were paid for but not delivered. This good internal audit work, plus the internal audit work done by the internal auditors at the Department of Public Works and Government Services identifying the sponsorship scandal (described below), has educated the government on the value of good internal auditing. It will take some time before the internal audit communities in most governments receive that much recognition.

Internal auditing in North America

In Canada the Office of the Auditor General revealed a federal sponsorship scandal after two internal audit reports had been ignored by the government (Government of Canada 2003). The media got wind of the problem when one of the internal auditors became a whistle-blower. The government called in the auditor general to investigate in 2002. Her first report was a scathing denunciation of abuse in which financial administration systems and rules were ignored. The explosive report used words such as "scandalous" and "appalling" to describe how the government abused the system.

The auditor general found that Can$100 million ($85 million) was paid to a variety of communications agencies in the form of fees and commissions and that the program was designed to generate commissions for these companies rather than to produce any benefit for Canadians. She told the Public Accounts Committee that officials in Canada's Public Works Department and Government Services "broke just about every rule in the book" when it came to awarding contracts to a marketing agency. She found instances in which the government paid Can$550,000 ($440,000) for reports that did not exist.

A year later the auditor general went even further, tracking the flow of funds and assisting the national police. Additional abuses were revealed, and the Public Accounts Committee held inconclusive hearings. The new prime minister set up a commission to investigate. The televised hearings and the report of the commission engrossed Canadian taxpayers during much of 2005. In the end, several recipients of fraudulent funds pleaded guilty, went to jail, and provided some restitution. Most Canadians believe that the auditor general's report on the scandal played a major role in toppling the government, which fell following these revelations.

Recently, the media reported a large (more than Can$100 million [$85 million]) procurement fraud regarding software development in the Department of Defence, in which companies were apparently paid for work not done (Bagnall and McGregor 2006). The fraud occurred despite repeated management letters from the auditor general pointing out weaknesses in the procurement processes.

Neither of the Canadian fraud reports arose from a financial audit. Both were originally identified by internal auditors.

In March 2003, the U.S. General Accounting Office (GAO) reported that the federal government's accounting practices are unreliable and may not meet widely accepted accounting standards. It reported that the information in the consolidated financial statements could not be relied upon to express an "opinion" because of deficiencies in accounting and reporting across the executive branch (GAO 2003).

In August 2005, the GAO (the name was changed to Government Accountability Office on July 7, 2004) faulted a defense contractor's performance in Iraq. The contractor had been awarded more than $10 billion in contracts. Auditors found significant cost overruns, the overcharging of the Defense Department by $61 million, illegal kickbacks, failure to police subcontractors' billing, and unauthorized expenses at the Kuwait Hilton Hotel. The GAO found that despite billions of taxpayer dollars spent on reconstruction efforts, oil and electricity production in Iraq remained below prewar levels (GAO 2005).

Internal auditing in Europe

Britain's National Audit Office reported that the government's innovative individual learning account (ILA) failed because corners were cut, causing an £80 million ($200 million) training scandal. The ILA program collapsed after ministers rushed the program into place without a business plan, crafted an imperfect contract, and used insecure information technology systems, all of which contributed to fraud and abuse.

The European Union (EU) has suffered a number of highly public fraud and corruption scandals. A recent one involved funding diverted by the Palestinian Authority into the pockets of terrorists. Auditors allege that money intended for use by the Palestinian Authority for legitimate purposes was siphoned off by corrupt officials to pay the wages of 7,000 nonexistent public servants.

European Court and internal auditors reported fraud in almost all EU institutions and all of its funding programs. Recently, 230 cases were sent to court for filing false expenses, submitting claims for work not done, evading customs duties, misappropriating funds, and padding contracts to suppliers, leading to kickbacks (Mobray 2003).

Internal auditing in China and the Russian Federation

The Chinese National Audit Office (CNAO), which has targeted fraud and corruption and sought out problems, has uncovered many instances of fraud and corruption that were not picked up by financial attest audits. Almost Y 9.1 billion ($1.1 billion) was misused in 38 central government departments, through embezzlement and misuse of funds in departments relating to hospitals, universities, water projects, highway construction, and scientific research. CNAO also reported that the lottery division of the national sports body overpaid two of its own companies so much for printing and distributing lottery tickets in 2003 and 2004 that they turned profits of Y 558 million ($67 million) (*China Daily* 2005).

The Air Traffic Management Bureau of the General Administration of Civil Aviation used Y 207 million ($25 million) of government money to circumvent national regulations and buy an office building in Beijing. It then paid annual rent of Y 13.5 million ($1.6 million) to use the building.

According to China's auditor general, "There are holes in the budget management system of some departments. They make use of their funds to improperly make profits for themselves, and he commented that the CNAO audits in 2004 resulted in savings of Y 1 billion [$120 million]" (Liu Li 2005).

In the Russian Federation, the Audit Chamber has reported fraud and corruption. In 2005 its chair reported that financial offenses uncovered by audit amounted to Rub 77 billion ($2.7 billion) and that his office had issued remedies that recovered Rub 1.5 billion ($50 million). The Audit Chamber also exposed contractual underpricing worth $275 million for sulfur, gas, coal, and petrochemicals exported from the Russian Federation through the Southern Customs Department in 2004–05 (Accounts Chamber of the Russian Federation 2005).

Whistle-Blowers

One of the most useful sources for finding fraud and corruption is information provided by whistle-blowers. Hotlines are being set up in some countries to

> **BOX 10.1** The Risks of Whistle-Blowing
>
> Paul van Buitenen, an internal auditor for the European Union, tried to bring his concerns to his superiors at the European Commission. He was demoted for his efforts. He went over the heads of his supervisors, taking his evidence directly to the European Court of Auditors. He was disciplined by his superiors and lost pay. Eventually, his evidence was supported and many senior EU officials resigned (van Buitenen 2000).
>
> Martha Andreasen claimed EU accounts were open to fraud. She found herself facing discipline charges by the European Union. In 2002 she was suspended from her post as chief accountant after publicly declaring that the Commission's accounts were faulty and open to fraud and abuse. According to Andreasen, there was "very little documentation to support contracts," "no check-up on accounting information," "missing progress and final reports," or simply "no contract files" (Sumberg 2002).
>
> Allan S. Cutler, an internal auditor in Canada, became concerned about the blatant abuses of the system for the sponsorship program. He claimed he was threatened with reprisals from his supervisor for having expressed concerns about the integrity of contract management within the sector. Cutler testified that he was ordered to backdate contracts to match the dates appearing on requisitions, that appropriate signing authorities were not adhered to, and that financial authorities had not been received from the client at the time contracts were issued. While Cutler raised issues of contract manipulation and management concerns, he did not allege any illegal activity. He identified that issues were systemic in nature and warranted further examination. After he brought his concerns to the attention of his superiors, his salary was frozen and he was no longer promotable. Eventually, his concerns were reviewed by the auditor general and Cutler was vindicated. He unsuccessfully ran for Parliament in the next election (Cutler 2007).

make whistle-blowing convenient. In the past whistle-blowing was often done by using brown envelopes that could not be traced to the author. In many cases the whistle-blower simply spoke out to authorities. Speaking out has led many whistle-blowers to be punished (box 10.1).

Ethics Programs and Hotlines

Two effective programs that can advance a fraud prevention agenda are ethics programs and hotlines. An ethics program addresses fraud and corruption in a comprehensive fashion that goes beyond a simple code of conduct. Governments that want to help employees make the correct ethical choices relating to environmental, legal, and social decisions may consider establishing an ethics program. Through courses, policies, ethics call lines, and other means, such programs help employees align bureaucratic practices with government values and beliefs.

One effective deterrent to fraud is a strong perception of being detected. A complaint or tip hotline can help strengthen the perception of detection, as calls are monitored and acted upon and the results publicized. Available to constituencies both internal and external to the organization, this deterrent is valuable and relatively inexpensive. Outsourcing the phone line to a third-party vendor provides the added benefit of ensuring there is no organizational bias in its operations.

Ensuring that hotlines are not abused is critical. Disgruntled employees can provide information that is damaging to a person who may have caused the caller some distress. To avoid misuse of hotlines, they must be designed in such a way that sorts the wheat from the chaff, so that only legitimate issues are followed up. Much effort has to be made in designing the system to ensure that complaints are not fictitious or frivolous. Psychologically designed questions help auditors focus on legitimate claims.

Professional Bodies with Standards and Guidance for Detecting Fraud and Corruption

Many bodies have promulgated standards and guidance to combat corruption and fraud. These include the INTOSAI, IFAC, the Institute of Internal Auditors, the Institute of Forensic Auditors, and Transparency International. SAIs, which are already members of INTOSAI, should encourage membership in all of these bodies where practical.

Government Agencies with Antifraud and Corruption Mandates

Many governments throughout the world have set up special agencies, in addition to police forces, to combat fraud and corruption. Their main tasks are to find and prosecute companies and individuals engaged in transnational crime, cross-border crime, customs evasion, fraud, counterfeiting, tax evasion, organized crime, and other fraudulent activities. SAIs can be very helpful to these national anticorruption agencies if they have evidence to support criminal charges. SAIs should be very careful in dealing with such evidence, as improper handling may cause the evidence to be declared inadmissible in court.

Reporting Fraud and Communicating with Management

The reporting standard does not change if auditors put more emphasis on detecting fraud and corruption. Laws, regulations, or policies may require auditors to report promptly to law enforcement or investigatory authorities indications of certain types of fraud, illegal acts, violations of provisions of contracts or grant agreements, or abuse. In such circumstances, they should ask those authorities, legal counsel, or both if publicly reporting certain information about the potential fraud would compromise investigative or legal proceedings. Auditors then limit their public reporting to matters that would not compromise those proceedings, such as information that is already part of the public record.

Reporting fraud requires auditors to address the effect that fraud or illegal acts may have on the financial attest audit report. It is important that the Public Accounts Committee or others with equivalent authority and responsibility are adequately informed about fraud or illegal acts. When auditors detect minor, but reportable, violations of provisions of contracts or abuse that is not material from a financial attest perspective, they usually communicate the findings in a management letter to officials of the audited entity. If the auditor's report discloses deficiencies in internal control, fraud, illegal acts, violations of provisions of contracts or grant agreements, or abuse, auditors should obtain and report their views to responsible officials.

Recommendations for Improving SAI Anticorruption Performance

SAIs can take many actions to improve their anticorruption and fraud performance. Many progressive SAIs are already doing the following:

- Making more courses and conferences on combating fraud and corruption
- Strengthening investigative powers
- Establishing forensic audit units
- Establishing fraud auditing standards
- Encouraging more professional designation
- Supporting Transparency International
- Supporting and cooperating with national antifraud agencies
- Encouraging ethics and fraud awareness training programs
- Encouraging ministries, departments, and agencies to create fraud control plans

- Encouraging ministries, departments, and agencies to contract-out fraud control (hotlines, fraud risk assessment, fraud training, fraud control plan, and fraud investigation) if resources are unavailable in-house
- Encouraging lawmakers to pass whistle-blower legislation to protect people who provide legitimate information to public control agencies.

Much more can be done in SAIs that have not amended their approaches to fraud and corruption in recent years.

References

Accounts Chamber of the Russian Federation. 2005. "Address of Chairman of Accounts Chamber of the Russian Federation, Mr. Sergey V. Stepashin, January 27, 2005." Bulletin No. 3. Moscow.

Bagnall, James, and Glen McGregor. 2006. "Inside Job." *Ottawa Citizen*, March 12.

China Daily. 2005. "Report of Li Jinhua, Chairman of the Chinese National Audit Office to the Standing Committee of China's National Peoples Congress." Beijing, June 28.

Cutler, Allan S. 2007. *The Whistleblower Speaks—The Sponsorship Scandal*. Ottawa, Ontario, Canada: AS Cutler and Associates.

GAO (U.S. Government Accountability Office). 2003. "Truth and Transparency of the Federal Government's Financial Condition and Financial Outlook." Address by David M. Walker, Comptroller General of the United States, to the National Press Club, September 17, Washington, DC. Available at www.gao.gov/cghome/2003ngc917.pdf.

———. 2005. "Rebuilding Iraq: Actions Needed to Improve the Use of Private Security Contractors." GAO Report 05-737. Washington, DC. Available at www.gao.gov/newitems/d05737.pdf.

Government of Canada. 2003. *2003 Reports of the Auditor General of Canada*. Chapters 3, 4, and 5. Ottawa. Available at www.oag-bvg.gc.ca/domino/reports.nsf/html/03menu_e.html.

INTOSAI (International Organization of Supreme Audit Institutions). 1998. Reports and proceedings of the 16th International Congress of Supreme Audit Institutions, Montevideo, Uruguay, November. Available at www.nao.org.uk/intosai/edp/reportindex.html.

Kulluna Massoul. 1999. *Lebanon Anti-corruption Initiative Report*. Washington, DC: U.S. Agency for International Development. Available at www.kullunamassoul.org.lb/general/report/Final.doc.

Liu Li. 2005. *China Daily*, June 26.

Mobray, C. 2003. "Fraud against European Union Totaling More than Half a Billion Pounds Have Been Uncovered in the Past Year." *EU Weekly News*, November 30.

Sumberg, David. 2002. "Tories Fight Labour over Firing of EU Whistleblower." Posted online October 28. Available at www.davidsumberg.com/eu_whistleblower.htm.

van Buitenen, Paul. 2000. *Blowing the Whistle: One Man's Fight against Fraud in the European Commission*. London: Politico's.

11

Public Sector Performance Auditing in Developing Countries

COLLEEN G. WARING AND STEPHEN L. MORGAN

Performance auditing is a systematic, objective assessment of the accomplishments or processes of a government program or activity for the purpose of determining its effectiveness, economy, or efficiency. This determination, along with recommendations for improvement, is reported to managers, ministers, and legislators, who are responsible for enacting the recommendations or ensuring accountability for corrective action. Performance auditing is an important building block with which to improve accountable and responsive governance of public resources.

As government programs continue to grow in magnitude and complexity, public sector auditing has evolved and extended its scope beyond mere financial or compliance audits to the auditing of performance to support policy makers in their oversight role.[1] Performance auditing is a very new development in the history of auditing. Its growth parallels the evolution of politics and public administration from a one-dimensional focus on control of inputs (resources) toward broader attention to accountability for outputs and outcomes. This evolution of auditing represents both a means by which auditors can continue to be relevant and a move toward fulfilling their accountability role in governance.

Throughout its history, auditing has served an accountability function. It first developed as a risk-reduction strategy for the owner ("principal") who entrusted assets into the custody of an agent. The agent's responsibility was to make an accounting back to the principal as to the proper application of the assets. Because of the risks associated with physical distance or lack of expertise in the relevant activity, the principal employed an independent third party (the auditor) to attest to the believability of that accounting. Performance auditing is similar in its aims: it involves the examination of the performance of a public organization or program on behalf of a client—ultimately citizens—by an independent auditor.

This chapter is a practical guide to performance auditing. It focuses on auditing methods and practices that facilitate economy, efficiency, and effectiveness in the delivery of government services; the implementation of such programs in Sub-Saharan Africa; and the requirements to ensure that performance audits can be used by legislatures, civil society, and the managers of the audited organization or program to improve outcomes. The first section of the chapter identifies the objectives of performance audits and describes the types of audit findings. The second section outlines the steps involved in conducting a performance audit. The third section examines the challenges of institutionalizing a performance audit function in Sub-Saharan African countries.

Elements of a Performance Audit

Performance audits examine the extent to which government programs or activities have achieved expected performance. Despite the multiplicity of methods by which various organizations conduct performance audits, most descriptions of this branch of auditing converge around the concept of the three E's—economy, efficiency, and effectiveness. This type of audit examines

- the economy of administrative activities in accordance with sound administrative principles and practices, as well as management policies;
- the efficiency of utilization of human, financial, and other resources, including examination of information systems, performance measures and monitoring arrangements, and procedures followed by audited entities for remedying identified deficiencies; and
- the effectiveness of performance in relation to achievement of the objectives of the audited entity and audit of the actual impact of activities compared with the intended impact.

Performance auditing is based on decisions made or goals established by the legislature. It may be carried out throughout the whole public sector (Auditing

Standards 1.0.38 and 1.0.40 of the International Organization of Supreme Audit Institutions [INTOSAI]).

Performance Audit Objectives, Findings, and Findings Elements

Performance auditing works with the same performance management concepts used by program managers and their principals to plan, monitor, and evaluate how public resources are used to achieve public policy ends. The concepts of inputs, processes, outputs, outcomes, and impact, as well as their interface with the above goals of economy, efficiency, and effectiveness, are common tools for public managers and public performance auditors alike. However, as performance auditing represents an evaluation of public performance management processes, it uses an additional set of concepts that describe its component processes and outputs. Key to this language is the concept of an audit finding and its component elements.

The fundamental component of a performance audit is the audit finding. An audit finding is made up of standard elements, including criteria, conditions, effects, and causes. The structure of an audit finding is determined by its audit objective (the key query that needs answering) and the model on which the audit is constructed using these elements.

Criteria represent the ideal against which actual performance will be measured. They can include expectations, standards, rules, policies, benchmarks, program goals, or average performance in similar programs or institutions. In designing fieldwork methods, auditors design data collection and analysis procedures to meet the audit objectives and subobjectives. Criteria can be established by benchmarking to comparable programs, eliciting customer expectations or demands, determining the program intent, identifying internally established targets, comparing individual comparable units within the same organization, locating industry or sector standards, comparing to historical trends, identifying optimal or average performance achieved in a trend, comparing working time to actual elapsed time, or comparing an intervention group's performance to that of a control group.

Conditions are the actual state, as depicted by current performance, actual practices, or circumstances. Identifying condition involves collecting or creating data and information that allow comparison to the criteria. The primary methods for developing evidence of condition are analyzing existing performance data gathered by the auditee, analyzing performance data gathered by an outside organization, and developing an ad hoc performance measurement system. If an ad hoc measure is chosen, care should be taken to control for variables, or the audit results should be qualified.

The *effect* is the difference between the established criteria and the condition(s) or the consequences of the difference. Effect can also represent the measured impact of the condition, where the condition represents a program intervention. To develop evidence of effect, auditors must quantify the difference between the criteria and the condition and identify the impacts on the organization or its customers of not meeting the standard.

The *cause* describes why or how the condition came about, or the reasons why performance is not as expected when problems are found. Although it is tempting to assert cause by focusing on the absence of specific controls, to ensure their analysis of cause is valid, auditors must examine a variety of potential reasons for variances between condition and criteria. Auditors may find insight into causes by identifying and verifying barriers and constraints to achieving standards (inadequate resources, external variables, acts of providence). They should also assess the legal authority, support systems—that is, the clarity of expectations, the timeliness of feedback, empowerment and efforts to improve process—and accountability systems within which staff work. Other factors that should be considered are the qualifications and training needs of staff and critical shortages.

Although performance auditors are frequently tempted to assert that the cause for every deficiency found is an inadequate control system, several potential reasons must be explored. The theoretical framework may be flawed, a direct relation between program processes and outputs and desired outcomes may not exist, program goals may be unrealistic, or inputs or resources may have been inadequate. Intervening or external variables may exist that negate, deflect, or mask the program's effect. These variables may be related to an act of providence that could not be foreseen by program planners, such as a drought that negates the effects of an agricultural support program.

Types of Audit Findings and Relevant Elements

The elements of a particular finding vary based on the audit objective. Findings can be descriptive, normative, traditional or causal, or impact (table 11.1). A descriptive finding refers to the condition only. A normative finding involves both criteria and condition. A traditional finding constructs a causal argument involving the criteria, condition, cause, and effect. An impact finding compares the condition with and without the program intervention.

Program "footprints" and their performance auditing aspects

Performance auditing is frequently based on decisions made or goals established by the legislature. It may be carried out throughout the public sector.

TABLE 11.1 Types and Examples of Audit Findings

Type of finding	Elements	Sample audit finding
Descriptive	Condition only	Annual cost to incarcerate a prisoner was $67,800 in 2005.
Normative	Criteria and condition	Annual cost to incarcerate a prisoner was $67,800 in 2005, compared with $52,000 at comparable prisons.
Traditional/causal	Criteria, condition, cause, and effect	Annual cost to incarcerate a prisoner was $67,800 in 2005. Budget appropriation authorized $58,000 per prisoner, resulting in a deficit of $17.8 million. The additional costs were caused primarily by a significant increase in labor and benefit costs following implementation of the May 2005 union contract.
Impact	Condition with cause (intervention) compared with condition without cause (effect)	Recidivism (re-arrest) rates among alcohol-dependent inmates who participated in the alcohol treatment program before release were significantly lower than rates among alcohol-dependent inmates who did not receive the treatment.

Source: Raaum and Morgan 2001.

However, whether or not the government has explicitly stated the expectations against which achievements are examined through public instruments such as plans or budget statements has little bearing on the legitimacy of undertaking performance audits. Those who provide government with its authority and resources—for example, the electorate and their representatives in parliament—expect that the authority and resources will be used in accordance with certain values. Those values—economy, efficiency, and so on—are referred to as *performance aspects*.

Performance aspects tie directly to the basic "footprint" of any government program—the program elements. The elements of every government program are the inputs used to support the program, the processes that carry out the program, the outputs produced by the process, and the outcomes. This footprint is represented by a model that characterizes the relations among program elements (figure 11.1). Each element of the program links to a specific aspect of performance that describes the expectations for performance. Specifically,

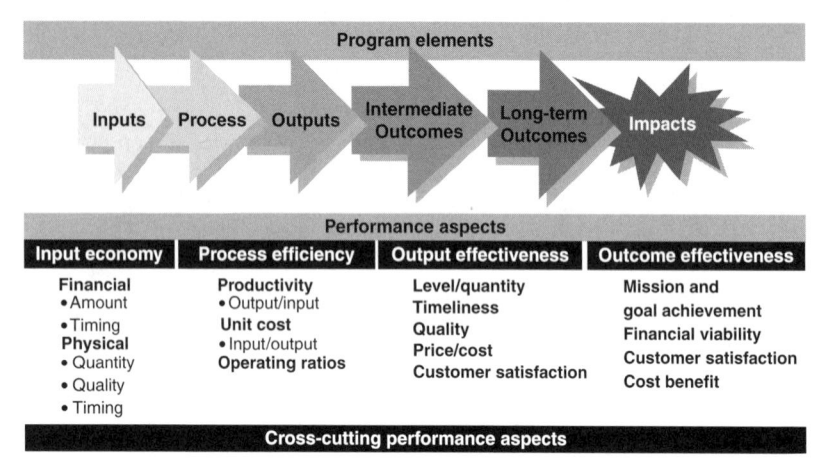

Figure 11.1 Government Program Elements and Performance Aspects Subject to Audit

Program elements: Inputs → Process → Outputs → Intermediate Outcomes → Long-term Outcomes → Impacts

Performance aspects

Input economy	Process efficiency	Output effectiveness	Outcome effectiveness
Financial • Amount • Timing Physical • Quantity • Quality • Timing	Productivity • Output/input Unit cost • Input/output Operating ratios	Level/quantity Timeliness Quality Price/cost Customer satisfaction	Mission and goal achievement Financial viability Customer satisfaction Cost benefit

Cross-cutting performance aspects

Compliance with laws and regulations
reliability, validity, and availability of information
maintaining underlying values

• Individual ethics and integrity • Societal equity • Cooperation and partnership
Continuous improvement

Source: Authors.

governments are expected to obtain and use inputs economically, conduct processes efficiently, and produce effective outputs that result in effective achievement of intended outcomes.

In addition to the aspects of performance that are relevant to a specific program element, there are cross-cutting performance aspects that apply as expectations to every element of the program. These include compliance with laws and regulations; reliability, validity, and availability of information; maintenance of underlying governmental values, such as ethics, integrity, and equity; and continuous improvement.

Because these performance aspects represent the expectations for government performance, they are relevant both to the planning and ongoing monitoring that should be carried out by government managers themselves and to the conduct of performance audits.

Examining the economy of inputs

Inputs are the financial resources (measured in monetary units) and physical resources (such as staff, equipment, and building space) used in a program. The performance that is expected with respect to acquisition of inputs is called *economy*. *Input economy* describes the expectation that governments minimize the cost of program resources (relative to required levels of resource quality). Methods for measuring input economy include comparison of cost or prices paid for inputs to benchmark costs, such as private sector charges, historical costs, or costs as a ratio, such as the ratio of the audited program's resources to total organizational resources or expenditures. An audit of input economy can focus on economy in the use of financial resources, physical resources, or both.

Auditing economy in the use of financial resources entails determining the extent to which cash expenditures for specific nonmonetary resources, such as staff, facilities, and equipment, were reasonable or minimized relative to the quality needs of the program. Where borrowed funds are used for the program, it may also evaluate the economy of the financing cost. Overhead costs can also be evaluated, by comparing them with costs in similar programs.

Examining economy in using physical resources includes determining, for example, whether space is used optimally (measured as square feet per full-time staff equivalent compared with benchmarks, standards, or comparable operations). Equipment costs can also be evaluated. (Are fleet expenses directly relatable to the program activities? Are equipment features directly relevant to program needs, or has the program "gold-plated" its equipment acquisition?)

Examining the efficiency of processes

Processes are the systems, steps, tasks, and management decisions involved in providing government services. Processes include not only activities associated with the direct delivery of services (such as solid waste pick-up or police patrol) but also the planning, organizing, monitoring, and decision making associated with the program under audit.

Process efficiency is technically measured as the relation between outputs and inputs. Outputs are the services or products produced by government program. Inputs are the resources expended or consumed. Inputs are measured by such units as person days, person hours, staff time, or full-time staff equivalents. The relation between outputs and inputs is measured by two primary efficiency ratios: unit cost and productivity. It is also measured through the use of surrogates, such as utilization rates or backlogs.

Unit costs express the number of inputs used to produce an output. (How does the cost per client vary across health clinics? Is the local government's clinic cost per client at or below the national health insurance reimbursement rate per client?) Productivity measures the number of units (outputs) produced per unit of input. A productivity audit could seek to determine, for example, if there are significant variances across branch offices in the number of passports issued per staff-year. Utilization ratios include measurements such as rates of equipment use, percentage of hospital beds occupied, and recreation center occupancy.

Evaluating the effectiveness of outputs

Outputs are the units of service actually provided, such as the number of construction permits issued or the number of students completing a training class. Even a government's internal service functions (such as the accounting function) produce outputs, although they may be provided to or internally consumed by the organization's direct service providers rather than the government's ultimate clients. An output of the payroll function, for example, is the number of payroll checks issued.

Output effectiveness represents the quality of the services or products produced. In addition to the expectation that government programs should obtain inputs economically and conduct processes efficiently, citizens, taxpayers, and parliamentarians also expect governments to produce effective outputs. Expectations for output effectiveness can be established in a variety of forms, including output quantity, quality, and timeliness.

In auditing output quantity performance, the key question is the extent to which the number of units is congruent with demand or need. One method for determining the adequacy of a program's output quantity is to examine backlogs or work in process. Another is to measure outputs as a ratio of demand (requests for service). Output quality is achieved if there are no defects in the units completed and the services are adequate. Quality might be an attribute of the unit of output itself or of the delivery of the output. It can be audited in relation to accuracy (does the construction inspection process accurately identify all critical violations?); reliability (can citizens count on their hospital staying open?); consistency (do safety inspections consistently address key safety conditions?); durability (how does the average pothole failure rate in an area compare with industry standards?); serviceability (what is the average return rate for vehicle repairs?); and appearance (how do bus riders rate the cleanliness of public buses?). Auditors may also choose to measure the cost of quality, by examining the resources spent on correcting failures, controlling quality, and collecting delinquent payments; waste; injury and mortality rates; and warranty expenses, for example.

Output timeliness refers to the speed of work completion and delivery. In the safety and security sector, an important audit objective may be how average police response time compares with other cities.

Auditors can also measure output timeliness in terms of cost of delays, variance from established deadlines, and various dimensions of customer wait times.

Evaluating outcome effectiveness

Outcomes are the results achieved by the program intervention. They often represent the most difficult performance aspect to measure, for both government managers and auditors.

One means of distinguishing the program output from the outcome is by identifying the actor: the output is the product or service created or delivered by the program itself. The outcome represents the change in state or action of the recipient of the program services. For example, the outputs in an education program would be the number of students enrolled or attending classes. The immediate outcome is the number of students graduating (or successfully completing) the program. The longer-term program outcome is the percentage of graduates employed in the field of their degree.

It is sometimes difficult to distinguish between output quality and near-term or intermediate outcomes. The key is to define or map the inputs-processes-outputs-outcomes chain to show what products or services are produced by the program's processes.

Outcome effectiveness measures the quality of outcomes and the extent to which program results are directly related to the program. Characteristics that can be measured for assessing outcome effectiveness are the results of a program or the degree to which the program mission was achieved. For example, key audit questions in the education and integrated justice sectors might be whether a school's tutoring program increased the graduation rate of the target population and what percentage of inmates who received drug treatment were rearrested for drug-related offenses. The performance audit can also examine cost-benefit or cost-outcome relations, such as the total cost for each job training graduate who is still gainfully employed after three years, or financial condition indicators, such as the extent of unfunded benefits in a pension program.

Financial results can also be relevant to outcome effectiveness. In public transport investment, for example, a performance audit may examine the degree to which user charges cover the cost of the system. Key characteristics for measurement are profit, cost recovery, and return on investment.

Customer satisfaction is another method used to ascertain outcome effectiveness. In services that become necessary as a result of external events, such as military, fire, police, hospital emergency, ambulance, and snow removal services, readiness presents another performance dimension that can be measured. A common measure is the percentage of services mobilized within a target response time.

Impact, the ultimate measure of a program's outcome effectiveness, is measured as the proportion of the problem that has been reduced as a result of a program. In housing, for example, impact can be measured by determining the extent to which the need for affordable housing has been reduced each year.

Relation between Audit Objectives, Audit Structure, and Audit Steps

The underlying model for undertaking a performance audit involves first clarifying the objective of the audit (box 11.1). This involves determining whether the performance audit is aimed at auditing the economy of input use, the efficiency of program processes, or the effectiveness of program outputs and outcomes—in other words, the aspects of performance to be examined.

In principle, the audit objective determines what steps need to be followed. For instance, a performance audit objective that requires a descriptive finding as to the efficiency of a specific activity would involve a simplified process of evaluating and establishing the measures to be used, collecting the relevant

---

BOX 11.1 Does the Drug Abuse Resistance Education (DARE) Program Work?

Drug Abuse Resistance Education (DARE) is a drug abuse prevention program that aims to reduce drug use among school-age children in the United States. The performance audit of the program measured the extent to which it was achieving its goals.

The audit used an experimental design, comparing juvenile arrest rates for youth who participated in the program (the intervention group) with those who did not (the control group). The demographic profiles (ethnicity, income levels, age) of both groups of students were identical. The audit found that students who participated in the program were actually arrested more frequently than the control group, for both drug-related and non-drug-related offenses.

The design of this audit was heavily dependent on the existence of sufficient amounts of reliable data for determining student involvement in the program and identifying their arrest information in the local juvenile correctional system. These conditions are often difficult to meet, unless such comparisons have been planned from the initiation of the government program itself.

Source: Location fictionalized from the 1994 audit of the Austin DARE Program, Office of the City Auditor, Austin, Texas.

data, and formulating a finding. In contrast, if the objective is to measure the efficiency of a program and to provide a causal finding involving the criteria, the condition, the cause, and the effect, the performance audit would involve the following steps:

- *Establish the efficiency measures (or indicators) that will be used for the audit.* Auditors need to evaluate the existing measures used by the program itself, construct ad hoc efficiency measures, or both. A key step is critiquing existing measures against standard criteria for good measures and identifying where measures are deficient.
- *Establish the criteria to be used.* Auditors need to establish what ideal will be used to measure process efficiency. Will the audit use the program's own stated ideal or a standard or rule, or will it construct a benchmark by measuring efficiency using the selected measures in other similar institutions or programs? Is the stated goal adequate, or should it be changed?
- *Determine the validity of the efficiency reports produced by the program.* Auditors need to assess the quality of the measure and the quality of the data. Are measures consistent over time? Do they represent the output? Do the data have integrity (are they open to manipulation or collected independently from the function being measured)?
- *Determine whether the achieved efficiency levels meet the established goals or criteria.*
- *Determine what causes the efficiency rates to vary from the criteria.* Auditors must try to determine what is responsible for variances in efficiency from the standard or average.
- *Formulate the performance audit finding and recommend efficiency improvements.* As part of its recommendations, the performance audit can calculate the projected savings to be achieved if the efficiency improvements are implemented.

Conducting the Performance Audit

Performance auditing is carried out in three phases: planning, fieldwork, and reporting. The methods used to carry out the phases vary widely among auditing organizations around the world.

Performance audits are well suited to being conducted in a team environment, as a diversity of perspectives and experiences can enhance the value of the product. To ensure harmonious functioning, all parties involved in the assignment must understand and accept their roles and responsibilities.

Most fundamentally, they must agree on and share a basic understanding of the performance audit's objectives.

Throughout the audit, performance auditors will need to communicate actively with members of the audited institution. The auditor's motto in terms of auditee relations should be "no surprises." The audit begins with an "entrance conference," which is used to introduce the audit team to the management staff and key employees of the institution being audited. Following the entrance conference, auditors should brief managers at all levels on a periodic basis: one of the worst mistakes an audit team can make is to assume that the liaison or manager most closely involved with the audit will keep his or her peers and upper management informed about the audit's findings. This rarely, if ever, happens in the real world of audit communication.

Planning

Unlike financial audits, performance audits are seldom repeated (box 11.2). Consequently, audit tests and procedures that apply to one audit will not necessarily be relevant or useful in the next audit. For example, the measures for success of a school—such as the completion rate for students entering the program or the ultimate percentage of graduates who become gainfully employed—have no relation to the measures of success for a road construction activity. This variation among the government's programs means that auditors must create a unique audit to evaluate the most significant issues of each program.

Unlike in audits of financial statements, in a performance audit the objective of fieldwork is often developed after the audit begins, based on an assessment of the risks and vulnerabilities associated with the activity being audited. However, in some cases the performance audit is initiated at the request of parliamentarians or ministers. When this is the case, the audit's objective can be established at the outset, based on their specific questions or concerns.

Auditors must ensure that their own managers participate actively and continuously raise questions during the planning phase. They can encourage this participation by submitting a written plan that details the steps, schedule, and resources that will be used to accomplish the five phases of planning: (a) gathering information; (b) conducting a risk assessment; (c) assessing the vulnerabilities to the significant risks of the program; (d) defining/refining the audit objectives; and (e) developing the audit scope, audit methodologies, fieldwork programs, and audit budget/resources. The process of developing an audit that best fits the relevant and most critical issues of the particular

> **BOX 11.2** Conducting a Performance Audit of Child Immunization Services at the Local Level
>
> A national law requires all children to be immunized before enrolling in school, and the national budget authorizes funds for conducting immunization programs. The goal of the national immunization program is to eliminate preventable childhood diseases, including measles (rubella), whooping cough (pertussis), tetanus, polio, and diphtheria. At the national level, the National Health Ministry (NHM) conducts awareness marketing aimed at educating parents on the importance of immunization. At the local level, the NHM provides funds for local government immunization services. The NHM sets regulations that prescribe limits on the use of funds: health care providers must use the NHM sliding-fee scale to charge for immunizations based on income ability. The NHM also sets standards for safe handling and appropriate administration of vaccines. Local governments are responsible for monitoring to ensure compliance with regulations.
>
> The NHM allocates funds annually on a formula basis, using census data to calculate a fixed amount for each school-age child in the receiving jurisdiction. The local Health Bureau uses these funds to contract with private sector providers and to supplement the costs of municipal health clinics. For fiscal year 2006, the total allotment from the NHM to the city of B—was $5.94 million. The city's Health Bureau paid $1.23 million to local private clinics (as reimbursement for vaccinations), using the remaining $4.71 million to supplement the operating expenses of city-owned clinics. The Health Bureau reported that 72,366 vaccinations were performed, at a cost of $82 per vaccination.
>
> *Source:* Authors.

activity or program involves learning about the program, assessing its risks and vulnerabilities, and using the information to develop audit objectives, scope, and methodology. (To illustrate each step of the audit process described below, a fictional case study audit of a local government's immunization program is described in text boxes and tables at relevant points.)

Step 1: Gathering information

To begin tailoring the audit to the activity being audited, auditors conduct background research into relevant literature on the type of activity, review the activity's enabling legislation, and familiarize themselves with its plans, budget and expenditure trends, and program processes (table 11.2). All of the auditors' activities are enriched by interviews of relevant program staff and managers, which can provide insights into the culture, context, and nuances of the environment.

TABLE 11.2 Pre-audit Information-Gathering Activities and Their Benefits

Activity	Benefit
Literature review	Understanding of issues and risks inherent in activity, accepted management practices, and performance standards
Study of enabling legislation, other rules and regulations	Insights into authorized scope of activity and its legal environment
Study of activities plans	Understanding of intended mission and expected results; mapping strategies and processes developed to achieve results
Study of budgets and expenditure trends	Insights into scope of operations and real priorities of activity
Study of policies and procedures, operating manuals, performance reports, activity logs, organization charts	Insights into formal rules of operation and actual processes
Flowcharting to observe how activities are carried out	Understanding of front-line experiences and barriers to service delivery

Source: Authors.

Step 2: Assessing risk

Most performance audits are customized to the nature of the activity or program being audited. This tailoring process begins with assessing risks associated with the activity, in order to focus the audit effort on the most relevant issues. As used in performance auditing, *risks* are events that, if they occurred, would have a negative impact on the organization or its ability to achieve its objectives.

Auditors consider two types of risk: "inherent" and "control" risk. Inherent risks are the events that face the organization by the very nature of its activities. Police officers, for example, face safety risks in engaging in law enforcement activities. Risks of loss or misappropriation of funds are inherent in a cash-handling operation, such as might exist in a health clinic or a bureau that collects traffic fine payments. Control risk (also called *vulnerability*), addressed in the next section, is the risk that remains in the activity after the effects of any internal controls are considered.

Risk assessment involves two steps. The first step is identifying the inherent risks associated with or arising from the type of activity being audited. Auditors will have collected much of the inherent risk information during the background review process.

The second step is ranking the risks based on their potential impact on the organization. Risk ranking can be done through a variety of methods and at various levels of rigor. Basic risk assessment involves asking the commonsense question, how great will the impact be if this risk event occurs? The impact of the risk event focuses on the activity or organization being audited and can range across any of the standard program performance aspects. What is the impact on the program if it fails to obtain inputs economically? What is the impact if its processes are inefficient? Risk ranking prioritizes the list of inherent risks, ranking each risk as high, medium, or low impact. Whatever factors or means are used, the criteria or reasoning used to rank the risks should be documented in order to ensure that future questions about the decisions made in this crucial phase of the audit can be answered fully.

The product of the risk assessment is a prioritized list of inherent risks, any of which might ultimately become a key focus of the audit objectives. A performance audit of child immunization services, for example, might identify risks that threaten program impact: excessive staff cost for city health clinics, a low rate of children immunized per full-time-equivalent staff, underutilization of government-owned immunization facilities, and prohibitively high fees for immunizations.

Step 3: Assessing vulnerability to risks

Once the risks are assessed and ranked, the next step is to determine how vulnerable the organization is to each risk. Vulnerability represents the probability that a specific risk will occur, given the control procedures that are in place (or not) to prevent it. Auditors assess vulnerability by evaluating the controls and making judgments about whether the controls are likely to be effective. The control risks should be clearly linked to the inherent risks that exist in the ministry, department, or agency being audited.

The output of the vulnerability assessment (table 11.3) will be an additional dimension incorporated into the original risk assessment ranking results. This dimension is critical in determining the issues to focus on during audit fieldwork. Vulnerability assessment is an essential aid in preventing auditors from wasting valuable audit resources examining high-risk issues that already have well-developed controls in place.

Step 4: Defining/refining the audit objectives

With the completion of the risk and vulnerability assessments, auditors must determine what focus their fieldwork should take to add the most

TABLE 11.3 Vulnerability Assessment of Risks Facing Child Immunization Services

Risk/controls	Is control present?	Risk level	Vulnerability level
Excessive staff costs for city health clinics			
■ Human resource management system that identifies appropriate professional grades, establishes competitive market pay rates, tests candidates, and determines placement	No		
■ Separation of duties for establishing position pay grades and hiring decisions	No	4.5	High
■ Objective process for determining pay grade for new hires	No		
Lower-than-benchmark rate of children immunized per full-time-equivalent staff			
■ Collection and monitoring of data on clinic productivity	No	4.0	High
■ Evaluation of productivity data during contract renewals	No		
Underutilization of government-owned immunization facilities			
■ Use of objective population criteria for location decisions	No		
■ Local placement of facilities based on availability of public transportation and proximity to concentrations of target population	No	4.0	High
Prohibitively high fees for immunizations of target population			
■ National Health Ministry regulations requiring clinics to charge on sliding-fee scale	Yes		
■ City Health Bureau monitoring of fees in contract clinics	No	4.0	High
■ Review of fees and charges during contract renewal	No		

Source: Authors.
Note: Risk is scored on a scale of 1–5. The highest risk score (5) indicates that a risk event could significantly impair achievement of objectives.

value. Audit objectives focus the fieldwork phase of the audit. Ultimately, the audit report will answer the question posed by the audit objectives.

The objective queries should be phrased in as specific terms as possible, posed in a close-ended rather than open-ended format. That is, rather than asking, "How is the city's immunization program performing?" the objective query should ask, "To what extent is the immunization program providing full coverage for the eligible population, as measured by the percentage of local children 2–7 who receive the full series of required vaccinations?"

Objectives should also be framed keeping in mind the realistic scope and methodology of the audit. If, for instance, more than one element of performance is to be reviewed, the objectives should be separated.

The steps for developing audit objectives can be summarized as follows:

- Understand the primary report user.
- Identify the subject, problem, or concern that will be explored.
- Create an "input-process-output-outcome" diagram, and determine if it concerns processes, outputs, or outcomes.
- Decide which aspect or aspects of performance to include in the audit (economy, efficiency, effectiveness).
- Decide which elements of the audit finding to develop, and link them to subobjectives.
- Develop subobjectives as a series of separate questions addressing each finding element required to meet the audit objective.

Before selecting an audit objective for fieldwork, the audit team must evaluate the "auditability" of potential objectives. A variety of constraints can limit the auditors' ability to answer the question posed by an audit objective in time for the information to be relevant. For example, an audit question may require considerable staff resources or specialized expertise in order to find the answer. Issues to be considered in determining auditability include audit skill, audit power, the availability of evidence and information, the required audit hours, the audit morale, and the time frame within which the results must be provided to the decision maker. Based on the risk and vulnerability assessments, a series of objectives is formulated (table 11.4).

Step 5: Determining the audit scope, methodology, fieldwork program, and audit budget

The audit scope defines the depth and coverage of audit work and any limitations to that depth or coverage. Auditors typically determine scope based on a compromise between the ultimate objective of the audit and the time, cost, and expertise constraints. Scope decisions include the time period covered by the audit, the kinds and sources of evidence, the universe (population) that will be examined, the sample size and site selection rationale, and the need for and means of obtaining expert advice. In selecting evidence

TABLE 11.4 Performance Objectives Based on Assessed Risks of Child Immunization Program

Risk	Objective question
Staff costs for city health clinics are excessive.	Are staff costs in city health clinics comparable to market rates for pay and benefits for similar work, experience, and education?
Rate of children immunized per full-time-equivalent staff is lower than benchmarks.	What is the immunization rate per full-time equivalent in city-owned clinics? How does it compare to local private sector clinics and the national average?
Government-owned immunization facilities are underutilized.	To what extent are city immunization clinics used? If utilization is lower than capacity, what is the impact on the clinics' average unit costs? If utilization rates are lower than capacity, what are the causes?
Fees for immunizations are prohibitive for target population.	Are all subsidized clinics charging the National Health Ministry sliding-fee scale for immunizations? If so, are the fees correct with respect to the actual income level of the patient's family (that is, are income levels correctly reported)? If not, what is the total amount charged incorrectly to families or inappropriately subsidized to families?

Source: Authors.

types and sources, auditors consider the type and number of records to be collected, the location of operations that will be visited, what new data need to be created, the form of the information to be collected, and the reliability of the data that will be collected.

Methodologies are the data collection and analysis techniques used in performing the audit (table 11.5). For each type of methodology, audit plans (sometimes called "audit programs") spell out the detailed steps to implement the methodology. Audit methodologies may involve collecting and analyzing data or forms routinely kept by an organization for purposes other than the audit or analyzing information collected by auditors.

TABLE 11.5 Methodologies for Gathering and Analyzing Data

Methodologies for gathering data	Methodologies for analyzing data	
	Quantitative methods	Qualitative methods
▪ Sampling ▪ Automated data retrieval ▪ Questionnaires, surveys, focus groups ▪ Trained observer ratings ▪ Interviews ▪ Benchmarking	▪ Content analysis ▪ Ratio analysis ▪ Trend analysis ▪ Flowcharting ▪ Cost-benefit analysis ▪ Inferential statistics ▪ Variance/comparative analysis ▪ Regression ▪ Interrupted time series	▪ Case studies ▪ Expert judgment ▪ Document examination ▪ Case studies

Source: Authors.

The audit team considers several variables in choosing the appropriate methodology with which to answer the audit objective questions:

▪ *What information is needed to answer the objective question?* For example, if the audit objective relates to the unit cost performance of an environmental inspection program, the data required will be the number of outputs (number of inspections) and the inputs (cost data).
▪ *Where will auditors obtain the information they need?* Before authorizing and initiating an audit methodology, auditors should anticipate any barriers, such as the location, availability, and reliability of information and information sources.
▪ *How will auditors obtain the information they need?* Once the specific types and sources of data are identified, the data collection method must be determined. If original data must be collected, a data collection instrument should be designed and pretested during the planning phase.
▪ *What will auditors do with the information once they have it?* Auditors must ascertain the specific data analysis methods they will use to answer the audit objective question.
▪ *What questions will the information answer?* This critical question helps ensure that the auditors begin with the end in mind. Without it, relevant information that was not previously considered might go ignored, or time might be wasted collecting information that proves to be inadequate to meet the audit objective.

■ *What are the limitations of the audit?* It is important to communicate with clients about the limitations of the work to be done.

An important principle of performance auditing is to select methodologies that will accomplish the audit objectives at the least cost. The methodology should be linked to the fieldwork program by specifying the evidence to be collected and the techniques for analyzing the evidence.

When selecting methodologies, auditors must choose whether to conduct the audit as a measurement-based or process-based audit. A process-based approach entails a review of the control system over performance. This type of audit focuses on the way things are done, the systems that are in place, and the procedures that are used. The measurement-based approach focuses on the achievement of specific aspects of performance. It provides findings that describe actual performance, such as the unit cost to provide a service or the percentage of clients who are satisfied. In an ideal audit world, the most comprehensive and persuasive audit would combine both approaches. However, auditability considerations generally make this too expensive or time consuming to be practical.

Once the audit objectives, scope, and methodology have been selected, the audit team develops an audit fieldwork program. A fieldwork program worksheet should present a clear chain from the audit objectives and sub-objectives through the scope description to the required tasks, the sampling methodologies, the data collection and analysis methodologies, and the proposed data sources, documents, and systems. It should also contain confirmation of supervisory approval, an audit budget and allocation of resources, a time line, and the means to be used to involve external resources and communicate with the audited organization or program. The fieldwork program should be presented to and discussed with the audit organization's management before fieldwork begins, ideally leading to agreement on its main parameters. A sample matrix for making the linkage from the audit objective to the design of the audit structure and the fieldwork is provided for the immunization case study (table 11.6)

Fieldwork

The fieldwork program sets out the required tasks and maps out processes for each aspect of fieldwork (box 11.3). While the exact steps to be followed are specific to each audit and determined in the fieldwork plan, some data collection considerations are common to all audits. The rigor and security of data collection play an important role in the data's ultimate credibility as

TABLE 11.6 Finding Elements, Data, and Analysis Methods Needed to Conduct Performance Audit of Child Immunization Program

Objective question	Finding element	Data needed	Analysis method
Process based			
Does city have system in place to ensure that staff costs in city health clinics are comparable to market rates for pay and benefits for similar work, experience, and education?	*Criteria:* Best-practice human resources procedures and recommended controls for compensation programs *Condition:* Actual city practices	■ Policies and procedures for pay determination ■ Actual practices of human resource and hiring managers ■ Hiring documents for compliance with pay range thresholds	■ Evaluate controls or processes to determine if they are adequate to ensure comparable pay and benefits. ■ Conduct content analysis of policies, hiring forms, and procedures and compare it against actual hiring documents to assess congruence between policy and practice. ■ Compare pay rates paid to authorized pay rates for specific positions.
Measurement based			
How does actual utilization of immunization clinics compare with capacity? If utilization is under capacity, what is the impact on clinics' average unit costs?	*Criteria:* Optimum utilization rate of city clinics *Condition:* Actual utilization rates of city clinics *Effect:* Unit cost differential for underutilized clinics	■ Number of clinic visits per day, week, month, and year ■ Current average service time per clinic visit (sign-in and sign-out logs) ■ Available clinic hours	■ Calculate average number of daily and weekly clinic visits for selected seasonal months in the year. ■ Compute average time per visit. ■ Multiply number of visits times average time for actual utilization.

(continued)

TABLE 11.6 (*continued*)

Objective question	Finding element	Data needed	Analysis method
If utilization rates are lower than capacity, what are the causes?	*Cause*: Reasons for underutilization	■ Clinic staff schedules ■ Number of examination rooms	■ Compute optimum number of possible visits based on hours, staffing, and available exam rooms. ■ Compare optimum to actual. ■ If actual usage is less than capacity, interview staff and customers to determine causes.

Source: Authors.

> **BOX 11.3 Cost of Child Immunization Services Clinic Staff: Site Visit Fieldwork Plan**
>
> To determine each position's title and pay rate, auditors will collect current job descriptions and personnel files for every staff member employed during the year. From each job description, they will record the position's primary duties, required types and years of experience, required amount of education, and any licenses or other required certifications.
>
> From each employee's personnel file, auditors will
>
> - collect pay status documents and record the current authorized salary amounts and any supplemental pay (mileage allowance, telephone allowance, and so forth);
> - assemble job application and resumé documents, and record the date of hire, reported experience, education, and licenses and certifications at time of hire; date and type of additional education, licenses, or certifications since hire date; and ratings from last three performance appraisals; and
> - collect last three months' canceled payroll checks for all staff currently on payroll.
>
> They will then compare actual pay amounts with authorized salary amounts from pay status documents and resolve variances while on site.
>
> *Source:* Authors.

audit evidence. The audit team's composition, characteristics, and training must be adequate to minimize bias and interpretation errors. Ensuring that the sampling strategies are appropriate for the evaluation questions improves credibility. The audit manager can also elect to obtain an opinion on the adequacy of the methodology from an independent party.

When undertaking data analysis and interpretation, it is important to ensure that all competing explanations for effect and cause are considered. Teams should be trained to look for data that will negate their initial findings. Important values that apply to all stages of the fieldwork process are to be careful and precise and to limit the final interpretation and description of the data to the boundaries set by the characteristics of the methods used and data obtained.

Auditors classify the information they collect into four types: testimonial, documentary, analytical, and physical (in order of increasing strength). As the audit team begins to plan the audit procedures, it should consider the types of evidence and information it will be collecting and build in means to ensure that the information will be relevant to the audit objective and sufficient and competent to support expected conclusions. Some of these means including paying attention to interviewing strategies (eliminating leading questions, for example); triangulating, by combining data sources, methods, and other factors to examine the question under study; performing consistent analysis (by compiling complete, rigorous, and accurate field notes, for example); weighting evidence; using debriefings and feedback; and carefully documenting audit processes, data, and findings.

Reporting

For each audit, the audit team will have determined the means of reporting the audit findings at the beginning of the fieldwork. The decision on reporting medium will be based on the audit organization's relevant auditing standards and the customer's needs—both for timeliness in receiving the audit results and for the ultimate use to which the findings will be put. Audit reports may take the form of a complete report that describes the audit objectives and fully describes the conclusions along with the evidence that supports those conclusions, or they may be provided in the form of a high-level presentation that highlights the objectives and results in a series of headlines. Other, less conventional media for audit reporting include video- or audio-taped presentations by the auditors and one-on-one briefings by the auditors to the requesters of the audit.

The performance audit report is not a prewritten, fill-in-the-blank form. In order for it to be used effectively, the audit report should be clearly understandable to its intended audiences. Just as the audit itself was tailored to the specific issues and vulnerabilities of the activity being audited, the audit report must present the specific conditions along with the particular audit procedures used and results obtained. All audit reports must contain an explanation of the origination or reason for conducting the audit; sufficient background on the audited activity to enable readers to understand its findings; a clear statement of the audit objectives; a description of the scope and methodologies; the audit findings; and conclusions and comments by the responsible managers over the audited activity. However the results of the audit are communicated, auditors should take care to ensure that the results are documented in a form that is retrievable, to ensure that the public and other interested parties have appropriate access, in accordance with the government's transparency laws, and to enable oversight authorities to review and provide ultimate accountability for the findings and audit recommendations.

Government audit reports usually have a variety of audiences, each of which has different needs and levels of preexisting understanding of the issues presented. Each audience will have a different amount of time available to devote to reading and digesting the audit report's contents. These differences in needs and level of attention to findings can best be served by providing the audit report information at various levels of detail. The primary audiences for audit reports are the managers and decision makers within the audited activity, policy makers over the audited activity, the public (through the media), special interest groups, and civil society organizations. More and more, audit organizations are also providing press releases with their audit reports as a way of helping the media discern the key points and understand the context of the findings.

Communicating audit findings

Because every performance audit is unique to the environment and issues it covers, the corresponding audit report must also be unique. This presents challenges to auditors, who must decide what information and how much detail to include in the report, how to organize the information, and which words to choose that will accurately and precisely portray their conclusions without overstating or obscuring the nature of the problems they found.

Key requirements for effective audit report writing involve presenting an understanding of the relations among the elements of the finding so that those relations can be clearly portrayed and organizing information in a manner that corresponds with readers' existing conceptual frameworks. Describing audit findings clearly involves determining and conveying the finding elements in their proper logical relations. The specific elements needed for any single finding will depend on that particular audit objective. However, the logical relation among the elements of a finding is fixed. Understanding that relation is the key to establishing which element is which. This logical relation is best portrayed graphically (figure 11.2).

The audit team must examine and sort its findings before drafting its report, in order to determine the most appropriate organizational structure. Using a logical order and classification in presenting the findings can help readers understand the report. Reports can be organized chronologically (presenting findings in the same order as the steps of the process), in order of importance, or by themes (categorical).

Audit findings need to be both understandable and readily accessible in the report. Toward this end, auditors should organize the material deductively and provide different report elements to meet the differing needs of various audiences. This means that although the audit process itself proceeds inductively (from the collection of detailed data and information to the development of a general rule or conclusion), the report

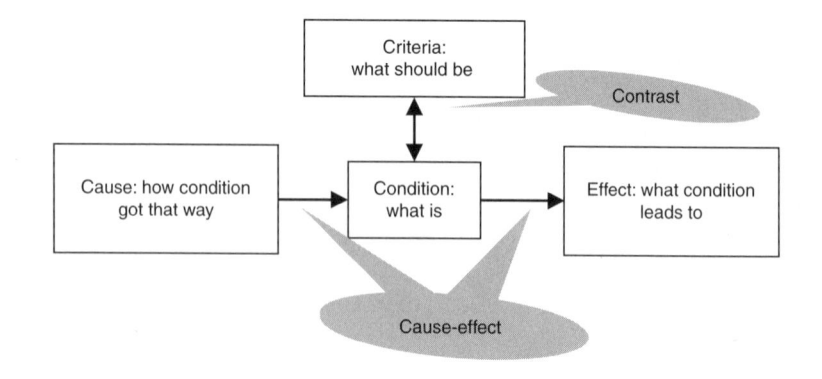

```
                    ┌─────────────────┐
                    │   Criteria:     │
                    │ what should be  │         Contrast
                    └─────────────────┘
                             ↕
┌──────────────────┐  ┌─────────────────┐  ┌──────────────────┐
│ Cause: how       │→ │   Condition:    │→ │ Effect: what     │
│ condition got    │  │    what is      │  │ condition leads  │
│ that way         │  │                 │  │ to               │
└──────────────────┘  └─────────────────┘  └──────────────────┘

                         Cause-effect
```

Source: Authors.

FIGURE 11.2 Interaction among Elements of an Audit Finding

should first present the key messages or conclusion and then provide the evidence to support that conclusion. The report also needs to provide headlines and summary information that accurately and clearly convey key messages.

Designing an effective audit report begins with audience analysis. Who will be reading the audit report? What are their preexisting understandings and questions about the report? How much time will they be able to devote to reading the findings? Because different audiences have different needs, questions, and time constraints, audit reports are often segmented into several separate "documents," each designed to meet specific audience needs and often presenting the same information in different formats. Formats include the following:

- A one-page summary with bulleted messages summarizing the findings to provide for a quick scan.
- Deductive headlines that summarize findings to allow readers to quickly find a section of interest. Longer reports list these headlines in a table of contents to support quick access to particular issues or findings.
- A background section describing processes, environmental characteristics, and program scope and design characteristics, such as budget, staffing, locations, program goals, and strategies.
- The main text, which details the supporting evidence for each conclusion, to allow staff and management of the organization being audited to examine and understand the audit's messages.
- A list or table of audit recommendations or corrective actions identified, which enables readers to quickly scan the solutions. The auditee's

concurrence with the recommendation and action plan for implementation can be included here.
- Appendixes, which amplify and provide reference information for the reader's use. These may include detailed methodology descriptions, tables and charts with supporting data, and reference material about the audited activity.

A new technology currently being explored by educators—the podcast (a videotaped message of any length, recorded and available for replay by clicking a Web link)—may become a powerful means for auditors to explain and present their findings at the user's convenience.

Facilitating positive reception by the auditee

Regardless of the degree of independence accorded to the audit function, auditors must balance their role of watchdog with the goal of improving the program. Both auditors and auditees can benefit from a collaborative approach to the performance audit, by focusing on the improvements that can be made from a thorough and critical evaluation of the activity being audited.

Although the primary role of a government audit is to ensure accountability for meeting citizens' expectations, performance audits also provide an excellent opportunity to set out a road map for change. The audit organization that focuses its attention and report solely on deficiencies and weaknesses will ultimately find that the auditees' natural defensiveness overcomes the desire to improve. The delicacy of balancing between being a watchdog on behalf of the principal and being a constructive agent for change underscores the importance of effective communication skills. Auditors need to be helpful and constructive, even as they maintain their integrity to the government's laws and the highest values of public service.

An effective way to achieve this balance during the final stages of the audit is by including auditees' comments in the body or appendix of the audit report. Other means include recognizing improvements made by auditees during the audit, citing best practices exhibited by the auditee, and highlighting instances of exemplary performance. Citing these achievements in the audit scope produces a more balanced audit report, and it increases the likelihood of achieving the desired outcomes for accountability and improvement.

Conducting Performance Audits in Sub-Saharan Africa

Despite overwhelming challenges, many countries in Sub-Saharan Africa have succeeded in establishing many features of good public governance. In governments that have not documented their operations or established tracking mechanisms for recording and monitoring the outputs they produce, both process- and measurement-based performance audits can help establish some of these foundations. Although auditors must maintain their objectivity about the activity being audited, at the end of the project they often share with managers the information and systems they have created to carry out the audit steps. For instance, where flowcharts and process descriptions did not exist, audit documentation has often served as the initial basis for a training or policy manual that helps establish routine practices. In a measurement-based audit for which ad hoc systems were developed to collect performance information, auditors often share copies of their data collection instruments (forms, surveys, and so forth) or reproduce copies of analysis tools used in the audit for managers or staff to adopt.

When performance auditing is first introduced, it is advisable to focus audits on readily measurable indicators, such as the reliability of reported information or the effectiveness of selected processes to achieve specified outputs. Until the audit function has built sufficient credibility and established its expertise in advanced methodologies, it may be overreaching to perform program effectiveness audits on experimental or long-term impact programs (such as research or disease prevention).

The most valuable performance audits that can be conducted in countries in Sub-Saharan Africa, at the local, regional, or national level, include the following:

- Effectiveness of revenue-collection processes, as measured by the percentage of assessed taxes or fees collected and received by the government, the timeliness of debt collections, and the accuracy of reporting by taxpayers
- Reliability of reported performance data (are services provided, clients eligible, program funds spent as reported?)
- Asset management (equipment and infrastructure maintenance, repair, utilization, and replacement)
- Validity of performance measures (do measures indicate real performance, important or relevant elements of performance?)
- Cost of services, such as cost per patient visit in health clinics, cost per household for sanitation and solid waste pick-up, and cost per thousand gallons of water
- Service timeliness, access, equity, and availability
- Staffing ratios compared with benchmarks (teacher/student, nurse/patient, doctor/patient, jailer/prisoner)
- Utilization rates (hospital beds, school desks, fleet vehicles)

- Regulatory enforcement effectiveness, measured by real change in regulated activity or by ability of regulators to assess penalties, enforce corrective actions, and provide meaningful coverage of regulated industry
- Effectiveness of procurement processes (compliance with competitive requirements to ensure least cost, means to ensure the quality of goods or services purchased, and equity in opportunities to all qualified vendors for government purchasing dollars).

Performance audits are capable of providing information and accountability about the provision of services that is not available from the financial and regularity audit alone. However, the decision to implement a performance audit program should be predicated on the existence of certain prerequisites that form the foundation from which to apply accountability to government actions or omissions. These include the rule of law, clearly defined government organizations with well-understood roles and responsibilities, and the existence of policy planning and budgeting structures and basic accounting systems capable of and used in the tracking, categorization, and reporting of economic transactions (Adamolekun 1999; Madavo 2005). In addition, certain caveats should be borne in mind (table 11.7).

Addressing the broader role of audit in public sector governance, a new practice guide by the Institute of Internal Auditors entitled *The Role of Auditing in Public Sector Governance* (Waring and others 2006) cites several key requirements to an effective audit function. These include organizational independence, a legal mandate, unrestricted access to information, sufficient

TABLE 11.7 Caveats about Conducting a Performance Audit

Before you...	You should...
Move to performance auditing	Have effective financial auditing
Seek to control outputs	Control inputs
Install an integrated financial management system	Operate a reliable accounting system
Introduce internal control	Establish external control
Insist that managers efficiently use the resources available to them	Adopt and implement predictable budgets
Introduce performance or outcome budgeting	Foster an environment that supports and demands performance
Introduce performance contracts in the public sector	Enforce formal contracts in the private sector

Source: Adapted from Schick 1998, cited in World Bank 1998.

funding, competent leadership, competent staff, stakeholder support, and professional audit standards. A few of these elements are present in some countries in Sub-Saharan Africa. Even the most advanced countries around the world will not have all of them fully in place.

Some good examples of strong legal mandates exist in Sub-Saharan Africa. South Africa's 1999 public finance management legislation, directed to the national and provincial governments, includes requirements and strong support for public sector audit. The East and Southern African Association of Accountants-General (ESAAAG) has adapted the Institute of Internal Auditors standards and promulgated public sector internal audit standards that provide a solid foundation for professionalism. Several pieces of supreme audit institution and internal audit legislation include language mandating unrestricted access to data and information to the auditors.

Challenges remain, however, in creating an institutional environment that is conducive to reaping the benefits of a regular performance audit function. These challenges include the needs for competent staff and leadership, stakeholder support, and organizational independence, none of which can be met by mandates or pronouncements.

The barriers to conducting and reaping the benefits of an effective government performance audit function stem from the fundamental challenges facing development in Africa, including corruption, poverty, poor governance, poor infrastructure, and a continuous brain drain to developed countries in Asia, Europe, and the Americas (Madavo 2005). All of these challenges constrain the introduction and effective functioning of a performance audit function in the public sector. Some, such as poverty and infrastructure problems, can be incorporated into the performance audit plan. The tractability of other challenges—primarily corruption and poor governance—depends on the level at which they occur. If the highest levels of government are corrupt or incompetent, it will probably not be possible for the performance auditor to be effective. However, if the audit function enjoys unwavering support at the highest levels of government, it can serve as a powerful tool in rooting out corruption and identifying needed improvements in management practices. This is especially true if the performance auditors combine forces with fraud investigators, forensic accountants, and law enforcement officials.

Support at the highest level is the most important requirement for conducting a performance audit. Second in importance is finding and retaining competent staff. Given that the role of the audit is to evaluate government activities and identify ways to improve them, auditors need to be among the best and brightest in the public service—the very people who can most easily find well-compensated work anywhere. In addition, as in some developed countries, some African countries have evolved a civil service bureaucracy that can limit audit organizations.

To attract and retain the best and the brightest, governments must be able to provide competitive salaries and conditions of service. (Competitive public service salaries would also help support efforts to reduce corruption, insofar as petty kickbacks or bribes are tied to public servants' inability to survive on their salaries.)

Other challenges to staffing a performance audit function lie in the education and competencies of the candidate pool. Performance auditors should be well educated and capable of continuous learning.

Opportunities for strengthening the knowledge base could be improved and the skills for successful performance auditing improved by establishing performance audit boot camps—one- or two-month on-the-job immersion programs supported by systems or capacity development groups, such as the African Capacity Building Foundation. The boot camp approach would allow participants the opportunity to conduct a narrow-scope performance audit under the tutelage of experienced senior auditors.

Another strategy would be to endorse university programs or establish communities of practice, such as the South African Institute of Internal Auditors (SAIIA). SAIIA's current expertise and service array is oriented toward private sector auditing. However, with the advent of strong, new financial management and audit legislation for all levels of government, South Africa's public sector auditors are becoming more involved with SAIIA and requesting more capacity development assistance.

The East and Southern African regions have also begun to assemble government auditors to discuss their challenges and develop strategies for the way ahead. The primary support group for government auditing outside of South Africa appears to be ESAAAG, whose focus is financial audits. It recently approved an updated internal audit guideline that parallels the Institute of Internal Auditing's *Standards for the Professional Practice of Internal Auditing*. Together with the INTOSAI standards, these standards can provide a general foundation for performance audit training.

Governments may also individually or regionally develop toolkits. Respondents to a survey of central government internal audit functions in five southern African countries (Botswana, Malawi, Namibia, Zambia, and Zimbabwe) reported that their greatest needs were for an up-to-date audit manual, tailored to local needs, that could be used to conduct training within their organizations. Respondents also reported that their libraries were limited and expressed a desire for more access to books and periodicals.

Information on management practices and other criteria is essential to the credibility and usefulness of the performance audit (Wynne 2001).

The development of an effective performance audit function in Sub-Saharan Africa should be preconditioned by the existence of some basic administrative systems. Where administrative systems are weak and ineffective, sponsors of the performance audit function will need to evaluate whether their resources would be better directed at designing and putting in place effective systems than at attempting to use resources to create audit evidence where none has been created or retained. The large number of backlogged financial audits (in Kenya and Zambia, for example) may be attributable to inadequacies in the accounting systems (Stephens [2004] details some fundamental systems that are needed to build capacity for adopting more advanced practices).

Administrative systems do not need to be functioning optimally to begin developing a performance audit function—if fully integrated and functional administrative systems were a necessary precondition, even many developed countries' governments would be years away from adopting them. Performance audits can be used to evaluate system capacity and help guide priorities for corrective action. Moreover, in environments in which the performance audit staff are proficient at measurement-based auditing, their work has sometimes served as the foundation for nascent monitoring or performance measurement systems.

Reporting and organizational relations should be well designed and clear. Government audit functions are organized in a wide variety of ways in Africa. Many of the national audit functions have evolved from their original colonial histories, taking their initial shapes from either the francophone (public law) or anglophone (Westminster) model.[2] From these initial roots, each country has evolved and hybridized different structural arrangements and scopes of responsibility for the supreme audit institution, as well as for the provincial/regional audit functions and the individual internal audit activities of the ministry, department, or agency. The structures of the supreme audit institution evolving from both models have generally resulted in environments that are supportive of the independence of the audit function. Among the more effective mechanisms is the (anglophone) use of a Public Accounts Committee, drawn from parliamentarians who serve on the audit committee of the supreme audit institution. These committees have proven effective in Botswana, South Africa, and Uganda (Adamolekun 1999).

Other organizational structures have placed internal auditors in the role of a pre-auditor of financial transactions. A survey of government internal audit organizations in Botswana, Malawi, Namibia, Zambia, and Zimbabwe notes that "internal audit in each country, except for Namibia, spends a significant proportion of its time undertaking pre-audit checks, that is, ensuring that payments are valid, accurate, and proper before the payment is made" (Wynne 2001: 3). Transferring the auditors' focus from pre-audits of payment transactions to the more complex and demanding performance audit process may involve a sweeping change in culture or at least necessitate reorganizing the allocation of staff resources between the accounting and auditing functions. Moreover, internal audit laws in several countries (Malawi, South Africa, Tanzania) place the internal audit function within the purview of the accounting officer of the ministry, department, or agency, a circumstance that can limit the ability to reallocate resources toward conducting audits of performance.

Auditor independence is the foundation on which the audit's credibility is built. Achieving independence involves addressing three dimensions: structural, environmental, and personal. Structural independence arises from the organizational placement of the audit function. It is independent when it is appointed by and makes its reports to officials outside the hierarchy of the organization and activities under audit. Environmental independence is ensured when auditors are free to conduct their work without interference, limits, or pressure from the auditee, such as limitations on access to records or employees, auditee control over budget or staffing for engagements, or auditee authority to overrule or modify audit reports. Personal independence means that auditors are free from conflicts of interest or biases that could affect their impartiality, the appearance of impartiality, or how they conduct their work or report results. In countries in Sub-Saharan Africa with strong informal governance systems or tribal influences, the challenge of ensuring personal independence, particularly in local governments, takes on added significance.

Regardless of the country or continent, government auditors face tremendous challenges in speaking the truth to authorities. Supreme audit institutions are not always free to take the strongest critical positions. In countries whose democratic trappings are too new or too superficial to have taken root, the supreme audit institution may find its independence shaky. In cases where the supreme audit institution reports to a weak, submissive parliament or is appointed by and reports directly to the president, audits criticizing the administration can require tremendous personal courage to publish. These difficulties are exacerbated for the internal audit function whose head is appointed by the chief executive of the ministry, department, or agency, especially if the reports must be tabled in parliament or forwarded to a central oversight body, such as the ministry of finance. This concern is not as great in countries in which internal auditors' reports are not distributed outside the audited organization's hierarchy, but in these conditions a more dangerous risk exists—that of unresolved performance problems or irregularities. Stories abound of government performance failures in which the internal auditor had been finding and reporting problems internally for years before the conditions became public.

Financial independence poses another challenge to the integrity of performance audit results that must be addressed—worldwide—if auditors are to be capable of reporting sensitive findings about the government's performance to a public audience. At a 2004 INTOSAI symposium of the Organization of Supreme Audit Institutions, participants discussed challenges to independence. Highlighted in the discussion was the need for a budget process and sufficient resources that are outside the control of the organization subject to audit.

The preconditions for conducting performance auditing in Sub-Saharan Africa reflect the same capacity-development challenges faced for improving governance more generally. Accordingly, once fully mapped out, the process for building the appropriate foundations to support performance auditing may facilitate strengthening or developing the full range of governance capacity. In the long run, an effective and well-supported program of performance auditing can contribute to the growth and strengthening of public administration, as well as to the public's faith in the honesty and effective administration of government.

Notes

1. Although private sector audit organizations do conduct performance audits, their purpose is to provide their clients with the means to better manage their operations in order to ensure regulatory compliance or improve the return on investment. By contrast, while public sector performance audits offer advice or recommendations on operational improvements, the audit is more likely to concurrently represent a form of accountability for the government entity. "It is true that related new variants of audit have emerged which are used mainly in the private sector, such as operative audits, management audits, quality audits, or environmental audits. The essential difference between these and performance audits as carried out by the supreme audit institution is that these are characteristically internalized forms of corporate control, whereas performance or value-for-money audits are a part of the external control system operating on public organizations" (Girr and others 1999: 19).
2. The francophone model places the supreme audit institution in a court of accounts, which examines (audits) the financial accounts and may also authorize expenditures and assess judgments (including fines) for irregularities. The underlying philosophy of the pure francophone model relies on the assignment of responsibility to public

servants through carefully defined administrative regulations. Accordingly, the audit role is narrowly focused on procedural and judicial examination of compliance with dictates. While the anglophone model also carries primary responsibility for auditing financial accounts, it is premised on the philosophy that public servants exercise wide latitude and discretion in decision making. The philosophical underpinnings of the anglophone model were initially more amenable to the more comprehensive approach of performance auditing. Despite the differences in philosophical approaches, many courts of accounts have embraced performance auditing.

References

Adamolekun, Ladipo, ed. 1999. *Public Administration in Africa: Main Issues and Selected Country Studies.* Boulder, CO: Westview Press.

Girr, Xavier, Jeremy Lonsdale, Robert Mul, Christopher Pollitt, Hilkka Summa, and Marit Waerness. 1999. *Performance or Compliance? Performance Audit and Public Management in Five Countries.* Oxford: Oxford University Press.

Madavo, Callisto. 2005. *Building Effective States, Forging Engaged Societies.* Report of the Task Force on Capacity Development in Africa, World Bank, Washington, DC.

Raaum, R.B., and S.L. Morgan. 2001. *Performance Auditing: A Measurement Approach.* Altamonte Springs, FL: The Institute of Internal Auditors.

Schick, Allen. 1998. *A Contemporary Approach to Public Expenditure Management.* (World Bank Local Government Organization and Management Participants' Manual.) Washington, DC: World Bank.

Stephens, Mike. 2004. *Institutional and Incentive Issues in Public Financial Management Reform in Poor Countries.* Washington, DC: World Bank.

Waring, Colleen, Jacques Lapointe, Joseph Bell, Jerl Cate, Jeanot deBoer, Mark Funkhouser, Steve Goodson, Jerry Heer, Ann-Marie Hogan, and Robert Schaefer. 2006. "The Role of Auditing in Public Sector Governance." Practice Guide. Institute of Internal Auditors, Altamonte Springs, FL.

Wynne, Andy. 2001. "Internal Audit in Southern Africa." *ACCA Internal Audit Bulletin.* Association of Chartered Certified Accountants, Glasgow, United Kingdom.

12

The Growth of Parliamentary Budget Offices

JOHN K. JOHNSON AND F. RICK STAPENHURST

Legislatures play a wide variety of roles in the budget process (Santiso 2005). While legislatures all over the world play at least a formal role in overseeing implementation of the budget they enact, their impact on the formulation of that budget varies dramatically in different systems. Some are very actively involved; others are not involved at all. Moreover, the role that the legislature plays in the budget process in many countries has changed over time and is expected to continue to change in the future (Schick 2002). These changing roles call into question the sources of information that are or may be made available to help the legislature participate in the budget process. Legislatures require reliable, unbiased information to be able to participate in a constructive manner in formulating the budget, as well as in overseeing its implementation.

This chapter discusses the value of a nonpartisan, independent, objective analytic unit to the legislative role in both enacting and overseeing implementation of the budget. It describes legislative budget offices in four regions, showing how such offices can contribute to the budget process and suggesting reasons for the growing (albeit still small) number of such units.[1]

The chapter does not address how significant a role legislatures should play in amending proposed executive budgets. Some have argued that significant legislative budget amendment powers may weaken fiscal discipline (von Hagen 1992) or increase the level of pork-barrel spending and that these powers should therefore be limited (Wehner forthcoming). As fundamental as this issue is, this chapter focuses only on the potential value of a nonpartisan objective unit, not the larger issue of the balance of power between the executive and legislative branches in preparing the budget.

The Role of Legislatures in the Budget Process

The roles that legislatures play in national budget processes vary widely across the globe. Several factors influence these roles, among them the type of political system (presidential, parliamentary, hybrid); the type of electoral system (plurality-majority, proportional, semiproportional); the legislature's formal powers (the extent of its powers to amend the executive budget); the combination of the political environment within which the legislature functions and the political will of legislators to exert the legislature's powers; and the technical capacity of the legislature (see Johnson 2005; Johnson and Nakamura 1999).

Norton (1993: 50) identifies three types of legislative roles in the budget process: budget approving, budgeting influencing, and budget making. Budget-approving legislatures lack the authority or capacity to amend the budget proposed by the executive and therefore approve whatever budget the executive presents. Budget-influencing legislatures have the capacity to amend or reject the executive budget proposal, but they lack sufficient capacity to formulate a budget of their own. Budget-making legislatures have both the legal authority and the technical capacity to amend or reject the executive's budget proposal and to substitute a budget of their own.

Since budget-approving legislatures simply rubber-stamp budgets submitted by executives, they have little need for independent offices to assist them in analyzing those budgets, challenging executive assumptions, or making changes to draft budgets. By contrast, several budget-making and budget-approving legislatures have established independent, nonpartisan budget units over the past half century or so. California's Legislative Analyst's Office (LAO), established in 1941, was the first such office. It was followed by the U.S. Congressional Budget Office (CBO), established in 1974. The Philippines Congress created its independent budget office—the Congressional Planning and Budget Department (CPBD)—in 1990.

The rate at which legislative budget offices are being established has increased over the past decade. Mexico's Chamber of Deputy's Centro de Estudios de las Finanzas Publicas (CEFP), or Center for Public Finance Studies, began operation in 1999. The Ugandan Parliament's Parliamentary Budget Office (PBO) was established in 2001. Two years later, the National

Assembly of the Republic of Korea passed legislation creating the National Assembly Budget Office (NABO). Both Kenya and Nigeria were in the process of creating parliamentary budget offices in 2006.

Examples of Specialized Legislative Budget Offices

Independent, nonpartisan legislative budget offices were beginning to be established as long as 60 years ago in the United States. In recent years, legislatures in Africa, Asia, and Latin America have begun developing similar offices. This section describes several.

The Legislative Analyst's Office in California

According to Elizabeth Hill, the director of the LAO, the California legislature had been concerned that the balance of budget power had been shifting to the executive since the early 1930s. Rather than rely exclusively on the executive for budget information, the legislature desired an independent source of budget information and analysis and professional assistance to help it conduct oversight and to ensure that its programs were being implemented effectively. It also sought to reduce the growing costs of state government and to make government more efficient and economical. In 1941 the Senate and Assembly passed legislation to establish their own budget office, but the governor vetoed the bill on the recommendation of his fiscal office. Undeterred, the legislature effectively overruled the governor by establishing the office through a joint rule of the Senate and Assembly the same year.[2] The legislature later established the LAO by statute.

The LAO reviews and analyzes both the finances and the operations of California state government. Unlike the U.S. Congressional Budget Office, described in the next section, the LAO performs specific oversight functions on behalf of the legislature, ensuring that legislative policy is implemented effectively and in a cost-effective manner. The specific functions of the LAO include the following:

- Analyzing and publishing a detailed review of the governor's budget bill (*Analysis of the Budget Bill*) that includes department reviews, as well as recommendations for legislative action
- Publishing *Perspectives and Issues*, an overview of the state's fiscal status that identifies major policy issues
- Assisting the budget committees throughout the budget process
- Reviewing administration requests to make changes to the budget after it is enacted and presenting these findings to the budget committees

- Publishing special reports on the state budget and on topics of interest to the legislature
- Conducting fiscal analyses of initiatives and ballot measures[3]
- Conducting legislative oversight, including evaluations of programs or agencies and issuing recommendations to the legislature
- Developing policy alternatives on public policy issues and making recommendations on policy matters.

LAO services are available to all committees and members of the legislature (see www.lao.ca.gov/LAOMenus/LAOFacts.aspx).

The Joint Legislative Budget Committee, made up of 16 members (8 from each house), oversees the LAO's operation. By tradition, a senator chairs the committee and a member of the Assembly serves as vice-chair. Funding comes equally from each house. The legislative analyst, as the head of the LAO is known, serves at the pleasure of the Joint Legislative Budget Committee and has tended to occupy the position for many years. The current legislative analyst has served for nearly 30 years.

With a staff of 50 (about 44 professionals and 6 administrative staff), the LAO is divided into subject area sections (such as health, criminal justice, social services) headed by directors who train staff and review their work. Professional staff members generally have master's degrees in fields such as public policy, economics, public administration, and business, as well as strong analytical and quantitative backgrounds. Each professional staff person is responsible for and becomes expert in a specific portion of the state budget. In 1999 the LAO budget was $4.6 million.

The U.S. Congressional Budget Office

The Congressional Budget Office (CBO) was established as part of the Congressional Budget and Impoundment Control Act of 1974. The Budget and Accounting Act of 1921 had centralized the budget process under the authority of the executive; over the next half century the president had acquired greater and greater influence over the budget by virtue of his growing control over budget and economic information.[4] Congress, by contrast, had not developed a similar capacity. It worked through a fragmented web of committees, relying on the president as its principal source of budget and economic information. The 1974 Act created a new, more coherent congressional budget process and created House and Senate Budget Committees to oversee the new budget process. The act also created the Congressional Budget Office to provide committees with independent budget and economic information.

Each year the CBO issues three major reports designed to assist the budget committees and to aid Congress in its work on the budget:

1. A report on the economic and budget outlook for the United States, estimating spending and revenue over the next 10 years
2. A report, usually released within a month of the release of the president's budget proposal, analyzing and independently reestimating the president's budget
3. A report presenting various options for the budget, including spending cuts and increases, tax cuts and increases, and suggested implications of broad policy choices.

In addition to these annual reports, the CBO analyzes the spending and revenue effects of legislative proposals and estimates the costs of pending legislation. As part of the Unfunded Mandates Reform Act of 1995, the CBO is also responsible for identifying the costs related to legislation containing federal mandates on state, local, and tribal governments, as well as on the private sector.

The CBO produces reports and studies analyzing specific policy and program issues related to the budget. These in-depth studies, designed to inform the congressional budget process, may cover longer-term issues not dealt with in the annual budget process. In-depth studies have included reports on the long-term budgetary pressures likely to develop with the aging of the baby-boom generation (people born between 1946 and 1964), a spending issue far beyond the budget horizon lawmakers generally consider. The statute creating the CBO requires agencies of the executive branch to provide the CBO with the information it needs to perform its duties and functions.

The CBO carries out its responsibilities with a staff of about 230 and a 2005 appropriation of just under $35 million. The director of the CBO is appointed jointly by the speaker of the House of Representatives and the president pro tempore of the Senate based on the recommendations of the budget committees of each house. They serve four-year terms; there is no limit on the number of times they can be reappointed.

The work of the CBO is carried out through seven divisions (for example, the division of tax analysis, the division of budget analysis). About 70 percent of the CBO's professional staff hold degrees in economics and public policy; all are officially employees of the House of Representatives (www.cbo.gov/organization/).

Each year the CBO completes about 2,000 formal or informal cost estimates of pending legislative proposals before the Congress, publishes

70–80 major reports, and testifies dozens of times before congressional committees. It makes its findings, methods of analysis, and assumptions widely available over the Internet (Anderson 2006).

The Congressional Planning and Budget Department of the Philippines

The Philippines Congress created its independent budget office in 1990, under the Secretariat of the House of Representatives. The office is modeled after the U.S. CBO.[5]

The CPBD has the following three major functions:

1. It assists the House of Representatives in formulating its agenda.
2. It provides House leaders and members with technical information, analyses, and recommendations on important social and economic policy issues.
3. It conducts analyses on the impact of legislation and conducts research and in-depth studies on identified policy issues.

CPBD publications are designed to inform House members about the implications of government policies and legislation.[6] Among its publications are policy advisories (updates on emerging policy issues), an annual macro analysis of the budget, and an analysis of the medium-term economic development plan. The CPBD gathers information to assist the House in conducting oversight and provides technical assistance to the Speaker and the Legislative Development Advisory Committee and other interagency committees. It publishes occasional papers reviewing and analyzing macroeconomic data and other information on the Philippine economy, as well as a "facts and figures" publication signaling trends and providing statistics on socioeconomic conditions in the Philippines.

The CPBD is headed by a director general, who is assisted by an executive director. Three divisions, each headed by a service director, report to the director general and the executive director. The Congressional Economic Planning Service conducts policy research on macroeconomic policy, competitiveness, and reform measures in infrastructure, industrial development, trade, and investments. The Congressional Budget Services conducts research and analysis on fiscal measures, including the macroeconomic implications of government taxing and spending. Special Project Services focuses on policy analysis and research on labor and employment, education, agriculture, and environment-oriented committees of the House of Representatives. The CPBD also has a division for support services.

Professional staff members generally hold advanced degrees in economics, finance, or public administration. In addition to its in-house staff, the CPBD makes regular use of consultants.

The Center for Public Finance Studies in Mexico

After functioning as a rubber-stamp legislature during the many decades of Partido Revolucionario Institucional (PRI) rule, the Mexican Congress became a more independent and assertive institution as the PRI's power waned in the late 1990s.[7] The Center for Public Finance Studies (CEFP), established by the House of Deputies in 1998, has helped the House play a more effective role in the budget process.

The CEFP is a technical, nonpartisan office staffed by specialists in public finance. Like the CPBD in the Philippines, it serves the House but not the Senate. It provides budget-related assistance to committees, groups within Congress, and individual members of the House. Its specific functions are to

- analyze the executive's trimester reports on the national economic situation, public finance, and public debt;
- analyze the executive's annual report on implementation of the national development plan and provide relevant information to subject area committees; and
- analyze the budget initiatives, tax laws, fiscal laws, and finance information the executive presents to the House.

In addition, the CEFP provides budget information to committees, parliamentary groups, and individual deputies as needed and maintains a library of copies of reports on finance and public debt.

A 22-member committee comprising members of the different political parties in the House of Deputies oversees the CEFP. The committee makes its decisions by consensus and, when necessary, by majority vote. The Center's director is selected by the whole House through an open competitive application process. He or she serves a five-year term, which can be renewed once. Staff are selected through an open, competitive process, not according to political affiliation.

The CEFP is divided into four divisions: macroeconomic and sectoral studies, treasury (or budgetary) studies, public budget and expenditure studies, and technology and information systems. Its Web site lists a professional staff of 27.

Mexico's more independent Congress has made additional changes to strengthen its role in the budget process since establishing the CEFP in the late 1990s. Amendments to the Mexican Constitution that became effective in 2005 require the executive to present its budget to Congress more than two months earlier than before, giving Congress more time to consider and make amendments to the draft budget. Amendments also require that the national budget be approved a month earlier (November 15 rather than December 15), giving state and local governments more time to plan for the upcoming fiscal year, which begins January 1.

The Parliamentary Budget Office of Uganda

In an effort to cool Uganda's heated and violent politics, President Yoweri Museveni instituted a no-party political system in 1986, prohibiting political parties from fielding candidates for office. A constitutional referendum ended this practice in 2005.

The Parliamentary Budget Office (PBO) was established by an act of Parliament in 2001. Like the U.S. Congressional Budget and Impoundment Control Act of 1974, the act not only created a budget office, it also created a centralized budget committee and made major changes in the role of the parliament in the budget process.

Beatrice Kiraso, primary author of the bill establishing Uganda's PBO, believes that Uganda's no-party system actually helped the National Assembly establish its budget office, because "there was no government or opposition side in Parliament, there was not majority or minority. It was easier for Members of Parliament to support a position favorable to Parliament against the Executive if it benefited or strengthened Parliament as an institution. Government was in a weaker position to whip members to its side" (Kiraso 2006: 4).

Annual PBO reports analyze local revenues, foreign inflows, expenditures, and other issues. The PBO analyzes the monthly reports that the Uganda Revenue Authority submits to the Budget Committee and the PBO, identifying whether revenue collections were on target, reasons for shortfalls (if any), and whether revenue targets should be adjusted. Using information from these reports, it has proposed to Parliament ways to widen the tax base and suggested possible methods to reduce taxes that would increase consumption.

The 2001 Budget Act requires the president to present information to the Parliament on state indebtedness. The PBO analyzes indebtedness reports on behalf of the Budget Committee and identifies issues for committee attention.

The Budget Act also requires that ministers submit an annual policy statement to Parliament showing the funds appropriated for the ministry, the funds released, and the use to which funds were put. The PBO produces quarterly budget performance reports, enabling Parliament to follow the general budget performance of different sectors during the year. It also provides Parliament with a yearly economic indicator report, as well as a report recording all of Parliament's recommendations to the government, whether the government was expected to respond, whether or not it complied, and the reasons for noncompliance.

The Budget Act expanded Parliament's role in the budget process; technical expertise provided by the PBO helps the National Assembly fulfill this new role. The new budget process gives Parliament an opportunity to review, comment on, and propose amendments to a draft executive budget, and it gives the executive time to respond by amending the draft budget and negotiating changes with the National Assembly—all before the budget is officially released.

Previously, the National Assembly's first glimpse of the government's budget figures was when the budget was read, about June 15, just before the new fiscal year, which begins July 1. Under the new system, by April 1—a full three months before the fiscal year begins—the president presents the National Assembly with an indicative revenue and expenditure framework for the next financial year. Parliament's sessional (also known as *portfolio*) committees, with the assistance of PBO economists, consider the indicative allocations and prepare reports to the Budget Committee, which may include recommended reallocations within sector budget ceilings.

The Budget Committee—on which the chairs of the 10 sessional committees sit—considers all proposals and may propose reallocations within and across sectors. The PBO helps the Budget Committee prepare a comprehensive budget report to the Speaker, who must forward it to the president by May 15. During the discussions between the executive and the legislature during the month leading up to the formal budget presentation, the executive generally makes a number of budget changes in response to the Parliament.

The PBO has positions for 21 experts, 4 of which have not been filled due to budget constraints. Professional staff members are economists with expertise in macroeconomics, data analysis, fiscal policy, and tax policy. They were drawn primarily from the Ministry of Finance, the Uganda Revenue Authority, the Central Bank of Uganda, and the Uganda Bureau of Statistics.

The Budget Act, along with the technical assistance provided through the PBO, has strengthened Parliament's role in the budget process in several ways (Kiraso 2006):

- Government now provides Parliament with three-year revenue and expenditure projections. The Budget Committee, with the expert assistance of the PBO, reports to Parliament any inconsistencies in these projections. It also reports on revenue and expenditure provisions for the following three years.

- Policy statements from ministries are now reported on time (by June 30), allowing sessional committees to scrutinize them. The PBO, in partnership with the Ministry of Finance, standardized the policy statement format. With assistance from PBO economists, committees review the policy statements. The statements must include value for money information (not just spending data) and report on the extent to which sectoral targets were achieved.
- The new Budget Act requires that every bill introduced in Parliament be accompanied by a certificate of financial implications. The PBO verifies the accuracy of these certificates and advises on the implications of the budget for that financial year. The National Assembly has made the government delay several initiatives after the PBO determined that they were not included in the current-year budget.
- The Budget Act requires that government keep supplementary expenditures to within 3 percent of what is budgeted. The PBO works closely with the ministries to ensure that these limits are adhered to.
- The PBO drafts an easy-to-understand version of the president's report on state indebtedness.

The National Assembly Budget Office of the Republic of Korea

The Republic of Korea's National Assembly Budget Office (NABO) was created through an act of the National Assembly on October 20, 2003.[8] It has two purposes: to encourage greater discipline in public spending and to allow the legislature to play a larger role in determining how the state obtains and spends its revenue. Those who drafted the act considered expanding the duties of the Budget Policy Bureau in the National Assembly Secretariat but concluded that NABO budget assistance was sufficiently unique that it merited establishing a separate agency within the Assembly.

NABO provides nonpartisan, objective information and analysis to committees and members of the National Assembly. It performs the following functions:

- Conducts research and analysis on the budget and on the performance of the government's fiscal operations
- Estimates the cost of bills proposed in the legislature
- Analyzes and evaluates government programs and medium- and long-term fiscal needs (audit function)
- Conducts research and analysis at the request of legislative committees or members of the National Assembly.

The Speaker, with the approval of the House Steering Committee, appoints the chief of the NABO, who appoints and directs a staff of 92 full-time employees (about 70 professional and 20 administrative). Professional staff members hold advanced degrees in accounting, economics, public policy, law, and related fields. Staff members are selected solely on the basis of professional competence (not political affiliation). The NABO's 2006 budget was about $12 million.

Budget offices are only as good as the information government provides them; if government ministries are unwilling to give them financial information, they cannot perform effectively. The legislation establishing the NABO requires executive agencies to provide it with the information it needs to carry out its functions. This has proven very useful in convincing reluctant agencies to provide necessary data.

Each year NABO conducts 80–90 formal cost estimates of pending legislative proposals and issues 30–40 major reports and other publications. Like the CBO in the United States, its analyses and work products are available to all members of the Assembly, as well as to the public over the Internet. Also like the CBO, NABO shares its methodologies and assumptions freely.

Proposed Budget Offices

Two national assembly budget offices appear to be very close to being established. Both are in former British colonies in Africa.

The Parliamentary Office of Fiscal Analysis of Kenya

A private member bill by Hon. Oloo Aringo, author of Kenya's "independence of Parliament" Act, was introduced in Kenya's National Assembly in March 2006.[9] The bill, which is similar to Uganda's Budget Act 2001, has the support of the government (Benson 2006).

The bill seeks to ensure that government follows principles of prudent fiscal management, including by reducing government debt, increasing transparency, and establishing predictable tax rates. It requires the government to set before the National Assembly a detailed budget statement well in advance of the new fiscal year. It establishes a Fiscal Analysis and Appropriations Committee and an Office of Fiscal Analysis, and it requires the finance minister to provide the National Assembly with specific economic and fiscal reports. It grants the permanent secretary of the Finance Ministry specific authority to obtain information required under this legislation from public officers and sets severe penalties for public officers who fail to comply. According to the bill, the Office of Fiscal Analysis "will comprise qualified budgeteers and economists," while the Fiscal Analysis and Appropriations Committee will "ideally be composed of members who have demonstrated competence or interest in the subject. Thus the two institutions will not only be reservoirs of expertise and continuity but also the fulcrum of the budgetary mechanism in the National Assembly."

While the bill has not yet been enacted into law, in 2006 Kenya's parliament created the Fiscal Analysis and Appropriations Committee, through the authority provided in its standing orders, and nominated 15 members from across party divides to sit on it. The committee is now reviewing and making some amendments to the bill, which is expected to pass in 2007 (SUNY 2006).

The National Assembly Budget and Research Office of Nigeria

The National Assembly of Nigeria is moving toward establishing a budget office.[10] The two chambers of Nigeria's National Assembly have agreed to enact legislation reforming the budget process and creating an independent, nonpartisan National Assembly Budget Office. The legislation will clarify roles and responsibilities of the legislative and executive branches of government and require that government present its budget to the National Assembly at least three months before the end of the budget year, giving the Assembly ample time to consider and pass the appropriations bill before the new fiscal year begins. The Assembly has a budget line and earmarked funds to establish the budget office.

According to the agreement worked out in the National Assembly, the National Assembly Budget and Research Office will have the following responsibilities:

- Review the budget submission of the executive to ensure that it is realistic and objectively defensible
- Provide technical assistance and briefings to relevant committees to help them understand and appraise the proposed budget
- Review, monitor, and evaluate the government's budget performance of the previous year
- Forecast economic trends, draft budget impact briefs and statements, and support committee oversight functions.

Nigeria's parliament had not passed the legislation establishing the National Assembly Budget and Research Office as of the beginning of 2007, but it appeared committed to doing so.[11]

Potential Value and Functions of Independent Budget Offices

What benefits do legislative-based, independent, nonpartisan, objective analytic budget units provide for legislatures, committees, and citizens?[12] First, independent legislative budget units break the executive's monopoly on budget information, placing legislatures on a more equal footing with the executive. In the cases of the California legislature and the U.S. Congress, legislative leaders were concerned that their budget powers were being eclipsed by those of the executive. They established budget offices to help redress that imbalance.

Budget offices simplify complexity. Executive budget agencies often fail to provide legislatures with the budget information they need; even when they provide information, it may be presented in a form too complex for legislators to understand. Effective legislative budget offices simplify complex budget information provided by executives so that legislators can understand and use it.

Independent budget offices also help promote budget transparency—not just from the executive to legislatures but to the public as well. Many legislative budget offices publish national budget information and analyses on the Internet (see, for example, reports by the CEFP at www.cefp.gob.mx and the CBO at www.cbo.gov/). Greater transparency discourages executives and executive agencies from subterfuge.

Effective budget offices can also help enhance the credibility of the budget process. Because these services encourage simplification and transparency, they help make budget forecasts easier to understand and more credible. Nonpartisan budget offices often reveal their assumptions and methods along with their findings, enabling everyone to understand the bases on which the projections are made.

Budget offices can increase accountability. Scrutiny of estimates by the executive enhances accountability. The realization that their assumptions and figures will be carefully reviewed by budget experts from a separate branch of government encourages executive branch budgeters to be more careful and precise than they might otherwise have been. In addition, the simpler, more transparent, and accountable budget resulting through the work of a legislative budget unit makes the budget process more straightforward and easier to follow. Effective legislative budget offices may also lead to greater discipline in public spending.

According to a former CBO official (Anderson 2006), independent analytic budget units have the following four core functions:

1. Make independent budget forecasts. These forecasts should be objective; take into account the forecasts of private forecasters, bankers, and experts;

and be a bit conservative, as politically it is easier to use the results of a better than forecasted economy to reduce deficits than to find last-minute spending cuts or tax increases to deal with unanticipated deficits.
2. Establish baseline estimates. These estimates should be projections, not predictions. That is, they should assume that laws in place will stay in place; possible changes should not factor into policy proposals.
3. Analyze budget proposals of the executive branch by conducting technical (not political) reviews of the budgetary estimates contained in the budget.
4. Conduct medium-term analyses. A medium-term analysis alerts policy makers and the public to possible future consequences of proposed policy actions. It also provides a basis upon which to build long-term analyses.

Independent budget units may also perform several other functions, including the following:

- Estimating costs of both executive and legislative policy proposals
- Preparing spending-cut options for legislative consideration
- Analyzing the costs to corporations, subnational governments, and the economy of regulations and mandates
- Conducting more in-depth and longer-term economic analyses
- Analyzing the impacts of proposed and actual tax policies
- Producing policy briefs explaining complex budget proposals and concepts.

In addition to these functions, some of the budget offices examined in this chapter have taken on other roles. California's LAO makes recommendations to the legislature on ways government can run more efficiently and economically. It also acts as a watchdog, ensuring that the executive complies with the letter and spirit of legislative intent. Uganda's PBO keeps a record of how well the executive has complied with parliamentary recommendations to government. The Philippines' CPBD helps formulate the legislative agenda of the House of Representatives.

Why Is the Number of Independent Budgeting Offices Growing?

Why are the numbers of legislative-based nonpartisan, independent, objective analytic budget units increasing? One reason may be that, using Schumpeter's procedural (electoral) concept of democracy,[13] there are simply more democracies today than at any other time in history. With the demise of the Soviet Union and the resulting proliferation of new nations, the dramatic reduction in military governments in Africa and Latin America, and the sharp decline in one-party states in Africa, there are also more legislatures than ever before in history—several of them with the potential to exercise some level of independent power. Independent financial expertise, such as that provided by professional nonpartisan budget units, aids them in exercising that power.

A second reason is an extension of what Huntington (1991) calls "demonstration effects" or "snowballing," the phenomenon in which successful democratization in one country provides a powerful incentive to other nations, especially countries geographically proximate and culturally similar. The demonstration effect applies not only to democracy itself but also to the spread of its infrastructure. The Philippines' CPBD is patterned after the U.S. CBO; Kenya's private member Fiscal Management Bill 2006 has much in common with Uganda's Budget Act 2001. Hon. Beatrice Kiraso, author of the Uganda act, conferred with her Kenyan counterpart, Hon. Oloo Aringo, in developing his legislation. Indeed, much of the work of the international community encouraging parliamentary strengthening involves the sharing of best parliamentary practices across regions.[14]

A third reason for the growing number of parliamentary budget offices may be the increasing demand worldwide for government transparency and accountability. The proliferation of Transparency International offices, the growth of anticorruption agencies and watchdog organizations, and the increasing number of budget transparency think tanks all indicate greater interest in and scrutiny of government finances. Legislatures need the assistance of budget experts if they are to play their role in the development and oversight of the budget and the control of government spending.

Considerations in Establishing Effective Legislative Budget Units

Independent budgets must be nonpartisan if they are to be effective. Anderson (2006) distinguishes between bipartisan (or multipartisan) and nonpartisan services. A bipartisan or multipartisan service attempts to analyze matters from the perspective of both (or all) political parties; a nonpartisan office attempts to present information objectively, not from a political perspective at all.

Legislatures employ several means to ensure that their budget units start, and stay, nonpartisan. In some (California and Mexico, for example), bipartisan or multipartisan committees oversee the units. Unit staff are selected for their professional expertise, not their political affiliation.

Nonpartisan, independent budget offices should serve all parties in the legislature, potentially providing minority parties a greater voice in the budget process than they would otherwise enjoy. Anderson notes that as independent budget units age and executives adjust to their presence, their information may become more valuable to minority than to majority powers in the legislature. Parties in power should resist the temptation to underfund, undermine, or politicize independent budget units, realizing that they may be in the opposition some day and will need access to professional budget services.

Effective legislative budget units will have their existence and their core functions codified in law, so that they cannot be easily shut down or changed to suit some political purpose. According to Anderson (2006), legislative budget units should avoid making recommendations to their legislatures; serve committees and subcommittees principally, rather than individual members; meet with representatives from all sides of an issue in order to be able to present informed and balanced analyses; and avoid the limelight.

Budget units need access to government budget information. In some countries, including the Republic of Korea and the United States, the statutes establishing the units grant them authority to compel the executive to provide it. The legislation in Kenya has taken a creative approach to meeting this need. Rather than grant the National Assembly the authority to compel government to provide budget information, it grants the Finance Ministry the authority to obtain budget information requested by the National Assembly. Public officers who do not comply face heavy fines and jail terms.

In some places the legislature established the budget office as a standalone reform to the budget process. In others legislatures established budget offices as one component of a larger budget reform. The U.S. Congressional Budget and Impoundment Control Act of 1974 not only established the CBO, it also established a new congressional budget process and budget committees in each house to manage the process. Uganda's PBO was a part of a similar reform, which, for the first time, made the National Assembly a major player in the budget process. Kenya's new budget legislation and Nigeria's proposal include parliamentary budget offices as part of a broader budget process reform.

What is an appropriate size for a legislative budget unit? Those examined in this chapter range from 21 to about 200 professional staff (table 12.1). Their size helps determine the number and frequency of services they provide, but even nations as poor as Uganda consider a parliamentary budget office a good investment. Legislatures that pay their staffs very low salaries may find it difficult to attract the level of expert budget staff needed in a budget office and may need to consider adjusting their pay levels.

Should unit responsibilities extend beyond pure budget work? Other services that some of these offices provide to legislatures are valuable.

TABLE 12.1 Characteristics of Selected Independent Budget Offices

Office	Year established	Size of professional staff	Unit evaluates programs	Unit was associated with a larger budget reform process	Unit makes policy or budget recommendations to legislature
California Legislative Analyst's Office	1941	44	Yes	No	Yes
U.S. Congressional Budget Office	1974	205	No	Yes	No
Congressional Planning and Budget Department, Philippines	1990	—	Yes	No	Yes
Center for Public Finance Studies, Mexico	1998	27	No	No, but reformed budget timetable followed a few years later	No
Parliamentary Budget Office, Uganda	2001	21	Yes	Yes	No
National Assembly Budget Office, Republic of Korea	2003	70	No	No	No

Source: Authors.
— Not available.

However, architects of new legislative budget offices should focus on their central mission and avoid diluting their effectiveness by asking budget offices to do too much.

Conclusion

Given the increasing rate at which independent parliamentary budget offices are being established, several more will probably appear over the next decade. In addition to Kenya and Nigeria, which appear close to establishing budget units, interest has been expressed in Ghana, Guatemala, Thailand, Turkey, and Zambia. Other countries may also be interested in establishing such bodies.

Legislatures with longstanding traditions of nonpartisan parliamentary services (as exist in many Commonwealth nations with professional secretariats) may have an easier time establishing professional, nonpartisan budget offices than other countries. Legislatures in systems of divided government—where the legislative and executive are elected independently of each other—will have more incentive to develop independent budget offices than will their counterparts in true parliamentary systems. In a true parliamentary system, when the party or coalition controlling the legislature selects a government to represent it, it has little incentive to use parliament's resources to develop professional capabilities to challenge that government. Legislatures without a tradition of nonpartisan staff, and those whose entire administrations consist of political appointees replaced after each election, may also find it difficult—albeit not impossible—to establish independent budget offices. The U.S. Congress and state legislatures in the United States have developed such professional services, and they are becoming increasingly common in Latin America.

Once legislative-based independent, professional, nonpartisan budget units are established, a critical challenge for institution builders is to keep them nonpartisan. When and where they succeed, they will improve the quality of government budgeting and budgets, make the budget process more transparent and easier to understand for both legislators and the public, and generally enhance the credibility of government.

Notes

1. The terms *legislative budget office* and *parliamentary budget office* are used interchangeably in this chapter.
2. Much of the information on California's Legislative Analyst's Office is taken from Hill (2003a, 2003b); Vanzi (1999); and www.lao.ca.gov.

3. California is one of the U.S. states that allows citizens to petition the government to place special initiatives (such as tax cuts) on statewide ballots. The LAO prepares fiscal analyses of all such measures.
4. Much of the information for this section comes from CBO Director Dan Crippen (2002).
5. Much of the information on the CPBD comes from the Congressional Planning and Budget Department Web site (www.geocities.com/cpbo_hor/).
6. Unlike the LAO and the CBO, the CPBD serves only one house of the nation's two-house legislature.
7. This shift in power is illustrated by the dramatic reduction in the percentage of executive branch (relative to legislative branch) proposals enacted into law in the early years of the 21st century. In the spring 2001 term, 48 percent of legislation enacted into law was initiated by the president. Just four years later, in the spring 2004 term, that percentage had fallen to 7.1 percent (Weldon 2004).
8. This section draws on Park (2006).
9. Much of the information on the proposed Kenya Budget Office comes from the Fiscal Management Bill 2006, introduced in the National Assembly on March 24, 2006.
10. This section draws on Nzekwu (2006).
11. The chair of the House of Representatives Committee on Media, the Honourable Abike Dabiri, stated in a January 2007 interview, "We want to ensure that we have a National Assembly Budget Office. It is a legacy that we must ensure that this current National Assembly leaves behind, because without the budget office we cannot function effectively, we can't really perform the oversight functions and monitor the budget as it should be" (Akinola 2007).
12. Several of these benefits were presented by Barry Anderson, former Acting and Deputy Director of the U.S. Congressional Budget Office (Anderson 2006).
13. Samuel Huntington (1991) uses the Schumpeterian minimal definition of *democracy* when he defines a political system as democratic to the extent that its most powerful collective decision makers are selected through fair, honest, and periodic elections in which candidates freely compete for votes and in which virtually all the adult population are eligible to vote.
14. The World Bank Workshop on Parliamentary Budget Offices, held in Bangkok on May 15–17, 2006, was designed to share international practices regarding the establishment of parliamentary budget offices.

References

Akinola, Wale. 2007. "Nigeria: Why House Won't Intervene in Obasanjo/Atiku Feud Now." *Vanguard* (Lagos), January 23.

Anderson, Barry. 2006. "The Value of a Nonpartisan, Independent, Objective Analytic Unit to the Legislative Role in Budget Preparation." Paper presented at the World Bank Institute Workshop on Parliamentary Budget Offices, May 15–17, Bangkok.

Benson, Kathuri. 2006. "MPs Get Green Light on the Budget Office." *The Standard*. (Kenya), May 16.

Crippen, Dan. 2002. "Informing Legislators about the Budget: The History and Role of the U.S. Congressional Budget Office." Available at www.cbo.gov/ftpdocs/35xx/doc3503/CrippenSpeech.pdf.

Hill, Elizabeth G. 2003a. "California's Legislative Analyst's Office: An Isle of Independence." *Spectrum: The Journal of State Government.* www.lao.ca.gov/staff/journal_articles/lao_island.aspx.

———. 2003b. "Nonpartisan Analysis in a Partisan World." *Journal of Policy Analysis and Management.* www.lao.ca.gov/staff/journal_articles/NonPartisan_Analysis.aspx.

Huntington, Samuel. 1991. *The Third Wave: Democratization in the Late 20th Century.* Norman: University of Oklahoma Press.

Johnson, John K. 2005. "The Role of Parliament in Government." World Bank Institute, Washington, DC.

Johnson, John K., and Robert Nakamura. 1999. "A Concept Paper on Legislatures and Good Governance." United Nations Development Programme, Management Development and Governance Division, New York.

Kiraso, Beatrice Birungi. 2006. "Establishment of Uganda's Parliamentary Budget Office and Parliamentary Budget Committee." Paper presented at the World Bank Institute Workshop on Parliamentary Budget Offices, May 15–17, Bangkok.

Norton, Philip. 1993. *Does Parliament Matter?* New York: Harvester Wheatsheaf.

Nzekwu, Greg. 2006. "Nigeria: Role of National Assembly in Budget." Paper presented at the World Bank Institute Workshop on Parliamentary Budget Offices, May 15–17, Bangkok.

Park, Jhungsoo. 2006. "Budget Control and the Role of the National Assembly Budget Office in Korea." Paper presented at the World Bank Institute Workshop on Parliamentary Budget Offices, May 15–17, Bangkok.

Santiso, Carlos. 2005. "Budget Institutions and Fiscal Responsibility: Parliaments and the Political Economy of the Budget Process." Chapter prepared for the 27th Regional Seminar on Fiscal Policy, United Nations Economic Commission for Latin America, Santiago.

Schick, Allen. 2002. "Can National Legislatures Regain an Effective Voice in Budget Policy?" *OECD Journal on Budgeting* 1 (3): 15–42.

SUNY (State University of New York) Albany. 2006. *Quarterly Activity Report* 6 (July–September).

Vanzi, Max. 1999. "Liz Hill: Here Today, Here Tomorrow. *California Journal* (July). Available at www.lao.ca.gov/staff/press_awards/lhill_cal_journal_7-99.html.

Von Hagen, J. 1992. "Budgeting Procedures and Fiscal Performance in the European Communities." Commission of the European Communities, Directorate-General for Economic and Financial Affairs, Economics Paper 96.

Wehner, Joachim. Forthcoming. "Back from the Sidelines? Redefining the Contribution of Legislatures to the Budget Cycle." World Bank Institute, Washington, DC.

Weldon, Jeffrey. 2004. "The Spring 2004 Term of the Mexican Congress." Center for Strategic and International Studies, Washington, DC.

13

Strengthening Public Accounts Committees by Targeting Regional and Country-Specific Weaknesses

RICCARDO PELIZZO AND F. RICK STAPENHURST

Two sets of factors appear to be critical to the success of a public accounts committee (PAC): its institutional design and the behavior of its members (Stapenhurst and others 2005). This chapter examines these factors in a broad set of regions in order to determine whether PACs can be strengthened to target regional and country-specific weaknesses. The first section describes the role of legislatures in financial oversight and presents a general concept of public financial accountability. It underlines the critical role PACs play and their widespread use throughout the Commonwealth and elsewhere. The second section discusses the institutionalization of PACs, their terms of reference, and the activities they perform. The third section summarizes the findings of a survey of PACs that sought to identify the factors associated with success. The last section identifies obstacles to effective performance and suggests possible ways of overcoming them.

Legislatures and Public Financial Accountability

Legislatures perform three functions: representative, legislative, and oversight (Pasquino and Pelizzo 2006; Sartori 1987). They perform a representative function in that they represent the will of the people, the legitimate source of authority in democratic countries. They perform a legislative function because, in addition to introducing legislation on their own, they have the power to amend, approve, and reject government bills. They perform an oversight function, ensuring that governments implement policies and programs in accordance with the wishes and intent of the legislature. They can undertake this oversight function by overseeing the preparation of a given policy (ex ante oversight) and by overseeing the execution and implementation of a given policy (ex post oversight) (Maffio 2002).

Though most legislatures have the power to hold the government accountable for its actions and policies, differences in the form of government and other constitutional arrangements create considerable variation in the tools they use to perform their oversight function. These tools include legislative committees, questions in the legislature, interpellations, debates, the estimates process, scrutiny of delegated legislation, private members' motions, and adjournment debates that allow legislators to raise issues relating to the use or proposed use of governmental power, to call on the government to explain actions it has taken, and to require it to defend and justify its policies or administrative decisions (Pelizzo and Stapenhurst 2004a, 2004b).

One tool a legislature can use to enhance oversight of the financial operations of government is a specialized committee. In the "Westminster model" of democracy (Lijphart 1999), the committee is known as a PAC.[1] The PAC is the audit committee of the legislature, the core institution of public financial accountability.

Legislatures need useful information to perform their representative, legislative, and oversight functions effectively, as Frantzich (1979) pointed out more than two decades ago. PACs, like legislatures and legislative committees, need information to perform their task effectively. This information is generally provided by the legislative auditor, or auditor general. The auditor reports to the legislature and the public at large on whether public sector resources are appropriately managed and accounted for by the executive branch of the government.

Following implementation of a government's budget, a legislative auditor audits government accounts, financial statements, and operations. In most countries, this audit is followed by the legislature's consideration of the audit findings, which may include value-for-money and performance auditing as well as financial or compliance auditing. If the legislatures' role in the budget process is effective, legislative recommendations to the executive—based on the deliberation on audit findings put forward by the auditor—are reflected in future budgets, thus allowing for continuous improvements in public financial accountability.

The exact nature of the relation and interaction between the legislature and the auditor depends partly on the model of the legislative auditor and the reporting relationship to the legislature. In most Commonwealth countries, the legislative auditor is the auditor general, whose office is a core element of parliamentary oversight; he or she reports directly to parliament and the PAC. In some countries, such as Australia and the United Kingdom, the auditor general is an officer of parliament, which guarantees his or her independence from the executive. In other countries, such as India, the auditor general is independent of both the executive and the legislature.

Organization of PACs across the Commonwealth

PACs are usually legislative standing committees of the lower chamber of parliament. In Australia and India, the PAC is a bicameral committee.

In some countries, the PAC is established by the country's constitution. This is the case in Antigua and Barbuda, Bangladesh, the Cook Islands, Kiribati, the Seychelles, St. Vincent and the Grenadines, Trinidad and Tobago, and Zambia. In other countries, the existence of the PAC is institutionalized by the standing order of the legislature. This is the case in Canada, Guyana, India, Jamaica, Malta, Tanzania, and Uganda. In a third group of countries, which includes Australia and the United Kingdom, the PAC is instituted by an act of parliament.

The size of the PAC varies from country to country. There are 17 members in Canada, 22 in India, and 7 in Malta. The distribution of seats within the PAC corresponds, as much as possible, to the distribution of seats in the legislature. This means that the government party (or the government coalition) controls a majority of the seats in the PAC.

To counterbalance the power of the majority in the PAC, the opposition party is generally given the chairmanship of the PAC. This was the case in two-thirds of the PACs studied by McGee (2002). In some countries, such as India and the United Kingdom, this practice is the result of "a very strong convention" (McGee 2002: 66). In other countries it is codified by the same norms and rules that establish the PAC itself. For example, the standing orders of Malta's parliament establish "one of the members nominated by the Leader of the Opposition and so designated by him in consultation with the Leader of the House shall be appointed as Chairman of the Public Accounts Committee." The standing orders of Tanzania's parliament establish that "the Chairperson for the Public Account Committee shall be elected from amongst the Members of the Committee from the Opposition."

Giving chairmanship of the PAC to the opposition suggests that it performs two basic functions. First, it reequilibrates the balance of power between the government and the opposition. Second, it performs a symbolic function. The fact that the chair of the PAC is a member of the opposition indicates the willingness of both the majority and the minority to operate within the PAC in a perfectly bipartisan manner.

Australia represents an interesting exception to this general trend. There the chair of the PAC is generally a member of the parliamentary majority. This choice is motivated by the fact that "in Australia it is considered advantageous to have a government Member as Chair, as this can assist with the implementation of the PAC's recommendations. It is regarded as the duty of the Chair to advocate that the PAC's recommendations be taken up and implemented by the government. This can involve behind the scenes work persuading reluctant ministers to act. A government Member can do this more effectively than an opposition Member who as political opponent will not have the confidence of the ministers" (McGee 2002: 66).

Across the Commonwealth, there is considerable variation in PACs' terms of reference and modus operandi. In some countries the terms of reference are narrowly defined; in these countries PACs concentrate exclusively on financial probity. In other countries PACs look not only at financial probity but also at the efficiency and effectiveness of programs in achieving the objectives for which they were established. Like any other standing committee, the PAC has the power to investigate and examine all the issues referred to it by the legislature. It can also investigate some specific issues, such as the government's accountability to the legislature with regard to the expenses approved by the government, the effectiveness and the efficiency of the policies enacted by the government, and the quality of the administration.

There is considerable variation regarding the relation between the auditor general and the PAC, the status of the PAC within the legislature, how the PAC conducts its business, how the PAC reports to the legislature, and how the government is required to follow up on PAC recommendations. (These and related issues are examined in detail in McGee 2002.) An important feature in virtually all jurisdictions is the fact that PACs do not question the desirability of a particular policy; this remains the mandate of legislative departmental committees. Rather, PACs examine the efficiency and effectiveness with which policy is implemented.

Depending on the scope of their mandate, PACs may be given additional and more specific powers to perform their tasks. They may, for example, be given the power to examine the public accounts, the comments on the public accounts, and all reports drafted by the auditor general and the national audit office. The PAC may also have the power to conduct, directly or indirectly, some investigations; to receive all documentation it considers necessary to adequately perform its functions; to invite government members to attend the meetings of the PAC and respond to PAC members' questions; to publicize its own conclusions; to report to the legislature; and to suggest to government how to modify its course of action when necessary.

What Factors Contribute to the Success of a PAC?

Until recently, very little was known about the effectiveness of PACs. No comparative study had systematically investigated whether, and to what extent, PACs contributed to effective oversight of government activities and expenses. Recent research conducted by the World Bank Institute and the Commonwealth Parliamentary Association has generated interesting survey data (Pelizzo and others 2006; Stapenhurst and others 2005). The survey questionnaire was sent to the chairs of 51 national and state/provincial parliaments in Commonwealth countries in Africa, Asia, Australasia, Canada, the Caribbean, and the United Kingdom. These data are used here to assess the achievements of PACs and to identify conditions and factors that help PACs work well.

The success rate of PACs varies significantly both across and within regions, depending on the nature of the results the PAC seeks to achieve. PACs seem to be most successful acting as catalysts for enhancing implementation of policy decisions and improving the availability of government information to the legislature. They are less successful at catalyzing legal or disciplining action against errant civil servants. However, survey evidence indicates substantial regional variations (table 13.1). In Australasia, Canada, and the Caribbean, the acceptance and implementation of the recommendations of the PAC are regarded as the most frequently achieved results. In Africa and South Asia, by contrast, the acceptance of the recommendations and the government's provision of better information are considered the two most frequently achieved outcomes. In the United Kingdom, the acceptance and implementation of the PAC's recommendations as well as the government's provision of better information are regarded as the most common results achieved.

TABLE 13.1 Percentage of PAC Chairs Who Report that PAC "Frequently" Achieved Various Results, by Region

Result	Africa	Australasia	Canada	Caribbean	South Asia	United Kingdom
Recommendations accepted	36	75	50	50	90	100
Recommendations implemented	18	75	50	50	70	100
Legislation modified	20	12	0	25	20	33
Information improved	36	57	25	25	80	100
Legal action taken	9	0	25	25	40	0
Disciplinary action taken	30	0	25	25	56	0
Sample size	11	9	4	7	10	3

Source: Stapenhurst and others 2005.

Survey respondents were also given a list of factors that could be beneficial to the PAC's effective performance and asked to indicate whether they considered those factors very important, important, or not important. Following Stapenhurst and others (2005), these factors are grouped into three categories: the formal powers of the PAC, the composition of the PAC, and the practices and procedures of the PAC.

Formal Powers

Five formal powers of the PAC emerge as most important: the power to make recommendations and publish findings; freely choose the subjects for examination; investigate all past, present, and committed government expenditures; hold the government accountable for its spending; and examine the public accounts (table 13.2).

Composition

The second set of factors concerns the composition of the PAC. These factors include the balanced representation of all major political parties and the exclusion of government members. The mission of a PAC is to investigate the activities of the government, especially with regard to the use of public funds and resources. In order to perform its oversight activity, the PAC has

TABLE 13.2 Percentage of PAC Chairs Who Consider Various Formal Factors "Very Important" to PAC Success, by Region

Factor	Africa	Australasia	Canada	Caribbean	South Asia	United Kingdom
Power to make recommendations and publish findings	91	100	100	100	100	100
Power to choose subjects for examination	73	100	100	71	100	100
Power to investigate or review all past, current, and committed government expenditures	64	100	75	100	100	100
Clear focus on holding government accountable for spending	90	87	100	86	90	100
Permanent reference to examine public accounts	64	78	100	100	80	100
Power to compel witnesses to answer questions	100	78	75	71	100	100
Power to call independent witnesses	82	100	75	100	78	33
Power to compel officials to attend and be held accountable for administrative performance	73	56	25	100	67	67
Power to make legislative auditor perform specific tasks	56	57	75	100	67	67

(*continued*)

TABLE 13.2 (*continued*)

Factor	Africa	Australasia	Canada	Caribbean	South Asia	United Kingdom
Power to hold in camera meetings if dealing with sensitive issues	55	78	50	86	75	67
Permanent reference to examine all reports of legislative auditor	86	50	100	86	83	100
Clear focus on administrative policy and not on whether policies are good or bad	50	44	25	43	78	100
Power to hold meetings and conduct inquiry even when legislature not in session	64	56	100	43	90	33
Power to hold press conferences and issue press releases	64	33	50	86	57	67
Sample size	11	9	4	7	10	3

Source: Stapenhurst and others 2005.

to be free to conduct its business without government interference. Freedom from government interference would be difficult to achieve if government members also served as members of the PAC. If members of parliament (MPs) already serving in the cabinet were allowed to serve on the PAC, they might try to slow or mislead the investigative action of the commission in order to protect the cabinet. Even if they did not do so, their presence in the PAC would impair the proper functioning of the committee.

McGee's (2002) study reveals that PACs are not the most appealing commissions on which MPs can serve. Some MPs fear that serving on a PAC requires much work with little visibility, that serving on a PAC is not adequately rewarded at the ballot box, and that there is, therefore, no electoral incentive to serve on a PAC. The absence of electoral incentives is also coupled with the absence of partisan incentives (or the presence of partisan disincentives). MPs fear that serving on a PAC may get them in trouble with their own parties. MPs belonging to the majority party (or coalition) worry that serving on a PAC may force them to choose between loyally serving their party (by not performing the committee duties) and loyally serving the PAC (and alienating their own party). If MPs with appointments in the cabinet were allowed to serve in the PAC, their presence would provide younger MPs with an incentive to favor partisan interests over the interests of the committee. The committee would end up functioning in a very partisan manner or become totally unable to function as it should.

A third reason why cabinet ministers (and undersecretaries) should not be permitted to serve on a PAC is that even if the presence of government officials would not negatively affect the functioning of the PAC, it would affect the credibility of the PAC and its deliberations, which are the PAC's true assets. For these reasons, government members should not be allowed to serve.

How important are these factors for a PAC's successful functioning? Most respondents in the World Bank Institute/Commonwealth Parliamentary Association survey reported that the composition of the PAC is important. There was some cross-regional variation as to whether maintaining balanced representation was more important than excluding MPs with cabinet posts (table 13.3). Chairs from Canada, the Caribbean, and South Asia agreed that achieving balanced representation of the various parties in the committee is more important than excluding MPs with cabinet posts. In contrast, PAC chairs from Africa and Australasia reported that excluding MPs with cabinet appointments is more important than maintaining balanced partisan representation within the committee. Chairs from the United Kingdom were evenly divided.

TABLE 13.3 Percentage of PAC Chairs Who Consider Alternative Compositional Factors "Very Important" to PAC Success, by Region

Factor	Africa	Australasia	Canada	Caribbean	South Asia	United Kingdom
Balanced representation of various parties	91	63	100	86	100	100
Exclusion of MPs with cabinet posts	100	89	75	83	80	100
Sample size	11	9	4	7	9	3

Source: Stapenhurst and others 2005.

Practices

A third set of factors—the practices adopted by the PACs and their members—may facilitate success. To identify which practices and dynamics could improve PAC performance, the survey conducted by the World Bank Institute and the Bank's South Asia Region Financial Management Unit asked respondents to assess the importance of 18 practices (table 13.4).

Respondents reported that keeping the records of the meetings was one of the most important ways to improve PAC performance. They also noted that PAC performance was greatly enhanced when members were appointed to the committee for the whole term of the legislature. Respondents suggested that PAC performance was significantly improved when committee members did their homework before attending PAC meetings. These practices were considered important or very important by almost all respondents. Keeping transcripts was considered very important by all PAC chairs from Canada, the Caribbean, South Asia, and the United Kingdom; by 89 percent of chairs from Australasia; and by 73 percent of African chairs. This feature was the most important condition for the success of a PAC's activities. The appointment of the committee for the whole legislative term was regarded as very important by all chairs from Canada and the United Kingdom. It was also considered very important by chairs in the Caribbean (86 percent), South Asia (83 percent), Australasia (75 percent), and Africa (56 percent).

The second most important condition for the success of a PAC was appointing a committee for the entire duration of the legislature. Preparation before the meetings was unanimously regarded as very important by British

TABLE 13.4 Percentage of PAC Chairs Who Consider Various Practices and Procedures "Very Important" to PAC Success, by Region

Factor	Africa	Australasia	Canada	Caribbean	South Asia	United Kingdom
Transcripts kept	73	89	100	100	100	100
Committee appointed for life of parliament	56	75	100	86	83	100
Advance preparation before the meetings	91	67	75	57	100	100
Close working relationship between members from different parties	82	56	50	83	100	100
Comprehensive response from government	64	89	67	71	90	67
Annual report to the legislature; report debated	100	43	25	100	100	67
Effective follow-up procedures	82	63	75	57	90	67
Close working relationship and research reports from legislative auditor	55	33	75	71	100	100
Independent technical expertise and research support for hearings	70	67	33	50	86	100
Separate subcommittees for groups of related departments	55	0	33	67	40	0
Strategic prioritization of items for committee review	63	22	0	43	70	33

(*continued*)

TABLE 13.4 (continued)

Factor	Africa	Australasia	Canada	Caribbean	South Asia	United Kingdom
Meeting place suitable for media and public access	56	75	75	50	66	67
Televised public hearings	33	0	0	80	40	67
Committee members with at least two years of prior committee experience	56	14	0	14	33	0
Committee members with prior administrative or business experience	38	13	0	29	33	0
Extra pay or other incentives for members to participate in hearings	75	14	0	0	67	0
Sample size	11	9	4	7	10	3

Source: Stapenhurst and others 2005.

and South Asian respondents. It was important to 91 percent of respondents in Africa, 75 percent in Canada, and 67 percent in Australasia.

Preparation before the meeting was the third most important condition for a PAC's effective performance. Bipartisanship and the bipartisan functioning of the PAC were considered to be the fourth most important practice (or dynamics). All of the British and South Asian chairs reported that a close working relationship across party lines is a very important determinant of success. Chairs from all other regions except Canada agreed. More than 80 percent of the African and Caribbean respondents consider it very important that there be a close working relationship between the committee members regardless of their partisan affiliation.

Across regions a comprehensive response to the recommendations from government was regarded as the fifth most important determinant of effectiveness and success. This factor is regarded as more important than making an annual report to the legislature, having effective follow-up procedures to check whether the government acted on the PAC's recommendations, and having a close relationship with the legislative audit.

Obstacles to Effective Performance and Possible Ways of Overcoming Them

Oversight potential does not always translate into effective oversight. This section identifies which conditions may prevent PACs from functioning effectively.

The first obstacle is partisanship, whereby some PAC members use the investigative powers of the PAC to promote their own political fortunes (along with those of their respective parties). This problem is not due to institutional factors; it is a behavioral problem. However, insofar as institutions provide incentives for (political) behavior, it is possible to find some institutional solutions to these problems. To minimize the risk of partisan conflicts within a PAC, for example, in many legislatures the chairmanship is assigned to a member of the opposition. In Australia, where the chair belongs to the majority party, the importance of reaching unanimous decisions on suggestions and recommendations is emphasized. To minimize partisan tensions within the PAC, many PACs stress that their mandate is not to assess the political value or the content of the policies enacted by the government but to determine whether policies are implemented in an efficient and effective manner.

These steps are not sufficient to ensure bipartisan cooperation. Additional steps must therefore be taken.

Upon joining the PAC, new members could be asked to agree to a (formal or informal) code of conduct in which they pledge their loyalty to the efficient, nonpartisan functioning of the committee. PAC chairs could use this pledge to induce members to perform their functions and respect their institutional duties.

A second, and more serious, problem impinging on the effectiveness of the PAC's activity is the fact that governments sometimes have little interest in (if not open aversion to) the legislative oversight of their activities. Some governments consider legislative oversight as an improper intrusion into their own sphere of influence. Others think that PAC members are not sufficiently informed or competent to formulate suggestions, criticisms, or observations worthy of their attention. This is a serious problem, as it indicates a very poor understanding of the functions that executives and legislatures perform in parliamentary systems, in which the government is supposed to govern and the parliament is supposed to check on how it does so. Governments that try to avoid legislative controls or consider them as obstacles to effective government action have an imperfect understanding of how a parliamentary system works.

This imperfect understanding represents a problem not only in newly established democracies or democratizing regimes, which have, by definition, limited experience in the functioning of democratic institutions, but also in established and consolidated democracies. The Australian case is emblematic. Between 1932 and 1951, the PAC of the Australian Parliament never met because the government—which refused to recognize the benefits of the PAC—decided that the PAC's meetings were not necessary.

The sound functioning of the PAC is seriously threatened (and possibly compromised) in countries in which corruption and other forms of improper behavior (such as conflict of interests) are tolerated. If there is no demand for good governance—for efficient, effective, transparent, and honest governance—by civil society, the political class has no incentive to use oversight mechanisms to check and possibly improve the quality of governance.

Notes

1. The term *Westminster model of democracy* was coined by political scientist Arend Lijphart (1999), who used the term interchangeably with *majoritarian mode* to refer to a model of democracy defined by the concentration of executive power in one-party bare majority cabinets, cabinet dominance, a two-party system, majoritarian and disproportional systems of elections, pluralism of interest groups, a unitary and centralized government, the concentration of legislative power in a unicameral legislature, constitutional flexibility, the absence of judicial review, and a central bank controlled by the executive. The structure and function of the PAC date back

to the reforms initiated by William Gladstone, when he was chancellor of the exchequer in the mid-19th century. The first PAC was established in 1861 by a resolution of the British House of Commons. Replicated in virtually all Commonwealth and many non-Commonwealth countries, PACs are seen as the apex for financial scrutiny and have been promoted as a crucial mechanism for facilitating transparency in government financial operations.

References

Frantzich, Stephen E. 1979. "Computerized Information Technology in the U.S. House of Representatives." *Legislative Studies Quarterly* 4 (2): 255–80.

Lijphart, Arend. 1999. *Patterns of Democracy*. New Haven, CT: Yale University Press.

Maffio, Roberta. 2002. "Quis custodiet ipsos custodes? Il controllo parlamentare dell'attività di governo in prospettiva comparata." *Quaderni di Scienza Politica* 9 (2): 333–83.

McGee, David. 2002. *The Overseers: Public Accounts Committees and Public Spending*. London: Pluto Press.

Pasquino, Gianfranco, and Riccardo Pelizzo. 2006. *Parlamenti democratici*. Bologna: Il Mulino.

Pelizzo, Riccardo, and Rick Stapenhurst. 2004a. "Legislatures and Oversight: A Note." *Quaderni di Scienza Politica* 11 (1): 175–88.

———. 2004b. "Tools of Legislative Oversight." Policy Research Working Paper 3388, World Bank, Washington, DC.

Pelizzo, Riccardo, Rick Stapenhurst, Vinod Sahgal, and William Woodley. 2006. "What Makes Public Accounts Committees Work? A Comparative Analysis." *Politics and Policy* 34 (4): 774–93.

Sartori, Giovanni. 1987. *Elementi di teoria politica*. Bologna: Il Mulino.

Stapenhurst, Rick, Vinod Sahgal, William Woodley, and Riccardo Pelizzo. 2005. "Scrutinizing Public Expenditures: Assessing the Performance of Public Accounts Committees in Comparative Perspective." Policy Research Working Paper 3613, World Bank, Washington, DC.

Index

Boxes, figures, notes, and tables are indicated by b, f, n, and t, respectively.

accountability, 3, 4, 184, 373
   alternatives to traditional mechanisms of, 261, 262t8.2
   answerability and enforcement aspects of, 138–40
   bias as source of failure of, 141–44
   and Bolivia's Law of Popular Participation, 213–20, 229nn15–17
   and budget offices, 371
   capture as source of failure in, 141–44
   changes in roles of actors in, 171
   and civil service, 162–64, 179n3, 293–94, 300–301nn7–8
   and committee systems, 155–57
   concepts in accountability systems, 136–48, 179n1
   definitions of, 60, 136
   and democracy, 17–18, 60–61
   and donor-government relationships, 173–75, 179nn4–6
   and elections, 148–54
   to electorate, 169–70
   external, 7, 61
   failures in, 141–44, 176–78
   financial and programmatic, 117–18
   formal vs. informal institutions of, 144–46, 191–93, 227–28nn5–8
   forms of, 16–17
   functions of, 140
   and governance, 60–62, 84n1
   horizontal, 140–41, 160, 241
   hybrids of, 178
   and legislatures, 154–57, 179n2, 380–81, 392–93n1
   link to effectiveness, 18
   link to efficiency, 18
   link to performance management, 26–27
   opposition to innovations for, 175–76
   and oversight functions, 155
   in parliamentary systems, 154–55
   and participatory budgeting in Brazil, 157b5.3
   in Philippines' Local Government Code (1991), 220–22, 229nn18–19
   political benefits of, 20
   and political parties, 158–59, 179n2
   of power-holders, 171–72
   in presidential systems, 154–55
   promotion of, 78–81, 84nn4–6
   public financial accountability, 380–81, 392–93n1
   and rule-making functions, 155
   and sale of jobs, 258–60
   in South Africa's Local Government Transition Act, 222–23

standards of, 172–73
technocratic approach to, 28
trends to improve, 170–76, 179nn4–6
vertical, 140–41, 241
weaknesses of conventional forms of, 19–20
See also audits and auditing; political institutions
accountability committees, 268–69, 279
accountability institutions, 242–43
accounting reports, 16
activists, role in preventing corruption, 278–79
actors, 171–72, 331
ADB. *See* Asian Development Bank (ADB)
administrative corruption, 7–8, 235, 285
administrative fixers, 166
administrative frameworks, 80, 203–5, 354
  accountability in, 148
  link to national laws, 199–201
  nature of, 194
  of tax policies, 288–90
  See also tax administration
Agar, Mehmet, 275, 282n6
agencies
  agencification, 68, 84n2
  antifraud and corruption mandates, 319
  central, 24, 43–44, 271
  devolution of management responsibility to, 42–43
  independent agencies to combat corruption, 296b9.4
  investigative agencies, 160–61
  as location of performance management, 24
  in United Kingdom, 68, 70
  watchdog agencies, 245t7.2, 246
agencification, 68, 84n2
agenda setting institutions, 209–10
agents
  politicians as, 138
  See also principal-agent theory
aid and aid programs, 146, 156
  and donor-government relations, 173–75, 179nn4–6

and governance ratings, 280
role in preventing corruption, 279–80
Alabama, 74
Anderson, Barry, 377n12
Andreasen, Martha, 318b10.1
Anglo Leasing, 275
anglophone model, 354, 356–57n2
Annual Operation Plan (POA), Brazil, 198, 214–18
annual reports, of public accounts committees, 391
answerability, link to accountability, 138–40
anticorruption commissions, 296–97
anticorruption strategies, 49, 51, 243–46, 319
  dealing with systemic corruption, 260–72, 281–82nn2–4
  design and implementation of, 249–50
  evidence on success of, 244, 245–46t7.2
  and the judiciary, 308–9
  policies for, 310–11
  priorities for reforms in, 243t7.1
  recommendations for improving SAIs, 320–21
  relevance of, 247–48t7.3
  as suggested by economics of crime vs. principal-agent theory, 257t8.1
Argentina, electoral process in, 152–53b5.1
Aristotle, 234
Arnstein, Sherry, 188
ARVIN framework, 194, 225–26t6A.1
Asian Development Bank (ADB), 35b2.1
  aspects of performance, 326–28
  assets, public declaration of, 267
  audit budget, 342
  auditees, 349
  audit findings, 325–36
    communicating of, 347–49
    types of and relevant elements of, 326–32
  audit objectives, 332–33
    based on assessed risks of immunization program, 340t11.4
    defining and refining of, 337–39, 340t11.4, 343–44t11.6

Index   397

auditors general, 380–81
audit reports, 315–16, 346–49, 354
audits and auditing, 8, 118, 356n1
  as accountability function, 323–34
  auditors general, 380–81
  and combating corruption, 259b8.1
  compliance audits, 312
  computer audits, 314
  controls audits, 312–13
  detecting fraud, 314–19
  findings of, 325–36, 347–49
  need for change in audit emphasis, 305–7
  objectives of, 332–33, 337–39, 340t11.4, 343–44t11.6
  a priori audits, 312
  and public sector, 8–9
  randomized, 267
  reports of, 315–16, 346–49, 354
  structure of, 332–33
  types of, 311–14
  See also performance audits and auditing; supreme audit institutions (SAIs)
Australia, 75, 160, 246, 382, 392
Azfar, Omar, xxi, 6–7, 255–83

ballot measures, 362, 377n3
Bank of Credit and Commerce International, 235
barriers
  to access, 144
  to entry, 166
  to implementation of performance management, 27–28
behavior
  of bureaucrats, 297–98
  of civil servants, 16–17, 30, 304
  corruption as form of, 308
  of officials, 16–17
  of politicians, 50, 297–98
Belarus, 272–73, 274t8.3
benchmarks of performance, 114–15
Benin, 37–38, 46
Bernstein, Carl, 269
Bhutto, Benazir, 267

biases, 177–78
  antipoor, 162–63
  and civil service accountability, 162–63
  in judicial proceedings, 161–62
  and legislatures, 154
  as source of accountability failure, 142, 143–44
bipartisanship, and public accounts committees, 391
blacklisting, 293
Bolivia, 197, 202, 227n2
Botswana, 52
bottom-up corruption, 238
bottom-up reforms, 250
Brazil, 54, 213, 229n16
  laws on local government, 197
  local participatory mechanisms in, 203–4
  media in, 270–71
  participatory budgeting in, 157b5.3, 224, 227n2, 229n20
  presidential systems, 158
  systemic corruption in, 173
bribery, 235, 236–37, 238–39
  as regressive tax, 300n3
  and sale of jobs, 259
British Broadcasting Company, 270
Bucak, Sedat, 282n6
budget offices, 9–10
  creation of, 360–61
  See also legislative budget offices
budgets and budget processes
  budget management system in China, 317
  citizen participation in, 157, 157b5.3, 184, 185–87, 208, 227nn1–2
  credibility of, 371
  and e-government, 75
  importance of citizen-centered governance on, 187, 227n2
  linking performance management to, 25–26
  link to performance targets and measures, 24, 31n2
  outputs, 118n13
  reporting, feedback, and evaluation of, 211

role of legislatures in, 360–61
Uganda, 367–68
See also participatory budgeting
Bulgaria, corruption in tax administration, 286*b*9.1
bureaucracies and bureaucrats, 7, 161
 behavior of, 297–98
 corruption in, 235, 239
 discretionary powers of, 166
 in emerging countries, 67–68
 as independent monopolies, 238
 street-level bureaucrats, 17

California, Legislative Analyst's Office, 360, 361–62, 377*n*3
Cambodia, 78
campaign finance, 150
Canada, internal audit reports, 315–16
capacity, of community-based organizations, 110–13
Capgemini, 65
capture, 235, 237
 by bureaucratic agents, 170
 and civil service accountability, 162–63
 determinants of, 239–40
 and legislatures, 154
 as source of accountability failure, 141–42
CARD. *See* Computer-Aided Administration of Registration Department (CARD), India
Cavalcanti, Severino, 273
CBO. *See* Congressional Budget Office (CBO), United States
CBOs. *See* community-based organizations (CBOs)
CEFP. *See* Center for Public Finance Studies (CEFP), Mexico
censorship, 270
Center for Global Integrity, 276, 277
Center for Public Finance Studies (CEFP), Mexico, 360, 365–66, 377*n*7
central agencies, 271
 as location of performance management, 24
 remit of, 43–44

centralization, link to corruption, 51
CenVAT, 289*b*9.2, 290
Chambers of the Attorney-General, Singapore, 48
checkposts, 290, 295*b*9.3
Chile, 246
China, 82, 317
Chr. Michelsen Institute, Bergen, Norway, 110
CIC. *See* Citizen Information Centre (CIC), India
citizen-centered governance, 186–87, 241
Citizen Information Centre (CIC), India, 295*b*9.3
citizens and citizen participation, 5, 92–93, 141, 156
 and Bolivia's Law of Popular Participation, 213–20, 229*nn*15–17
 in budgeting process, 157*b*5.3, 208–12, 228–29*nn*11–14
 and coproduction, 107–9
 and e-government, 69*t*3.3, 73–76
 in electoral process, 152–53*b*5.1
 forms of, 188
 and government performance, 122–24
 in Philippines' Local Government Code (1991), 220–22, 229*nn* 18–19
 and relationship to public officials, 188, 191, 227*n*4
 role in fighting corruption, 277
 in South Africa's Local Government Transition Act, 222–23
 through collaborative networks, 125–27
 See also citizen voice mechanisms; participatory mechanisms; voice mechanisms
citizenship, 185
citizen-state relationship, 146
citizen voice mechanisms, 184, 205–7
 and critical background constraints, 193–95, 278*nn*9–10

direct and indirect national-level frameworks for, 196–203
evaluation of, 212
formal vs. informal institutions in, 191–93, 227–28nn5–8
functional processes to maximize impact of, 207–12, 228–29nn11–14
importance of in budgeting, 185–87, 227nn1–2
local-level laws, 203–5
overview of effectiveness of, 212–13
See also citizens and citizen participation; voice mechanisms
Civic Alliance, Mexico, 156*b*5.2
civic engagement, 76
civic groups, role in accountability, 171
civic infrastructure, 125–26
civil charges, 264–65, 271
civil rights, and e-government, 76–77
civil servants
  accountability of, 244, 293–94, 300–301*nn*7–8
  behavior of, 16–17, 30, 304
  control of, 300*n*2
  salaries of, 244, 293–94, 300–301*nn*7–8
civil service, 141, 153
  accountability and the political process, 162–64, 179*n*3
  codes of practice, 41
  Malaysia, 53
  raising prestige of, 51–52
  United Kingdom, 42, 53–54
Civil Service Commission, United Kingdom, 42
civil service commissions, 42, 163–64
civil service reform, 39
  in Morocco, 38, 38*t*2.2
  in Sri Lanka, 34, 35*b*2.1, 36, 37*t*2.1, 55*n*2
civil society, 89–90
  and account4ability implications, 174–75
  achievements in Mexico, South Africa, and Zambia, 156*b*5.2

and e-government, 67*t*3.3, 69*t*3.3, 70, 73–76, 76
empowerment of, 79
and political parties, 158–59, 179*n*2
Sub-Saharan Africa, 94–95
civil society organizations (CSOs), 184, 186
  and local participatory mechanisms, 204–5
  role in voice mechanisms, 195
clientelism, 149–50, 236, 242
  reduction in, 164–70
  and reform, 167–68
clients' charter, 244
code of ethics, 297–98
codes of conduct
  operationalizing of, 48–49
  Singapore, 48
  United Kingdom, 50
collaborative networks, 3–4
  and CBOs, 110–12
  and community development, 107
  redefining performance through, 125–27
  and strategic planning, 115
collusion, 290
Colombia, 71*b*3.1
commitment, to public management reform, 34–40, 55*n*2
committee systems, 155–57
Committee to Protect Journalists, 270, 278
Commonwealth model, 43
Commonwealth Parliamentary Association (CPA), 383, 387
communities
  meetings of, 223
  and self-interest, 94–95
  See also community-based organizations (CBOs); Fairfax County, Virginia
Community and Recreation Services (CRS) programs, Fairfax County, Virginia, 100*t*4.4, 108–9, 110–19, 120–21
community-based organizations (CBOs), 90, 126

building capacity of, 110–13
link to citizen engagement, 122–23
community development, 107,
    110–13, 126
community improvement, 89, 90–95
competence, improvement of, 72–73
competition, interdepartmental, 119
complaint institutions, 212, 218
compliance audits, 312
Computer-Aided Administration of
    Registration Department (CARD),
    India, 295b9.3
computer audits, 314
Congressional Budget Office (CBO),
    United States, 360, 362–64, 373
Congressional Planning and Budget
    Department (CPBD), Philippines,
    360, 364–65, 373, 377n6
Consolidated Community Funding Pool,
    111
constituents, 209
constitutions
    and citizen voice mechanisms,
        196–97
    and PACs, 381
continuous evaluation model, 120
control risks, 336, 337
controls audits, 312–13
cooperation, and e-government, 72–73
coproduction, 90, 101
    and community development, 107
    as form of citizen engagement, 123
    transforming citizens through, 107–9
corruption, 6, 47, 52, 178, 319
    administrative, 7–8, 235, 285
    categories of, 285
    and civil service accountability link to
        political process, 162–64,
        179n3
    in Columbia, 71b3.1
    combating of
        activists, NGOs, and universities roles
            in, 277–79
        commitment of national leaders
            to, 243
        evidence on control of, 259b8.1
        independent agencies role in, 296b9.4

information technology role in,
    295–96
policy makers role in, 243–49
conclusions concerning, 249–50
costs of, 291
definition of, 234–36
detection of, 311–14, 319
distinctions in, 142–43
drivers of, 242–43
and e-government, 70, 71–72b3.1
and elections, 276–77
forms of, 235–36
in Germany, 71b3.1
grand, 7–8, 142, 235, 285
historical perspective, 234–35
Hong Kong (China), 49–51
impact of, 235, 290–91, 300nn3–5
incidental corruption, 256–58, 607
India, 71b3.1
and INTOSAI, 309–10, 311
Republic of Korea, 71b3.1
Malawi, 162b5.4
Mexico, 71–72b3.1
Namibia, 72b3.1
and need for change in audit emphasis,
    305–7
and neoinstitutional economics
    frameworks, 241–42, 250n4
and new public management
    frameworks, 240–41
overview, 233–34
petty, 7–8, 142, 235, 285
Philippines, 72b3.1
political, 7–8, 237, 285
and principal-agent models, 236–40
and revolutions, 276–77
rise in, 303–5
Singapore, 49–51
in tax administration, 292–98,
    300–301nn6–8
term usage, 307–9
Thailand, 72b3.1
United Kingdom, 50
See also anticorruption strategies;
    patronage; systemic corruption
Corruption Perception Index
    (CPI), 308

Corrupt Practices Investigation Bureau, Singapore, 49, 50
Costa Neto, Waldemar, 273
cost-benefit analysis, 331
cost centers, 100t4.4, 108–9
costs
  of accountability innovations, 175–76
  of corruption, 291
  of fieldwork programs, 345b11.3
  of participatory mechanisms, 192
  and productivity measures, 101–3
CPA. See Commonwealth Parliamentary Association (CPA)
CPBD. See Congressional Planning and Budget Department (CPBD), Philippines
CPI. See Corruption Perception Index (CPI)
creaming, 29
credibility concept, 150
crime, 97, 103
  corruption as a national crime, 292–93
  crime and punishment models, 236–37
  criminal law systems, 266
  economics of, 255, 256–58
  See also legal frameworks
Croatia, 268
CRS. See Community and Recreation Services (CRS) programs, Fairfax County, Virginia
CSOs. See civil society organizations (CSOs)
cultural factors, 150, 194–95
cultures of probity, 141
customer satisfaction, 99t4.3, 105, 331–32
customs administration, 288–89
Cutler, Allan S., 318b10.1

Dallas County, Texas, 120
DARE. See Drug Abuse Resistance Education (DARE)
data
  analysis and interpretation of, 345–46
  collection of, 104–5, 340–41, 343–44t11.6
  to conduct performance audits, 343–44t11.6
  quality of, 119
  security of, 77
  voice and nonvoice, 84n5
  warehousing of, 77
debt servicing, 290
Decamatan Development Program, Indonesia, 279
decentralization, 297
  and corruption, 51, 237, 238–39, 244, 246, 246t7.2
  impact of national-level laws on, 197–99
  and performance management, 24–25
  and service delivery, 212, 229n14
  South Africa, 191
  Uruguay, 198, 198b6.1
decision making
  biased, 143–44
  and citizen voice, 191
  institutions for, 211, 228n13
  and performance measures, 19, 118–19
Deliberative Democracy, 264
delivery of services. See service delivery
demand-side mechanisms, 184
democracy
  and accountability, 17–18, 60–61, 137, 149
  Belarus, 274t8.3
  definition, 372, 377n13
  Japan, 36
  material democracy, 65
  Schumpeterian concept of, 372, 377n13
  Westminster model of, 380, 392–93n1
democratic governance, 62, 152b5.1
democratization, 373
Department of Systems Management for Human Services (DSMHS), Fairfax County, Virginia, 110–11

descriptive findings, 326, 327t11.1
developed countries, and e-government, 64–65
developing countries, 6
  anticorruption strategies, 243
  auditing in, 8–9
  barriers to implementing performance management, 28
  and e-government, 65–66, 82
  public governance in, 66–68
  rise of fraud and corruption in, 303–5
  sale of jobs in, 259–60
development programs, conditionality-based, 173, 179n5
digital rights, 78–79, 83, 84n5
direct cost method, 101
disadvantaged groups, 143–44, 221, 229n19
discretionary powers, 166, 237, 287
divisions of labor, 140
documentation institutions, 210
domestic accountability, 146
domestic trade taxes, 289–90
donor agencies, 155–56, 156b5.2
  donor-government relationships, 173–75, 179n4
  international donor community, 300n5
downsizing, 35b2.1
Drug Abuse Resistance Education (DARE), 332b11.1
Drüke, Helmut, xxi, 3, 59–87
DSMHS. *See* Department of Systems Management for Human Services (DSMHS), Fairfax County, Virginia
Duarate, Lidio, 273
Dye, Kenneth M., xxi–xxii, 8, 303–21

e-administration, 63
East and Southern African Association of Accountants-General (ESAAAG), 352, 353
e-business, 82
economic independence, 125
economic policy regimes, and clientelism, 164–70
economic reforms, 167–68, 250

economics of crime, 255
  vs. principal–agent theory, 256–58
economics of e-government, 81
economy of inputs, 328–29
e-consultation, 74
Ecuador, 277
effectiveness, 93
  of citizen voice, 205–13
  importance of accountability for, 18
  of legislative budget offices, 373–76
  of outcomes, 331–32
  of outputs, 330–31
  of PACs, 383–91, 391–92
  of participatory mechanisms, 193–94
efficiency, 92
  efficiency of processes, 329–30
  importance of accountability for, 18
  measures of, 97–100tt4.1–4.4, 101–3, 333
  in public management, 1–4
  reports of, 333
efficiency measures, 97–100tt4.1–4.4, 101–3, 333
efficiency reports, 333
e-government, 3
  and civil society, 69t3.3, 73–76
  Columbia, 71b3.1
  conclusions concerning, 81–84
  contributions to good governance, 68–77, 84nn2–3
  and developed countries, 64–65
  and developing countries, 65–66
  effect of, 60
  funding initiatives for, 79
  in Germany, 71b3.1
  and government competence, 69t3.3, 72–73
  improving readiness for, 78–79, 84nn4–5
  India, 71b3.1
  Republic of Korea, 71b3.1
  and legal systems, 69t3.3, 76–77
  Mexico, 71–72b3.1
  Namibia, 72b3.1
  obstacles to success of, 80–81, 84n6
  overview, 62–63
  Philippines, 72b3.1

Index   403

and stakeholder involvement in, 70, 76, 79, 81
stimulating demand for, 79
Thailand, 72b3.1
used to fight corruption, 71–72b3.1
e-information, 74
elections, 148–54
  as anticorruption mechanism, 261–63, 281n3
  Belarus, 272–73
  to dismiss corrupt governments, 269
  electoral process in Argentina and United States, 152–53b5.1
  and extent of capture, 239–40
  indirect, 263, 281n3
  Indonesia, 281n3
  inspired by corruption, 276–77
  and political parties, 158–59, 179n2
  of prosecutors, 266–67
  rigged, 261
elements of performance auditing, 324–33, 343–44t11.6, 347, 348f11.2
elicitation methods, 210–11
El Salvador, 160–61
emerging countries, bureaucracy in, 67–68
employment
  absences, 257–58
  appointments of staff, 45–46
  ghost workers, 259–60, 300–301n8
  redeployment procedures, 45
  reduction in number of employees in public sector, 294, 300–301n8
  reform in, 40, 44–47, 55n4
  sale of jobs, 258–60
  and wages, 293–94, 300–301nn7–8
empowerment of citizens, 240, 241
  See also citizens and citizen participation; citizen voice mechanisms
enforcement mechanisms, 48–49
  and bias, 143
  law enforcement, 281n2
  link to accountability, 138–40
entrance conference, 334
e-participation, 69t3.3, 73–76, 81

e-procurement, 70, 72, 81, 82
equity, 94, 123–24, 125–26
e-readiness, 78–79, 84nn4–5
e-reporting, 73
ESAAAG. See East and Southern African Association of Accountants-General (ESAAAG)
e-skilling, 78
ethics
  establishing code of, 297–98
  programs for fraud prevention, 318–19
  and training for tax officers, 298
ethics offices, 246
e-transactions, 64–65
EU. See European Union (EU)
Europe, 65, 316–17
European Union (EU), 316–17, 318b10.1
evaluations, 211, 218
  of citizen voice mechanisms, 212
  continuous evaluation model, 120
  institutions for, 211
  of service delivery, 187
e-voting, 65
executives, and accountability, 17
expenditures, tracking systems of, 267
external accountability, 7, 61
external work, link to public administration, 68–70
extranet services, 76

Fairfax County, Virginia, 4
  and CBOs, 110–12
  community development through CBOs, 126
  goals and performance targets, 97–100tt4.1–4.4, 108t4.5, 113–16
  as model of performance-based budgeting, 91
  outcome measures, 97–100tt4.1–4.4, 103–5
  output measures, 96–101, 127n1
  output reporting, 108t4.5
  process measures, 105–6
  transparency and performance reporting, 120–22, 127n1

Web sites, 97–100*tt*4.1–4.4, 108*t*4.5, 121, 127*n*2
family approach to leadership, 55
feasibility of reform, 36–38
feedback, 211, 218
fieldwork programs, 334, 339, 342, 345–46
financial accountability, 117–18, 380–81, 392–93*n*1
financial administration systems, fraud in, 315–16
financial audits, 306–7, 311–12, 354
financial institutions, 279–80
financial management, 18, 24, 162–64
financial reporting, 305
findings of performance auditing, 326–32, 347–49
Finland, 65, 74–76
fire and rescue operations, output measures, 97, 98*t*4.2, 99
Fishkin, James, 264
footprints of government programs, 326–28
Ford Motor Company, 45
foreign assistance, 146
foreign governments, role in preventing corruption, 279–80
forensic audits, 313–14
formal accountability, 144–46
forums, accessibility of, 223
francophone model, 354, 356–57*n*2
fraud
  and anticorruption policies, 310–11
  Canada, 315–16
  detection of, 314–19
  government agencies antifraud mandates, 319
  and internal audits, 316
  and INTOSAI, 309–10, 311
  and need for change in audit emphasis, 305–7
  prevention programs, 318–19
  reporting of, 320
  rise in, 303–5
  standards for detecting, 319
  term usage, 307–9
  types of audits to detect, 311–14

fraud audit standards, 314
freedom of information, 76–77, 201–2, 271
freedom of information acts, 271
fringe benefits, 101–2
Fujimori, Alberto, 255, 261, 269
FUNDAR, Mexico, 156*b*5.2
funding, for e-government, 79

Gabon, 235
GAO. *See* General Accounting Office (GAO), United States
GDP. *See* gross domestic product (GDP)
General Accounting Office (GAO), United States, 316
Germany, 71*b*3.1, 73, 75, 79, 158
ghost workers, 259–60, 300–301*n*8
Githongo, John, 273, 275
Gladstone, William, 392–93*n*1
Glaser, Mark A., xxii, 3–4, 89–131
global integrity, 276
GNTP. *See* Grupo Nacional de Trabajo para la Partipacion (GNTP)
goals, Fairfax County, 97–100*tt*4.1–4.4, 108*t*4.5, 113–16
good governance
  and accountability, 61–62, 84*n*1
  contributions of e-government to, 68–77, 84*nn*2–3
  dimensions of, 62, 63*t*3.1
  significance of, 66
governance, 1, 2
  and accountability, 137
  and anticorruption strategies, 243–44, 247–48*t*7.3
  citizen-centered, 186–87, 241
  collaborative, 224
  definition of, 234
  democratic, 62, 152*b*5.1
  and e-government, 81–84
  and government auditing, 9
  impact on corruption networks, 238
  participatory, 263–64
  and performance auditing, 349–56
  and poverty reduction strategies, 174
  public governance, 60–62, 66–68, 84*n*1
  quality of, 290

related concepts of, 146–48
steering approach to, 19
survey-based system, 263–64
See also good governance
governance ratings, and aid allocation, 280
government management capacity, 215–16
government officials, use of public office for private gains, 285
Government Performance and Results Act, United States, 24, 25
governments
  accountability of, 17
  administrative environment in, 288
  anticorruption focus of, 281, 319
  antifraud mandates, 319
  audits of finances of, 267
  and community, 94–95
  competence of, 69t3.3, 72–73
  corruption in, 52
  effectiveness of, 93
  efficiency of, 92
  equity issues, 94
  improvement of performance in Sub-Saharan Africa, 124–25
  improving competence of, 72–73
  internal auditors in, 314–17
  problems in structure of, 161
  responsiveness of, 92–93, 94
  rules-driven, 237
  use of information technology to streamline services of, 295b9.3
  See also decentralization
grand corruption, 7–8, 142, 235, 285
Great Britain, internal audits in, 316–17
gross domestic product (GDP), 235
Grupo Nacional de Trabajo para la Partipacion (GNTP), 215
Guatemala, 160–61
Gutierrez, Luizo, 277

Hamburg, Germany, 75
history, 150
Hong Kong (China), 49–51, 160, 294, 296b9.4
horizontal accountability, 140–41, 160, 241

hotlines, 318–19
HRO. *See* Human Right Ombudsman (HRO)
human resource reform, 34–38, 40–41, 55n2
human resources
  appointments of staff, 45–46
  strategic framework for, 45
  See also employment
Human Right Ombudsman (HRO), 160–61
human rights, reform in, 146–47
hybrid accountability, 141

IFAC. *See* International Federation of Accountants (IFAC)
ILA. *See* individual learning account (ILA)
immunization programs, performance audits of, 335b11.2, 338t11.3, 340t11.4, 343–44t11.6, 345b11.3
impact findings, 326, 327t11.1
implementation data, 211
incentives, for improvement in performance, 258
incidental corruption, 6–7, 256–58
INCOSAI. *See* International Congress of Supreme Audit Institutions (INCOSAI)
independent agencies, 24
independent budget offices
  characteristics of, 375t12.1
  establishment of effective units of, 373–76
  growth of, 372–73, 377nn13–14
  value and functions of, 371–72, 377n12
Independent Commission against Corruption, Hong Kong, 49–50, 296b9.4
India, 8, 71b3.1, 166, 296b9.4
  civil society in, 159
  constitution, 197
  customs administration in, 289
  domestic trade taxes, 289–90
  freedom of information, 201, 202b6.3, 271

laws on local government, 197
local participatory mechanisms, 203–4
tax fraud in, 289b9.2
and taxpayers, 287
tax systems, 292, 300n6
use of information technology to combat corruption, 295b9.3
indicatorism, 29
indicators, 2, 22, 333
of good governance, 62, 63t3.1, 84n1
link to output measures, 97
individual learning account (ILA), 316
Indonesia, 159, 194, 205, 271
combating corruption in, 259b8.1, 265b8.2
elections, 281n3
influence peddling, 150, 235
informal accountability, 144–46
information
access to, 76–77, 271
and accountability, 139
asymmetry of, 149
availability of, 217–18
for budgeting, 374
dissemination of, 240
freedom of information laws, 201–22
gathering of for performance audits, 335, 336t11.2
role in performance-based budgeting, 116–17
types of in performance audits, 345–46
information and communication technologies, 64–65, 295–96
inherent risks, 336, 337
initiatives, 108t4.5, 362, 377n3
innovations, opposition to, 175–76
input economy, 328–29
inputs, 21, 329–30
inputs-processes-outputs-outcomes chain, 331
Institute of Internal Auditors, 351, 352
institutional capacity, 146–47
institutional frameworks, 5
conclusions concerning, 224, 229n20
overview, 183–85, 195–96

that support citizen voice mechanisms, 188–205, 227–28nn3–10
See also national-level laws and institutions
institutionalization, 227–28n6
institutional public-private partnerships, 84n3
institutional reform, 146–47
institutions, 188, 227n3
for citizen voice mechanisms, 209–13, 228–29nn13–14
and critical background constraints, 193–95, 278nn9–10
weaknesses in, 242–43
See also institutional frameworks; specific institution
integrated services community initiatives, 108t4.5
integrity, 1–4, 50–52
intergovernmental organizations, 151
intermediaries, in patron-client relationships, 165–67
internal accountability, 61
internal audits, 314–17, 353, 354–55
internal controls, evaluation of, 306–7
International Congress of Supreme Audit Institutions (INCOSAI), 309
International Country Risk Guide, 233–34
International Federation of Accountants (IFAC), 311
International Organization of Supreme Audit Institutions (INTOSAI), 309–10, 311, 353, 356
Internet, 76–77, 78, 83
See also e-government; information and communication technologies
Internet bus, 83
interoperable systems, 80
INTOSAI. See International Organization of Supreme Audit Institutions (INTOSAI)
investigations, 264
investigative agencies, 160–61
investments, and corruption, 291
Iraq, 316

Japan, 36, 79
Jefferson, Roberto, 273
Jenkins, Rob, xxii, 4, 135–81
Johnson, John K., xxii, 9, 359–78
journalists, 270, 273, 278
judges, random assignment of, 265–66
judicial systems, 7, 77
 and accountability, 160–62
 and anticorruption strategies, 308–9
 and e-government, 72b3.1
 to prosecute corrupt activities, 50
 random assignment of judges, 265–66

Kautiliya, 285
Kenya, 246, 374
 corruption in, 233
 leadership issues, 54–55
 Parliamentary Office of Fiscal Analysis, 361–62, 369–70
 systemic corruption in, 273, 275
Kibaki, Mwai, 273
Kiraso, Beatrice, 366
Republic of Korea, 71b3.1, 78
 National Assembly Budget Office, 360–61, 368–69

labor costs, 101–2
labor force, sale of jobs, 258–60
labor rights, 77
land records, India, 295b9.3
land-use planning, 75
LAO. *See* Legislative Analyst's Office (LAO), California
Latin America, 66
Latvia, 233
law. *See* legal frameworks
law enforcement, 281n2
Law of Popular Participation, Brazil, 213–20, 229nn15–17
law of provocation, 143
leadership
 and code of ethics, 297
 commitment to combating corruption, 243
 and performance-based budgeting, 116–17, 124–25
 and performance measures, 118–29

 and public management reform, 52–55
 and tax administration, 287–88
learning processes, initiation of, 23
legal frameworks, 5
 and accountability, 155
 anticorruption legislation, 49
 civil charges for mismanagement, 264–65
 complexity of tax laws, 286
 design of tax laws, 292, 300n6
 and e-government, 69t3.3, 76–77, 79
 enhancing for performance management, 41–44
 formal vs. informal institutions in citizen voice, 191–93, 227–28nn5–8
 impact of national laws on local government, 197
 local-level legislative frameworks, 203–5
 overview, 183–85, 195–96
 for participatory mechanisms, 193, 228nn7–8
 that support citizen voice mechanisms, 188–205, 227–28nn3–10
 See also judicial systems; national-level laws and institutions
Legislative Analyst's Office (LAO), California, 360, 361–62, 377n3
legislative budget offices, 359, 376n1
 Center for Public Finance Studies in Mexico, 360, 365–66, 377n7
 characteristics of, 375t12.1
 conclusions concerning, 376
 Congressional Planning and Budget Department of the Philippines, 360, 364–65, 373, 377n6
 establishment of effective units of, 373–76
 growth of independent budget offices, 372–73, 377nn13–14
 Legislative Analyst's Office in California, 277n3, 360, 361–62

National Assembly Budget Office of
 Republic of Korea, 360–61,
 368–69
Parliamentary Budget Office of
 Uganda, 360, 366–68, 373, 374
proposed budget offices, 361,
 369–70, 377n11
U.S. Congressional Budget Office,
 362–64, 373
value and functions of independent
 budget offices, 371–72, 377n12
legislators and legislatures, 154–57, 179n2
 accountability committees, 268–69
 and public financial accountability,
 380–81, 392–93n1
 question time, 268–69
 role of, 237
LGTA. *See* Local Government Transition
 Act (LGTA), South Africa
liberalization, and reduction in
 clientelism, 164–70
line agencies, 42–43
Local Government Code of 1991,
 Philippines, 220–22, 229nn18–19
local governments, 203–5, 222–23
 impact of national level laws on,
 197–99
 performance audit of immunization
 programs, 335b11.2
 role in preventing corruption, 271–72,
 280–81
Local Government Transition Act
 (LGTA), South Africa, 222–23
local-level legislative frameworks, 203–5
Lukashenka, Alyaksander, 272–73,
 274t8.3

Madagascar, 77
Mahathir, Mohamed, 53
Malawi, 162b5.4, 163–64, 246
Malaysia, 53, 244
Mali, 288–89
management
 civil charges for mismanagement,
 264–65
 devolution of responsibility for, 42–43
 managerial decisions, 227n4

reporting fraud and communicating
 with, 320
managerialism, 30, 80, 84n6
managerialist, 35b2.1
managers, participation in audits, 334–35
manipulation, as form of participation,
 188
Manse Forum, Finland, 74–76
market clientelism, 169
material democracy, 65, 83
Mauritius, 54
MCA. *See* Millennium Challenge
 Account (MCA)
McCourt, Willy, xxii, 2–3, 33–58
MDG. *See* Millennium Development
 Goal (MDG)
measurement-based audits, 342, 350
measurement mechanisms, 20
media, 276
 private ownership of, 282n4
 and reporting of audit findings,
 346–49
 role in controlling corruption,
 269–71, 273, 282n4
 role in preventing corruption, 277–78
members of parliament (MPs), 387
Mesic, Stjepan, 268
methodologies, 340–41, 343–44t11.6
Mexico, 54, 71–72b3.1
 Center for Public Finance Studies
 (CEFP), 360, 365–66, 377n7
 civil society achievements in, 156b5.2
Millennium Challenge Account
 (MCA), 280
Millennium Development Goal
 (MDG), 40
mobile health units, 83
mobility of economic agents, 239
modernism, 80, 84n6
modernization
 and e-government, 65
 in Latin America, 67
Moi, Daniel Arap, 273, 275
money laundering schemes, 306
monitoring, 218
 of poverty by citizens, 202–3
 of tax officials, 287

monopoly powers, 237
  and bureaucracies, 238
  and media, 282*n*4
  reduction of, 293
  of tax officials, 287
Montesinos, Vladimir, 255, 261, 269, 278
Morgan, Stephen L., xxii–xiii, 8–9, 323–57
Morocco, civil service reform in, 38, 38*t*2.2
Mozambique, 54
MPs. *See* members of parliament (MPs)
multinational corporations, 293
multiskilling, 45
multitier hierarchy approach to corruption, 237–38
Mumbai, Action Committee for Rationing, 204*b*6.4
Municipal Development Plan (PDM), Brazil, 198, 214–18
municipal governments, Brazil, 213–20, 229*nn*15–17
municipal sector strategy workshops, 2215–16
Museveni, Yoweri, 366

NABO. *See* National Assembly Budget Office (NABO), Republic of Korea
Naga City Empowerment Ordinance, Philippines, 221–22
Namibia, 72*b*3.1
Nampula province, Mozambique, 54
National Assembly Budget and Research Office, Nigeria, 361, 370, 374, 377*n*11
National Assembly Budget Office (NABO), Republic of Korea, 360–61, 368–69
National Counter Corruption Commission, Thailand, 70, 72
National Health Ministry (NHM), 335*b*11.2, 338*t*11.3, 340*t*11.4
national-level laws and institutions, 202–3
  and administrative procedures, 199–201
  constitutional provisions, 196–97
  freedom of information laws, 201–2
  laws on local government, 197–99

National Public Radio, 270
National Security Council, Turkey, 276, 282*n*5
NBOs. *See* neighborhood-based organizations (NBOs)
negative corruption, 142
neighborhood-based organizations (NBOs), 90, 93, 125–26
neoinstitutional economics frameworks, relationship to corruption, 241–42, 250*n*4
Nepal, 42–43
networked solutions, 3–4, 107, 110–12, 115, 125–27
new aid modalities, 173–75
New Institutional Economics, 227*n*3
New Public Management, 41, 42, 59, 67, 240–41
new public management frameworks, impact on corruption, 240–41
New South Wales, 296*b*9.4
newspapers, 270–72
New Zealand, 23, 73
NGOs. *See* nongovernmental organizations (NGOs)
NHM. *See* National Health Ministry (NHM)
Nicaragua, 205
Nigeria, 246, 361, 370, 374, 377*n*11
nongovernmental actors, 171–72
nongovernmental organizations (NGOs), 159, 216
  and elections, 151, 152–53*b*5.1, 153–54
  GNTP, 215
  role in preventing corruption, 278–79
nonpolitical institutions, 135
nonvoice data, 84*n*5
normative findings, 326, 327*t*11.1
North America, internal auditing in, 315–16
Norway, 110

objectives. *See* audit objectives
OECD. *See* Organisation for Economic Co-operation and Development (OECD)

officials
  elected, 237
  punitive action against corruption of, 294
  tax officials, 287, 293, 298
ombudsmen, 200, 200*b*6.2, 246, 249
online services, 65
ordinances, 221–22
Oregon, 152–53*b*5.1
Organisation for Economic Co-operation and Development (OECD), 40–41, 64, 173–74, 179*n*4, 186
organizational relations, 354
Organization of Supreme Audit Institutions, 356
organizations, choosing one for evaluation, 21–22
OTBs. *See* territorial grassroots organizations (OTBs)
outcome measures, 97–100*tt*4.1–4.4, 103–5
outcomes, 20
  effectiveness of, 331–32
  of voice mechanisms on accountability, 206–7
  and volunteerism, 108*t*4.5, 109
  vs. outputs, 331
output measures, 96–101, 127*n*1
  Fairfax County, 97*t*4.1
  and volunteerism, 108*t*4.5, 109
outputs, 20, 21, 119, 329–30
  and budgets, 228*n*13
  community and recreation services, 100–101
  effectiveness of, 330–31
  fire and rescue operations, 97, 98*t*4.2, 99
  integrated services community initiatives, 108*t*4.5
  park services, 99, 99*t*4.3
  vs. outcomes, 331
output timeliness, 330–31
oversight functions, 155, 157, 158
  and accountability, 171
  in Bolivia's Law of Popular Participation, 214, 216–20, 229*n*15
  Indonesia, 279
  and investigative agencies, 160–61
  LAO, 361–62
  of legislatures, 380–81
  Mumbai, 204*b*6.4
  and performance based–management systems, 163
  and specialized accountability institutions, 161
Ozbay, Mehmet, 275, 292*n*6

PACs. *See* public accounts committees (PACs)
Pakistan, 235, 246, 267
Palestinian Authority, 316–17
park services, output measures, 99, 99*t*4.3
Parliamentary Budget Office (PBO), Uganda, 360, 366–68, 373, 374
parliamentary budget offices. *See* legislative budget offices
Parliamentary Commissioner for Administration, United Kingdom, 50
parliamentary immunity, 269
parliamentary institutions, 154–55, 155–56, 156*b*5.2
Parliamentary Office of Fiscal Analysis, Kenya, 361–62, 369–70
participatory budgeting, 157, 157*b*5.3
  Brazil, 203–4, 224, 227*n*2, 229*n*13
  establishment of, 208–12, 228–29*nn*11–14
  See also budgets and budget processes
participatory governance, 263–64
participatory mechanisms, 191–93, 227–28*nn*5–8, 242–43
  costs of, 192
  factors in effectiveness of, 193–94
  noninstitutionalized participation, 204*b*6.4
  See also citizens and citizen participation
participatory poverty assessments, 124, 202–3
partisanship, and public accounts committees, 391–92
paternalism, 236, 285
patient records, 83
patronage democracy, 168, 169

patronage systems, 7–8, 34, 164, 236, 285
  expenditure and nonexpenditure forms of, 165
  and principal-agent relationships, 169–70
  and reform, 167–68
  role of intermediaries in, 165–67
patron-client relationships, 39, 165–67
PBO. *See* Parliamentary Budget Office (PBO), Uganda
PDM. *See* Municipal Development Plan (PDM)
Pelizzo, Ricardo, xxiii, 10, 379–93
performance
  benchmarking of, 114–15
  dimensions of, 91–95
  impact of performance-based budgeting on, 120
  improvement of, 114, 124–25
  of PACs, 383–91, 391–92
  redefining through collaborative networks, 125–27
  transparency in performance reports, 120–22, 127n2
performance appraisals, 119–20
performance aspects, 326–28
performance audits and auditing, 8–9, 313, 316
  caveats about conducting, 351, 351t11.7
  child immunization services, 335b11.2
  DARE program, 332b11.1
  description, 324–35
  elements of, 324–33, 343–44t11.6
  fieldwork programs, 342, 345–46
  findings and relevant elements of, 325–32, 347–49
  methodologies for, 340–41, 343–44t11.6
  objectives of, 325–26, 332–33, 337–39, 340t11.4, 343–44t11.6
  overview, 323–24, 333–34, 356n1
  phases of planning, 334–42
  in public sector, 8–9
  reporting findings, 346–49, 354
  steps of, 332–33
  structure of, 332–33
  in Sub-Saharan Africa, 349–56, 356–57n2
  vulnerability assessments, 337, 338t11.3, 340t11.4
  See also audits and auditing; supreme audit institutions (SAIs)
performance-based accountability, 2
  logic of, 20–21
  strategies for changes in, 21–27
performance-based budgeting, 4, 89
  and citizen involvement, 122–24
  collaborative processes of, 126
  and cost centers, 109
  Fairfax County as model of, 91
  financial and programmatic accountability in, 117–18
  and goals, 113–16
  link to community development, 111
  link to performance improvement, 120
  revenue side of, 95
  role of information in, 116–17
  and strategic planning, 115
  as tool for change, 91
  and transparency, 118–21, 127n2
performance-based management, 2
  barriers to implementation of, 27–28
  benefits of, 27
  conclusions concerning, 30–31
  enhancing legal framework for, 41–44
  establishing responsibility for, 23–25
  link with traditional forms of accountability, 26–27
  perverse consequences of, 29–30
  and salaries of civil servants, 300n7
  shift to, 19–20
  steps in, 20–21
performance contracts, 163, 179n3
performance management units, 23, 25
performance measurement, 2, 3–4
  and collaborative networks, 107
  difficulty of, 28
  and dimensions of performance, 91–92
  and effectiveness of government, 93
  link to transparency and stakeholder engagement, 118–20

output measures, 96–101
placing expertise for, 23–24, 25
process measures, 105–6
role of policy decisions in, 19
types of measures, 95–106, 127n1
unintended consequences of, 115–16
personalized corruption, 142
personnel, staffing reform programs, 40
personnel management, 24, 26, 43, 43t2.3
Peru, 200b6.2, 255, 278, 281n2
Peters, B. Guy, xxiii, 1–2, 15–32
PETS. *See* public expenditure tracking systems (PETS)
petty corruption, 7–8, 142, 235, 285
The Philippines, 72b3.1, 194, 246
    Congressional Planning and Budget Department, 360, 364–65, 373, 377n6
    corruption in, 233
    laws on local government, 197
    Local Government Code of *1991*, 220–22, 229nn18–19
POA. *See* Annual Operation Plan (POA)
podcasts, 349
Poder Ciudadano, Argentina, 152–53b5.1
police departments, output measures, 97t4.1
policies
    administration of tax policies, 288–90
    analysis of, 2–3
    for anticorruption, 310–11
    policy making mechanisms, 183
policy cycle, 5
policy makers
    role in combating corruption, 243–49
    steps to protect media, 270–72, 282n4
political accountability, 20, 148, 158–59, 162–64, 179n3
political appointments, 288
political awareness, 239
political brokers, 166–67
political corruption, 7–8, 237, 285
political cycle, and short-termism, 30
political economies, 2, 3, 55n4, 213
    and citizen voice, 192, 193
    and public management reform, 34–36, 55n2

political institutions, 4
    and accountability, 20, 158–59, 162–64, 179n3
    civil service accountability and the political process, 162–63, 179n3
    and clientelism, 164–70
    and committee systems, 156
    and elections, 148–54
    and failures in accountability, 176–78
    formal vs. informal accountability, 144–46
    and political instability in Tanzania, 291
    political parties, 158–59, 179n2
    role in promoting accountability, 139
    specialized accountability institutions, 159–62
    See also accountability; legislators and legislatures
political leadership, 287–88
political models, of public management reform, 36–40
political parties, 158–59, 179n2
    one-party system, 300n2
    and voice mechanisms, 194, 228n9
political rights, and e-government, 77
political will, 82
politicians
    as agents, 138
    behavior of, 50
    commitment to reform, 39
    electoral process, 152–53b5.1, 153–54
    and patron-client relationships, 165
    recall of as anticorruption mechanism, 261–63, 281n3
The Politics, 234
populism, 66
Porto Alegre model, 203
positive corruption, 142
poverty
    antipoor biases, 162–63
    assessments of, 124
    citizen participation in monitoring, 202–3
poverty reduction strategies, 163, 173–74
Poverty Reduction Strategy Papers (PRSPs), 186

power relations, 195
PPP. *See* public private partnerships (PPP)
presidential systems, 154–55
principal-agent theory, 7, 160, 255
  and accountability, 137–38
  and patronage distribution, 169–70
  relationship to corruption, 236–40
  vs. economics of crime, 256–58
principal-supervisor-agent model, 238
a priori audits, 312
private sector, 300*n*1, 356*n*1
process-based audits, 342
process efficiency, 329–30
process measures, 45, 105–6
procurement, 70, 72
productivity, 92, 97–100*tt*4.1–4.4, 101–3
professional citizens, 119*n*16
program accountability, 117–18
program budgeting, 117–18
program delivery protocols, 106
program footprints, 326–28
program logic models, 96
program mission, 331
programs
  choosing one for evaluation, 21–22
  link to outputs and outcomes, 20–21
Project Votesmart, Oregon, 152–53*b*5.1
property rights, 77
proportional representation, 262–63
prosecutors
  election of, 266–67
  random assignment of, 265–66
PRSPs. *See* Poverty Reduction Strategy Papers (PRSPs)
Public Accounts Committee, South Africa, 354
Public Accounts Committee of Parliament, Malawi, 162*b*5.4
public accounts committees (PACs)
  composition of, 384, 387, 388*t*13.3
  factors contributing to success of, 383–91
  formal powers of, 384, 385–86*t*13.2
  Malawi, 162*b*5.4
  obstacles to effective performance of, 391–92

organization of, 381–83
overview, 379
practices of, 388–91
size of, 381
South Africa, 354
public administration
  and e-government, 63–64, 73
  and e-skilling, 78
  initiatives to modernize, 59
  link to external world, 68–70
public expenditure tracking systems (PETS), 267
public finance management, 352
public finances, 163
public governance
  accountability in, 60–62, 84*n*1
  in developing countries, 66–68
public management, 1–4
  and central agencies, 43–44
  holistic approach to integrity in, 47–50
  legal framework for, 41–44
  new public management frameworks, 240–41
public management reforms, 2–3
  approaches to, 33, 55*n*1
  conclusions concerning, 55
  creating conditions for, 40–52, 55*nn*3–4
  generating commitment to, 34–40, 55*n*2
  introduction and sequencing of, 52–55
  phases of, 40–41, 55*n*3
  political economy of, 34–36, 55*n*2
  political model of, 36–40
  Sri Lanka model, 37*t*2.1
  strategy for sequencing of, 52, 53*t*2.4
public office, use of for private gains, 285
public officials, 4
  and accountability, 148
  behavior of, 16–17, 285
  commitment to reform, 39
  declarations of assets, 267
  monitoring of, 171
  and new public management frameworks, 240–41

relationship to citizen participation, 188, 191, 227*n*4
and systemic corruption, 142
public performance management processes, 325
public private partnerships (PPP), 68, 68–70, 84*n*3
public resources, diverted to private consumption, 291, 300*n*4
public sector, 1–2
and accountability, 17, 186
and corruption link to governance, 234, 236
malfeasance in, 244
reduction of number of employees in, 294, 300–301*n*8
public sector auditors, 306–7
public sector performance auditing. *See* performance audits and auditing
public service
establishment of values for, 47–48
raising prestige of, 51–52
public service commissions
Malawi, 164
Nepal, 42–43
Sri Lanka, 34, 35*b*2.1, 36, 41
Purohit, Mahesh C., xxiii, 7–8, 285–302

question time, 268–69

radio, 270–71
record keeping, of PAC meetings, 388
recovery strategies, 44
redeployment procedures, 45
redress institutions, 212, 218
redundancy of procedures, 45
reforms, 117*n*1
and accountability costs, 176
and aid modalities, 173–74
antecedents of, 39–40
bottom-up, 250
and clientelism, 167–68
commitment to, 38
economic, 167–68, 250
in employment, 34–38, 40–41, 44–47, 55*n*2, 55*n*4
feasibility of, 36–38

in human rights, 146–47
institutional, 146
and order of priorities, 249
and participatory budgeting, 227*n*2
See also civil service reform; public management reform
regulatory capture, 235
reliability, 103
rent seeking, 7, 66, 255, 281*n*1, 291
report cards, 172, 227*n*2
Reporters without Borders, 270, 278
reports and reporting, 211
annual reports of PACs, 391
of audit findings, 315–16, 346–49, 354
efficiency reports, 333
and e-government, 73
financial, 305
formats for, 121–22
of fraud, 320
performance reporting, 120–21, 127*n*2
transparency in, 120–22, 127*n*3
representation institutions, 209
representatives, link to ordinary citizens, 151
response time, 332
responsibility concept, 16
definition of, 21
establishing responsibility for performance management, 23–25
link to accountability, 147
responsiveness concept, 16–17, 92–93, 94, 147
restricted stateness, 66, 67*t*3.2
results-based management systems, 163, 179*n*3
retrospective accountability, 149
revolutions, inspired by corruption, 276–77
risk
assessing for performance audit, 336–37
assessing vulnerability to, 337, 338*t*11.3, 340*t*11.4
risk ranking, 337

The Role of Auditing in Public Sector Governance, 351
rule-making functions, 155
rule of law, 146–47, 242, 244
rules-driven government, 237
Russell-Einhorn, Malcolm, xiii, 5, 183–232
Russian Federation, internal auditing in, 317

SAIIA. *See* South African Institute of Internal Auditors (SAIIA)
SAIs. *See* supreme audit institutions (SAIs)
salaries. *See* wages
sale of jobs, impact on accountability, 258–60
sales taxes, 289–90
Salinas, Carlos, 54
sanctions, 139
Schumpeterian concept of democracy, 372, 377*n*13
scope of audits, 339
Senegal, 288–89
service delivery, 329–30
  accountability for, 18, 117–18
  assessment of performance of, 249
  bias in, 144
  and Bolivia's Law of Popular Participation, 213–20, 229*nn*15–17
  demand for, 123
  and DSMHS, 110–12
  and e-government, 72–73
  importance of citizen participation in, 185–87, 227*nn*1–2
  link to patronage, 165
  overview of case studies on citizen voice mechanisms, 212–13,
  in Philippines' Local Government Code (1991), 220–22, 229*nn*18–19
  in South Africa's Local Government Transition Act, 222–23
  and steering approach to governance, 19
service quality, 98*t*4.2, 99*t*4.3, 100*t*4.4, 104

Shah, Anwar, xxiii–xxiv, 1–11, 233–53
Sharif, Nawaz, 267
short-termism, 29–30
Sierra Leone, 246, 300*n*2
Singapore, 52, 294, 296*b*9.4
  Chambers of the Attorney-General, 48
  controlling corruption in, 50–51
single-window solutions, 64
social accountability, 186, 215–16
social capital, 126, 192
social norms and structures, 195
social structure, 150
sociocultural factors, 5, 6, 194–95
Soglo, Nicephore, 37–38
Somalia, 294
South Africa, 160
  citizen voice mechanisms in, 191, 227*n*5
  civil society achievements in, 156*b*5.2
  Local Government Transition Act, 222–23
  voice mechanisms, 206–7
South African Institute of Internal Auditors (SAIIA), 353
South Asia Region Financial Management group, World Bank, 388
specialized accountability institutions, 159–62
Sri Lanka, civil service reform in, 34, 35*b*2.1, 36, 372.1, 41, 55*n*2
staff management, 43, 43*t*2.3
stakeholders
  and community development, 107
  and e-government, 70, 76, 79, 81
  expectations gap between stakeholders and SAIs, 305
  functional institutions for effective participation of, 209*f*6.3
  and strategic planning, 115
  and transparency, 118–20
standardized testing, 115–16
standards
  of accountability, 172–73
  of accounting, 316
  for audit work, 311
  of behavior, 16, 31*n*1

for citizen participation, 228n8
for detecting fraud and corruption, 319
for e-government, 80
for fraud audits, 314
of measures and measurement systems, 115
for park service, 105
of performance, 21
Standards for the Professional Practice of Internal Auditing, 353
Stapenhurst, F. Rick, xxiv, 9, 10, 359–78, 379–93
state
  development of, 176
  and e-government, 76–77, 78–81, 84nn4–6
  and freedom of information, 201
  and governance, 66–68
  as guardian of public interest, 242
  nature of administration of, 194
  reforming state tasks, 68–72, 84nn2–3
  restricted stateness, 66, 67t3.2
  state-socialist attitudes, 80
state capture, 235, 237
strategic model, 44–45
strategic planning, 93, 115
street-level bureaucrats, 17
structural independence, 125
structure of audits, 332–33
Sub-Saharan Africa, 3–4
  benchmarking performance of, 114–15
  and CBOs, 110
  and citizen engagement, 122–23, 125
  and community, 94–95
  coproduction in, 107–9
  improving government performance of, 124–25
  performance audits in, 9, 349–56, 356–57n2
  responsiveness of government in, 93
supervision, of tax officials, 287
supreme audit institutions (SAIs), 8, 303, 354
  anticorruption policies, 310–11
  detecting fraud, 314–19

INTOSAI, 309–10, 311
  recommendations for, 320–21
  See also audits and auditing
survey-based governance system, 263–64
Swaziland, 39
Sweden, 160
systemic corruption, 142, 260
  and alternatives to traditional mechanisms of accountability, 261, 262t8.2
  case studies on
    Belarus, 272–73, 274t8.3
    Brazil, 273
    Kenya, 273, 275
    Turkey, 275–76, 282nn5–6
  mechanisms to deal with, 260–72, 281–82nn2–4
  and role of local government, 271–72
  role of media in, 269–71
systems-approach to community improvement, 90–91

Tanzania, 44, 94, 95, 195, 246
  aid to, 300n5
  constitution, 197
  corruption in, 233
  political appointments, 288
  political instability in, 291
targets
  of accountability, 138
  for performance in Fairfax County, 97–100tt4.1–4.4, 108t4.5, 113–16
  and strategic planning, 115
tax administration, 7–8
  causes of corruption in, 286–88
  combating corruption in, 292–98, 300–301nn6–8
  conclusions and policy recommendations for, 298–99
  online processing, 72
tax bases, 94, 95
tax competition framework, 239
tax-demand discontinuity, 123

taxes, integrated system of, 296
tax fraud, India, 289b9.2
tax laws, 286, 292, 300n6
  See also legal frameworks
tax officials, 287, 293, 298
taxpayers, 287, 290, 298
tax policies
  administration of, 288–90
  conclusions and recommendations for, 298–99
TeamWest project, Australia, 75
technical capacity, 125
technological frameworks, 78–79
television, 270–71
territorial grassroots organizations (OTBs), 198, 214–18
Texas, 120
Thailand, 70, 72, 72b3.1, 197–98
Thatcher, Margaret, 54
theft, and corruption, 143
top-down corruption, 238
total quality management (TQM), 187
traditional findings, 326, 327t11.1
training
  and personnel management, 26
  retraining, 45
transactions, and e-government, 64–65
transfers, 94–95
transformational leadership, 53
transparency, 91, 184, 210
  and e-government, 63–64
  global, 373
  of government actions, 22
  in performance reporting, 120–21, 127n2
  promotion of, 15–16
  and stakeholder engagement, 118–20
  and use of information technology to combat corruption, 295
Transparency International, 51, 52, 278, 308
Transparency International Annual Bribe Payers, 308
trends in performance, 114
triangulation of measures, 95–96, 101, 109, 124
Turkey, 275–76, 282nn5–6

Uganda, 160, 202–3, 246, 300n4
  constitution, 197
  laws on local government, 197–98
  Parliamentary Budget Office, 360, 366–68, 373, 374
  PETS in, 267
  reduction in employees, 294, 300–401n8
UNDP. See United Nations Development Programme (UNDP)
undue influence, 142
UNESCAP. See United Nations Economic and Social Commission for Asia and the Pacific (UNESCAP)
UN Global E-Government Readiness Report 2005, 83
Uniontown, Alabama, 74
United Kingdom, 23
  civil service, 42
  controlling corruption in, 50
  and e-government, 72–73, 76, 79
  public agencies in, 68, 70
  question time in Parliament, 268
  redundancy agreement, 45
  staffing reforms, 53–54
United Nations Department of Economic and Social Affairs, 78, 84n4
United Nations Development Programme (UNDP), 35b2.1
United Nations Economic and Social Commission for Asia and the Pacific (UNESCAP), 61–62
United Nations Global Programme against Corruption, 308
United States
  Congressional and Impoundment Control Act of 1974, 374
  Congressional Budget Office, 360, 362–64, 373
  DARE program, 332b11.1
  and e-government, 74
  electoral process in, 152–53b5.1, 262
  General Accounting Office, 316
  Government Performance and Results Act, 24, 25

presidential systems, 158
Wireless Philadelphia Executive
    Committee, 76
units of service, 330–31
universities, role in preventing
    corruption, 278–79
Uruguay, 198, 198*b*6.1, 309–10
U.S. Agency for International
    Development (USAID), 179*n*1
utilization ratios, 330

validity, 103, 333
value added tax (VAT), 290, 294
value-for-money audits, 356*n*1
values, establishing of public service
    values, 47–48
van Buitenen, Paul, 318*b*10.1
VAT. *See* value added tax (VAT)
Veja magazine, 273
Venezuela, 257
vertical accountability, 140–41, 241
veto power, 191
Vietnam, 159
village development councils,
    Philippines, 229*n*18
Virginia Beach, Virginia, 65, 70
vision, link to leadership, 53
voice data, 84*n*5
voice elicitation institutions, 210–11
voice mechanisms, 5, 6, 137
    legal and institutional frameworks that
        support, 188–205,
        227–28*nn*3–10
    role in CSOs, 195
    See also citizen voice mechanisms
volunteerism, 108*t*4.5, 109
voters and voting, 148–54, 165
    citizen efforts to improve,
        152–53*b*5.1, 153–55
    and decision-making
        institutions, 211
    e-voting, 65

and patronage, 169–70
registry of, 77
vulnerability assessments, 337, 338*t*11.3,
    340*t*11.4

wages, 245*t*7.2, 246
    of civil servants, 244, 293–94,
        300–301*nn*7–8
    and price of jobs, 260
Waring, Colleen G., xxiv, 8–9, 323–57
watchdog agencies, 245*t*7.2, 246
Web-based technologies, 60
Web sites
    CBO capacity building, 111–12
    Fairfax County, 97–100*t*4.1–4.3,
        108*t*4.5, 121, 127*n*2
Weeks, Edward C., 123
Westminster model of democracy, 380,
    392–93*n*1
whistle-blowers, 315,
    317–18
Wireless Philadelphia Executive
    Committee, United States, 76
Woodward, Bob, 269
workload measures. *See* output
    measures
World Bank, 35*b*2.1, 148
    ARVIN framework, 194,
        225–26*t*6A.1
    Assessing Aid report, 36
    definition of corruption, 308
    role in preventing corruption,
        279–80
    staffing reform programs, 40
World Bank Institute, 8, 10, 383, 387, 388
World Development Report, 2004, 186

Zambia, civil society achievements in,
    156*b*5.2
Zardari, Asif, 267
zero-sum behavior, 119
Zuzul, Miomir, 268

ECO-AUDIT
Environmental Benefits Statement

The World Bank is committed to preserving endangered forests and natural resources. The Office of the Publisher has chosen to print **Performance Accountability and Combating Corruption** on recycled paper with 30 percent postconsumer fiber in accordance with the recommended standards for paper usage set by the Green Press Initiative, a nonprofit program supporting publishers in using fiber that is not sourced from endangered forests. For more information, visit www.greenpressinitiative.org.

Saved:
- 13 trees
- 9 million Btu of total energy
- 1,110 lb. of CO_2 equivalent greenhouse gases
- 4,607 gal. of wastewater
- 592 lb. of solid waste

green press
INITIATIVE